SCRIPTURE AS SOCIAL DISCOURSE

SCRIPTURE AS SOCIAL DISCOURSE

Social-Scientific Perspectives on Early Jewish and Christian Writings

Edited by
Jessica M. Keady, Todd E. Klutz and C. A. Strine

t&tclark

LONDON • NEW YORK • OXFORD • NEW DELHI • SYDNEY

T&T CLARK
Bloomsbury Publishing Plc
50 Bedford Square, London, WC1B 3DP, UK
1385 Broadway, New York, NY 10018, USA

T&T CLARK and the T&T Clark logo are trademarks of Bloomsbury Publishing Plc

First published in Great Britain 2018

Library of Congress Cataloging-in-Publication Data
Names: Keady, Jessica M., editor.
Title: Scripture as social discourse : social-scientific perspectives on
early Jewish and Christian writings / Jessica M. Keady, Todd E. Klutz, and Casey Strine.
Description: 1 [edition]. | New York : Bloomsbury Academic, 2018. |
Includes bibliographical references and index.
Identifiers: LCCN 2017053721 (print) | LCCN 2018012168 (ebook) |
ISBN 9780567676054 (ePDF) | ISBN 9780567676047 (hardback : alk. paper)
Subjects: LCSH: Bible–Social scientific criticism.
Classification: LCC BS521.88 (ebook) | LCC BS521.88 .S37 2018 (print) |
DDC 220.6/7–dc23
LC record available at https://lccn.loc.gov/2017053721

ISBN: HB: 978-0-5676-7604-7
ePDF: 978-0-5676-7605-4
ebook: 978-0-5676-8499-8

Typeset by Newgen KnowledgeWorks Pvt. Ltd., Chennai, India
Printed and bound in Great Britain

To find out more about our authors and books visit www.bloomsbury.com
and sign up for our newsletters.

CONTENTS

PREFACE

All of the chapters in this volume are, in various ways, the product of a biblical studies colloquium held in Manchester and Sheffield on 24–25 April 2014, and include contributions by specialists in biblical studies and related areas at the Universities of Manchester, Sheffield, Lausanne and Geneva. The theme of that year's colloquium, and thus the topic of the present collection, was suggested by our good friend Christophe Nihan (Lausanne) in consultation with eventual contributors George J. Brooke, Thomas C. Römer and David Hamidović. It was quickly agreed that since all of the anticipated participants were already pursuing research influenced in one way or another by the social sciences and social-scientific interpretation, all of us were likely to have done a lot of thinking on the suggested theme already and to have ideas about it worth sharing with other parties in the form of a published collection.

The volume's three editors are grateful to everyone involved in the colloquium and its afterlife as an edited volume. George Brooke deserves special thanks both for having taken the lead role in organizing the programme for the 2014 colloquium, and for entrusting to us the work of editing the essays. Much gratitude is also owed and hereby registered both to Richard Benda for his skilful rendering of three essays originally given in French and requiring English translation; and to Eliot Klutz, for his efficient and timely assistance in producing the abbreviations list and the fifteen separate essay bibliographies.

Jessica M. Keady, Todd E. Klutz and C. A. Strine

ABBREVIATIONS

AB	Anchor Bible
ABD	*The Anchor Bible Dictionary*. Edited by David Noel Freedman (New York: Doubleday, 1992)
Adv. Haer.	*Adversus Haireses* (Irenaeus)
ANTJ	Arbeiten zum Neuen Testament und Judentum
AOAT	Alter Orient und Altes Testament
ATD	Das Alte Testament Deutsch
BASOR	*Bulletin of the American Schools of Oriental Research*
BETL	Bibliotheca ephemeridum theologicarum lovaniensium
BibInt	*Biblical Interpretation: A Journal of Contemporary Approaches*
BN	*Biblische Notizen*
BNTC	Black's New Testament Commentary
BTB	*Biblical Theology Bulletin*
BZAW	Beihefte zur *ZAW*
CBQ	*Catholic Biblical Quarterly*
CD	The Damascus Document from the Cairo Genizah
CRBS	*Currents in Research: Biblical Studies*
DHR	Dynamics in the History of Religions
DJD	Discoveries in the Judaean Desert
DSD	*Dead Sea Discoveries*
ExpTim	*Expository Times*
FAT	Forschungen Alten Testament
FRLANT	Forschungen zur Religion und Literatur des Alten und Neuen Testaments
Gos. Phil.	*Gospel of Philip*
HSM	Harvard Semitic Monographs
HTR	*Harvard Theological Review*
IJS	Institute of Jewish Studies
IOS	Israel Oriental Studies
JBL	*Journal of Biblical Literature*
JECS	*Journal of Early Christian Studies*
JHS	*Journal of Hellenic Studies*
JJP	*Journal of Juristic Papyrology*
JSJ	*Journal for the Study of Judaism in the Persian, Hellenistic and Roman Period*
JSJSUP	Supplements to the Journal for the Study of Judaism
JSNT	*Journal for the Study of the New Testament*
JSNTSUP	*Journal for the Study of the New Testament*, Supplement Series
JSOT	*Journal for the Study of the Old Testament*
JSOTSUP	*Journal for the Study of the Old Testament*, Supplement Series

JSPSUP	*Journal for the Study of the Pseudepigrapha*, Supplement Series
JSS	*Journal of Semitic Studies*
JTS	*Journal of Theological Studies*
LAPO	*Littératures anciennes du Proche-Orient*
LCL	Loeb Classical Library
LHBOTS	Library of Hebrew Bible/Old Testament Studies
LNTS	Library of New Testament Studies
LSTS	Library of Second Temple Studies
NHS	Nag Hammadi Studies
NHMS	Nag Hammadi and Manichean Studies
NICNT	New International Commentary on the New Testament
NovT	*Novum Testamentum*
NTOA	Novum Testamentum et orbis antiques
NTS	*New Testament Studies*
NTT	New Testament Theology
NTTS	New Testament Tools and Studies
OBO	Orbis biblicus et orientalis
OTE	Old Testament Essays
OTL	Old Testament Library
PG	J. P. Migne (ed.) *Patrologia cursus completa ... Series graeca* (166 vols.; Paris: Petit-Montrouge, 1857–83)
Pol.	*Politica* (Aristotle)
P Teb.	*Tebtunis Papyri* (1902–76)
PW	August Friedrich von Pauly and Georg Wissowa (eds), *Real-Encyclopädie der classischen Altertumswissenschaft* (Stuttgart: Metzler, 1894–)
1Q14	*Pesher Micah*
1QH	*Hymns / Hodayot*
1QM	*War Scroll*
1QPHAB	*Pesher Habakkuk*
1QS	*Community Rule*
4Q171	*Pesher Psalms^a*
4Q173	*Pesher Psalms^b*
4Q267	*Damascus Document^b*
4Q270	*Damascus Document^e*
4Q416	*Sapiential Work A^b / The Children of Salvation*
4Q428	*Hymns*
11Q19(–20)	*Temple Scroll*
RB	*Revue biblique*
REJ	*Revue des études juives*
RevQ	*Revue de Qumran*
RSR	*Recherches de science religieuse*
SAC	Studies in Ancient Chronology
SBL	Society of Biblical Literature
SBLDS	Society of Biblical Literature Dissertation Series
SBLEJL	SBL Early Judaism and Its Literature
SBLMS	SBL Monograph Series

SJOT	*Scandinavian Journal of the Old Testament*
SNTSMS	Society for New Testament Studies Monograph Series
SPCK	Society for Promoting Christian Knowledge
STAC	Studien und Texte zu Antike und Christentum
STDJ	Studies on the Texts of the Desert of Judah
Sull.	*Pro Sulla* (Cicero)
SUNT	Studien zur Umwelt des Neuen Testaments
Symp.	*Symposium* (Plato)
TDNT	Gerhard Kittel and Gerhard Friedrich (eds), *Theological Dictionary of the New Testament* (trans. Geoffrey W. Bromiley; 10 vols.; Grand Rapids: Eerdmans, 1964–)
TLZ	*Theologische Literaturzeitung*
Tri. Trac.	*Tripartite Tractate*
TSAJ	Texts and Studies in Ancient Judaism
TU	Texte und Untersuchungen
Tusc.	*Tusculanae disputations* (Cicero)
TynB	*Tyndale Bulletin*
TynBul	*Tyndale Bulletin*
VC	*Vigiliae christianae*
VT	*Vetus Testamentum*
VTSUP	*Vetus Testamentum*, Supplements
VWGTH	Veröffentlichungen der Wissenschaftlichen Gesellschaft für Theologie
WBC	Word Biblical Commentary
WUNT	Wissenschaftliche Untersuchungen zum Neuen Testament
ZAW	*Zeitschrift für die alttestamentliche Wissenschaft*

CONTRIBUTORS

Chen Bergot
Faculté de Théologie
University of Geneva
Switzerland

George J. Brooke
Department of Religions and Theology
University of Manchester
United Kingdom

Philip R. Davies
Sheffield Institute for Interdisciplinary
    Biblical Studies
University of Sheffield
United Kingdom

Kimberley A. Fowler
Centre National de la Recherche
    Scientifique
Aix-Marseille University
France

David Hamidović
Institut romand des sciences
    bibliques
University of Lausanne
Switzerland

David S. Harvey
Westside King's Church, Calgary,
    Alberta and Visiting Lecturer in
    New Testament at Mattersey Hall
    College
United Kingdom

Walter J. Houston
Centre for Biblical Studies
University of Manchester
United Kingdom

Jaeyoung Jeon
Institut romand des sciences bibliques
University of Lausanne
Switzerland

Jessica M. Keady
Faculty of Humanities and
    Performing Arts
University of Wales Trinity
    Saint David

Todd E. Klutz
Department of Religions and
    Theology
University of Manchester
United Kingdom

Peter Oakes
Department of Religions and
    Theology
University of Manchester
United Kingdom

Julia Rhyder
Institut romand des sciences bibliques
University of Lausanne
Switzerland

Thomas C. Römer
Institut romand des sciences bibliques
University of Lausanne
Switzerland

C. A. Strine
Sheffield Institute for Interdisciplinary
    Biblical Studies
University of Sheffield
United Kingdom

Chapter 1

INTRODUCTION: THE STRUCTURE OF SOCIAL-SCIENTIFIC AND GRAMMATICAL INTEGRATIONS

Todd E. Klutz

1.1 *The Closing of Ravelstein's Mind*

Abe Ravelstein, according to his fictional friend and biographer Chick in the last of Saul Bellow's published novels, was 'out to undermine the social sciences'.[1] In addition to inoculating as many of his students as possible against the social-science virus destroying the souls of impressionable students at his prestigious Midwest university, Ravelstein 'felt himself deeply and vitally connected' with Chicago Bulls superstar guard Michael Jordon – 'a genius to watch . . . the artist',[2] Ravelstein would muse, the athletic equivalent, in fact, of Ravelstein's own high-flying act in the coliseum of intellect – and considered professional basketball more generally, along with jazz, as among the highest expressions of twentieth-century American culture. Whenever an important Chicago Bulls game was to be aired on NBC television, Ravelstein would invite his graduate students to his apartment, order prodigious quantities of pizza, and host basketball parties that created 'a common ground between the fan clubs of childhood and the Promised Land of the intellect toward which Ravelstein'[3] himself, like some Hellenistic hybrid of New Moses and Socrates *redivivus*, was leading them.

The character Ravelstein's romance with basketball has a much firmer basis than his ambivalence towards the social sciences does in the life of Bellow's late friend, the American philosopher Allan Bloom; it therefore also goes far towards explaining why I remain charmed by Bellow's roman-à-clef at least as much as I do by Bloom's 1987 bestseller, *The Closing of the American Mind*,[4] a richly informed and self-consciously unfashionable work whose foreword was provided by Bellow

---

1. Saul Bellow, *Ravelstein* (London: Penguin Books, 2000), 160.

2. Ibid., 56.

3. Ibid., 56–57.

4. Allan Bloom, *The Closing of the American Mind: How Higher Education Has Failed Democracy and Impoverished the Souls of Today's Students* (New York: Simon and Schuster, 1987).

as a ringing endorsement, and whose twenty-fifth anniversary recently was an occasion for largely favourable reappraisals, suggesting that Bloom's argument has aged surprisingly well.[5] What Bloom's bestseller and Bellow's Ravelstein can at best only begin to explain, however, is how the present writer – someone still sympathetic in many respects to Bloom's critique of Western (not merely American) academia, and thus also of the the various social sciences in that larger enterprise – can now find himself cheerfully writing the introduction to a collection of essays united in the conviction that the social sciences offer conceptual tools indispensable for the best varieties of exegesis and interpretation of biblical and related literatures from antiquity.

Vivid memories of two particular experiences, both of them involving Bloom, in the early days of my engagement with social-scientific approaches to the Bible and its early reception would seem to make my present situation even more difficult to explain; but since both of those experiences, upon even brief reflection, offer insight into the recent intellectual history and context assumed by the present volume, they are worthy of recollection as part of an effort to situate and preview the essays that follow.

The setting of the first of those experiences is an academic conference I attended in England in 1989, near the beginning of my PhD programme at the University of Sheffield. I had come to Sheffield, and thus also to this particular conference, with comparatively strong training in biblical languages, taught and learned in a spirit of evangelical sobriety and fervour at Dallas Theological Seminary, but also with growing interest in method and theory – both social-scientific and literary-theoretical – in the study of Bible and religion, the latter interest having been nurtured at Wheaton College Graduate School by a mandatory reading of Wayne Meeks's *The First Urban Christians* (1983) and, immediately afterwards, by my reading of Philip Esler's *Community and Gospel in Luke-Acts* (1987), a socio-redactional interpretation that made creative and illuminating use of Peter Berger and Thomas Luckmann's influential work, *The Social Construction of Reality* (1966).[6]

Seated next to me at dinner on the first evening of the conference is a very learned but also sociable mid-career American scholar who, in response to a question shaped by my then recent reading of Bloom's work, strongly assures me that however emphatically Bloom may have understood his topic to be the closing of the American mind, the decisive factor in the context of Bloom's argument is,

---

5. See 'Conference on the 25th Anniversary of Allan Bloom's *The Closing of the American Mind*, on Students', Program on Constitutional Government at Harvard, 17 August 2017, https://www.youtube.com/watch?v=VLGTSo-9JwA.

6. Wayne A. Meeks, *The First Urban Christians: The Social World of the Apostle Paul* (New Haven: Yale University Press, 1983); Philip Esler, *Community and Gospel in Luke-Acts: The Social and Political Motivations of Lucan Theology*, SNTSMS 57 (Cambridge: Cambridge University Press, 1987); and Peter L. Berger and Thomas Luckmann, *The Social Construction of Reality: A Treatise in the Sociology of Knowledge* (Garden City, NY: Anchor Books, 1966).

tragically, the closing of Allan Bloom's own mind. My new acquaintance's critique of Bloom, articulated as it is with a nearly ideal mix of eloquence, good humour and relevant knowledge, opens my mind to the possibility that Bloom's criticisms of the social sciences might be neither adequately informed nor fair-minded. But while I am becoming at this time more and more aware of the analytical potential afforded by the social sciences to serious readers of the Bible, I am not persuaded that Bloom's analysis is as crude and weak as this American visitor is suggesting; for among other things, neither my conference co-attendee nor even Bloom/Ravelstein's dear friend, Bellow/Chick, shows adequate awareness of a subtle but highly important distinction in Bloom's argument that will become significantly more substantial to me in the years ahead: namely, Bloom is in fact not accurately understood if he is interpreted as trying to undermine the social sciences at all;[7] instead, his argument is that despite the validity of many of the now familiar criticisms of the Great Books approach to liberal education, the potential satisfactions provided by that approach are vastly to be preferred to the incoherent, intellectually parasitic and economically languishing lot that passes for humanistic studies in the universities of today.[8] In Bloom's vision of the good university, a curriculum in which the Great Books are used as instruments for the foregrounding of big, enduring and potentially humanizing questions could be designed and implemented at little or even no cost to the social sciences; indeed, in order to enrich understanding and prevent naïve reading of such texts, the ever-growing reservoir of social-scientific theorizing and related critical concepts would be recognized by any serious student as including powerful tools for the description, interpretation and explanation of the books.

The value and relevance of that discussion both for the contemporary university and for the present collection cannot be overestimated. The enduring human need and desire to understand critically and as well as possible the manifold discursive energies actualized by the so-called Great Books – biblical and related literatures such as those treated in the present volume are among the most obvious examples – will properly inspire literate consumers of those texts to interpret them with the aid of every pertinent body of knowledge at their disposal, not least the various disciplines constituting modern social science. On that point, at least, Bloom, most of his critics, a great many (if not all) social scientists and all the contributors to the present collection would almost certainly agree, forming thereby a pool of theoretical and procedural commitments shared by the essays published herein.

As indicated above, another experience involving Bloom's controversial work might have discouraged any involvement on my part in a social-science friendly work such as this one. For purposes of the present discussion, the complicated setting of this second experience is best simplified as a scholarly

---

7. A powerful antidote to the many unhealthy caricatures of Bloom's stance on the social sciences is the vastly richer, holistic but also detailed, highly appreciative but also critical, statement in Bloom, *The Closing of the American Mind*, 354–71.

8. Ibid., 344–46.

interchange between American sociologist Rodney Stark, whose work *The Rise of Christianity: A Sociologist Reconsiders History* (1995)[9] was stimulating a great volume of discussion in the latter half of the 1990s, and three of that study's most recent reviewers – namely, Keith Hopkins, Elizabeth Castelli and myself – with our respective reviews and a response from Stark being published as a group in the summer issue of the *Journal of Early Christian Studies* in 1998.[10] From the larger conversation between *The Rise of Christianity*, its reviewers, and Stark's response, a small handful of points possess notable significance for the context assumed here.

First, and especially in light of the sorts of concerns registered not only by Bloom but also, more recently and from a significantly different philosophical point of view, by Martha Nussbaum, over the direction and comparative strengths/weaknesses of the humanities in contemporary higher education,[11] issues of comparative power and prestige in the relationship between humanistic disciplines such as literary criticism and ancient history on the one hand and the social sciences on the other played a subtle but significant and very revealing role in the conversation between Stark and his humanist interlocutors. More specifically, although the argument of *The Rise of Christianity* is marked by a self-advertising rhetoric of science that positions the rationality of its own 'up-to-date and . . . rigorous brand of social science'[12] over the methods of humanists and the 'older generation of social "scientists" ',[13] it also acknowledges the inspiration its author drew from the published efforts of historians and New Testament scholars to utilize social science with a view to illuminating the early Christian era.[14] In balance, while the collective valorization of social science in Stark's book, its interdisciplinary precursors and some of its scholarly reviews is undoubtedly an indication of a whole syndrome of deficits still afflicting the humanities, it simultaneously bears loud witness to the unique power of humanities scholarship to inspire and nurture the kinds of real interdisciplinary conversations that create cohesion across university faculties, and suggests the word 'university' might be something other than a sophistic label for what, in the eyes of some institutional managers and their governmental auditors, might fairly be described as a cacophonous assortment of mutually unintelligible fiefdoms.

9. Rodney Stark, *The Rise of Christianity: A Sociologist Reconsiders History* (Princeton: Princeton University Press, 1995).

10. See Todd Klutz, 'The Rhetoric of Science in *The Rise of Christianity*: A Response to Rodney Stark's Sociological Account of Christianization', *JECS* 6, no. 2 (1998): 162–84; Keith Hopkins, 'Christian Number and Its Implications', *JECS* 6, no. 2 (1998): 185–226; Elizabeth Castelli, 'Gender, Theory, and *The Rise of Christianity*: A Response to Rodney Stark', *JECS* 6, no. 2 (1998): 227–57; and Rodney Stark, '*E Contrario*', *JECS* 6, no. 2 (1998): 259–67.

11. Martha C. Nussbaum, *Not for Profit: Why Democracy Needs the Humanities* (Princeton: Princeton University Press, 2010), especially pages 1–26.

12. Stark, *The Rise of Christianity*, xi.

13. Ibid., 26.

14. Ibid., xi.

Disappointingly, Stark's response in 1998 to the present reviewer's comments about the rhetoric of science in his work was less a serious engagement with the problem of his methodological formalism than a forgivably misjudged but largely irrelevant grumble about postmodern nonsense.[15] In that connection, and more specifically in terms of Clifford Geertz's distinction between those social scientists who reject the widespread science/historicism dichotomy and perpetuate the dream of a *science humaine*, on the one hand, and those now in the ascendant – 'the paradigm hunters ... pronouncing themselves "mainstream" ... nicely preadapted to the bottom-line mentality now pervading our public life', who would transform the field into 'some sort of social physics, complete with laws, formalisms, and apodictic proofs',[16] on the other, Stark made no secret of his commitment and contributions to the winners of that phase of the war.

1.2 *Science, Universalism and the Pull of Shiny New Theories*

Isolated from its wider discursive context down to the present, and as hinted above, Stark's reply might not have seemed to bode well for the duration and mutual enrichment of the relationship between the humanities and the social sciences, or more particularly between ancient history and sociology. Interpreted in the context of the ongoing conversation, however, both the aforementioned points about the rhetoric of science and even Stark's reply to it are worth revisiting in the context of the present collection and its publication. Very helpfully and with admirable clarity, for instance, Stark responded to the challenge about his rhetoric of science not merely by asserting that 'sociology is a social *science*' (emphasis his), 'science' being a word whose meaning, we are reminded, should not be reduced to that of 'rhetoric', but also by committing himself to a position that sees science as consisting specifically of 'the formulation of general theories

---

15. Since the publication of my 'The Rhetoric of Science' in 1998, and while I remain appreciative of the stimulating contribution made by Stark's book, my reservations about the latter have been reinforced and hardened by my reading in conceptual metaphor theory – notably, the influential works of George Lakoff and Mark Johnson – and more especially in cognitive science and conceptual blending, whose insightful critiques of so-called formal approaches to various areas of modern research (e.g. Claude Lévi-Strauss, Noam Chomsky, Alan Turing) are highly applicable to Stark's work, with its emphatic subscription to '*formal* methods of analysis' and '*formal* rational choice models' (*The Rise of Christianity*, xii, emphasis mine). On the influence and limitations of formal methods, and especially their underestimation of the contribution of imagination to processes of making and interpreting meaning, see Gilles Fauconnier and Mark Turner, *The Way We Think: Conceptual Blending and the Mind's Hidden Complexities* (New York: Basic Books, 2002), 3–15.

16. Clifford Geertz, *Available Light: Anthropological Reflections on Philosophical Topics* (Princeton: Princeton University Press, 2000), 94–95.

which give rise to observable predictions and of the testing of those predictions against appropriate data'.[17]

To some, that particular formulation will seem uncontroversial and thus uninteresting; but to those informed by recent debates in physics, the history and philosophy of science, the philosophy of the social sciences more particularly, and the modern history of social-scientific influence upon the formulation of Western economic and foreign policy,[18] the question of what real 'science' actually consists of – what distinguishes it from other modes of human thought and practice – is rather more complicated than Stark suggests, notwithstanding the respectability and clarity of his assertion in that regard. Psychology, for instance, including the practices of psychoanalysis, is widely assumed to belong to the social sciences, while serious academic debates surrounding that discipline's ability to satisfy scientific criteria such as prediction and falsifiability continue to rage.[19] Allan Bloom, to his credit, observed that while most social scientists aspire to imitate the natural sciences by having the power to make reliable predictions, the aspiration has been achieved by almost none of them.[20] The question of criteria for science as a category therefore includes, but also goes beyond, the late social anthropologist Ernest Gellner's question whether the social sciences are really 'scientific';[21] more particularly, it invites questions about what we mean nowadays when we speak of 'science', what sorts of things we are trying to do with that word, to what degree (if at all) those things are reasonable or theoretically defensible, and whether the most recent descriptions of methods and theories in humanities scholarship as 'social-scientific' have the discursive potential to prompt roughly the same

17. Stark, '*E Contrario*', 262.

18. For interesting discussion of some of these areas, see e.g. Patrick Baert, *Philosophy of the Social Sciences: Toward Pragmatism* (Cambridge: Polity Press, 2005), especially pages 131–35, regarding Richard Rorty and Thomas Kuhn on the 'myth of scientific method'; George Lakoff and Mark Johnson, *Philosophy in the Flesh: The Embodied Mind and Its Challenge to Modern Thought* (New York: Basic Books, 1999), 88–93, 467–68, on postmodern philosophy of science from the perspective of embodied realism; Michael Carrithers, *Why Humans Have Cultures: Explaining Anthropology and Social Diversity* (Oxford: Oxford University Press, 1992), 146–55, on the role of epistemologically naïve views of science in the dichotomist construction of the relationship between the natural sciences and anthropology; Geertz, *Available Light*, 143–66, on physics and other natural sciences in the thought of Kuhn and Charles Taylor; and Noam Chomsky, *American Power and the New Mandarins* (New York: Pantheon Books, 1969), 268–77, 283, on the ideological functions of social science in American policy-formation during the Vietnam War.

19. Still unsurpassed is the statement by Ernest Gellner, *The Psychoanalytic Movement: The Cunning of Unreason* (London: Paladin, 1985).

20. Bloom, *The Closing of the American Mind*, 360.

21. Ernest Gellner, 'The Scientific Status of the Social Sciences (und leider auch Sociologie)', in *Relativism and the Social Sciences* (Cambridge: Cambridge University Press, 1987), 101–27.

meanings – and purchase approximately the same prestige – that such talk used to prompt and purchase.

Because the questions just raised are partly matters of definition and in some quarters could therefore be devalued as little more than quibbles over words and thus as not very deep, they could be summarily dismissed as not deserving discussion in essays such as this one. There is, however, good reason for seeing them as having much greater importance than that. Perhaps most importantly, wherever the use of social-scientific concepts is attended by the assumption that a particular set or sequence of human social happenings has at least a general predictability about it, one version or another of cultural universalism will almost certainly be lurking nearby and demanding that it be given some form of ideological work to do. Indeed, the presumption of predictability stands upon (or, less optimistically, falls down from) the shoulders of the universalism thesis, which in turn can be seen as validated or reinforced every time it generates a prediction that proves to possess power. But most importantly, as exemplified not only by Bloom but also by George Brooke in the present volume and a host of other scholars in diverse disciplines, universalism and the gang of abstractions it often hangs out with are increasingly suspected of being impatient towards the discursive particular – the historically singular detail – and of being indulgent towards overgeneralization.[22]

A large and growing volume of intellectually serious work has been produced by different sides in that debate, whose subtleties and academic range defy useful summarization in the present context; but for purposes of identifying, understanding and perhaps even correcting some of our worst intellectual habits in regard to generalization, fresh inspiration might be derived from Bloom, who understood our preference for abstractions, sameness and similarity over the concreteness of differences to be a consequence of our democratic assumptions and the egalitarian implications we so fondly infer from them:

> The very universality of democracy and the sameness of man presupposed by it encourage this tendency [to embrace inadequately grounded abstractions and general theories] and make the mind's eye less sensitive to differences . . . Simulacra of thought and experience, hardly better than slogans . . . take the place of reflection . . . Our temptation is to prefer the shiny new theory to the fully cognized experience.[23]

By contrast, Bloom continues, 'Concreteness, not abstractness, is the hallmark of philosophy. All interesting generalization must proceed from the richest awareness of what is to be explained, but the tendency to abstractness leads to simplifying the phenomena in order more easily to deal with them'.[24] In the context of the present volume, as in the situation addressed by Bloom, with his

22. See, e.g. Geertz, *Available Light*, 133–40.
23. Bloom, *The Closing of the American Mind*, 254.
24. Ibid., 255.

old-fashioned interest in 'Great Books', the phenomena to be dealt with – to be explained, preferably of course without abstractions that oversimplify – are very largely ancient texts, along with whatever evidence can justifiably be identified as belonging to their early contexts of production and reception; and thus comes into view the problem of how to achieve the optimal interplay between appropriate social-scientific generalization on the one hand, and the mass of grammatical and discursive particulars that constitute our ancient texts and require close attention *qua* language on the other hand.

A general answer which, although it certainly needs more elaboration than I can give it here, has the honour of being favoured in one way or another by every essay in the present volume can be summed up in a single word: namely, 'exegesis'. Despite its abstractness and ring of fustiness, the word is less obvious and has greater value in relation to the question than we might be inclined to imagine. For starters, although it is certainly true that a lot of modern exegesis of the Bible has been much too idea-centred, too theologically orientated, too individualistic and too little interested in the wider social and cultural dialectics of the ancient texts, it is equally true that theological and related ideas constitute a foregrounded level of meaning in most of those texts, and that the best exegesis has always made room for careful consideration of contextual matters – albeit not always in a systematic or optimally illuminating way. Accordingly, wherever basic or even old-fashioned exegesis gives ample space not only to the concerns of lexis, morphology and syntax but also to wider contextually relevant insights from the social sciences, it should and almost certainly will have an honourable seat at the table of interpretation.

1.3 *Seductive Abstractions, Grammatical Particulars and the Paradigm of Paradigms*

Another reason exegesis fully deserves mention in the present context is that just as social-scientific approaches to biblical interpretation are now acquiring greater and greater visibility in the academic study and teaching of the Bible, so the art and skills of biblical exegesis – the close reading, analysis and synthesis of the verbal minutiae, the particulars, of biblical and other writings from antiquity in their original languages – are simultaneously suffering a long and worrying decline. The contrast in fortunes could arouse suspicions worthy of investigation outside the present context. What is more important for my immediate purpose is that, like Stark's sociological account of the rise of Christianity, a growing volume of published biblical scholarship, MA and PhD writing in biblical studies, and undergraduate essays in the same field shows signs of having been produced on the assumption that ancient texts and their meanings are relatively straightforward phenomena that can be handled responsibly without proper training in their original languages, and without painstaking attention to their grammatical details in particular. Instead of the difficult but still essential wrestling with Greek, Hebrew, Aramaic and other relevant language grammars, we increasingly find the repetition of abstractions such as multiple scope integration networks, motor schemas, the cognitive unconscious, acquired honour, limited good, dyadic personality, the folk theory of general kinds, typology of exchange, shamanic altered states of consciousness (ASC), initiation crisis, negative reciprocity, guilt culture, androcentrism, patriarchy, phallocentrism, the communicative presumption, the relevance principle, the mirror stage, cognitive dissonance, deep/shallow taxonomies of knowledge, sociocultural accommodation/ tension and many more. In my own interpretative work, several of these abstractions have proved to be well-suited to given topics and data that interested me, their use and application thus proving to be illuminating;[25] indeed, the potential of each of those just mentioned to be helpful in a range of analytical projects is not to be doubted. But like many or perhaps even all abstract categories, those just noted and numerous others have dangerous potential to seduce us by their blend of opacity and mystery, to dupe us into crying out their names before the time is right, into forcing them down upon innocent particulars whose distinctive qualities have been poorly observed and for whom they are not well-matched, and eventually (if our senses and conscience remain intact) into feelings of embarrassment and regret over our reckless, hasty, exegetically unchecked longing for social-scientific consummation.

Is exegesis the only patrol on duty for checking the IDs of social-scientific interpreters needing to prove they are not carriers of the dreaded contagion *abstractionitis*? If exegesis is understood not as a lone patrolperson but rather as the parent of a large and growing family of criticisms – a whole police force of closely interrelated but distinct strategies of analysing and interpreting texts – it might relieve us of our concerns for a time and even give us reasons for feeling that, at least right now, our borders are secure. An entire household of those criticisms can be seen at work in the present volume and is given attention below in my preview of its constituent essays. Other types of criticism and exegesis, having contributed to notable advances in scholarship, deserve the attention of all serious students of method and theory in biblical studies but cannot be given more than brief mention here. The socio-literary approach advanced in 1985 by Norman K. Gottwald,[26] for instance, in his monumental introduction to the Hebrew Bible, was an outstanding attempt at integrating social-scientific and literary approaches to the study of biblical texts as two of the four major paradigms he identified in scholarly study up to that time. For Gottwald's socio-literary method was constructed partly as an answer to a serious (but also widely overlooked) problem to which brief attention is given below: namely, in a context where social-scientific approaches to the Bible constitute only one of several distinct paradigms influencing the field, how

---

25. See, e.g. the appropriation of anthropological models of shamanic ASCs and spirit possession, for interpreting Lk. 9.37-43a and its parallels, in Todd Klutz, *The Exorcism Stories in Luke-Acts: A Sociostylistic Reading*, SNTSMS 129 (Cambridge: Cambridge University Press, 2004), 194–205.

26. Norman K. Gottwald, *The Hebrew Bible: A Socio-Literary Introduction* (Philadelphia: Fortress Press, 1985).

might interpreters best move back and forth between the different enterprises and achieve a coherent synthesis of their results?[27] But just as importantly, Gottwald's method also has much in common with a different approach which, through long and patient development from the 1970s to the present, has come to influence scholarly interpretation of the Bible (especially the New Testament) as much as any other approach used in the last twenty-five years: namely, socio-rhetorical criticism, whose chief architect has been Vernon K. Robbins.[28]

The success of socio-rhetorical criticism in attracting scholarly interest and enriching biblical interpretation stems partly from its effort to bring together social-scientific criticism – especially modern anthropology and sociology – rhetorical criticism and other varieties of analysis (e.g. narratology and, more recently, cognitive science) in a manner that facilitates multilevelled and often richly observed readings of texts.[29] More particularly, with its postulate that any given unit of biblical discourse can be analysed fruitfully in terms of several different layers of 'texture' (inner texture, intertexture, social and cultural texture, ideological texture and sacred texture), socio-rhetorical criticism offers the interpreter a way of negotiating the problem noted above in connection with Gottwald – how best to negotiate and conceptualize the necessary movement across multiple and distinct levels of analysis pertinent to rounded interpretation of a single text – and simultaneously discourages rigid attachment to any one particular method of analysis.[30] In this regard, socio-rhetorical criticism can make a comparatively strong claim to fulfil an increasingly recognized need created by the recent proliferation of methods incorporated into biblical studies: namely, the intellectual need for what Gottwald aptly denoted a 'paradigm of paradigms',[31] a higher-order model of interpretation that can integrate the conceptual tools of the various methods now on offer and the results of their conjoined application.

Despite socio-rhetorical criticism's numerous merits, however, it has weaknesses that not only explain its absence from the foreground of the present collection but also alert us to the need for continued methodological reflection on the use of

27. Ibid., 7–8, 30–34.

28. The volume of pertinent publications by Robbins, his students, and others is too great for judicious survey here; but for the most influential syntheses see especially Vernon K. Robbins, *The Tapestry of Early Christian Discourse: Rhetoric, Society, and Ideology* (London and New York: Routledge, 1996); Robbins, *Exploring the Texture of Texts: A Guide to Socio-Rhetorical Interpretation* (Valley Forge, PA: Trinity Press, 1996); and Robbins, 'Social-Scientific Criticism and Literary Studies: Prospects for Cooperation in Biblical Interpretation', in *Modelling Early Christianity: Social-Scientific Studies of the New Testament in its Context*, ed. Philip Esler (London and New York: Routledge, 1995), 274–89.

29. The architect's own more recent, well-considered reflection in Vernon K. Robbins, 'Socio-Rhetorical Criticism', in *The Blackwell Companion to the New Testament*, ed. David Aune (Chichester: Wiley-Blackwell, 2010), 192–219 (esp. 192–93).

30. Ibid., 192–93.

31. Gottwald, *The Hebrew Bible*, 34.

social science in the interpretation of biblical and related texts. For instance, in both the theorizing and critical practice of Robbins and many other socio-rhetorical interpreters, the prominence assigned to historically specific Greco-Roman theories and practices of rhetorical composition in connection with the 'rhetorical' aspects of the method[32] have almost certainly resulted in doubts regarding its value and utility for purposes of interpreting Jewish Scripture, and especially the Hebrew Bible, much or all of which was composed and edited in contexts untouched by classical rhetoric; the approach has, not surprisingly, made its mark very largely in studies of the New Testament and post-biblical writings. Furthermore, while the heuristic value of conceptualizing texts as complex tapestries of multiple varieties of 'texture' is not in doubt, the various types of texture differentiated in socio-rhetorical criticism are organized and presented more in the form of an exegetical checklist[33] – a highly helpful checklist, to be sure – than as a properly systemic, organized grammar of analytical and interpretative foci; the latter sort of system, one example of which will be recommended presently, has numerous advantages over even the best of checklists, the most important edge being that it offers much greater potential for exploring and conceptualizing the precise relations between the different types of functional and contextual particulars of a given text, as opposed to merely ensuring that a good range of different perspectives are brought to bear on the act of interpretation.

Third, and finally, although the scholarly publications in socio-rhetorical criticism show occasional awareness of linguist M. A. K. Halliday's school of systemic linguistics and functional grammar as relevant to their own approach, their use of it tends to be limited to general comments about 'wordings'[34] and rarely exploits its analytical potential in a disciplined or detailed way; and while in theory Robbins's concept of inner texture allows room for serious analysis of the grammatical facets of texts, the backgrounding or even near-absence of grammatical aspects of texts and exegesis in various accounts of the socio-rhetorical approach and in many of its published results suggests that grammar is not a visible priority for this approach – a curious tendency for an enterprise that in other respects seems genuinely intent on facilitating comprehensive readings of the sources.[35] By what stroke of theoretical or other magic, previous generations of exegetes would surely marvel, has the best and most thorough form of exegesis become possible without

32. See, e.g. Robbins, 'Socio-Rhetorical Criticism', 192, 194, 207; and Robbins, *Jesus the Teacher: A Socio-Rhetorical Interpretation of Mark with a New Introduction* (Minneapolis: Fortress Press, 1992), 29.

33. Indicative is the structure of the method and its proposed levels of texture in Robbins, *Exploring the Texture*, vii–viii.

34. See, e.g. Robbins, *Exploring the Texture*, 5.

35. Perhaps to be seen as a symptom is the absence of the words 'grammar', 'syntax' and 'morphology' in Robbins, 'Socio-Rhetorical Criticism' – words moreover that are comparably difficult to find in the fuller treatment of inner texture, where such terms and the concerns they signify should find a home, in Robbins, *Exploring the Texture*, 7–39.

detailed engagement with lexis, the standard lexica, morphology, syntax and the major grammars of the biblical and related languages of antiquity? The oddness of all this is only increased when we consider that neither Halliday's functionalist approach to language, nor the formalist grammatical theories of Noam Chomsky, nor more recently the various articulations of cognitive grammar view language as intelligible, either psychologically or sociologically, without reference to its structuring as a grammatical system. As Halliday observes, the notion that a text can be analysed as discourse without considering grammar is a linguistically naïve illusion.[36]

And yet, the backgrounding of grammar in socio-rhetorical criticism is not so odd after all, for in the last few decades grammar has become less and less visible in most other approaches to biblical exegesis as well, including the various types of social-scientific criticism.[37] Indeed, because most social scientists are not required to study modern linguistics in depth and thus often display a lack of what is now often called 'critical language awareness',[38] the deficiency in that regard has motivated British linguist Norman Fairclough to develop Halliday's framework into a powerful method of linguistically cognizant criticism (known more widely as 'critical discourse analysis', or CDA) for use most especially in contemporary social research but potentially of great value to anyone in need of a rigorously theorized approach to the analysis of discourse in texts more generally, whatever the precise nature and origins of those texts might be.[39] Because both Halliday and Fairclough view the discipline of linguistics as a branch of sociology and appreciate its relationships with other social sciences such as psychology and social/cultural anthropology,[40] their approaches to the analysis and interpretation of language as social discourse provide excellent tools both for managing the dialectic of social-scientific generalization and properly observed discursive particulars, and

---

36. M. A. K. Halliday, *An Introduction to Functional Grammar* (London: Edward Arnold, 1985), xvi–xvii.

37. There are, of course, noteworthy exceptions; and one rightly singled out by Philip Esler ('The Context-Group Project: An Autobiographical Account', in *Anthropology and Biblical Studies: Avenues of Approach*, ed. Louise J. Lawrence and Mario I. Aguilar [Leiden: Deo, 2004], 57) is John Elliott's outstanding commentary, *1 Peter: A New Translation with Introduction and Commentary*, AB (New York: Doubleday, 2000).

38. Norman Fairclough, *Discourse and Social Change* (Cambridge: Polity, 1992), 1–2.

39. Many of Fairclough's numerous publications have the potential to enrich the analytical toolkit of the biblical exegete; but the most useful of them are his synthetic descriptions of critical discourse analysis as providing a framework for the integration of insights from system linguistics, the social sciences and critical theory, for which see especially Norman Fairclough, *Language and Power*, 3rd edn (London and New York: Routledge, 2015); Fairclough, *Critical Discourse Analysis*, 2nd edn (London and New York: Routledge, 2013); and Fairclough, *Discourse and Social Change*, esp. 225–40.

40. See, e.g. M. A. K. Halliday, *Language as Social Semiotic: The Social Interpretation of Language and Meaning* (London: Edward Arnold, 1978), 38–39.

for integrating the procedures and results of distinct levels of analysis carried out on a single text. More particularly, Halliday and Fairclough's sociolinguistic conceptualization of a text's extratextual environment as consisting of concentric spheres of ideological, cultural and situational context[41] does not merely allow but strongly encourages incorporation of whatever relevant insights a biblical critic might discover through their engagement with the scholarship of sociologists, anthropologists, ethnographers and other types of social scientists.

It is not within my aims here to describe all the methodological riches available in the published work of Halliday, Fairclough and related theorists; but I have provided an introduction to a good range of their leading ideas and put them to interpretative use in *The Exorcism Stories in Luke-Acts: A Sociostylistic Reading* (2004).[42] The lack of explicit reference to those ideas in the ensuing essays of the present volume should not be understood, therefore, as indicative of a judgement concerning their worth but rather is a mere accident of the contributors' particular interests (including my own) at the time of their essays' original drafting and presentation.

1.4 *Social-Scientific Perspectives on Jewish Scripture*

Half of the ensuing fourteen essays focus on matters pertaining to Jewish Scripture. The first of those, Philip R. Davies's 'Literary-Historical Exegesis as a Social Science', is especially interested in the contributions that both archaeology and the sociological subdiscipline of 'social memory' can make to exegetical scholarship concerning ancient Israel and the ideological construction of Israel in the Hebrew Bible. Like the present writer and many others, Davies sees the scholarly work of Norman Gottwald (see above) as having effected a bold advance from the major historical-critical studies by Von Rad and Noth towards a social-scientific mode of exegesis less interested in either the religious

---

41. See, e.g. Halliday, *Language as Social Semiotic*, 109, 122–26; and Fairclough, *Language and Power*, 58–60; in the same systemic tradition, the clearest account of the different levels of context is perhaps Suzanne Eggins, *An Introduction to Systemic Functional Linguistics* (London: Pinter Publishers, 1994), 34, 113, 330–32.

42. Like nearly all published monographs in biblical studies, my study of the exorcism stories was reviewed with a blend of approval (or even enthusiasm) and critical challenge; but in the present context, one of the book's qualities that in various ways seemed to be appreciated by all of its reviewers is the way in which my adapted methodology, sociostylistics, facilitated a rich integration of relevant theory, pertinent contextual data and various levels of linguistic and grammatical phenomena. See, e.g. Robert Brawley, review of *The Exorcism Stories in Luke-Acts: A Sociostylistic Reading*, by Todd Klutz, in *The Journal of Religion* 85, no. 4 (2005): 653–54, whose most relevant comment for my present purposes was his praise for the study's results as 'an outstanding weaving together of the linguistic, structural, and cultural dimensions of the text' (653).

distinctiveness of Israel or theological concepts such as 'the mighty acts of God'. Davies furthermore argues that optimal integration and dialectic of archaeology and literary analysis entails that the critical distance achieved by Gottwald in relation to historical-critical constructions of Israel (e.g. John Bright) needs to be increased. Particularly since Davies's own move in that direction strongly encourages a shift of critical interest away from establishing historical referents for the language *in* the texts to the types of rhetorical situations implied *by* the texts, it simultaneously contributes to the formulation of what Davies considers 'the essential interrogation' to be pursued in any application of social memory theory; namely, and in regard to any text that can be analysed as mnemonic performance, a properly social-scientific exegete will ask, 'Why deploy this particular repertoire?' From the platform of mnemo-repertoire, moreover, it is a very short journey to a methodological station similar to it but also interestingly different, namely, the relevance principle, and more particularly the question: To what blend of historical and social circumstances might the performance of a given repertoire of memories have been optimally relevant?

In 'The Concepts of "Counter-History" and Mnemohistory Applied to Biblical Sciences', Thomas Römer conceptualizes social-scientific criticism of the Bible as less a departure from the collective practices of historical criticism than a member of their set; yet, because historical criticism has served to highlight *inter alia* enormous complexities in the task of contextualizing and establishing firm datings for most parts of the Hebrew Bible in particular, it has created big problems for that prominent facet of social-scientific criticism which construes most of the biblical text's communicative meaning in terms of its orientation to particular specifiable audiences and precise configurations of social circumstances, an agenda comparatively less complicated for social-scientific readings of early Christian writings and the texts from Qumran. Because a comparatively high degree of spatio-temporal and experiential distance stands between the assumed context of reference and the implied context of mnemonic performance in most portions of the Hebrew Bible, much of that collection is well-suited to the types of analysis made possible by mnemohistory and 'counter-history' – the former, largely without interest in the verification of historical events, being defined chiefly by its focus upon the roles of tradition and social memory in the construction of group identity (a focus wholly consonant with its intellectual roots in the Durkheim-Halbwachs-Assmann genealogy); the latter being concerned primarily with the more specific mechanisms whereby tradition and memory construct the social other, a collective enemy, and thus indirectly also 'us', or a collective self. Römer's use of mnemohistory in particular serves to adduce fresh support for the Midianite-Kenite hypothesis concerning the origins of Yahwistic religion, while his application of both mnemohistory and counter-historical imagination to Exod. 4.6-7 contributes to a strong reading of those verses as a counter-historical reaction to earlier anti-Jewish discourse, closely related to Manetho's account in Flavius Josephus (*Against Apion*), to the effect that Moses was the leader of a group of lepers.

In 'Your Name Shall no Longer Be Jacob, but Refugee: Involuntary Migration and the Development of the Jacob Narrative', C. A. Strine looks at the characterization of Abraham, Isaac, Jacob and the matriarchs of Genesis 12–36 from a perspective informed by the emerging social-scientific discourse of refugee and forced migration studies (FMS). From that sort of angle, argues Strine, all of the characters just mentioned can be seen as resembling, in ways significant for exegesis of the ancestral narratives, the many refugees now receiving more and more attention from anthropologists, policymakers and experts in international law. The Jacob Narrative (Gen. 25.19–33.20) is explored by Strine as a specific test case, with a view to casting new light both on difficult features in the narrative and on its diachronic development. The fruit of that effort is, in effect, something genuinely distinctive in the history of scholarship on the ancestral narratives: namely, an FMS commentary on Gen. 25.19–33.20, the power of Strine's distinctive approach being illustrated best, perhaps, in his reading of (1) the deceitfulness of Isaac and Rebekah as typical of refugee behaviour studied in recent settings, (2) the high cost of Jacob's long-term commitment to Laban for the acquisition of Rachel as partly explicable in light of the arrangement's implicit provision of seven years of refugee protection for Jacob and (3) the more general asymmetry of the relationship between Jacob and Laban as representative of the tenor of migrant–host dealings observed by specialists in FMS with reference to a variety of other settings.

Walter Houston's essay, '"To Share Your Bread with the Hungry": Justice or Charity?', begins as an experiment in the use of economic anthropology, and more specifically the trio of modes of exchange conceptualized by Karl Polanyi and Marshall Sahlins (reciprocity, redistribution and exchange), with a view to explaining an observable constriction across time of concepts of justice in the Hebrew Bible; but in order to account for both the moral dimension and the power dynamics of almsgiving in particular, as a conceptual latecomer in the given process of constriction, Houston reminds us of our need for engaging with more than one or two favoured theorists; for in order to understand the long and historically particular process in question, the models provided by Polanyi and Sahlins are judged by Houston as requiring supplementation and correction – needs substantially satisfied by the anthropologist David Graeber's distinctive analysis of economic relations, which sees charity as entailing both a hierarchical relationship between the participants and thus operative principles antithetic to reciprocity and justice. In that light, the process whereby justice becomes identified in Jewish Scripture with almsgiving is to be explained at least partly by the historic shift in political structure from native Israelite monarchy in the pre-exilic era to the experience of non-Israelite imperial rule; for the function of Israel's monarchy in repressing destitution and even negative reciprocity (e.g. manipulative varieties of patronage) shows no evidence of having been performed later, during the Persian and Hellenistic periods, by foreign imperial rulers.

The increasingly approved distinction in scholarship on the book of Leviticus between ritual text and ritual praxis is the initiative supposition in Julia Rhyder's 'Space and Memory in the Book of Leviticus'. Recent scholarship based on that distinction, however, is evaluated by Rhyder as having shown inadequate awareness of important differences between 'actual' or empirical spaces on the one hand, and cultic spaces located in a mythic and thus distant past such as that described in Leviticus on the other; even the best of recent scholarly treatments of social and ritual space in Leviticus, Rhyder shows, presuppose that the conceptualization of space in the text of Leviticus directly mirrors either existing or desired cultic space. Rhyder argues that in order to give a better account of the role of Leviticus in constructing a socially relevant memory of Israel's cultic past, a methodology is required which integrates a blend of social-scientific studies of memory and interdisciplinary research on ritual space; for that purpose, recent anthropological and other appropriations of philosopher Henri Lefebvre's model of space as the product of an interaction between physical, mental and symbolic fields enables Rhyder's analysis of space in Leviticus to deal not merely with spaces as places – that is, as relatively stable or even static phenomena – but more subtly as dynamic environments in, around and through which participants in ritual events move with a rich variety of meanings. Of the several noteworthy results produced by Rhyder's application of her methodological synthesis, the three most illuminating might be her reading of Leviticus 16, the Yom Kippur text, as designed to help non-priestly Israelites imagine the processes of movement in all the spaces required for the ritual; her inference that the many differences between the wilderness context of reference in Leviticus and a Jerusalemite context of early textual reception would require any practice of ritual imitation to be imaginative and contextually adapted; and finally, her interpretation of the absence of discourse concerning either a king or royal patronage for the cult in Leviticus as indicative of an authorial interest in constructing a paradigmatic memory for a people under foreign rule – in order to participate meaningfully in the cult, Rhyder infers from Leviticus, all that is needed are priests, the law and the people themselves.

Norman Fairclough, mentioned briefly above in connection with critical discourse analysis, adds considerable value to M. A. K. Halliday's systemic-functionalist account of human language by incorporating insights from a wider range of major social and political theorists than Halliday's writings consider, including most especially the Italian political theorist Antonio Gramsci (1891–1937), whose thought concerning cultural hegemony provides the essential core of theoretical concepts employed by Jaeyoung Jeon in 'The Zadokite and Levite Scribal Conflicts and Hegemonic Struggles'. The appropriateness of a Gramscian analysis of select biblical writings from the Persian period is defended by Jeon partly on the ground that, with the various groups of Judahite competitors for influence at that time possessing neither a native kingship nor effective instruments of military and administrative power, their strategies both for seeking authority and for countering it depended very heavily on a combination of social, religious and cultural resources typical of those at play in hegemonic conflict more generally. Jeon interprets the two layers of tradition identified by many scholars in Numbers 16 as instantiating hegemonic conflict between established priestly authority and an influential group of lay challengers over control of the Jerusalem temple and, therewith, local governance and taxation. Both the literary structure of the P document as a whole, moreover, and its foregrounding of specifically temple-oriented and priestly interests, is construed by Jeon as exemplifying the sort of attempt that hegemonic groups characteristically make to universalize their perception of their own well-being as serving the interests of the entire community. When Jeon reads the Deuteronomistic History from the same Gramscian perspective, he is able to contextualize the ideology of that work as representing the interests of a group of elders, the lay challengers, within the same historical process of hegemonic struggle, and thus as an attempt to counter the Aaronide-priestly opponents. Closely related hegemonic struggles are inferred by Jeon from the relationships between the Phinehas story in Num. 25.6-15 and the anti-Aaronism of Exod. 32.8; and between Ezekiel 44, with its Zadokite criticism of the Levites, and the positive characterization of the Levites in 2 Chron. 11.13-17, the latter having strong potential to be read as a class-conscious correction of the former. From a Gramscian point of view, suggests Jeon, the entire history of implied conflict between the Zadokites and the levitical alliance both assumes and entails an ideological development on the levitical side from false consciousness (i.e. acceptance of the subordinate role assigned to them in the Zadokite world view) to class consciousness (i.e. critically aware opposition to the Zadokites' non-universal, group-specific interests).

In 'The Concept of Utopia and the Psalm of Habakkuk: An Alternative Reading', Chen Bergot approaches the prophetic book of Habakkuk from a methodological angle informed by recent thought about utopia, a concept that has spawned an entire field of academic discourse attracting interest not only from sociologists (e.g. Ruth Levitas) and political scientists (e.g. L. T. Sargent) but also literary theorists and philosophers. Bergot's attention is focused in particular upon the recognized difficulty of the ambiguous relationship between the prophetic collection of Habakkuk (chs 1–2) and the immediately ensuing psalm (Habakkuk 3). Because part of that ambiguity arises from differences between the two sections in regard to their respective contexts of reference, the interdiscursive blend of the book of Habakkuk as a whole (most especially ch. 3) is read by Bergot as inviting comparison with utopian writing – a category whose most defining characteristic is, propitiously for Bergot's inquiry, understood by many theorists to be marked by ambiguity in the relationship between 'the reality of the text' (i.e. the better reality to which all or part of the text refers) and 'the now of its composition' (i.e. the immediate situation assumed by its composition). Against readings that construe the psalm in particular both as eschatological discourse concerning an indefinite future and as the product of a stage of redaction later than the composition of the prophetic collection, Bergot's utopia-theoretical analysis enables her to develop an alternative synthesis that, among other things, makes Habakkuk as a literary whole more textually cohesive, ideationally coherent and pragmatically effective: the psalm, she argues, is best interpreted not eschatologically but instead as utopian discourse about an alternative reality better than the familiar world described in the prophetic collection and achievable in the present time of the book's intended audience.

1.5 *Social-Scientific Perspectives on the Dead Sea Scrolls and Early Christian Literature*

An interest uniting the two parts of the present volume and its introductory essay is the desideratum of a methodological synthesis that not only encourages use of the full range of the social sciences but also cultivates development of the highest levels of textual analysis and historiographical reflection. That interest is not merely assumed but underscored in various ways by George Brooke in 'The Social Sciences and the Dead Sea Scrolls'. A survey and critical assessment of the use of the social sciences in Qumran studies to date, Brooke's analysis gives students of the Dead Sea Scrolls nearly everything they might need to know about what sorts of questions ought to be asked in social-scientific readings of the ancient sources, which of the social-science disciplines have been used to good effect (and which have not) thus far, what results have been achieved, and where analytical pitfalls in the field will be anticipated by the wary. A noteworthy contribution from scholarly efforts to use Bryan Wilson's sociology of sectarianism, Brooke observes, is that it has enabled multiple identities to be inferred from the sectarian compositions and, thereby, to add some appropriate complexity to our understanding of the movement that produced them; in recent scholarly interest, a discernible movement away from the sociology of sectarianism to various types of identity theory may point to a field of fruitful inquiry for future research. By comparison with sociological approaches, attempts to employ anthropology have impacted upon a wider variety of questions, the areas of greatest influence identified by Brooke including most especially ritual, the contribution of scripture in prayer and liturgy to community identity, gender and the construction of male and female identities, the interplay of geography and social location, and systems of purity/impurity. The spatiality and implicit hierarchy of seating arrangements at the eschatological meal is singled out as an especially promising domain for future study. Equally useful treatments are given in turn to psychology, politics and economics, none of which are seen by Brooke as having been utilized in ways that exploit more than a small part of their potential. Brooke sees the social sciences as having assisted Qumran studies in the construction of etic categories that facilitate translation and sometimes even point to universal (or at least very widely shared) features of human experience; but he also joins the chorus of several other contributors to the present volume who warn that universalism – especially in texts from the distant past – is better discovered than assumed, and that social-scientific interpretation will always need to be wedded to careful exegesis if unhappy losses of semantic subtlety and historical particularity are to be prevented.

In 'Reviewing Purity and Impurity from a Gendered Perspective: The War Scroll (1QM) as a Case Study', Jessica Keady takes Mary Douglas's still influential study, *Purity and Danger: An Analysis of the Concepts of Pollution and Taboo* (1966), as her methodological point of departure but finds Douglas's tendency to downplay the material bodies of human agents ill-suited to her own particular interest in the Qumran male's embodied experience of impurity. That area of inquiry is, Keady argues, better matched with modes of analysis associated with the interdisciplinary fields of masculinity studies and gender analysis. From the perspective of those fields, the dynamism and instability of purity in everyday life entails that the status and measure of masculinity of the Qumran male must likewise have been experienced as inconstant and mutable; moreover, because conditions of impurity precluded participation in war and thus constituted obstacles between the impure male and the principal theatre for performing and demonstrating ideal masculinity, they impacted very strongly upon the Qumran male's honour rating in families and the wider community. Keady further illuminates the importance and function of war as an arena for the performance of masculinity by highlighting similarities between the War Scroll and comparative material from classical Athens where, in regard to armed conflict, disability seems to have functioned much like impurity at Qumran.

David Hamidovic, in 'The Teacher of Righteousness from the Perspective of the Sociology of Organizations', provides what is, among many other things, a valuable example of the ways in which the social sciences not only can keep us mindful of the historical processes of socio-religious change assumed and implied in our ancient primary sources but also enable us to model, understand and sometimes even explain those processes. Hamidovic's essay is interested above all in identifying processes of social change whose reality is necessitated by close reading of a few passages dealing with the Teacher of Righteousness at Qumran, and in explaining the role played by the Teacher, as individual agent, in bringing about those changes within his group, the Qumran community. For those purposes, Hamidovic's analysis makes fruitful use of the sociology of organizations, and most especially the work of Michel Crozier and Erhard Friedberg, whose seminal treatise *L'acteur et le système* (1977) is devoted chiefly to theorizing both the relationship between the individual agent and the group or organization to which they belong, and the ways in which that relationship conditions the realities of organizational change. Crozier and Friedberg's modelling of the interplay between collective organizational goals and the strategies of individual agent-members is viewed as a suitable and potentially illuminating resource for understanding the relationship between the Qumran community and the Teacher; more specifically, and in contrast to previous sociologically oriented studies of the Dead Sea Scrolls and the Qumran community – studies that have tended to put nearly all of their emphasis on collective aspects of the evidence – Hamidovic's use of Crozier and Friedberg is consciously motivated by a desire to explore the agency and strategies of an individual *acteur*, the Teacher of Righteousness, at the time of his arrival in the community. The characterization of the Teacher in the *Damascus Document*, CD A 1.3-11, as arriving in the community at Qumran twenty years after the group's birth is seen by Hamidovic as a potential clue to one of the historical Teacher's personal strategies and contributions to change and development in the group; for the reference in that text to the period of twenty years stoutly resists explanation as either a form of symbolic discourse or an echo of one potential intertext or another – instead, the reference satisfies the familiar historical-critical test of the criterion of embarrassment by entailing that the community experienced shameful difficulties in the two decades or so directly following its founding, a key implication being that the reference constitutes a reliable piece of social memory for use in Hamidovic's project of historical reconstruction. That line of interpretation has additional support from comparative analysis of *Pesher* Psalms[a], 4Q171 III 15-17, insofar as the identification of the Teacher in the latter text as the group's founder conflicts with the account in CD A 1.3-11. Partly on the basis of the contradiction between those two texts, Hamidovic builds a model of sociocultural change in the history of the Qumran community's memory of the Teacher: namely, a change from remembering the Teacher as a paradigm for non-Essene Jews joining the existing community – a memory close to the historical Teacher's own self-understanding – to remembering him as authoritative interpreter of Torah.

David Harvey's 'Saving Face in Galatia: Εὐπροσωπέω and Concern for Honour in the Argument of Paul's Letter' assesses critical scholarship on Galatians as having failed thus far to provide appropriate contextualization for the apostle's 'face' discourse in Gal. 6.12. Harvey's essay steps into that gap and quickly begins to fill it by, first, properly locating the 'face' lexis of ancient comparative sources within the larger semantic field concerning honour, an understanding often backgrounded or sometimes even altogether missing in the scholarly literature. The contextual relevance of honour having thus been clearly established, Harvey is unwilling to take the easy path of uncritically accepting the standard discussions of honour in the ancient Mediterranean world but instead engages with an impressive range of Greco-Roman sources in order to construct his own, contextually adapted model of honour. What emerges from that engagement is, among other things, the discovery that honour in general and face discourse in particular is very often embedded in larger registers or situation types which include overtones of challenge and riposte, competition for status, and social hierarchy. All of that has value, of course, for a reading of Galatians and perhaps beyond; but it shows its greatest significance when it enables Harvey to look afresh at his key passage in Gal. 6.12 – Paul's discourse about his opponents wanting to make a 'good face' – and to read it as broadly synonymous with the apostle's evaluation of the same people as 'boasting in the flesh' (Gal. 6.13); as implying concern on their part, shameful from Paul's point of view, for honour; as contributing to a salient chain of textual cohesion and coherence across much of the letter, from 1.22 (Paul as unknown 'by face') through 2.6 (God's rejection of human 'facework') to 6.12; and as being more social in force than either legal or even theological, though the implications for both theology and ethics stand very much at the centre of Paul's aims. As Harvey himself highlights, a noteworthy implication of his analysis is that from Paul's point of view, the problem with his opponents in Galatians has less to do with bad theology than with an addiction to the honour game, social competition and differentiation, a problem that is worsened when seen in the light of their own God's repudiation of all forms of facework.

In 'The Use of Social Models in Biblical Studies: Philippians 1.27–2.5 as a Case Study', Peter Oakes draws attention to the pervasiveness and practical necessity of everyday models as reality-simplifying strategies for managing complexity. On that basis of daily human experience, Oakes reminds us, the scholarly enterprise of carefully and reflectively constructing explicit social-scientific models for the analysis and interpretation of texts can be understood as continuous with what human beings effectively do in largely unconscious ways all the time, and thus also as an activity worth understanding by anyone interested in dealing responsibly with complex writings from social environments very different from our own. With models being intrinsic to the way we think, the constraints on human choice regarding models is not whether or not to employ them but pertains rather to how consciously and deliberatively we choose, revise and use them for managing whatever task is at hand. In addition to highlighting a range of very attractive advantages to be gotten from careful attempts to use models in our interpretative activities, Oakes helpfully alerts us to a particular subtlety to be noted by anyone eager to utilize social-scientific kinds of modelling in interpretative work: namely, the existence of significant differences between prominent practitioners of social-scientific interpretation in New Testament studies, a tension perhaps best represented by exchanges published several years ago between Philip Esler and David Horrell, whose wide-ranging debate included disagreement over usage of the term 'model' itself. An example of the ways in which explicit construction of models can facilitate significant interventions in biblical scholarship is provided by Oakes in a paradigmatic critical reflection on his own earlier use of models for contextualizing Paul's letter to the Philippian church, a community often modelled (not very carefully or deliberatively) as consisting almost entirely of either Roman citizens or Roman military veterans. A more conscious modelling of the Philippians letter's audience, Oakes argues, exposes such models as highly improbable and supports an alternative picture that includes far greater social diversity in the church at Philippi; and that higher degree of diversity has several very significant implications for interpreting Paul's letter, the most noteworthy perhaps being that a substantial part of the audience to whom Paul's letter offers a new exalted identity in Christ consisted of non-elites, of people whose status outside Christ was low.

My own essay, 'Inside the Bridal Chamber: Individual, Group, and Intertextuality in the *Gospel of Philip* 65.1-26', is partly an implicit integration of methodological concepts imbibed from sociologists (e.g. Emile Durkheim and Rodney Stark), their scholarly interpreters (e.g. Michael A. Williams), and sociologically oriented linguists (e.g. Norman Fairclough and Roger Fowler); and partly the continuation of an attempt initiated several years ago to explore the implications of the rethinking of 'Gnosticism' for the reading and contextualizing of early Christian texts.[43] By conscious design, the methodological synthesis in my essay is firmly subordinated to my interest in reading as well as possible the target text and the chosen comparative sources (especially Gen. 2.18-24; Plato, *Symp.* 189-193; Eph. 5.31-32). Against possible misunderstanding of my use of 'individualism' in the essay, it is worth highlighting here that my interpretation of *Gos. Phil.* 65.1-26 as instantiating a comparatively individualistic variety

---

43. See Todd Klutz, 'Re-Reading the Corinthian Correspondence After Rethinking "Gnosticism"', *JSNT* 26, no. 2 (2003): 193–216.

of discourse is not a consequence of unawareness on my part of the important scholarship of Bruce Malina and others highlighting the group-oriented character of the ancient Mediterranean world;[44] instead, my thesis regarding individualism in *Gos. Phil.* 65.1-26 tacitly takes for granted the general validity and usefulness of Malina's model – that explains why I do not even bother to mention it – in addition to illustrating (albeit only obliquely) its broad correspondence to the perspectives represented in my main comparative sources. But it is precisely for those reasons that the assumptions and rhetoric of *Gos. Phil.* 65.1-26 in particular stand out as worthy of special attention – the discourse of that text, in comparison with my handful of key comparative sources, fits Malina's model to a much lesser degree; thus, a methodologically significant implication of my essay is that, while the explanatory models of social scientists and social-scientifically oriented interpreters do very often fit and illuminate the ancient evidence that interests us, their degree of suitability can and should be understood as varying from case to case. But almost as importantly, even (or perhaps especially) when a given model fits poorly, something valuable can be learned from the same process of inquiry.

Methodologically, the starting point for Kimberley Fowler's 'Shifting Social Contexts at Nag Hammadi: Imagining a Fourth-Century Monastic Response to the Roles of Knowledge and Love in the *Gospel of Philip*' is common ground shared with Hugo Lundhaug's recent appropriation of cognitive science, and more particularly current theorizing about conceptual metaphor and conceptual blending, in a study of soteriological tropes in the *Gospel of Philip* and the *Exegesis on the Soul*. In Fowler's own more tightly focused study, critical awareness of metaphor and conceptual blending contributes to a reading of the *Gospel of Philip*'s discourses about love and knowledge which militates strongly against the increasingly wobbly notion of a 'Valentinian' church setting for the text as a whole. Against the Valentinian hypothesis, and partly by means of a disciplined comparative study of the *Gospel of Philip* and fourth-century Pachomian literature in specific regard to the key pair of motifs, Fowler builds a case for contextualizing her target text not merely in a broad context of fourth-century Egyptian Christianity but more particularly within a setting of late antique Egyptian monasticism. Much to the delight of the present writer, Fowler's critique of the Valentinian hypothesis converges in significant ways with my own essay on the *Gospel of Philip* near the end of this volume; but for any readers who feel that my own piece might press the case for a comparatively individualistic ideology in that tractate too far, Fowler's nuanced argument for a monastic setting might be found more palatable. In balance, though, the difference may very well be less substantive than it seems; for if the argument of Larry Siedentop's *Inventing the Individual: The Origins of Western Liberalism* (2014) should be allowed into the conversation, it might tell

---

44. See Bruce J. Malina, *The New Testament World: Insights from Cultural Anthropology*, 3rd edn (Louisville: Westminster John Knox, 2001), 43–46, 58–80; and more recently Philip Esler, 'The Mediterranean Context of Early Christianity', in *The Early Christian World*, vol. 1 (London and New York: Routledge, 2017), 16–17.

us that the late antique and early medieval monastic ideal of 'solitude in company' was both an instantiation of existing individualistic tendencies in the Christian tradition, and an important contribution to their further development.[45]

1.6 *Concluding Integrative Postscript*

As implied at the very beginning of the present essay, and like both Abe Ravelstein and thus also the late American political philosopher Allan Bloom, the present writer not only has a long-standing interest in the social sciences – in my own case, an interest encouraged by how very much the social sciences bring to the table of interpretation devoted to early Jewish, Christian and other literatures, but also more generally because of the social sciences' collective prominence, influence and sheer intellectual heft in the institutional environments in which I have studied and taught throughout much of my adult life – but also continues to nurture an even longer passion for the game of basketball, the beautiful game, as it is known to many of its enthusiasts, but particularly to fans of the San Antonio Spurs, and even more especially in reference to the Spurs' distinctively cohesive, group-oriented style of play. Accordingly, I sometimes wonder what one or another of the beautiful game's greatest talents might think or say upon hearing or reading any of my thoughts about the kinds of topics treated above. Indeed, upon hearing nothing more than the title of the present essay, for instance, the most promising current heir to the hoops throne once occupied by Michael Jordan – I am referring here, of course, to the 2016–17 Most Valuable Player in the National Basketball Association, Mr Russell Westbrook – can easily be imagined responding, 'What? Bro, what you talking about, man?'[46] My remaining comments below are therefore intended to sum up the discussion above in a manner that might clarify the sense of 'The Structure of Social-Scientific and Grammatical Integrations' for the benefit of any reader wanting the help, but especially for the sake of intelligent non-specialists like Russell Westbrook and their fans, a significant portion of whom read biblical and other ancient sources of wisdom and terror, take them very seriously, and sometimes even dip into academic books like this one.

---

45. Larry Siedentop, *Inventing the Individual: The Origins of Western Liberalism* (London: Allen Lane, 2014), 92–99. On the prominence of individualism as one of the two main attitudes characterizing Pachomius's regime, and thus as a feature in the relevant emerging culture, see Philip Rousseau, *Pachomius: The Making of a Community in Fourth-Century Egypt* (Berkeley: University of California Press, 1985), 94–95.

46. Westbrook's response to a sports journalist who asked whether the outcome of a particular game between Westbrook's team, the Oklahoma City Thunder, and the Utah Jazz was a matter of the Thunder losing the game or, instead, of the Jazz winning it; see 'Russell Westbrook Funny Interview, "Bro, what you talking about?"', Titas Bielskis, 17 August 2017, https://www.youtube.com/watch?v=OHy7s-2UA0k.

In the present essay, one of my two main interests is the question, how best to integrate both our use of appropriate social-scientific generalizations in the reading of biblical and related texts, and the ever-necessary grammatical analysis of linguistic and literary details in those same writings, with a view to interpreting them as well as they can be interpreted; but at the same time, the present essay is also interested in setting up and previewing a collection of imaginative attempts to achieve that very sort of integration – a collection, in other words, of social-scientific and grammatical integrations. The matter of the 'structure' of those integrations – the question, that is, of how or in what way(s) the dialectic of social-scientific generalizations and grammatical particulars might be suitably designed for our particular interpretative projects – pertains likewise both to the present essay and to the larger collection of which it is a part; for while the present introduction is explicitly interested in the kinds of available frameworks that might help us to optimize the configuration of our integrative projects, it also previews the structure, sequencing and contents of the other fourteen essays in the volume, each of which in its own distinctive ways instantiates strong interest in the challenges of methodological integration.

But finally, in addition to being unified by an interest in methodological integrations and their structure, both the individual essays offered here and the volume as a whole are, alike, products of the particular type of dialectical integration that often results from good conversation, where exchanges of knowledge, ideas and experience take place between people who do not merely share a common pool of communicative resources but also differ from each other in significant ways. Those sorts of exchanges and conversations afford us many of our best opportunities for growth and refinement in our experience of meaning. The present volume is therefore offered as a contribution to a larger conversation about the integration and use of the social sciences and other bodies of knowledge for interpreting biblical and related writings from antiquity; and it is offered more specifically in the hope that both its contributors and its readers might be able to carry that conversation forward into the future, to continue to learn from it, and to do so as integratively as possible.

Bibliography

Baert, Patrick. *Philosophy of the Social Sciences: Toward Pragmatism*. Cambridge: Polity Press, 2005.

Bellow, Saul. *Ravelstein*. London: Penguin Books, 2000.

Berger, Peter L., and Thomas Luckmann. *The Social Construction of Reality: A Treatise in the Sociology of Knowledge*. Garden City, NY: Anchor Books, 1966.

Bloom, Allan. *The Closing of the American Mind: How Higher Education Has Failed Democracy and Impoverished the Souls of Today's Students*. New York: Simon and Schuster, 1987.

Brawley, Robert. Review of *The Exorcism Stories in Luke-Acts: A Sociostylistic Reading*, by Todd Klutz. *The Journal of Religion* 85, no. 4 (2005): 653–54.

Carrithers, Michael. *Why Humans Have Cultures: Explaining Anthropology and Social Diversity*. Oxford: Oxford University Press, 1992.

Castelli, Elizabeth. 'Gender, Theory, and *The Rise of Christianity*: A Response to Rodney Stark'. *JECS* 6, no. 2 (1998): 227–57.

Chomsky, Noam. *American Power and the New Mandarins*. New York: Pantheon Books, 1969.

Eggins, Suzanne. *An Introduction to Systemic Functional Linguistics*. London: Pinter Publishers, 1994.

Elliott, John. *1 Peter: A New Translation with Introduction and Commentary*. AB. New York: Doubleday, 2000.

Esler, Philip F. *Community and Gospel in Luke-Acts: The Social and Political Motivations of Lucan Theology*, SNTSMS 57. Cambridge: Cambridge University Press, 1987.

Esler, Philip F. 'The Context-Group Project: An Autobiographical Account'. In *Anthropology and Biblical Studies: Avenues of Approach*, edited by Louise J. Lawrence and Mario I. Aguilar, 46–61. Leiden: Deo, 2004.

Esler, Philip F. 'The Mediterranean Context of Early Christianity'. In *The Early Christian World*, edited by Philip F. Esler, 3–26. London and New York: Routledge, 2017.

Fairclough, Norman. *Discourse and Social Change*. Cambridge: Polity, 1992.

Fairclough, Norman. *Critical Discourse Analysis*. 2nd edn. London and New York: Routledge, 2013.

Fairclough, Norman. *Language and Power*. 3rd edn. London and New York: Routledge, 2015.

Fauconnier, Gilles, and Mark Turner. *The Way We Think: Conceptual Blending and the Mind's Hidden Complexities*. New York: Basic Books, 2002.

Geertz, Clifford. *Available Light: Anthropological Reflections on Philosophical Topics*. Princeton: Princeton University Press, 2000.

Gellner, Ernest. *The Psychoanalytic Movement: The Cunning of Unreason*. London: Paladin, 1985.

Gellner, Ernest. 'The Scientific Status of the Social Sciences (und leider auch Sociologie)'. In *Relativism and the Social Sciences*, edited by Ernest Gellner, 101–27. Cambridge: Cambridge University Press, 1987.

Gottwald, Norman K. *The Hebrew Bible: A Socio-Literary Introduction*. Philadelphia: Fortress Press, 1985.

Halliday, M. A. K. *Language as Social Semiotic: The Social Interpretation of Language and Meaning*. London: Edward Arnold, 1978.

Halliday, M. A. K. *An Introduction to Functional Grammar*. London: Edward Arnold, 1985.

Hopkins, Keith. 'Christian Number and Its Implications'. *JECS* 6, no. 2 (1998): 185–226.

Klutz, Todd. 'The Rhetoric of Science in *The Rise of Christianity*: A Response to Rodney Stark's Sociological Account of Christianization'. *JECS* 6, no. 2 (1998): 162–84.

Klutz, Todd. 'Re-Reading the Corinthian Correspondence after Rethinking "Gnosticism"'. *JSNT* 26, no. 2 (2003): 193–216.

Klutz, Todd. *The Exorcism Stories in Luke-Acts: A Sociostylistic Reading*. SNTSMS, no. 129. Cambridge: Cambridge University Press, 2004.

Lakoff, George, and Mark Johnson. *Philosophy in the Flesh: The Embodied Mind and Its Challenge to Modern Thought*. New York: Basic Books, 1999.

Malina, Bruce J. *The New Testament World: Insights from Cultural Anthropology*. 3rd edn. Louisville: Westminster John Knox, 2001.

Meeks, Wayne A. *The First Urban Christians: The Social World of the Apostle Paul*. New Haven: Yale University Press, 1983.

Nussbaum, Martha C. *Not for Profit: Why Democracy Needs the Humanities*. Princeton: Princeton University Press, 2010.

Program on Constitutional Government at Harvard. 'Conference on the 25th Anniversary of Allan Bloom's *The Closing of the American Mind*, on Students'. Accessed 17 August 2017. https://www.youtube.com/watch?v=VLGTSo-9JwA.

Robbins, Vernon K. *Jesus the Teacher: A Socio-Rhetorical Interpretation of Mark with a New Introduction*. Minneapolis: Fortress Press, 1992.

Robbins, Vernon K. 'Social-Scientific Criticism and Literary Studies: Prospects for Cooperation in Biblical Interpretation'. In *Modelling Early Christianity: Social-Scientific Studies of the New Testament in its Context*, edited by Philip Esler, 274–89. London and New York: Routledge, 1995.

Robbins, Vernon K. *The Tapestry of Early Christian Discourse: Rhetoric, Society, and Ideology*. London and New York: Routledge, 1996.

Robbins, Vernon K. *Exploring the Texture of Texts: A Guide to Socio-Rhetorical Interpretation*. Valley Forge, PA: Trinity Press, 1996.

Robbins, Vernon K. 'Socio-Rhetorical Criticism'. In *The Blackwell Companion to the New Testament*, edited by David Aune, 192–219. Chichester: Wiley-Blackwell, 2010.

Rousseau, Philip. *Pachomius: The Making of a Community in Fourth-Century Egypt*. Berkeley: University of California Press, 1985.

Siedentop, Larry. *Inventing the Individual: The Origins of Western Liberalism*. London: Allen Lane, 2014.

Stark, Rodney. *The Rise of Christianity: A Sociologist Reconsiders History*. Princeton: Princeton University Press, 1995.

Stark, Rodney. 'E Contrario'. *JECS* 6, no. 2 (1998): 259–67.

Titas Bielskis. 'Russell Westbrook Funny Interview, "Bro, what you talking about?"'. Accessed 17 August 2017. https://www.youtube.com/watch?v=OHy7s-2UA0k.

Part I

SOCIAL-SCIENTIFIC PERSPECTIVES
ON JEWISH SCRIPTURE

Chapter 2

LITERARY-HISTORICAL EXEGESIS AS
A SOCIAL SCIENCE

Philip R. Davies

2.1 *History, Bible and Archaeology*

The deployment of social-science models within literary-historical exegesis is an inevitable consequence (if not universally recognized) of the consensus that archaeology provides the most secure body of historical data on first millennium BCE Palestine. Archaeology is a social science: hence the history of ancient *Israels*[1] must be grounded in a social-scientific enterprise. However, there also exist 'Israels' in the Hebrew Bible less straightforwardly represented in the material culture and assuming, partly or wholly, the character of social constructs. These appear within the literary record, mainly but not exclusively in the Hebrew scriptures. However, unless judged as purely ideal creations of authors, they correspond to historical identities shared by certain groups and recognized by others. While directly accessible only through literary analysis, these 'Israels' comprise an important constituent of the social history of central Palestine and are therefore also amenable to a social-scientific investigation, and historical-critical exegesis should direct itself accordingly. This argument will be expanded in the following essay.

The now discredited 'biblical archaeology' movement,[2] whatever its faults, clearly accepted the principle that archaeology was the basis for reliable historical reconstruction, even if its rather positivistic mindset did not adequately acknowledge the extent of subjective interpretation necessary to convert the data into a historical narrative. A further defect was, of course, its assumption that the biblical stories of the past constituted reliable historiography, this assumption serving as both premise and conclusion to the entire enterprise. Its fundamental methodological flaw was its asymmetrical comparison of biblical and artefactual

---

1. On the necessary use of the plural, see P. R. Davies, *The History of Ancient Israel: A Guide for the Perplexed* (London: T&T Clark, 2015), 65–100.

2. B. O. Long, *Planting and Reaping Albright: Politics, Ideology, and Interpreting the Bible* (University Park, PA: Pennsylvania State University Press, 1997); T. W. Davis, *Shifting Sands: The Rise and Fall of Biblical Archaeology* (Oxford: Oxford University Press, 2004).

data. Scientific archaeology proceeded by stratigraphy, ceramic typology and other analytical methods that eventually, instead of merely recovering objects and displaying features, exposed the underlying traces of human occupational history and developed an appropriate history from these. But the biblical narratives were not dealt with in a similar way: only their surface was read. The texts were unexamined, unexcavated, the traces of their own history disregarded. This disregard was not entirely innocent: underlying, and in some cases encouraging, biblical archaeology was an aversion to 'higher criticism', creating an impulse to bypass its methods. The aversion was not methodological, but arose from a deep cultural affection for the biblical stories and a rejection of conclusions that drove a wedge between the sacred narrated *in* the texts and the critically reconstructed history *of* the texts, which offered a rather different account of the past.

Beyond the 'biblical archaeology' circle, notably in Germany, the correct alignment of archaeological data with the results of 'higher criticism' remained a crucial component of historical research. The necessary reconciliation of the different histories implied by archaeology and biblical narrative was resolved in a manner that served theological rather than sociological interests. We may take the treatment of the exodus, wilderness wanderings and military conquest as primary examples. The biblical narratives about the past came to be seen as representing *tradition*, a term that recognized a certain distance in both time and content between real events and their biblical recollection, yet allowed a positive evaluation of that recollection. As articulated supremely by von Rad,[3] it was the 'traditions' that provided the basis for theological evaluation, not the history – a direct reversal of the priority given to the historical events by biblical archaeology. While the source-critical basis of the 'New Documentary Hypothesis' remained uncontested, a new approach emerged that traced the history of *traditions*. The modern reader of Noth's great *Überlieferungsgeschichte des Pentateuch*,[4] however, can see how uneasily the approach fitted the source-critical substructure, as the division of the 'tradition' into themes ran alongside a *Grundschrift* in which they were combined in the manner of classical Pentateuchal source theory. More significant, however, was the abandonment of this approach in confronting the books of Samuel–Kings. One of Wilhelm de Wette's arguments for the relative lateness of the Mosaic law was its absence from the religious practice implied in these books, where Julius Wellhausen, following suit, found a description of that early, more spontaneous form of Israelite religion that in his view characterized the prophets. Thus, the historical reliability of Samuel–Kings did not yield that same distinction between 'history' and 'tradition' as in the Pentateuchal/Hexateuchal writings. Noth, for example, despite a fully tradition-historical commentary on Joshua,[5] adopted the book of Judges as depicting the historical basis for the

---

3. G. von Rad, *Old Testament Theology* (London: SCM Press, 1975); German original, Munich: Kaiser, 1957–60.

4. M. Noth, *A History of Pentateuchal Traditions* (Englewood Cliffs: Prentice-Hall, 1972); German original, Stuttgart: Kohlhammer, 1948.

5. M. Noth, *Das Buch Josua* (Tübingen: Mohr, 1938), 59.

formation of Israelite traditions in an amphictyony. Von Rad, meanwhile, argued that the 'Solomonic enlightenment'[6] provided the setting for the work of the Yahwist. The 'united monarchy', the reigns of the Judahite and Israelite kings, the exile and the 'return' were unproblematically free of the need for reconstruction; Noth's *History of Israel* was only slightly less a midrash on these books than John Bright's.[7]

After the advent of archaeology, as before, 'higher criticism', whether as source-, form- or tradition criticism, operated as a literary discipline. While we should not ignore the attempts to correlate certain 'traditions' with historical contexts (the amphictyony, the reign of Solomon), these contexts were themselves part of the biblical construction of history. Despite the assumptions of 'biblical archaeology', very little of that construction constituted an archaeological fact, and the juxtaposition of literary and archaeological methods was incapable of generating a true synthesis. The language of 'correspondence' or 'confirmation' betrayed their essential independence, pointing to occasional moments of conjunction but not to an integrated approach that required an alliance of methodologies. The proponents of 'biblical archaeology' were no more interested in such a methodological alliance, being uninterested in the texts as historical products but only as testimony to 'history'. Moreover, the kind of history to which 'biblical archaeology' was being led was itself a literary kind of history, not only drawn from texts but also focusing on persons and events that in many cases were simply not capable of being inferred purely from the material remains. The challenge of constructing an appropriately archaeological kind of history was to emerge only as ceramic typology and stratigraphy were supplemented by techniques that illuminated the contours of human life and aimed at a different conception of 'history'.

But in the late twentieth century archaeology rapidly developed as a social science, not least in becoming more theory-driven as well as technically competent, and as a branch of anthropology rather than of history. Somewhat belatedly, and as yet incompletely, biblical-related archaeology caught on. In the field of literary-historical criticism, biblical studies witnessed a turn towards literary theories that were indifferent or even hostile to historical dimensions. Yet paradoxically, this turn led to an increasing awareness of literary theory in general and informed the practice of literary-historical criticism, itself a practice that was beginning to adopt social-scientific questions and methods. The reasons for this shift towards social science cannot all be identified, but with the publication of the results of the West Bank survey in the 1970s, a clear breach was made between what had been identified as 'Israelite traditions' and archaeological history. Not only the stories of patriarchs and conquest – pillars of biblical archaeology already under attack – but the entire edifice of origin traditions could no longer be related to the historical period to which they claimed to refer. Simply put, the 'Israel' that supposedly

---

6. Von Rad, *Old Testament Theology*, I, 57.
7. J. Bright, *A History of Israel* (Philadelphia: Westminster Press, 1959).

developed the 'traditions' did not exist. How such stories could have come about, when and why, posed a more acute problem. The origins of the earliest population widely interpreted as forming the basis for 'Israel' were explicable not by reason of divine election, nor immigration to an originally discrete culture or ethnicity, but to socio-economic causes.

Gottwald's *Tribes of Yahweh*,[8] which explicitly addressed a social-scientific challenge to a practice dominated by theology, represents a landmark in the journey towards social-scientific exegesis. It retained many elements of what had gone before, including tradition-historical argumentation and especially a positive evaluation of religious distinctiveness in 'early Israel'. But this distinctiveness was explained by reference to social structures and not 'mighty acts of God'. Since then, both archaeological and literary research into the history of Iron age Palestine have developed quite dramatically. It is still the case that archaeological history of ancient Palestine is dominated by the theme of 'Israel', but it is increasingly attending to the interaction of numerous political and social groupings and a recognition that interaction among these, together with the impact of external powers, is the plot, and not the rise and fall of two small kingdoms. Literary research is not only addressing the process by which 'traditions' – now being recast as 'memories' in order to exploit the theories, methods and results of interdisciplinary research on social memory – arise and develop, but also the purposes they serve. In both areas, some common themes can be discerned, of which identity is perhaps the most significant. Archaeologically, the basic issue is whether ethnicity (sc. the ethnicity 'Israel') can be identified through material cultural remains; literarily, the question is how identity is reflected, created and modified through the production of stories about the past. And perhaps the most important development within historical-critical exegesis is the social location of the authorship of the scriptural writings, a focus that brings together the two aspects of text, its material production and its ideological configurations.

Despite the enormously enhanced sophistication of archaeological and literary methods, the fundamental challenge of the last hundred years of biblical criticism remains largely unresolved: how are the results of each approach to history to be integrated? According to the opinions of some scholars, the question is wrongly designed: each discipline addresses a different kind of evidence, and constructs a different kind of history. Such an opinion is not wholly wrong either. But if it rests on a classic distinction between 'ideal' and 'material', then it ignores both the insight that texts are also material artefacts and also a recognition that archaeology likewise seeks to understand the 'inner history' of societies, their mentalities, from material remains. Archaeologists search after lifestyles, the symbolic values implied in architecture, the social coding of diet, of interaction with the environment, and, in general, large-scale (*longue durée*)

---

8. N. K. Gottwald, *The Tribes of Yahweh: A Sociology of the Religion of Liberated Israel, 1250–1050 B.C.E.* (Maryknoll, NY: Orbis Books, 1979).

processes. The biblical stories deal with individuals, conversations, private transactions and discrete events, most of which are invisible to excavation and survey, but which, even when fictional (perhaps *especially* when fictional), shed light on that 'inner history'. Archaeological data and biblical texts together exhibit the functioning of households, the distribution of gender roles, belief systems, symbolic universes, ethnicity and many other issues upon which human society is constructed. There may exist areas of social life into which neither the text nor archaeology can adequately reach, but where each can seek the help of the other. At all events, the different kinds of data that each discipline deals with cannot be used as an excuse for non-engagement. On the contrary, the previously employed contrasts, even antagonisms, between text and spade have been rendered obsolete by the developments in each discipline just described. The competent historian of any human past – but especially of ancient Palestine – will now need to be accomplished in both archaeological and exegetical analysis. She or he will need to recognize her- or himself as, in large measure, a social scientist.

From the point of view of a historical-critical exegete, the most straightforward approach in a social-scientific agenda is to consider any text in the first instance as a product of history, as brought into existence by a historical society, by a particular kind of individual and at a particular moment. The complications become immediately apparent: as historical artefacts, texts by and large reflect not a single datable moment, but a period of time, perhaps entailing certain discrete moments of revision, during which they can be seen against different historical moments that may in some cases have prompted such revision. They are themselves rather like *tells* whose layers require stratification. Unlike excavation, however, any stratification has to be deduced. The literary critic's capacity to identify historical contexts purely from a critical analysis of a text is in any case limited, and consequently it is now archaeology that provides the more reliable basis for a historical reconstruction from which, where possible, the analysis of text as artefact can be undertaken. What may be added, however, are the insights from a body of sociological theory and data pertaining to the ways in which societies operate. A dramatic illustration of the shift from theology to sociology is the assumption that 'ancient Israel' is essentially approached as typical and not remarkable. This is necessary, of course, for the comparative nature of most social-science theory and argumentation. It is also, I would argue, necessary for the construction of any acceptable history, for without the application of norms of human behaviour, it is impossible to provide a meaningful historical narrative. While the 'mighty acts of God', a divinely elected 'nation', or even an inspired set of 'traditions' supported a great deal of writing about Israelite history before the latter part of twentieth century, now it can only promote a continued isolation of Palestinian history from the history of the rest of the world, in the same way that the 'Holy Land' is separated in Jewish and Christian imagination from the remainder of the globe.

2.2 *History and Sociology*

Historical-critical exegesis as conventionally practiced has a limited ability to correlate effectively with archaeological data and their interpretation. Biblical critics in the past have posited histories of the evolution of texts that entailed the postulation of creative authors, schools and editors, often denoted by sigla (J, P, D, with or without superscript numbers). The kind of history that such analyses produce cannot provide a reliable basis for either political or religious history. Historical-critical analysis must align with the procedures of archaeological interpretation: that is, to adopt a social-scientific approach by considering the manner in which texts as artefacts are produced. 'Texts as artefacts', however, implies two constructions of the meaning of 'text'. One is the physical, material product: an ancient inscription, an ostracon or a Qumran manuscript, for instance. The other is the intangible, the linguistic expression of ideas. The two aspects collude in a single act of inscription, a historical occurrence. The historical-critical exegete and the archaeologist surely meet with the same interrogation: what are the implications of the production of such texts, in terms of resources, be they material, political, intellectual, or cultural (i.e. 'social' in the widest sense)? Whether the assumption is always valid or demonstrable, we must presuppose that no text, in either connotation of the word, can entirely mask the historical moment of production. This does not mean the moment can be discerned, for a particular narrative may import a widely applicable character or may be a reworked assemblage of types and tropes devoid of any overt (or even covert) historical referentiality. But there remains the question: why tell this story, why tell it this way, why deploy this particular repertoire, why introduce these details and why tell it *now*? Even here, of course, we cannot always decode. By using the social science of memory studies, for example cultural memory,[9] we can focus on the interaction of ideology and politics, on the act, purpose and function of creating a particular image of the past.

This is not at present an agenda either widely or explicitly adopted by literary-historical critics. But it follows from the premise that both literary-historical exegesis and archaeology are human sciences and, indeed, ultimately seeking very similar goals. Both address the products of past human societies, investigating and analysing their material and symbolic interaction with their environment. The biblical texts give us no secure knowledge about the nature and activities of gods or the meaning of history, but they do inform us about how human beings, individually and collectively, imagined and lived in a world they conceived as overseen and determined by divine beings. They also demonstrate how the thoughts and behaviours of people could be informed and controlled by those who claimed to have access to these divine beings and their secrets, access that gave the power even to declare what had happened in the past, what was happening now

---

9. Biblical Studies has previously employed the term 'tradition' for this work.

and what would happen in the future. Divination pervaded every level of life in the first millennium BCE. But the biblical texts are not omens; they do not convey transcendental reality – or at least, such a notion has to be programmatically excluded by the historian or social scientist.

Models of how literary criticism can contribute to a social-science investigation of the human past are plentiful, and they are being exploited across biblical studies. The works of Marxist philosophers, of new historicists, of 'mnemohistorians', of anthropologists and sociologists, of cultural critics, have all been applied to the interpretation of biblical texts.[10] The characterization of historical-critical exegesis as a social-scientific approach is not a new insight, but perhaps it needs stating explicitly. Indeed, it needs more than asserting. What remains to be achieved is a recognition not only that literary-historical criticism aims to produce historical knowledge and therefore belongs within the discipline of history, nor just that literary-historical exegetes as historians must utilize other social sciences – especially archaeology – but also that archaeologists of first millennium BCE Palestine *need* historical-critical exegetes. Archaeologists need to embrace historical-critical work, to integrate it into their own historical narrative. The lack of competence in archaeology among biblical historical critics is problematic, but much less problematic than the lack of competence among archaeologists in handling biblical texts in a properly historical-critical manner. It is gratifying to see that the archaeologist Israel Finkelstein and the biblical scholar Thomas Römer have collaborated recently in two articles dealing with the historical background of selected Genesis narratives. Still, more and more persistent collaboration between those studying textual and material artefacts is needed.

By way of postscript, attention can also be drawn to another similarity between biblical texts and archaeology, namely, the ways in which material remains and biblical texts operate canonically within Jewish and Christian culture, each stimulating contemporary social memory. The ideologies that once fashioned temples, prompted inscriptions, informed diet and shaped ritual are now replaced by ideologies that refashion scriptures and stones in the service of ethnic or religious affiliation. We may deplore the way in which our particular part of human history is so relentlessly subject to ideological demands, but it is a reminder to us about the kind of passion with which the past was created. It does not need repeating that history is really about the present. The struggle for the historian is to try to use historical studies as a way to inform the present, and not to be enslaved to them. In this endeavour, the united resources of the exegete and the archaeologist, as twin social sciences, are needed. Hopefully, together they can bring the message that common humanity should unite people rather than that different religions should divide it. Social science carries its own cultural message.

---

10. For a review of methods, see Davies, *History of Ancient Israel*, 119–36.

Bibliography

Bright, J. *A History of Israel*. Philadelphia: Westminster Press, 1959.

Davies, P. R. *The History of Ancient Israel: A Guide for the Perplexed*. London: T&T Clark, 2015.

Davis, T. W. *Shifting Sands: The Rise and Fall of Biblical Archaeology*. Oxford: Oxford University Press, 2004.

Gottwald, N. K. *The Tribes of Yahweh: A Sociology of the Religion of Liberated Israel, 1250–1050 B.C.E.* Maryknoll, NY: Orbis Books, 1979.

Long, B. O. *Planting and Reaping Albright: Politics, Ideology, and Interpreting the Bible*. University Park, PA: Pennsylvania State University Press, 1997.

Noth, M. *Das Buch Josua*. Tübingen: Mohr, 1938.

Noth, M. *A History of Pentateuchal Traditions*. Englewood Cliffs: Prentice-Hall, 1972; German original, Stuttgart: Kohlhammer, 1948.

Von Rad, G. *Old Testament Theology*. London: SCM Press, 1975; German original, Munich: Kaiser, 1957–60.

Chapter 3

THE CONCEPTS OF 'COUNTER-HISTORY' AND MNEMOHISTORY APPLIED TO BIBLICAL SCIENCES

Thomas C. Römer

3.1 Introduction: The Challenge of Using Social-Scientific Criticism in the Study of the Old Testament

In the last decade and especially in Anglo-Saxon circles, biblical studies has become increasingly interested in the social sciences and now includes among its established methods 'social-scientific criticism'. This approach falls within the scope of the school of historical criticism in biblical exegesis. According to Elliott:

> Social-scientific criticism investigates biblical texts as meaningful configurations of languages intended to communicate between composers and audiences. In this process it studies not only (1) the social aspects of the form and content of texts but also the conditioning factors and intended consequences of the communication process, (2) the correlation of the text's linguistic, literary, theological (ideological), and social dimensions and (3) the manner in which this textual communication was both a reflection of and a response to a specific social and cultural context, that is, how it was designed to serve as an effective vehicle of social interaction and an instrument of social as well as literary and theological consequence.[1]

Apparently, this method/approach has been more successful in New Testament studies and the Qumran literature than in the exegesis of the Hebrew Bible. There is a relatively simple explanation for this fact: whereas the New Testament books, the Qumran texts and the early Christian writings can be easily dated with a few years' margin of error, this is far from being the case for most of the texts in the Hebrew Bible (henceforth, HB). For many passages of the Pentateuch in particular,

---

1. John H. Elliott, 'Social-Scientific Criticism: Perspective, Process and Payoff. Evil eye accusation at Galatia as illustration of the method', *HTS Teologiese Studies* 67, no.1 (2011), http://www.hts/article/view/858/1454 (27 April 2014).

but not exclusively, dating can vary by many centuries. Even once a date has been chosen, socio-historical analysis of the same text can lead to very different, if not contradictory, results. The problem can be illustrated by means of 'the king's law' in Deut. 17.14-20, the only passage in the book of Deuteronomy which takes a detailed interest in the institution of monarchy.[2]

[14] When you have come into the land that the 'Lord' or 'Yhwh' your god is giving you, and have taken possession of it and settled in it, and you say 'I will set a king over me', like the nations that are around you [15] You may indeed set over you a king whom the lord your god will choose. One of your own community you may set as king over you; you are not permitted to put a foreigner over you, who is not of your own community. [16] Even so, he must not acquire many horses for himself, or return the people to Egypt in order to acquire more horses, since the Lord has said to you, 'You must never return that way again.' [17] And he must not acquire many wives for himself, or else his heart will turn away; also silver and gold he must not acquire in great quantity for himself.[18] When he has taken the throne of his kingdom, he shall have a copy of this law written for him in the presence of the Levitical priests.[19] It shall remain with him and he shall read in it all the days of his life, so that he may learn to fear the 'Lord' or 'Yhwh' his god, diligently observing all the words of this law[3] and these statutes. [20] Neither exalting himself above other members of the community nor turning aside from the commandment, either to the right or to the left, so that he and his descendants may reign long[4] over his kingdom in Israel.

This law is quite peculiar in the ancient Near East. As shown by the Code of Hammurabi, it is the king who is the mediator chosen by the gods to enlighten the people, by guaranteeing their welfare, upholding the law and justice, caring for the weak, and so on. Here, the king is indeed chosen by Yhwh, but he is himself subjected to a law that drastically limits his authority and his privileges. Is there an explanation for this law? In what sort of historical context should it be located? Such a text would evidently appeal to an approach interested in political structures and power conflicts among different communities.

If one considers the hypothesis that this 'law' belongs to the first edition of Deuteronomy in the seventh century before the Christian era, probably under the reign of Josias, it is possible to follow the sociological analysis of Patricia Dutcher-Walls who sees in this law a strategy for corporate power, the attempt by the Deuteronomists who belonged to the palace elite in Jerusalem to limit the king's power. These officials sought to 'carefully balance loyalty toward Yhwh as toward Assyria; so that the king

---

2. Cf. also Deut. 33.5, where mention of the king in the expression ויהי בישרון מלך might refer to Yhwh himself or to a king chosen by Yhwh.

3. Most manuscripts of the Septuagint have the equivalent of את־כל־דברי התורה הזאת which brings to mind the beginning of the book of Deuteronomy.

4. The Samaritan Pentateuch adds על כסא thus reinforcing the parallel with verse 18.

could be at the same time a good servant to Yhwh and a good vassal to Assyria.[5] In the ancient Near East, high officials, especially the scribes, could exert a certain influence or power over the king who was often illiterate as was certainly the case with Josias. Thus restriction on the king's power can be easily explained. However, the presence of such a 'law' in the Josianic edition of Deuteronomy would be astonishing: in the first place, it does not have equivalents in other near-eastern legislative codes; and even if the Deuteronomists had sought to legitimize their power over the king, would they have dared to openly restrict the king's power?

A different reading has been suggested by R. Albertz, who thinks that the interdiction of v. 16 refers to the exchange of Judean mercenaries for Egyptian horses. Albertz thinks that he can place this interdiction very precisely in the context of an alliance between Pharaoh Psamtik II and the Judean king Zedekiah who would have sent Judean soldiers into Egypt to support the pharaoh in his Nubian campaign circa 593–92 BCE.[6] This interdiction would therefore reflect the opposition of the palace scribes against the king's foreign policy. However, the passage touches on a great deal more than that; and it is implausible that a key point would have been drowned in a panoply of interdictions. As a matter of fact, contrary to Albertz' assertion, events that occurred during Zedekiah's reign do not allow for a precise dating of this verse since there is evidence for the presence of Judean mercenaries during Persian and Hellenistic eras as well, as indicated in the Elephantine documents and the Letter of Aristeas. According to the latter, the presence of Jews in Egypt would date back from the time when Psamtik was at war against the Ethiopians, which means that this period marks the *terminus a quo* rather than *ad quem* of the interdiction in Deut.17.6.

It is, however, not certain that Deut.17.6 really makes reference to an exchange of mercenaries for horses.[7] Therefore, it is necessary to take into account the totality of the interdictions and prescriptions, and query their communicative context. In the first place, there is no doubt that the interdictions presuppose deuteronomistic texts on the beginnings of the monarchy, on the dark side of king Solomon, and on king Josiah as loyal keeper of the Torah. As such, it could well be a table of contents of sorts for the history of monarchy as it is told in the deuteronomistic history.

5. Patricia Dutcher-Walls, 'The Circumscription of the King: Deuteronomy 17:16–17 in its Ancient Social Context', *JBL* 121 (2002): 616. In previous publications, the author underlines the existence of conflicting factions among the elite in agrarian societies; see, e.g. Patricia Dutcher-Walls, 'The Social Location of the Deuteronomists: A Sociological Study of Factory Politics in Late Pre-Exilic Judah', *JSOT* 52 (1991): 77–94.

6. Rainer Albertz, 'A Possible *terminus ad quem* for the Deuteronomic Legislation? A Fresh Look at Deut.17:6', in *Homeland and Exile: Biblical and Ancient Near Eastern Studies in honour of Bustenay Oded*, ed. Gershon Galil, M. Geller and A. Millard, VTSup 130 (Leiden-Boston: Brill, 2009), 288.

7. In the Temple Scroll, Deut.17.6 is used with an addition according to which the king should never return the people to Egypt (רק לוא ירבה לוא סוס ולוא ישיב את העם מצרים; 11QA19 LVI 15–16). This may be making allusion to mercenaries; but it could also be a later use of Exod. 1.11, which expresses the idea that the Israelites might go to war against Egypt.

However, since neither 1 Samuel 8–12 nor 1 Kings 9–11 or 2 Kings 22–23 make reference to Deut. 17.14-20, it is possible to surmise that this passage was written after those texts. Similarly, given that in the context of the Pentateuch Deut. 17.14-20 is the only text that contains a discourse on monarchy as an institution, that same discourse can be interpreted as integral to internecine conflicts between factions within Judaism when the Torah was promulgated. The two dominant factions that are responsible for the promulgation of the Torah are most certainly the temple circle and the 'lay' branch of the local administration, to which the Persians had delegated managerial authority for political and religious affairs in the province. These circles did not support the return of a Judean monarchy, which was apparently desired within some prophetic circles (Jer. 33.17-23; Ezek. 37.15-27; Amos 9.11-12) that also echoed popular aspirations. In that context, Deut. 17.14-20 can be read as a concession to those who hoped for the return of a monarchy.

Restrictions to this monarchy were particularly informed by the knowledge of stories about the beginnings of monarchy in Samuel and Kings. Some of those limitations are not incompatible with the monarchic ideology of the Near East which also insists on some form of humility on the monarch's part, who must not exploit the people whom the gods have put in his care. What has radically changed is that the king in Deuteronomy 17 is no longer the supreme authority. He is certainly chosen by Yhwh (v. 15) but he is no longer the mediator of his commands, which are from now on consigned in a book whose authority he must respect and also ensure among his people. Therefore, the concession to the idea of restoring the monarchy tries to drastically reduce the powers of the king. The mention of Levitical priests who are the keepers of the Torah, of which the king must make a copy, seems to imply the idea of power sharing between those who are in charge of the Temple and the law and the king who from now on is a monarch with limited privileges.

This quick overview shows the difficulties surrounding sociological interpretation of any HB text, because the outcomes of the power play diverge depending on which historical context the biblical passage in question is placed in. This observation constitutes first and foremost a warning against any hasty application of sociological theories to the HB texts. Since the reconstruction of the historical contexts for many HB texts remains an extremely hypothetical endeavour, I would like to briefly explore two concepts which equally come from the field of social and cultural studies but find their origin either in their confrontation with a text or through the concession that there exists some distance between the text and the memory that it carries: namely the concepts of 'counter-history' and 'mnemohistory'.

3.2 Counter-History as a Concept

The concept of counter-history was used by Michel Foucault in many of his lectures at the College de France in the 1970s. According to him, counter-history arises against the official history of power which is a 'ritual for reinforcing sovereignty'.[8] Thus, he contrasts the 'political-legendary power of the Romans' and the 'mythical-religious power of the Jews', in order to underline the ability of biblical texts to oppose the powers that be.[9] This concept of counter-history was subsequently retrieved and redefined by Amos Funkenstein who understands the function of counter-history as polemical, its methodology consisting of 'systematic exploitation of the adversary's most trusted sources against their grains – "die Geschichte gegen den Strich kämmen." '[10] Funkenstein uses the concept mainly to describe the polemics of ideology between Jews and Christians since the first centuries of the Christian era. Against Foucault, he insists that the counter-histories of both groups do not reveal more historical truth since they rely on an ideological construct which they certainly overturn but equally, with an ideological aim, 'everything in them is a reflective mirror'. As the prime instance of counter-history in the context of anti-Jewish polemics, Funkenstein points to the story of Manetho as told by Flavius Josephus in Book I of *Against Apion*. According to Manetho, the Hyksos – he calls them shepherds-kings – were expelled from Avaris to Palestine under the leadership of a certain Osarseph who is identified as Moses in the end.[11]

[237]The men confined in the quarry mines had been suffering for quite a long time when the king, following their supplications that he grants them a home and a keep, consented to give them the old city of the Shepherds, Avaris, then deserted . . .[240] After having adopted these laws and many others which were in stark contradiction with Egyptian customs, he got a multitude of workers to repair the city walls and to get ready for war against King Amenhotep. [241]He formed an alliance with some of the priests who were similarly contaminated, sent a delegation to the Shepherds who were expulsed by King Tuthmosis, in the city called Jerusalem, presented to them his and his companions' plight who were similarly wronged, he invited them to join them and attack Egypt together. He promised to lead them to Avaris the first city of their ancestors, and to provide abundantly for the needs of the masses, that when the time came he would fight for them and easily conquer the land for them. [243]Overjoyed, all the Shepherds as many as two hundred thousand men were quick to set off and soon after they reached Avaris . . . [248]Things were happening in the same way in Ethiopia. However, the Solymites carried out a raid with the Egyptians and treated the people so sacrilegiously and so cruelly that in comparison the domination of

8. Michel Foucault, '*Il faut defendre la société*': *Cours du Collège de France, 1975–1976*, Hautes Etudes (Paris: Gallimard-Seui, 1997), 49.

9. Ibid., 50.

10. Amos Funkenstein, *Perceptions of Jewish History* (Berkeley: University of California Press, 1993), 36. Cf. also Funkenstein, 'History, Counter-History and Memory', in *Probing the Limits of Representation: Nazism and the 'Final Solution'*, ed. Saul Friedländer (Cambridge, MA and London: Harvard University Press, 1992), 66–81.

11. Cited according to http://remacle.org/bloodwolf/historiens/Flajose/Apion1.htm (25 April 2017).

the Shepherds seemed like a golden era to those who witnessed their impieties. [249]Not only did they burn cities and villages, or restrict themselves to looting the temples and mutilate the statues of gods, they continued to use the sanctuaries as kitchen to roast sacred animals, and they forced the priests and the prophets to immolate and slaughter them, then they stripped them and threw them outside. [250]It is said that the heliopolitan priest who gave them a constitution and laws, named Osarseph from the name of god Osiris worshiped in Heliopolis, changed his name to Moses after he came by these people.

According to Funkenstein, Manetho, who wrote these works in the early part of the third century BC, would have been well versed in the biblical narrative of Exodus and deliberately perverted it for the purpose of constructing an anti-Semitic counter-history. However, it is unlikely that Manetho would have read the Torah and equally unlikely that the Septuagint would have been already in wider circulation in his time. On the other hand, it is hardly possible that he would have made the story up. On the contrary, within the Pentateuch narrative there are a few passages which, in opposition to Funkenstein's analysis,[12] appear to presuppose the story used by Manetho and construct a counter-history from it. In fact, there are two passages in the book of Exodus that hardly make any sense in the biblical context, but which can be explained as polemical retrieval, the counter-history of a discourse that circulated in Hellenistic Egypt as early as the fourth century.

3.2.a *Exod. 1.10 and the War of the Hebrews against Egypt*

At the beginning of Exodus, Pharaoh is said to want to reduce the number of Hebrews in Egypt by using the following argument:

> [8] Now a new king rose over Egypt, who did not know Joseph. [9] He said to his people, 'Look, the Israelite people are more numerous and more powerful than we. [10] Come, let us deal shrewdly with them, or they will increase and, in the event of a war, join our enemies and fight against us and escape from the land.'[13]

The idea that Israel would join the enemies of Egypt and fight against the Egyptians is a blind motif in the narrative of Exodus and does not reappear anywhere. Such a motif makes sense, however, as a background to Manetho's discourse on the

---

12. Cf. also the critical assessment of Funkenstein's thesis on Manetho by Erich S. Gruen, *Heritage and Hellenism: The Reinvention of Jewish Tradition* (Berkeley: University of California Press, 1998), 41–72; and David Biale, 'Counter-history and the Jewish Polemics against Christianity: The *Sefer toldot yeshu* and the *Sefer zerubavel*', *Jewish Social Studies* 6 (1999): 132.

13. Some translate ועלה as 'they will take over the land' instead of escape, which is totally unnecessary. The initial translation is more than adequate.

'lepers'.[14] As already emphasized, it is hardly plausible to understand Manetho's history as a midrash on one half verse of Exod. 1.10 since that would presume that he was a keen reader of the biblical text. Therefore, it is more logical to understand the biblical text as an addition by an editor who wants to retrieve this tradition by putting in Pharaoh's mouth an oracle which foresees the exodus of the Hebrews. It is indeed easy to see 1.10b as an addition because it interrupts the direct transition from 1.10a to 1.11.

> [9] He said to his people: look, the Israelite people are more numerous and more powerful than we. [10] Come, let us deal shrewdly with them, or they will increase *and, in the event of a war, join our enemies and fight against us and escape.* [11] Therefore they set taskmasters over them to oppress them with forced labour.

The historical context of this addition might be sought in the period of Persian domination over Egypt, when the Judeans of Elephantine allied themselves with the Persians or were considered by the Egyptians to be allies of the Persians. Thus, a letter from an Elephantine community addressed to Bagohi, the Governor of Judea, recalls the war between Cambyses against Egypt. 'When Cambyses entered in Egypt, he found the sanctuary (of Yahô) already built, as well as the sanctuaries of the gods of Egypt, we ransacked all of them but no one damaged anything in that sanctuary' (letter no. 102).[15]

This paragraph can certainly evoke the tradition reported by Manetho with regard to the destruction of Egyptian temples. It is also possible to see behind Exod. 1.10 a theme of hostility between the Egyptians on the one hand, and an alliance of Egyptian Jews and Persian power during the Persian era on the other hand. However, above all else the paragraph just cited must be understood as a positive retrieval of an anti-Jewish tradition, with the intention of emphasizing the military might of the Hebrews, a fact which makes the king of Egypt panic at the beginning of the Exodus narrative.

3.2.b *Exod. 4.6-7: Moses's Leprous Hand*

Exodus 4.1-17 introduces new objections that arose much later, after Moses's calling and the revelation of god's name in 3.1-17.[16]

---

14. See also Jan Rückl, 'Israel's Alliance with the Enemies of Egypt in Exodus 1,10', in *La construction de la figure de Moïse – The Construction of the Figure of Moses*, ed. Thomas Römer (Transeuphratène Suppl. 13; Paris: Gabalda, 2007), 157–68.

15. English translation according to Pierre Grelot, *Documents araméens d'Egypte* (LAPO; Paris: Cerf, 1972), 102.

16. For this reason these verses are considered as part of the later redactions of the Pentateuch. Cf. e.g. Jan Christian Gertz, *Tradition und Redaktion in der Exoduserzählung: Untersuchungen zur Endredaktion des Pentateuch*, FRLANT 186

[1]Then Moses answered, 'But suppose they do not believe me or listen to me, but say, "The LORD did not appear to you." '[17] [2]The LORD said to him, 'What is that in your hand?' He said, 'A staff.' [3] And he said, 'Throw it on the ground.' So he threw the staff on the ground, and it became a snake; and Moses drew back from it. [4] Then the LORD said to Moses, 'Reach out your hand, and seize it by the tail' – so he reached out his hand and grasped it, and it became a staff in his hand – [5] 'so that they may believe that Yhwh,[18]. . . the God of Abraham, the God of Isaac, and the God of Jacob, has appeared to you.' [6] Again, the LORD said to him, 'Put your hand inside your cloak.' He put his hand into his cloak; and when he took it out, his hand was leprous[19] as white as snow. [7] Then God said, 'Put your hand back into your cloak.' So he put his hand back into his cloak, and when he took it out, it was restored like the rest of his body – [8]'If they will not believe you or heed the first sign, they may believe the second sign. [9] If they will not believe even these two signs or heed you, you shall take some water from the Nile and pour it on the dry ground; and the water that you shall take from the Nile will become blood on the dry ground.'

This first part is made of three parts:

4.1: They will not believe me

Sign: the staff becomes a snake then becomes a staff again ➜ 7.8-13 (Moses and Aaron before Pharaoh).

4.5: So that *they may believe*

Sign: Moses's hand becomes leprous, then becomes normal again.

4.8-9a: If *they do not believe you*

Sign (future, 4.9b): the water of the Nile will turn into blood ➜ 7.19-21 (first plague: water transformed into blood).

It is noticeable that the first and third scenes refer back to the first two scenes in the story of the plagues. They are 'interrupted' by the middle scene, which makes allusion to something shrouded in uncertainty. It is often associated with the story of Miriam who became a leper for a time in Numbers 12. It is difficult to see why

---

(Göttingen: Vandenhoeck & Ruprecht, 1999), 305–27. Jaeyoung Jeon, *The Call of Moses and the Exodus Story: A Redactional-Critical Study in Exodus 3-4 and 5-13*, FAT/II 60 (Tübingen: Mohr Siebeck, 2013), 194–97 has also made plausible the later character of these verses even if he does not attribute them to the final redaction of the Pentateuch.

17. The Septuagint (LXX) adds 'What will I tell them?'

18. Missing in LXX.

19. Missing in LXX most likely for theological reasons. Moses would not be presented as impure.

Moses would anticipate Miriam's fate. From a diachronic perspective, it is possible to see this passage as the result of a secondary insertion between 4.1-4 and 4.8-9 (the original text is indicated in italics):

> [5] *'so that they may believe that Yhwh, . . . the God of Abraham, the God of Isaac, and the God of Jacob, has appeared to you.'*
>
> [6] Again, the LORD said to him, 'Put your hand inside your cloak.' He put his hand into his cloak; and when he took it out, his hand was leprous as white as snow.
>
> [7] Then God said, 'Put your hand back into your cloak.' So he put his hand back into his cloak, and when he took it out, it was restored like the rest of his body –
>
> [8] *'If they will not believe you or heed the first sign, they may believe the second sign.*
>
> [9] If they will not believe even these two signs or heed you, *you shall take some water from the Nile and pour it on the dry ground; and the water that you shall take from the Nile will become blood on the dry ground.'*

This second sign is again preceded by 'Yhwh says again', and v. 8 is astonishing. It makes reference to the first sign, yet with the leprous hand we already have two signs. This indicates that v. 8 was originally written as a logical continuation of v. 5. All of a sudden, the redactor who introduced vv. 6-7 has modified the text at the start of v. 9 by speaking of two signs. The story of the leprous hand is therefore a very recent insertion in a recent text.

A convincing explanation of vv. 6-7 can again be found in Manetho's account according to which Moses was the leader of a group of lepers. This anti-Jewish discourse is well known to the editor of vv. 6-7 who reacted to the story by creating a counter-history. Yes, Moses was a leper but only for a short time and only as a sign of his god's power. The story of Moses's leprous hand is therefore to be read as the reversal of a narrative on impure Jews and the superiority of Moses over Egypt and its political and religious leaders. It is for this reason that Exod. 7.1 refers to Moses as Elohim for Pharaoh, a verse which likewise probably belongs to later redactions of the Pentateuch.

3.2.c *Later Rereading of the Pentateuch and the Construction of a Counter-History*

The use of the concept of a counter-history in order to explain a certain number of later redactions makes it possible to understand the constitution of the corpus of the Torah, not only as an intra-Judean and Samaritan process but equally as a reaction to narratives that circulated among non-Jewish or non-orthodox Jewish circles. The construction of a counter-history shared by all the groups out of which the Torah emerged, especially priestly and deuteronomistic groups, equally gives cohesion to these groups by creating a common 'enemy' who can only be fought against by means of this counter-history.

3.3 *The Concept of Mnemohistory Applied to the Tradition of the Exodus*

Let us return to the narrative put forward by Manetho. Although his discourse on the Hyskos has a strong orientation, it still contains the memory of a sixteenth-century BCE historical reality, namely the presence of a pharaonic dynasty of Semitic ancestry. If the name of Osarseph makes allusion to Akhenaten as it is commonly agreed, it refers to a historical figure who lived more than a thousand years before him. This means that recent texts can be vehicles of traces of memory (Gedächtnisspuren), to borrow from Jan Assmann.[20] In his book *Moses the Egyptian: The Memory of Egypt in Western Monotheism*, Assmann introduces a concept from the cultural sciences, namely mnemohistory, or the history of memory.[21] The aim of an inquiry on mnemohistory, or the collective memory of a group, is not to study the historical veracity of traditions but their role in the construction of a group identity. While its main focus is the function of traditions in the current context of recipients of a narrative or a story, mnemohistory also allows for taking exception with a school of thought within Old Testament studies which refuses to go beyond the context of the initial writing down of biblical traditions. There exists, especially within research circles on the Pentateuch and more particularly with exegesis in the German language, the idea that nothing can be said about either the origins of or the sources used by the authors of the Bible. However, it is evident that no text of the Pentateuch is made up in the modern sense of the term; instead, the Pentateuch presents us with a literature of traditions – the authors do not present themselves as individuals[22] – which constructs a collective memory precisely by using traces of memory.

3.3.a *The Calling of Moses and the Revelation of God's Name*

The two accounts of Moses's calling in Exodus 3 and 6 contain a number of significant differences but agree that the Israelites had not known the name of Yhwh before it was revealed to Moses. In Exodus 3, it is Moses who has to ask the name of the god who is talking to him, whereas in Exodus 6 Yhwh clarifies from the onset that he is revealing his name for the first time by stating, 'I am Yhwh, I revealed myself to Abraham, Isaac and Jacob as El shadday, but by my

---

20. Jan Assmann, *Das kulturelle Gedächnis: Schrift. Erinnerung und politische Identität in frühen Hochkuluturen* (München: C. H. Beck, 1992).

21. Jan Assmann, *Moses the Egyptian: The Memory of Egypt in Western Monotheism* (Cambridge, MA: Harvard University Press, 1998). For a precursor, see Maurice Halbwachs, *La mémoire collective*, ed. G. Namer, Bibliothèque de l'évolution de l'humanité (Paris: A. Michel, 1997).

22. In the HB, there are only a very few texts where the authors introduce themselves as individuals; e.g. the 'memory of Nehemiah' in the Book of Nehemiah, or the Book of Ecclesiastes.

name Yhwh I did not make myself known to them' (vv. 2-3). The revelation of Yhwh's name in Exodus 3 takes place on the 'Mountain of God' which, according to the narrative context, is located in Midianite territory. On the other hand, God's speech to Moses in Exodus 6 seems to happen in Egypt. In Exodus 3, the revelation of Yhwh's name is linked to a theological speculation about the meaning of his name based on the root 'be' (I will be who I will be). In Exodus 6 the priestly circles used this revelation to construct a theory of revelation in three steps or circles. To humanity as a whole, God reveals himself as 'Elohim', to Abraham and his descendants as 'El Shadday', and as Yhwh only to Moses and Israel. Despite their different intentions, both texts insist on the fact that the name of Yhwh was unknown before Moses's time. How does one explain this convergence and this idea which seems to be contradicted by other texts (such as Gen. 4.26, 'At that time, people began to invoke the name of Yhwh'). In the context of the promulgation of the Torah, it is possible to propose the explanation that this might be a strategy intended to consolidate the importance of Moses as a figurehead, and the only moderator between Israel and Yhwh. That is certainly one of the functions of this story.

However, these texts offer an instance of mnemohistory that reworks a tradition according to which Israel had not always had Yhwh as their god. The fact that Exodus 3 is flanked by episodes that highlight ties between Moses and the Midianites, and the story in Exodus 18 which, before the arrival at Sinai places the Israelites at the 'Mountain of God' where they receive the visit of Moses's Midianite father-in-law who is the first to offer a sacrifice to Yhwh, has led to the rise in the nineteenth-century of the so-called Midianite–Kenite[23] hypothesis which holds that 'Israel' would have known Yhwh through the mediation of a group of Midianites. It might be necessary to revive this idea which has become somewhat obsolete. To that end, I would highlight another astonishing motif in the narrative of the Exodus, namely the idea that Pharaoh must let the Israelites go, not to leave indefinitely but rather to serve their god Yhwh who lives no farther than a three days' journey in the desert (Exod. 5.1-3; 7.17; 8.23-24). In Exod. 5.1-3 this theme serves to introduce the conflict between Yhwh and the gods of Egypt.

> [1]Afterward Moses and Aaron went to Pharaoh and said, 'Thus says Yhwh, the God of Israel, "Let my people go, so that they may celebrate a festival to me in the wilderness." [2] But Pharaoh said, 'Who is Yhwh that I should heed him and let Israel go? I do not know Yhwh and I will not let Israel go.' [3]Then they said, 'The God of the Hebrews has revealed himself to us; let us go a three days' journey into the wilderness to sacrifice to Yhwh our God, or he will fall upon us with pestilence or sword.'

---

23. For details see Joseph Blenkinsopp, 'The Midianite-Kenite Hypothesis Revisited and the Origins of Judah', *JSOT* 33 (2008): 131–53.

However, it is possible that this motif hides the trace of memory about a god Yhwh who originates from somewhere between Egypt and Canaan, maybe in Midianite territory. After the failure of the first negotiation with Pharaoh in Exodus 5, v. 22 often goes almost unnoticed: 'Then Moses turned again to Yhwh and said: "O Lord, why have you mistreated this people? Why did you ever send me?"' Commentators often imagine that this remark has to be understood as though Moses prayed to God for a second time, but such a literal reading would mean that Moses returned to the place where Yhwh lives on the mountain of god in the desert. If that were the case, the second (priestly) revelation of Yhwh did not take place in Egypt as it is generally accepted, but on Yhwh's mountain, a three-day journey into the desert.

Stressing the possibility of Yhwh's connection to a mountain this much, which stands in tension with the exodus story, undoubtedly reflects a memory trace according to which Yhwh first resided between Egypt and Canaan. This memory can be related to inscriptions found in Egypt between the fourteenth and twelvth century BCE which make mention of Shasu nomads. Some of these are combined with a toponym which is most likely the Egyptian transliteration of the name of *Yhw*.[24] In these texts, *yhw'* appears to be a geographical term, maybe a sacred mountain. It appears that these Shasu of Yhw lived in Edomite or even Midianite territory.

This tradition of a Yhwh located in the 'South' is similarly echoed in a number of poetic texts of the HB that speak of a Yhwh from the south and often identified with the mountain of Sinai as in Judg. 5.4-5: 'Yhwh, when you went out from Seir, when you marched from the region of Edom, the earth trembled and the heavens poured, the clouds indeed poured water, the mountains quaked before Yhwh, the One of Sinai, before Yhwh the god of Israel'; and likewise in Deut. 33.2: 'He said: "Yhwh came out from Sinai, for them[25] he dawned from Seir, he shone for them from Mount Paran, he came forth from 'Meribat of Qadesh',[26] from the south to the Slopes,[27] for them."' A similar idea is found in Hab. 3.3: 'God came from

---

24. Martin Leuenberger, 'Jhwhs Herkunft aus Süden: Archäologische Befunde–biblische Überlieferungen–historische Korrelationen', *ZAW* 122 (2010): 1–19.

25. In reference to the tribes mentioned in verse 5.

26. The Hebrew expression *mēribbōt qōdeš* is difficult to understand. Some translate the Masoretic text as 'He came with myriads of holy ones', which frankly does not make any sense. The poetic figure of 'parallelism of members' supports a geographical context instead. The Septuagint has Qadesh as a proper name: 'with the myriads of Qadesh'.

27. The end of the verse is almost impossible to translate. The Masoretic vocalization suggests something like 'from his right hand comes a fiery law'. The term *dāt* ('law') is borrowed from the Persian language. In this case it could be a gloss or a latter addition. The LXX has 'angels with him' probably with the intention of creating a parallelism with 'the myriad of holy ones'. The opinion adhered to here is to consider the word as a plural *ašdāt* which approximately means 'slopes', i.e., the transition between high mountains and the desert.

Teman, the Holy one from Mount Paran. *Selah.* His glory covered the heavens and the earth was full of his praise.'

Despite their many differences, these texts agree on the affirmation that the god Yhwh came from the 'south'. It is therefore very possible that these four poetic passages reprise an ancient tradition to which Yhwh was a deity connected to a mountain in the desert, in the east or west of Arabia.[28]

What kind of mnemohistory do these texts evoke? In the context of the Persian era, the assertion of a southern origin for Yhwh can be understood as a narrative intended to mitigate the loss of Yhwh's Temple in Jerusalem by transferring it outside the land of Judah, in the desert even in enemy territory, thus underlining the mobility of the god of Israel who is not tied to a specific territory.[29] This same collective memory, however, when the tradition is used with due caution, helps the historian in the task of reconstructing the origins of Yahwistic religion.

3.4 *Conclusion*

The two concepts of counter-history and mnemohistory open historical criticism of the Hebrew Bible to new perspectives. The concept of counter-history makes it possible to explain the making of biblical texts in relation to extra-biblical narratives. The construction of a counter-history makes it possible to construct, out of different groups, an ingroup which finds cohesion in its opposition to the *outgroup.* Through the concept of mnemohistory, it is possible to use recent texts to analyse more ancient traditions. It makes possible the analysis of the function of these traditions at the time of their usage and to ask questions about the collective memory buried within these traditions.

Bibliography

Albertz, Rainer. 'A Possible *terminus ad quem* for the Deuteronomic Legislation? A Fresh Look at Deut.17:6'. In *Homeland and Exile: Biblical and Ancient Near Eastern Studies in Honour of Bustenay Oded*, edited by Gershon Galil, M. Geller and A. Millard. VTSup 130; 271–96. Leiden-Boston: Brill, 2009.

Assmann, Jan. *Das Kulturelle Gedächtnis. Schrift. Erinnerung und Politische Identität in frühen Hochkuluturen.* München: C. H. Beck, 1992.

Assmann, Jan. *Moses the Egyptian: The Memory of Egypt in Western Monotheism.* London, Cambridge, MA: Harvard University Press, 1998.

---

28. For more details, see Thomas Römer, *The Invention of God* (London-Cambridge, MA: Harvard University Press, 2015).

29. In this sense cf. Henrik Pfeiffer, *Jahwes Kommen von Süden: Jdc 5, Hab 3, Dtn 33 und Ps 68 in ihrem literatur- und theologiegeschichtlichen Umfeld*, FRLANT 211 (Göttingen: Vandenhoeck & Ruprecht, 2005). He however understands these texts as a theological fabrication by redactors from the Babylonian era, which seems anachronistic to me.

Biale, David. 'Counter-history and the Jewish Polemics against Christianity: The *Sefer toldot yeshu* and the *Sefer zerubavel*'. *Jewish Social Studies* 6 (1999): 130–45.

Blenkinsopp, Joseph. 'The Midinianite-Kenite Hypothesis Revisited and the Origins of Judah'. *JSOT* 33 (2008): 131–53.

Dutcher-Walls, Patricia. 'The Social Location of the Deuteronomists: A Sociological Study of Factory Politics in Late Pre-Exilic Judah'. *JSOT* 52 (1991): 77–94.

Dutcher-Walls, Patricia. 'The Circumscription of the King: Deuteronomy 17:16–17 in its Ancient Social Context'. *JBL* 121 (2002): 601–16.

Elliott, John H. 'Social-Scientific Criticism: Perspective, Process and Payoff. Evil Eye Accusation at Galatia as Illustration of the Method'. *HTS Teologiese Studies* 67, no. 1 (2011): 10 pages. Available Online: http://www.hts/article/view/858/1454

Foucault, Michel. *'Il faut defendre la société': Cours du Collège de France 1975–1976.* Hautes Etudes, Paris: Gallimard-Seui, 1997.

Funkenstein, Amos. 'History, Counter-History and Memory'. In *Probing the Limits of Representation: Nazism and the "Final Solution"*, edited by Saul Friedlander, 66–81. Cambridge, MA and London: Harvard University Press, 1992.

Funkenstein, Amos. *Perceptions of Jewish History.* Berkeley: University of California Press, 1993.

Gertz, Jan Christian. *Tradition und Redaktion in der Exoduserzählung: Untersuchungen zur Endredaktion des Pentateuch.* FRLANT 186. Göttingen: Vandenhoeck & Ruprecht, 1999.

Grelot, Pierre. *Documents araméens d'Egypte.* LAPO. Paris: Cerf, 1972.

Gruen, Erich S. *Heritage and Hellenism: The Reinvention of Jewish Tradition.* Berkley: University of California Press, 1998.

Halbwachs, Maurice. *La mémoire collective*, edited by G. Namer. Bibliothèque de l'évolution de l'humanité, Paris: A. Michel, 1997.

Jeon, Jaeyoung. *The Call of Moses and the Exodus Story: A Redactional-Critical Study in Exodus 3–4 and 5–13.* FAT/II 60. Tübingen: Mohr Siebeck, 2013.

Leuenberger, Martin. 'Jhwhs Herkunft aus Süden: Archäologische Befunde-biblische Überlieferungen-historische Korrelationen'. *ZAW* 122 (2010): 1–19.

Pfeiffer, Henrik. *Jahwes Kommen von Süden: Jdc 5, Hab 3, Dtn 33 und Ps 68 in ihrem literatur- und theologiegeschichtlichen Umfeld.* FRLANT 211. Göttingen: Vandenhoeck & Ruprecht, 2005.

Römer, Thomas. *The Invention of God.* London-Cambridge, MA: Harvard University Press, 2015.

Rückl, Jan. 'Israel's Alliance with the Enemies of Egypt in Exodus 1,10'. In *La construction de la figure de Moïse – The Construction of the Figure of Moses*, edited by Thomas Römer, Transeuphratène suppl. 13; 157–68. Paris: Gabalda, 2007.

Chapter 4

YOUR NAME SHALL NO LONGER BE JACOB, BUT REFUGEE: INVOLUNTARY MIGRATION AND THE DEVELOPMENT OF THE JACOB NARRATIVE

C. A. Strine

4.1 *Introduction*

Consider this atypical summary of the ancestral narrative in Genesis 12–36.

The narrative begins with Abraham,[1] who migrates to Canaan. On arrival in Canaan, famine forces Abraham to flee to Egypt (Gen. 12.10). Abraham eventually returns to Canaan, where his son Isaac also faces a famine that forces him to migrate (Gen. 26.1). Rather than leave Canaan, Isaac drifts within its boundaries, residing in various places to survive. Isaac's son Jacob grows up in Canaan, but spends his early adulthood as an asylum seeker avoiding the aggression of his brother Esau by taking refuge with his family in Mesopotamia. After twenty years, Jacob returns to Canaan to find a transformed, unrecognizable society. The conciliatory attitude of Esau – who seeks to reconcile with Jacob instead of killing him – exemplifies Jacob's reverse culture shock. Throughout, a *Leitwort* is gēr, 'sojourner', a term that connotes transitory residence, difference from the host population, and limited legal protection.

One might summarize the narrative with terms used by the United Nations High Commissioner for Refugees (UNHCR): Abraham is an environmentally induced externally displaced person; Isaac is an environmentally induced internally displaced person; and Jacob is an asylum seeker who subsequently repatriates by choice. Abraham, Isaac and Jacob are all self-settled involuntary migrants.[2]

---

1. For ease, I shall use Abraham throughout, though the first patriarch's name is Abram from his introduction until it is changed by Yhwh in Gen. 17.5.

2. The matriarchs in Genesis 12–36 are also involuntary migrants. When they seek respite from the famine in Canaan, Abraham coaches his wife Sarah to identify as his sister, thus protecting him from any Egyptian who might consider murdering him to take this beautiful woman as their wife. Abraham and Sarah do the same again when fleeing famine in Gerar. Like father, like son: when Isaac and Rebekah encounter a famine in Canaan and migrate to Gerar in order to survive it, they employ the same scheme for the same reasons.

When framed this way, there is little doubt that Genesis 12–36 invites the commentator to employ social-scientific research on involuntary migration. Though social-scientific approaches to Genesis are not new,[3] very little work on the ancestral narrative foregrounds the issue of migration. Perhaps the first to recognize the prominence of this theme in Genesis was John Van Seters, though it only informs his approach tangentially.[4] Recent volumes by David Frankel and Elizabeth Robertson Kennedy and an article by Guy Darshan give a larger role to migration in Genesis,[5] but none draws on the sub-discipline of the social sciences often known as refugee studies in order to deal with this theme.

In UNHCR's terms, Sarah and Rebekah are environmentally induced involuntary migrants; circumstances beyond their control compels them to engage in a form of sex work in order to provide for their families. For further details, see C. A. Strine, 'Sister Save Us: The Matriarchs as Breadwinners and Their Threat to Patriarchy in the Ancestral Narrative', in *Women and Exilic Identity in the Hebrew Bible*, eds. K. Southwood and M. Halvorson-Taylor (London: Bloomsbury T&T Clark: London, 2018) 53–66.

3. *Inter alia*, E. Theodore Mullen, *Ethnic Myths and Pentateuch Foundations: A New Approach to the Formation of the Pentateuch* (Atlanta, GA: Scholars Press, 1997), John Van Seters, *The Pentateuch: A Social-Science Commentary* (Sheffield: Sheffield Academic Press, 1999), Mark G. Brett, *Genesis: Procreation and the Politics of Identity* (London: Routledge, 2000), and Anselm C. Hagedorn, 'Hausmann und Jäger (Gen 25,27-28): Aus den jugendtagen Jakobs und Esaus', in *Die Erzväter in der biblischen Tradition: Festschrift für Matthias Köckert*, ed. A. C. Hagedorn and Henrik Pfieffer (Berlin: Walter de Gruyter, 2009). Beyond Genesis, the best examples are John Ahn, *Exile as Forced Migrations: A Sociological, Literary, and Theological Approach on the Displacement and Resettlement of the Southern Kingdom of Judah* (Berlin: Walter de Gruyter, 2011), Jill Middlemas and John J. Ahn, *By the Irrigation Canals of Babylon: Approaches to the Study of the Exile* (New York: T&T Clark, 2012), and Katherine E. Southwood, *Ethnicity and the Mixed Marriage Crisis in Ezra 9–10* (Oxford: Oxford University Press, 2012). For a broader justification for employing social-scientific research as an interpretative heuristic, see the argument of Philip Esler, 'Social-Scientific Models in Biblical Interpretation', in *Ancient Israel: The Old Testament in Its Social Context*, ed. Philip Esler (Philadelphia, PA: Fortress, 2006), 3–14.

4. For John Van Seters's most extended discussion of the issue, see *Prologue to History: The Yahwist as Historian in Genesis* (Zürich: Theologischer Verlag Zürich, 1992), 209–14.

5. David Frankel, *The Land of Canaan and the Destiny of Israel: Theologies of Territory in the Hebrew Bible* (Winona Lake, IN: Eisenbrauns, 2011), Elisabeth Robertson Kennedy, *Seeking a Homeland: Sojourn and Ethnic Identity in the Ancestral Narratives of Genesis* (Leiden: Brill, 2011), and Guy Darshan, 'The Origins of the Foundation Stories Genre in the Hebrew Bible and Ancient Eastern Mediterranean', *Journal of Biblical Literature* 133, no. 4 (2014). Frankel does not draw on the social sciences in a substantial way. Kennedy relies upon the work of Anthony D. Smith; this is helpful and her book offers important new ideas, but she sees migration as merely a precursor to a landed, national, static form of identity that fails to really engage with the lived experience of forced migration. Darshan

To some extent, this lacuna arises from the youth of forced migration studies. Some trace its origin to the 1951 UN convention relating to the status of refugees,[6] but a vast number place its foundation in the early 1980s.[7] Still in its infancy, the field of involuntary migration studies continues to grow and define its methods, only recently being capable of delivering findings that can be used in other disciplines. Bearing these limitations in mind, the preceding summary of the ancestral narrative indicates that Biblical Studies – especially work on the Hebrew Bible – offers a prime area for such interdisciplinary work.

Two potential contributions of this approach lie at the core of my work on Genesis. First, the insights that the study of forced migration provides on the migratory experience suggest new interpretations of difficult texts in the ancestral narrative. Second, built upon that exegetical work, one can reconsider questions of textual fractures indicating separate sources and, by examining the attitudes exhibited towards the experience of involuntary migration exhibited in these textual sources comprising Genesis, then work towards a fresh model for the diachronic growth of the book.

This essay shall focus on the Jacob narrative (Gen. 25.19–33.20), using it as a case study to demonstrate both contributions. The Jacob narrative lends itself to this effort particularly well because it presents a full 'lifecycle' of involuntary migration. In stage one, Jacob lives as an asylum seeker from Esau's threat of violence, receiving refuge in Haran/Padan-aram. In stage two, though Jacob is welcomed and protected by Laban, he remains an indentured labourer with limited rights. Typical of subordinated persons, Jacob does not acquiesce to this situation, but eventually finds a way to subvert his domineering host, even to benefit financially from the situation. In stage three, Jacob returns 'home' to Canaan. Anxiety consumes Jacob when he considers the hostility he will face from Esau when he returns; yet, when he arrives in Canaan he is astonished to find that Esau wants to reconcile with him. 'Home' is totally other than what Jacob remembers or imagines. Nonetheless, the patriarch proceeds with caution and a lack of trust for Esau, the same strategies that proved successful during his time as a refugee. In all three stages, Jacob resembles involuntary migrants from other cultures, whose experiences can, therefore, enhance our understanding of this narrative.

does not employ the social sciences, though his comparative method further underscores the potential for this approach to enhance our understanding of not only the biblical but also classical material.

6. Richard Black, 'Fifty Years of Refugee Studies: From Theory to Policy', *International Migration Review* 35, no. 1 (2001): 57–78; for the UN document see http://www.unhcr.org/pages/49da0e466.html (accessed 23 Feb. 2017).

7. Dawn Chatty, 'Anthropology and Forced Migration', in *The Oxford Handbook of Refugee and Forced Migration Studies*, ed. Elena Fiddian-Qasmiyeh et al. (Oxford: Oxford University Press, 2014), 74–80.

4.2 *Jacob the Involuntary Migrant (Gen. 25.19–29.14a)*

The Jacob narrative begins in Gen. 25.19 with the *Toledot* formula and a description of the struggle between Esau and Jacob during their birth. The continual nature of their conflict with one another is highlighted by the stew–birthright negotiation story in 25.27-34. The story of Isaac facing a famine, like Abraham before him, interrupts the developing rivalry; though it underscores the centrality of involuntary migration in the ancestral narrative, its role must remain a topic for another time.

After the story of Isaac's and Rebekah's time in Gerar, the narrative returns to Esau and Jacob. The details of Rebekah and Jacob's ruse to gain the patriarchal blessing for Jacob instead of Esau are familiar, but it is worthwhile to look at the end of Genesis 27 where the circumstances of Jacob's departure from Canaan are enumerated. Esau's bitterness towards Jacob produces homicidal intentions, which Rebekah discovers. She counsels Jacob to flee Canaan and seek safety with Laban in Haran for 'a while' – this amounts to recommending that Jacob seek asylum and become a refugee. 'A refugee', as defined now, 'is someone who has been forced to flee his or her country because of persecution, war, or violence',[8] and it is likely she or he 'cannot return home or are afraid to do so'.[9]

Staying with the final form of the text for now, Gen. 27.46–28.5 explains how Rebekah facilitates Jacob's departure by expressing her disgust at the idea that he would marry a Canaanite woman. From the perspective of involuntary migration studies, it is entirely logical that Jacob's mother would use her influence and knowledge to gain safe passage for her son. Caution is necessary to avoid anachronism, but research in various areas shows that asylum seekers and refugees – like all manner of marginalized people – see their claims succeed far more often when a qualified person takes forward their claim.[10] Today, this generally involves legal counsel; in antiquity, influential people played similar roles, though they did not have a professional qualification per se. Often, these people had a social status that allowed influence with a powerful person (e.g. Nathan's influence with David; Rehoboam's counsellors in 1 Kgs 12.1-17). It is not at all extraordinary that Jacob

---

8. http://www.unrefugees.org/site/c.lfIQKSOwFqG/b.4950731/k.A894/What_is_a_refugee.htm (accessed on 23 Feb. 2017); cf. Article 1, 1951 Convention Relating to the Status of Refugees, which says 'owing to a well-founded fear of being persecuted for reasons of race, religion, nationality, membership of a particular social group, or political opinion, is outside the country of his nationality, and is unable to or, owing to such fear, is unwilling to avail himself of the protection of that country'.

9. http://www.unrefugees.org/site/c.lfIQKSOwFqG/b.4950731/k.A894/What_is_a_refugee.htm (accessed on 23 Feb. 2017).

10. See Eleanor Acer, 'Making a Difference: A Legacy of Pro Bono Representation', *Journal of Refugee Studies* 17, no. 3 (2004): 347–66, and Katia Bianchini, 'Legal Aid for Asylum Seekers: Progress and Challenges in Italy', *Journal of Refugee Studies* 24, no. 2 (2011): 390–410, for discussion and further references.

relies upon his mother for this support: ethnographic research indicates that 'the *only* person a man can *really* trust is the one person who will not stand to gain by his death. This person is neither his wife nor his children; it is his mother'.[11]

Rebekah is a powerful figure by any estimation. Mark Brett notes that this story 'serves to emphasize her agency',[12] and John Anderson remarks that 'the narrative presents Rebekah as much more than a simple housewife'.[13] Indeed, no one knows better than Rebekah that Isaac's life was shaped by the requirement of endogamous marriage and, more recently, by distrust for the local population (e.g. the men of Gerar in Genesis 26). She acts in a way that is likely to persuade Isaac to allow Jacob's departure. Rebekah operates like a political figure or legal advocate, using her knowledge, access and influence to aid her 'client'.

The content of Rebekah's plea to Isaac represents a change in theme and style from Gen. 27.1-45, one of several reasons scholars allocate Gen. 27.1-45 to a non-Priestly source (non-P) and 27.46–28.9 to a Priestly source (P). Further attention to those issues will come later. For now, this fracture should neither obscure that the study of involuntary migration provides a sensible logic for the topical shift between the two sections nor overshadow the similarities between Rebekah's approach here and Isaac's pragmatic tactics with the men of Gerar in Genesis 26. Both Isaac and Rebekah exhibit a willingness to bend the truth and to use deception. It is relevant to note, then, that Barbara Harrell-Bond and Eftihia Voutira quote an involuntary migrant source remarking that: '[t]o be a refugee means to learn to lie'.[14] Whatever the process by which these texts arrive in their canonical form, the characters and actions depicted here correspond closely to behaviours observed among involuntary migrants facing similar challenges in other times and places.

As Jacob sets out for Canaan (Gen. 28.10), he spends a night in the place that he will name Bethel. His vision into the divine realm provides an aetiology for the sanctuary at Bethel, to be sure. However, approached from the perspective of involuntary migration, Jacob's vow forms the critical aspect of the experience:

> [20b] If God remains with me, if he protects me on this journey that I am making, and gives me bread to eat and clothing to wear, [21] *and if I return safe to my father's house* – YHWH shall be my God. [22]And this stone, which I have set up as a pillar, shall be the house of God; and of all that you give me, I will make a tithe to you.

---

11. Eftihia Voutira and Barbara E. Harrell-Bond, 'In Search of the Locus of Trust: The Social World of the Refugee Camp', in *Mistrusting Refugees*, ed. E. V. Daniel and J. C. Knudsen (Berkeley: University of California Press, 1995), 208.

12. Brett, *Genesis: Procreation and the Politics of Identity*, 88–89.

13. John E. Anderson, *Jacob and the Divine Trickster: A Theology of Deception and Yhwh's Fidelity to the Ancestral Promise in Jacob Cycle* (Winona Lake, IN: Eisenbrauns, 2011), 70.

14. Voutira and Harrell-Bond, 'In Search', 216. It should be stressed that necessity, not deficient morality, typically drives such dishonesty. Deceptive actions often constitute one of very few survival mechanisms available to people with a legitimate fear for their life.

This scene, coherent and unified despite much argument to the contrary,[15] does far more than offer a *hieros logos*; rather, it conveys the hopes and fears of an involuntary migrant fleeing mortal danger by travelling into an unknown place, without assurance things will be better there.

4.3 *Jacob the Refugee (Gen. 29.14b–32.1)*[16]

Upon arrival in Haran, Jacob meets Rachel, who then introduces him to her father, Laban. Laban welcomes Jacob into his house, where Jacob explains what has prompted his departure from Canaan to Laban (29.13b), who declares his willingness to protect Jacob by calling the newcomer 'my bone and my flesh' (29.14a). Recognized as family, Jacob falls under Laban's protection. He is, in an ancient form, granted asylum from his bloodthirsty brother, Esau.[17]

The relationship between Laban and Jacob is not one of full equality. After a month of service 'Laban said to Jacob, "Just because you are a kinsman, should you serve me for nothing?"' (Gen. 29.15a). Despite inviting Jacob to set the wage, the text leaves Laban's motivation ambiguous. Wenham remarks that Laban keeps 'his options open' and concludes that the extraordinarily large commitment Jacob is willing to make for Rachel suggests that he will pay handsomely for her.[18] Without disregarding that interpretation, one may add to it from the perspective of involuntary migration: Jacob's extended commitment assures him of protection for the foreseeable future. From one perspective, seven years constitutes an extraordinarily long term of service for a bride; from another, it affords Jacob security, assuring he retains protection against the violent retribution he seeks to avoid.

Moreover, bearing in mind Jacob's 'refugee status' illuminates the power dynamics at play. Asylum seekers in the United Kingdom, as just one example, do not choose where they live, cannot work legally, and must survive on about £6 a day in vouchers. Life is complicated by the constant threat of deportation. Even after receiving refugee status, forced migrants remain at the mercy of the government: they do not live as citizens, but on time-limited and revocable visas. Without uncritically applying modern circumstances to the ancient context, one may still highlight the fundamental dynamic that does cross cultures: the one granting protection to the asylum seeker possesses tremendous power over them. So long as the threat of expulsion exists, so does an asymmetric power relationship.

---

15. Erhard Blum, 'The Jacob Tradition', in *The Book of Genesis: Composition, Reception, and Interpretation*, ed. Craig Evans, A., Joel N. Lohr and David L. Petersen (Leiden: Brill, 2012), 197–203.

16. This division of the sections follows the BHS arrangement, where 29.14a concludes the preceding material and 29.14b opens a new movement in the narrative.

17. cf. cities of refuge, e.g. Num. 35; Deut. 23.16; Josh. 20.2, 21.13, 21, 27, 32, 38.

18. Gordon J. Wenham, *Genesis 16–50* (Nashville, TN: Thomas Nelson, 2000), 235.

This model explains Laban's duplicitous behaviour. When Laban takes advantage of Jacob's status as a refugee, Jacob has little recourse. 'Benevolent' Laban, remarks von Rad, is 'a master of deceit':[19] even though Laban agrees that seven years of service from Jacob will warrant a daughter in marriage (Gen. 29.19), without warning or regret he gives Jacob the older, unwanted daughter Leah. 'Laban said, "It is not the practice in our place to marry off the younger before the older. Wait until the bridal week of this one is over and we will give you that one too, *provided you serve me another seven years*"' (Gen. 29.26-27). Westermann remarks that 'Jacob agrees; he has no option.'[20]

Westermann is correct, but he neither elaborates on the reasons why nor considers the implications of the situation. Because Laban assures Jacob's livelihood and safety, Jacob lives in an asymmetric power relationship with him. He is, like all refugees, in a subordinate position to the one who grants this status. The refugee is marginalized, disempowered and circumscribed in their ability to pursue their rights for fear of expulsion. All of this is compressed into the short, dismissive comment with which Laban begins his explanation: 'It is not done thus in *our* place' (לא יעשה כן במקומנו ;Gen. 29.26a). Even though Laban has welcomed Jacob like family and granted him asylum, Jacob remains an outsider, not a part of the host community.

Jacob has severely limited options in this situation. His stated desire to marry Rachel is not irrelevant, but it is hard to avoid the conclusion that Jacob accepts Laban's one-sided offer to serve another seven years for Rachel without resistance or negotiation because of the asymmetric power relationship between them.

Jacob serves the additional seven years of service, sees the birth of twelve sons and then requests permission to leave (Gen. 30.25). Even after almost twenty years (cf. 31.38), Laban politely declines, suggesting instead that Jacob specify another 'wage'. This is not generosity, writes Westermann, but 'a rejection of Jacob's request'.[21] Laban imitates a loving father, but leverages his power to compel Jacob into yet another term of service that will benefit him far more than Jacob.

Whereas commentators interpret the confusing set of statements between Laban and Jacob in Gen. 30.25-34 through their kinship,[22] it is far more helpful to examine it through migration studies. Jacob expresses the desire to live on his own, to manage his own affairs, and to be treated as a fully capable agent (30.25-26, 30b). This desire is common to involuntary migrants, who prefer to self-settle and to survive by their own agency.[23] When Laban refuses Jacob's request

---

19. Gerhard von Rad, *Genesis: A Commentary*, trans. John H. Marks (London: SCM Press, 1961), 292.

20. Claus Westermann, *Genesis 12–36: A Commentary*, trans. John K. Scullion S. J. (Minneapolis, MN: Augsburg Publishing House, 1985), 467.

21. Westermann, *Genesis 12–36*, 481.

22. As an example, consider Bill T. Arnold, *Genesis* (Cambridge: Cambridge University Press, 2009), 271–72.

23. See, for instance, Barbara E. Harrell-Bond, *Imposing Aid: Emergency Assistance to Refugees* (Oxford: Oxford University Press, 1986), Liisa H. Malkki, *Purity and Exile: Violence,*

(30.31a), the patriarch resorts to a tactic common among subordinated groups across cultures: he employs Laban's paternalistic language against him, utilizing it to construct the ruse whereby he will acquire the majority of Laban's livestock.

American sociologist and political scientist James C. Scott has demonstrated that subaltern groups resist and deceive dominant groups in their daily practices.[24] In *Weapons of the Weak* and *Domination and the Arts of Resistance*, he establishes that dominated groups assert their rights through disguised behaviours that push the established boundaries of obedience for their benefit without breaking them so blatantly as to provoke punitive measures from the authorities. Particularly relevant to the Laban–Jacob relationship, Scott observes that when dominant powers portray themselves with 'paternalist flourishes about care, feeding, [and] housing',[25] subaltern groups happily employ this rhetoric in requests that suit their needs. Jacob's scheme against Laban depicted in Gen. 30.25-43 fits this profile.

Daniel Smith-Christopher previously suggested the relevance of Scott's work for interpreting the Jacob narrative, though he did not note the particular connection to Jacob's use of Laban's language. Smith-Christopher concludes that trickster narratives contribute to a 'subcultural ethics' that emerges from the social circumstances of exilic subordination, extol the subaltern's ability to successfully navigate problematic circumstances[26] and exhibit a willingness to use truth and falsehood to survive. Laban's disingenuous rhetoric furnishes Jacob an opportunity to resist his authority in this way. Jacob shrewdly capitalizes upon it in order to serve his ultimate aim to gain autonomy.

The importance of the asymmetric power structure between Laban and Jacob is highlighted by what happens when it is undone. Compare the final conversation between Jacob and Laban in Gen. 31.25-54. Although Laban feigns his desire to celebrate Jacob, still Jacob confesses that 'I was afraid because I thought you would take your daughters from me by force' (31.31). Furthermore, when Laban cannot prove his accusation that Jacob has his household gods, Jacob feels free to respond with anger (31.36). Now outside of Laban's home and his protection, Jacob is forceful, unafraid to assert his rights and even accusatory. This is not the same man

---

Memory and National Cosmology Among Hutu Refugees in Tanzania (Chicago: University of Chicago Press, 1995), and the synthesis in Elizabeth Colson, 'Forced Migration and the Anthropological Response', *Journal of Refugee Studies* 16 (2003): 7–10; for an anecdotal overview, cf. the recent lecture by Jeff Crisp at the Refugee Studies Centre in Oxford: http://www.rsc.ox.ac.uk/news/in-search-of-solutions-refugees-are-doing-it-for-themselves-refugee-voices-opening-plenary-jeff-crisp (accessed on 23 Feb. 2017).

24. James C. Scott, *Weapons of the Weak: Everyday Forms of Peasant Resistance* (New Haven, CT: Yale University Press, 1985); Scott, *Domination and the Arts of Resistance: Hidden Transcripts* (New Haven, CT: Yale University Press, 1990), 110–25.

25. Scott, *Domination*, 18.

26. Daniel Smith-Christopher, *Biblical Theology of Exile* (Minneapolis, MN: Augsburg Fortress, 2002), 167; cf. Susan Niditch, *A Prelude to Biblical Folklore: Underdogs and Tricksters* (Urbana, IL: University of Illinois Press, 2000).

who accepted a seven-year term of service for Rachel without negotiation because this is no longer a refugee dependent upon a protective power. Laban recognizes as much: though he wants to claim all Jacob possesses as his own (31.43), even he knows this is not possible, so he settles for a treaty that includes curses on Jacob should he mistreat Leah or Rachel (31.50).

4.4 Jacob the Return Migrant (Gen. 32.2–33.20)[27]

The narrative immediately pivots towards Canaan, and Jacob's demeanour changes as he contemplates returning 'home'. Jacob understandably dreads what he will find when he meets Esau; he lives with a nightmare of return, not the more common utopian dream of home called the myth of return.[28] On the night prior to crossing the Jordan, Jacob struggles with a divine being (Genesis 32). The fight dislocates his hip, providing the aetiology for the name Israel, but also affording him the courage to face Esau. Thus, Jacob's assessment, 'I have seen God face to face yet my life has continued' (Gen. 32.31) evokes the traumatized involuntary migrant remarking, 'if I can deal with this, I can deal with anything'. Jacob's encounter at the Jabbok does not change his character, but underscores his ability to endure even the most fearful circumstances.[29]

The positive impact on Jacob's courage comes to the fore when he encounters Esau again (33.1-11). Jacob remarks, 'to see your face is like seeing the face of God, and you have received me favorably' (33.10),[30] creating an explicit echo of 32.31. No less surprising than seeing the divine countenance and surviving, Jacob's confession to Esau reveals equal astonishment at confronting his aggrieved brother without open hostility. Lest the point escape notice, this suggests that the experience of involuntary migration remains absolutely central to the narrative even in the two divine visions (Gen. 28.10-20 and 32.23-33) that provide the *hieros logoi* for Bethel, Mahanaim and Penuel. At the same time as providing aetiologies, these texts offer assurance and hope to those facing the frightful trial of living among potentially hostile others.

Jacob does not live his nightmare when he meets Esau, but that does not mean his return 'home' fails to be disorienting. Nothing resembles either Jacob's memory or expectation of Canaan. Jacob remains confused that Esau seeks reconciliation and not revenge. Though one anticipates that Jacob will now behave differently towards Esau, the unexpected situation leaves Jacob facing yet another new place

---

27. The UN defines a returnee as a refugee who has returned to his or her home country. See http://www.unrefugees.org/site/c.lfIQKSOwFqG/b.4950731/k.A894/What_is_a_refugee.htm (accessed on 23 Feb. 2017).

28. Jesse Newman, 'Narrating Displacement: Oral Histories of Sri Lankan Women', *Refugee Studies Centre Working Papers* 15 (2003): 18–59.

29. cf. the discussion in Anderson, *Jacob and the Divine Trickster*, 160–69.

30. Following the JPS translation; cf. Westermann, *Genesis 12–36*, 522–23.

with yet another unfamiliar host. Laban appeared benevolent to Jacob initially before taking advantage of him; will Esau be any different?

Katherine Southwood examines Ezra–Nehemiah and not Genesis, but she establishes that the Hebrew Bible depicts return migrants reapplying the strategies they used to survive away from 'home' to navigate the unfamiliar circumstances they find when returning there.[31] Likewise, Jacob responds to Esau with the same strategies he employed for handling Laban. First, Jacob offers a material payment that is exceedingly large (Gen. 33.1-11; cf. 29.15-20), indeed apparently unnecessary (33.9), to his unfamiliar host. Second, Jacob treats Esau's generous offer to provide assistance for his journey to Seir with suspicion because he is wary of having Esau's representatives with him. When Jacob refuses their help, the logic of his refusal replicates his final dealing with Laban: Jacob recognizes the generosity offered (compare 30.31 and 33.15), but refuses to accept.[32] With Laban, this behaviour provides Jacob the opportunity to deceptively acquire wealth; with Esau, it provides Jacob protection by creating separation between him and someone he does not trust. Jacob acts the same way in circumstances that appear quite different to some, but are alarmingly similar to an involuntary migrant.

Though a similar analysis of Genesis 34–36 could show how the experience of involuntary migration colours the interaction between Jacob's family and the Shechemites, in order to demonstrate the second potential contribution of this approach it is necessary to explore how this interdisciplinary exegesis may be coordinated with further insights from the study of migration to examine the diachronic growth of the Jacob material.

4.5 Reassessing the Development of the Jacob Narrative

The relatively broad agreement on the sources that comprise the canonical form of the Jacob narrative makes it a good case study to expound how the study of migration may inform a fresh assessment of Genesis's diachronic development.

Perhaps the single point of consensus in Pentateuchal source criticism now is the division between P and non-P material. Owing to the relatively small amount of P material in Genesis 25–36, consensus is even more prevalent here. Erhard Blum enumerates an 'almost undisputed' list of 29 verses from P in the Jacob narrative: 25.19-20, 26b; 26.34-35; 27.46-28.9; 31.17-18; 33.aαא.β; 35.(6?) 9-15, 22b-29.[33] Scholars also generally agree that P's material dates to the period

---

31. Southwood, *Ezra 9–10*. For the social-scientific research basis of her argument, see pp. 49–56.

32. In 30.31 Jacob says 'pay me nothing!' and in 33.15 'Oh no, my lord is too kind to me!'

33. Blum, 'Jacob', 190–91.

after 586 BCE, most accepting that it binds the ancestral tradition and the exodus tradition into a single narrative for the first time.[34]

The question of what material may predate P remains highly debated, though scholars tend towards one of two groups. One group identifies major pieces of the non-P Jacob narrative as pre-priestly compositions that originate separately from the Abraham (and Isaac) traditions, emerging from the Northern Kingdom of Israel prior to the fall of Samaria in 722 BCE. This group includes Erhard Blum, Albert de Pury,[35] David Carr,[36] Israel Finkelstein and Thomas Römer,[37] along with many others. Blum, perhaps the most influential of this group, may serve as a representative of it here, though differences certainly exist between him and the others in this group.

Blum argues for three stages of development prior to the P edition (his Kp). The earliest edition (Blum's *Kompositionsschicht*) consists of a Jacob–Esau–Laban story, probably composed during the Omride era (*c*. 880–850 BCE). This version comprises the *Vorstufe* for the second edition, Blum's so-called *Jakoberzählung*, which expands the text into a tri-partite narrative with Jacob's two encounters with Esau framing his time with Laban. Crucial to Blum's dating of the *Jakoberzählung*, it now includes the *hieros logos* for Bethel (28.10-22), along with aetiologies for Mahanaim and Penuel (32.2-3, 23-33). Such material, Blum contends, must date from a time when the relevant sanctuary operated, making 722 BCE the *terminus ante quem* for this form of the narrative in his schema.[38] Blum speculates the likely provenance for the *Jakoberzählung* is 'under the second Jeroboam, probably in the realm of the sanctuary at Bethel'.[39]

This *Jakoberzählung* comes to the Southern Kingdom of Judah after the destruction of Samaria, where, in due course at some point after 586 BCE, Judahite tradents combine it with the existing Abraham traditions in order to form the

---

34. I bracket the Neo-Documentarian approach here. Insofar as these scholars offer a date for any source, there are indications they prefer a pre-586 date for P. This matter deserves further attention, but that is not possible here.

35. Albert de Pury, *Promesse divine et légende culturelle dans le cycle de Jacob: Genèse 28 et les traditions patriarcales* (Paris: J. Gabalda, 1975); Albert de Pury, 'Le cycle de Jacob comme légende autonome des origines d'Israël', in *Congress Volume: Leuven, 1989*, ed. J. A. Emerton (Leiden: Brill, 1991).

36. David M. Carr, *Reading the Fractures of Genesis: Historical and Literary Approaches* (Louisville, KY: Westminster John Knox, 1996).

37. Israel Finkelstein and Thomas Römer, 'Comments on the Historical Background of the Jacob Narrative in Genesis', *Zeitschrift für die alttestamentliche Wissenschaft* 126 (2014): 317–38; cf. Israel Finkelstein and Thomas Römer, 'Comments on the Historical Background of the Abraham Narrative: Between "Realia" and "Exegetica"', *Hebrew Bible and Ancient Israel* 3 (2014): 3–23.

38. Blum, 'Jacob', 208.

39. Blum, 'Jacob', 210.

ancestral history (*Vätergeschichte II* in Blum's earlier work on this material).[40] Though Blum's scheme details further development from this stage, both because that does not impact the current discussion and for brevity's sake that shall not be traced here.

Another group of scholars maintains that the Jacob narrative originates after the destruction of Jerusalem in 586 BCE. Recently and notably, Nadav Na'aman has argued that the pre-P Jacob material comes from 'about the mid-6th century B.C.E.' in Judah.[41] Despite problems in Na'aman's argument, he demonstrates a number of obstacles to a Northern, eighth-century setting for the composition of the Jacob material as outlined by Blum. Six of Na'aman's arguments shall be reviewed here in order both to specify the problems he identifies with Blum's view and also to provide a foundation for a fresh proposal regarding the composition of the pre-P Jacob material.

Three points can be catalogued quickly. One, Na'aman observes that the well-integrated beginning (26.23, 33) and ending (35.19) of the Jacob story occur in Judah, not the Northern Kingdom.[42] Two, he notes that '[t]he prominence of Haran in the story fits the reality of the late 8th-6th centuries, not that of the time of the Israelite monarchy'.[43] Three, Na'aman follows Jacob Hoftijzer, concluding that the promise texts, which form an important part of the story (12.1-3; 26.2-3b; 31.3; 31.13; 46.3-4), 'first arose at a time in which the Israelites' existence was seriously threatened, probably in the exilic period'.[44] While Na'aman correctly stresses a connection to a time when the community felt its control over its land was at risk, he fails to recognize this mood may have prevailed in Israel, and indeed Judah, anytime from about 730 BCE onwards.

Na'aman's fourth point constitutes his strongest objection to Blum's position: instead of postulating that the Bethel *hieros logos* (Gen. 28.10-22) must originate in a period when Bethel contained an active temple, Na'aman demonstrates the equal likelihood that the material seeks to engender hope for a future restoration of the Bethel sanctuary. According to him, Genesis 28 presents a 'foundation legend of the temple, which justifies its restoration and expansion', substantiating a 'hope that when Jacob/Israel returns home, "this stone, which

---

40. Erhard Blum, *Die Komposition der Vätergeschichte* (Neukirchen-Vluyn: Neukirchener Verlag, 1984); see Erhard Blum, *Studien dur Komposition des Pentateuch* (Berlin: de Gruyter, 1990), 214, n. 35, and the discussion of the Blum's revision of his position in Rainer Albertz, *Israel in Exile: The History and Literature of the Sixth Century B.C.E.*, trans. David Green (Atlanta, GA: Society of Biblical Literature, 2003), 251–52.

41. Nadav Na'aman, 'The Jacob Story and the Formation of Biblical Israel', *Tel Aviv: Journal of the Institute of Archaeology of Tel Aviv University* 41 (2014): 95.

42. Na'aman, 'Jacob Story', 99.

43. Na'aman, 'Jacob Story', 99.

44. Na'aman, 'Jacob Story', 99.

I have set up as a pillar, shall be God's house".[45] Na'aman's case hardly decides the issue; nevertheless, it shows the impossibility of dating this aetiology according to the operational status of the Bethel sanctuary.

Fifth, Na'aman argues that a positive description of a familial network connecting the Northern Kingdom to Haran sits uneasily with the proposed dating of the 'Story of Jacob' during the Israelite monarchy, a period of great hostility between the Israelites and the Arameans.[46] To this extent, Na'aman remains convincing, though he carries on into speculative claims he cannot substantiate.[47] Na'aman also observes that the Jacob narrative contains precious little material seeking to justify the role of the Israelite monarchy, which only strengthens his point. Whereas the material in Judges and Samuel, for which similar claims exist, obviously deals with political and military leadership, and even the Abraham material intimates similar themes (i.e. Genesis 14), Jacob never adopts such a role. Jacob lives subordinated to others. Whatever success Jacob does experience comes by trickery of the dominant power, never from obtaining that power himself. If the Jacob narrative intends to justify Israelite royal prerogative, it is an especially obtuse attempt to do so.

Finally, Na'aman discusses the varying locales of Rachel's tomb: placed alternately in the north (1 Sam. 10.2; Jer. 31.14) and in Ephrath/Bethlehem (Gen. 35.16-20), he contends that the link to Bethlehem 'strongly supports my suggestion that Jacob's story was written in Judah rather than in Israel. Otherwise', he continues, 'the tomb would have been identified in north Benjamin, near Bethel, where the inhabitants of the Northern Kingdom claimed its location to be'.[48] Na'aman correctly stresses the connection to Benjamin, but he moves too quickly to conclude this indicates a Judahite composition. Indeed, his assertion relies upon his own idiosyncratic view that Benjamin comprised part of Judah throughout both the Bronze and Iron ages.[49] That view disregards strong evidence

45. Na'aman, 'Jacob Story', 101; cf. Harald Wahl, *Die Jakobserzählungen. Studien zu ihrer mündlichen Überlieferung, Vorschriftung und Historizität* (Berlin: Walter de Gruyter, 1997), who suggests the story is written once Bethel is already destroyed.

46. Na'aman, 'Jacob Story', 105.

47. Na'aman speculates that the 'Arameans' that live beyond the river (Gen. 31.21-23) represent the 'descendants of the Israelites that the Assyrians deported to north Mesopotamia who, over the course of time, lost their former ethnic identity and became "Arameans"'. Na'aman attempts to support his speculation with an inscription from Sargon II, the account of 2 Kgs 17.6, and (admittedly) sparse evidence for Yahwistic names in this area during the seventh century, but the evidence will not support the claim (Na'aman, 'Jacob Story', 105). He presents this case as an extension of Mario Liverani's, *Israel's History and the History of Israel*, trans. Chiara Peri and Philip Davies (London: Equinox, 2005), 264, though there is little to nothing in Liverani's discussion to suggest this conclusion.

48. Na'aman, 'Jacob Story', 108.

49. Nadav Na'aman, 'Saul, Benjamin and the Emergence of "biblical Israel"', *Zeitschrift für die alttestamentliche Wissenschaft* 121 (2009): 211-24, 335-49.

that Benjamin constituted part of Israel and Judah at various times during the Iron Age, with Judahite control of the region demonstrable from the late eighth century until the fall of Jerusalem in 586 BCE.[50] So, while Na'aman accurately emphasizes the Benjamite connection, he incorrectly correlates this to the sixth century rather than sometime after roughly 730 BCE.

To summarize, Na'aman persuasively demonstrates the author of the Jacob narrative 'was familiar with places in south Judah and the neighboring southern regions and with Judahite oral traditions, and . . . was familiar with the North Israelite urban centers and cultural memories'.[51] One may appropriate this contribution without accepting his specious conclusion that the Jacob material is, then, 'a Judahite exilic composition' which 'might be read as a paradigm of a forced migration from the land, the hard life in the Diaspora and the return home'.[52] In sum, Na'aman effectively unmoors the Jacob narrative from a reigning Israelite monarchy and a functioning Bethel sanctuary while cogently connecting it to a community with knowledge of both Israel and Judah, living during a period of prominence for Haran (the late eighth to sixth centuries), and familiar with the experience of involuntary migration.

The preceding exegesis – showing the centrality that involuntary migration plays in the Jacob narrative – magnifies the importance of this final feature. Indeed, when one places the efforts at royal authorization and religious aetiology in proper perspective alongside the dominant theme of involuntary migration, the vital contribution that the social-scientific study of involuntary migration can make to identifying the provenance of Genesis 25–36 comes to the fore. The key question emerges in this form: did a community of involuntary migrants, familiar with prominent locations in Israel and Judah, positively disposed to the traditions about the patriarch Jacob, exist during the period of Haran's prominence between the late eighth and sixth century BCE?

Much remains unknown about the aftermath of the fall of the Northern Kingdom to Assyria around 720 BCE. Scholars largely agree, nevertheless, that the extant material and the textual evidence indicates a substantial number of Israelites (involuntarily) migrated into Judah as a result of these events. 'Resettlement of Israelite groups from the area of southern Samaria, including Bethel, in Jerusalem

50. Israel Finkelstein, *The Forgotten Kingdom: The Archaeology and History of Northern Israel* (Atlanta, GA: Society of Biblical Literature, 2013), 44–47, who argues in direct rebuttal to Na'aman's position as detailed in Na'aman, 'Saul, Benjamin'.

51. Na'aman, 'Jacob Story', 118.

52. Na'aman, 'Jacob Story', 109; cf. Bert Dicou, *Edom, Israel's Brother and Antagonist: The Role of Edom in Biblical Prophecy and Story* (Sheffield: Sheffield Academic Press, 1994). Indeed, Na'aman seems to undermine his own view in this last quote, which posits a community that has experienced diasporic living and, minimally, a desire to return home. Without objecting at all to Na'aman classifying those who remained in Judah after 586 BCE as involuntary migrants, because they remain in Judah they are, by definition, not part of a diaspora that yearns for a return home.

and Judah', comments Israel Finkelstein about this period, transformed Judah into 'a mixed Judahite-Israelite kingdom under Assyrian domination.'[53] Scholars primarily concern themselves with the process by which this generates a so-called pan-Israelite identity secured by combining Northern and Southern textual traditions, but this analysis overlooks the possibility for compositional activity during this period prior to such amalgamation.[54]

Blum originally located the initial combination of the Abraham and Jacob traditions into a patriarchal history (his *Vätergeschichte I*) during this period,[55] though he subsequently revised his view, opting to argue this occurred after 586 BCE.[56] Blum's move created something of a 'dark period' between roughly 720 and 586 BCE for him, and it would seem, for many others working on the Pentateuch as well. Recently, Finkelstein and Thomas Römer have revived the role of this period in the development of the Jacob narrative, though they consider it only as a time that might allow for the combination of the Abraham and Jacob traditions, not as an opportunity for independent development of the Jacob material occurring prior to any integration with the Abraham traditions.

Nevertheless, the social setting for the Israelite involuntary migrants in Judah between 720 BCE and approximately 630 BCE provides precisely the atmosphere in which one may account for the strengths in both Blum's and Na'aman's views. The Israelites who involuntarily migrated to Judah not only knew Samaria and Bethel, as Finkelstein observes, but also Shechem and perhaps Penuel, the main locations in the Jacob narrative. The oscillating affiliation of Benjamin with Israel and Judah makes it likely some of these Israelite involuntary migrants settled there, offering a possible logic for locating Rachel's burial there too. The small size of Judah and relative proximity of Jerusalem, Bethlehem and Beersheba (about 40 miles/65 km from the former two), even by ancient standards, accounts for knowledge about the key Southern sites in the Jacob narrative.

It is conjecture to speak about the social status and education of the Israelite involuntary migrants, but the fact that any Northern tradition survives at all strongly implies the presence of some literate elites, such as priests and scribes. It is no struggle to imagine some elites being sent ahead 'to safety', as it were, from Samaria, Bethel and other key locations in Israel as the Assyrian invasion commenced and defeat became more and more likely, even if this situation lies beyond what is demonstrable. Whatever the case, members of the Israelite involuntary migrant community would have known key components of the pre-existing Jacob traditions – for instance, some aetiological material along with some stories about migration – that enabled them to perpetuate the stories

---

53. Finkelstein, *Forgotten Kingdom*, 155.

54. Finkelstein, *Forgotten Kingdom*, 155.

55. Blum, *Die Komposition*, 273–97, especially pp. 296–97.

56. Blum, *Studien zur Komposition*, 214, n. 35; cf. Matthias Köckert, *Vätergott und Väterverheißungen: eine auseinandersetzung mit Albrecht Alt und seinem Erben* (Göttingen: Vandenhoeck & Ruprecht, 1988), 252–54.

after arriving in Judah, perhaps orally, perhaps in writing.[57] This community of Israelite involuntary migrants, even in such broad outline, provides a fitting social setting for all the features Na'aman highlights about the Jacob narrative's likely author.

What aim would an Israelite involuntary migrant seek to achieve by including existing traditions about Jacob the patriarch and key religious sites in the North into a new edition of the story after 720 BCE? Recall the major moves in the plot of the Jacob narrative from Genesis 25–33: conflict between Esau and Jacob produces hostility between them, so that Esau pronounces his homicidal intentions; Rebekah uses her access and influence with Isaac to arrange, with something between misdirection and dishonesty, Jacob's departure; Jacob travels to Laban, who he does not know but to whom he is related, and obtains refuge; though providing safety for Jacob, Laban accrues great power over Jacob, forcing Jacob to accept unfair treatment in order to retain his protection; after twenty years, Jacob cleverly escapes Laban's control, departs from this 'safe-haven', and returns to face his enemy; although the enemy's hostility appears to have dissipated, uncertainty prompts Jacob to employ trickery to protect himself and his family once again. In sum, the Jacob narrative describes how to successfully navigate the frightful challenges arising from life as an involuntary migrant caught between a hostile enemy (e.g. Assyria) and a host community to which one is related, but does not have your well-being at the top of their priorities (e.g. Judah).

Characterized thus, the Jacob story offers encouragement to and sustains hope for the Israelite involuntary migrants in Judah after 720 BCE. To illustrate this function, compare this objective with the aims of stories told by contemporary involuntary migrants. In her influential work with Hutu refugees in Tanzania, Liisa Malkki notes the unabashedly didactic nature of their historical narratives. Lasting from hours to several days, the stories 'were crafted with considerable oratorical eloquence' and 'clearly had a beginning, a development, a climax, and a closure'.[58] The stories facilitated discussions on the lessons contained in the material. The 'heavily moral stories' constructed an understanding of the world 'and the pragmatics of everyday life' as an involuntary migrant.[59]

By depicting Israel's eponymous ancestor Jacob as an asylum seeker, refugee and return migrant who successfully navigates the gauntlet between hostile enemy Esau and coercive host-protector Laban, the Jacob narrative accomplishes the didactic, pragmatic function of endorsing a mode of life suited to the situation of the Israelite involuntary migrants who find themselves in Judah after 720 BCE.

---

57. On the evidence for an 'oral-written literary matrix' lying behind the development of the texts in the Hebrew Bible, see David M. Carr, *Writing on the Tablet of the Heart: Origins of Scripture and Literature* (Oxford: Oxford University Press, 2005).

58. Malkki, *Purity and Exile*, 53.

59. Malkki, *Purity and Exile*, 53–55.

4.6 Conclusion

The Jacob narrative, as demonstrated, foregrounds the experience of involuntary migration. It follows sensibly, then, that the social-scientific study of that same phenomenon must illumine the meaning of the text. Furthermore, the same social-scientific research offers important inputs into the effort to reconstruct the diachronic development of the text by substantially clarifying the social setting(s) from which it likely arose.

This essay has employed findings from the study of involuntary migration to offer a fresh exegesis of the Jacob narrative, thereby justifying the need for scholars to recognize its central theme is involuntary migration. Additionally, this essay outlines a new argument for placing important diachronic developments in the Jacob narrative's history among Israelite involuntary migrants living in Judah during the period between 720 and 630 BCE.

The first stage of the argument – a synchronic exegesis – remains valid regardless of whether one accepts the second stage, namely, the diachronic reconstruction. This point deserves explicit statement, lest any disagreement on the more contentious issues of source criticism and provenance obscure the important contribution that occurs at this interpretative level.

That said, even scholars who disagree with the compositional history advocated on the basis of this exegesis will need to account for it – especially the finding that involuntary migration comprises a dominant theme of the Jacob narrative. The case for its role here should make it a common feature in future reconstructions of the diachronic development of the ancestral narrative. Indeed, one might define the central contribution of this article as its indication that the social-scientific study of migration, especially involuntary migration, can and should assume an important role in analysis of the ancestral narrative.

Bibliography

Acer, Eleanor. 'Making a Difference: A Legacy of Pro Bono Representation'. *Journal of Refugee Studies* 17, no. 3 (2004): 347–66.

Ahn, John. *Exile as Forced Migrations: A Sociological, Literary, and Theological Approach on the Displacement and Resettlement of the Southern Kingdom of Judah.* Berlin: Walter de Gruyter, 2011.

Albertz, Rainer. *Israel in Exile: The History and Literature of the Sixth Century B.C.E.*, trans. David Green. Atlanta, GA: Society of Biblical Literature, 2003.

Anderson, John E. *Jacob and the Divine Trickster: A Theology of Deception and Yhwh's Fidelity to the Ancestral Promise in Jacob Cycle.* Winona Lake, IN: Eisenbrauns, 2011.

Arnold, Bill T. *Genesis.* Cambridge: Cambridge University Press, 2009.

Article 1, 1951 Convention Relating to the Status of Refugees. Accessed on 23 Feb. 2017. http://www.unrefugees.org/site/c.lfIQKSOwFqG/b.4950731/k.A894/What_is_a_refugee.htm

Bianchini, Katia. 'Legal Aid for Asylum Seekers: Progress and Challenges in Italy'. *Journal of Refugee Studies* 24, no. 2 (2011): 390–410.

Black, Richard. 'Fifty Years of Refugee Studies: From Theory to Policy'. *International Migration Review* 35, no. 1 (2001): 57–78. Available online: http://www.unhcr.org/pages/49da0e466.html (accessed 23 Feb. 2017).

Blum, Erhard. *Die Komposition der Vätergeschichte*. Neukirchen-Vluyn: Neukirchener Verlag, 1984.

Blum, Erhard. *Studien dur Komposition des Pentateuch*. Berlin: de Gruyter, 1990.

Blum, Erhard. 'The Jacob Tradition'. In *The Book of Genesis: Composition, Reception, and Interpretation*, edited by Craig Evans, A., Joel N. Lohr and David L. Petersen, 197–203. Leiden: Brill, 2012.

Brett, Mark G. *Genesis: Procreation and the Politics of Identity*. London: Routledge, 2000.

Carr, David M. *Reading the Fractures of Genesis: Historical and Literary Approaches*. Louisville, KY: Westminster John Knox, 1996.

Carr, David M. *Writing on the Tablet of the Heart: Origins of Scripture and Literature*. Oxford: Oxford University Press, 2005.

Chatty, Dawn. 'Anthropology and Forced Migration'. In *The Oxford Handbook of Refugee and Forced Migration Studies*, edited by Elena Fiddian-Qasmiyeh et al., 74–80. Oxford: Oxford University Press, 2014.

Colson, Elizabeth. 'Forced Migration and the Anthropological Response'. *Journal of Refugee Studies* 16 (2003): 7–10.

Crisp, Jeff. 'In Search of Solutions: Refugees Are Doing It for Themselves (Refugee Voices, Opening Plenary)', at the Refugee Studies Centre in Oxford, 24 March 2014. Available online: http://www.rsc.ox.ac.uk/news/in-search-of-solutions-refugees-are-doing-it-for-themselves-refugee-voices-opening-plenary-jeff-crisp (accessed on 23 Feb. 2017).

Darshan, Guy. 'The Origins of the Foundation Stories Genre in the Hebrew Bible and Ancient Eastern Mediterranean'. *JBL*, 133, no. 4 (2014).

De Pury, Albert. *Promesse divine et légende culturelle dans le cycle de Jacob: Genèse 28 et les traditions patriarcales*. Paris: J. Gabalda, 1975.

De Pury, Albert. 'Le cycle de Jacob comme légende autonome des origines d'Israël'. In *Congress Volume: Leuven, 1989*, edited by J. A. Emerton. Leiden: Brill, 1991.

Dicou, Bert. *Edom, Israel's Brother and Antagonist: The Role of Edom in Biblical Prophecy and Story*. Sheffield: Sheffield Academic Press, 1994.

Esler, Philip. 'Social-Scientific Models in Biblical Interpretation'. In *Ancient Israel: The Old Testament in Its Social Context*, edited by Philip Esler, 3–14. Philadelphia, PA: Fortress, 2006.

Finkelstein, Israel. *The Forgotten Kingdom: The Archaeology and History of Northern Israel*. Atlanta, GA: Society of Biblical Literature, 2013.

Finkelstein, Israel, and Thomas Römer. 'Comments on the Historical Background of the Abraham Narrative: Between "Realia" and "Exegetica"'. *Hebrew Bible and Ancient Israel* 3 (2014): 3–23.

Finkelstein, Israel, and Thomas Römer. 'Comments on the Historical Background of the Jacob Narrative in Genesis'. *ZAW* 126 (2014): 317–38.

Frankel, David. *The Land of Canaan and the Destiny of Israel: Theologies of Territory in the Hebrew Bible*. Winona Lake, IN: Eisenbrauns, 2011.

Hagedorn, Anselm C. 'Hausmann und Jäger (Gen. 25,27-28): Aus den jugendtagen Jakobs und Esaus'. In *Die Erzväter in der biblischen Tradition: Festschrift für Matthias Köckert*, edited by A. C. Hagedorn and Henrik Pfieffer. Berlin: Walter de Gruyter, 2009.

Harrell-Bond, Barbara E. *Imposing Aid: Emergency Assistance to Refugees*. Oxford: Oxford University Press, 1986.

Kennedy, Elisabeth Robertson. *Seeking a Homeland: Sojourn and Ethnic Identity in the Ancestral Narratives of Genesis*. Leiden: Brill, 2011.

Köckert, Matthias. *Vätergott und Väterverheißungen: eine auseinandersetzung mit Albrecht Alt und seinem Erben*. Göttingen: Vandenhoeck & Ruprecht, 1988.

Liverani, Mario. *Israel's History and the History of Israel*, trans. Chiara Peri and Philip Davies. London: Equinox, 2005.

Malkki, Liisa H. *Purity and Exile: Violence, Memory and National Cosmology Among Hutu Refugees in Tanzania*. Chicago: University of Chicago Press, 1995.

Middlemas, Jill, and John J. Ahn. *By the Irrigation Canals of Babylon: Approaches to the Study of the Exile*. New York: T&T Clark, 2012.

Mullen, E. Theodore. *Ethnic Myths and Pentateuch Foundations: A New Approach to the Formation of the Pentateuch*. Atlanta, GA: Scholars Press, 1997.

Na'aman, Nadav. 'Saul, Benjamin and the Emergence of "biblical Israel"'. *ZAW* 121 (2009): 211–24, 335–49.

Na'aman, Nadav. 'The Jacob Story and the Formation of Biblical Israel'. *Tel Aviv: Journal of the Institute of Archaeology of Tel Aviv University* 41 (2014): 95–118.

Newman, Jesse. 'Narrating Displacement: Oral Histories of Sri Lankan Women'. *Refugee Studies Centre Working Papers* 15 (2003): 18–59.

Niditch, Susan. *A Prelude to Biblical Folklore: Underdogs and Tricksters*. Urbana, IL: University of Illinois Press, 2000.

Scott, James C. *Weapons of the Weak: Everyday Forms of Peasant Resistance*. New Haven, CT: Yale University Press, 1985.

Scott, James C. *Domination and the Arts of Resistance: Hidden Transcripts*. New Haven, CT: Yale University Press, 1990.

Smith-Christopher, Daniel. *Biblical Theology of Exile*. Minneapolis, MN: Augsburg Fortress, 2002.

Southwood, Katherine E. *Ethnicity and the Mixed Marriage Crisis in Ezra 9–10*. Oxford: Oxford University Press, 2012.

Strine, C. A. 'Sister Save Us: The Matriarchs as Breadwinners and Their Threat to Patriarchy in the Ancestral Narrative'. In *Women and Exilic Identity in the Hebrew Bible*, edited by. K. Southwood and M. Halvorson-Taylor. London: Bloomsbury T&T Clark, 2018.

Van Seters, John. *Prologue to History: The Yahwist as Historian in Genesis*. Zürich: Theologischer Verlag Zürich, 1992.

Van Seters, John. *The Pentateuch: A Social-Science Commentary*. Sheffield: Sheffield Academic Press, 1999.

Von Rad, Gerhard. *Genesis: A Commentary*, trans. John H. Marks. London: SCM Press, 1961.

Voutira, Eftihia, and Barbara E. Harrell-Bond. 'In Search of the Locus of Trust: The Social World of the Refugee Camp'. In *Mistrusting Refugees*, edited by E. V. Daniel and J. C. Knudsen. Berkley: University of California Press, 1995.

Wahl, Harald. *Die Jakobserzählungen. Studien zu ihrer mündlichen Überlieferung, Vorschriftung und Historizität*. Berlin: Walter de Gruyter, 1997.

Wenham, Gordon J. *Genesis 16–50*. Nashville, TN: Thomas Nelson, 2000.

Westermann, Claus. *Genesis 12–36: A Commentary*, trans. John K. Scullion S. J. Minneapolis, MN: Augsburg Publishing House, 1985.

Chapter 5

'TO SHARE YOUR BREAD WITH THE HUNGRY': JUSTICE OR CHARITY?

Walter J. Houston

5.1 *Prologue*

It is a commonplace in modern Christian advocacy for development charities to argue that giving to the poor, at least in a constructive manner rather than merely as a stopgap, is 'not charity but justice'. I take this to mean that it is not a voluntary act of benevolence, but an obligation. So understood, it is not only a modern idea. There are famous sayings by Christian preachers of the fourth and fifth centuries that categorize almsgiving as the exercise of justice, in that it is simply giving the poor what is due to them. So Basil of Caesarea: 'The bread you are holding back belongs to the hungry; the coat you keep in your wardrobe belongs to the naked; the shoes mouldering in your house belong to the barefoot; the money you are hiding underground belongs to the needy. So you are doing wrong (ἀδικεῖς) to all those whom you were in a position to help.'[1] That this may be more than a rhetorical flourish is suggested by John Chrysostom, who tells those with inherited wealth that if they go far enough back they will find their wealth arises from some injustice.[2] To share one's bread with the hungry is no voluntary charitable act, but a restoration to the poor of what belongs to them.[3]

5.2 *In the Hebrew Bible: Under the Monarchy*

While almsgiving is in these sources argued to be justice, if we look at the issue from the perspective of the Hebrew Bible, we find that a far wider concept of justice or righteousness has been progressively narrowed to that of almsgiving

1. Basil of Caesarea, 'On the saying of the Gospel according to Luke, "I will pull down my barns and build bigger ones"', *PG* 31, 277.
2. John Chrysostom, 'In Epistulam I ad Timotheum Cap. IV, Homilia 12', *PG* 62, 562–63.
3. See Gary A. Anderson, *Charity: The Place of the Poor in the Biblical Tradition* (New Haven/London: Yale, 2013).

or 'charity'. I shall argue in this essay that this development results from social changes over the whole period of the Old Testament, and is only complete in the deutero-canonical writings. I shall be using concepts in economic anthropology; initially the well-known trio of modes of exchange postulated by Karl Polanyi and refined by Marshall Sahlins: reciprocity, redistribution and exchange.[4] But for the analysis of almsgiving itself I find more helpful the fascinating work of David Graeber, *Debt, the First 5,000 Years*.[5] (This is only one way of approaching the question: I have in my *Contending for Justice* used a more sociological analysis of the underlying development.[6])

In writings usually supposed to be from the monarchic period (leaving out of account the virtually undatable wisdom sentences in Proverbs), we do not find the feeding of the hungry and the clothing of the naked as even an *aspect* of justice. The prophets' condemnations, for example, are not directed against those who have failed to feed the hungry or clothe the naked, but against more active wrongs. This idea first appears in Ezekiel and Trito-Isaiah. The book of the covenant, likewise, apart from the sabbatical injunctions, is concerned to counsel against active injustice: 'you shall not exploit . . . you shall not oppress . . . do not act like a moneylender, do not impose interest . . . return [the pledge] before sunset . . . do not pervert the justice due . . . do not accept a bribe' (Exod. 22.20–23.9). Deuteronomy, which we shall come to in a moment, is rather different.

Why should this be? In peasant society it is unusual for individuals to be left to starve. There is a strong tendency for households to help one another when in difficulty, if only because of 'the hard-headed realization that some aid to one's neighbour may simply be a form of insurance against the rainy day'.[7] In monarchic Israel and Judah this tendency may well have been strengthened and formalized through the institution of the מִשְׁפָּחָה, a real or fictive kinship group that often embraced all or most of the inhabitants of a village.[8] 'Generalized reciprocity', to use Sahlins's rather unwieldy term – 'indefinite reciprocity' would be better – would have applied, as usual, between kin, especially with gifts of food.[9] But this is not what we generally understand by 'charity'. Giver and receiver are equals and

4. Karl Polanyi, 'The Economy as Instituted Process', in *Trade and Market in the Early Empires: Economies in History and Theory*, ed. K. Polanyi, Conrad M. Arensberg and Harry W. Pearson (Glencoe, IL: Falcon's Wing, 1957), 243–69.

5. David Graeber, *Debt, The First 5,000 Years* (Brooklyn: Melville House, 2011).

6. Walter J. Houston, *Contending for Justice: Ideologies and Theologies of Social Justice in the Old Testament*, rev. edn (London & New York: T&T Clark, 2008), 18–51.

7. Eric R. Wolf, *Peasants*, Foundations of Modern Anthropology Series (Englewood Cliffs, NJ: Prentice-Hall, 1966), 80.

8. S. Bendor, *The Social Structure of Ancient Israel* (Jerusalem: Simor, 1996), 67–86; Avraham Faust, *The Archaeology of Israelite Society in Iron Age* II (Winona Lake, IN: Eisenbrauns, 2012), 170–75.

9. Marshall Sahlins, *Stone Age Economics* (London: Tavistock Publications, 1974), 185–219.

members of the same community, and in the medium term each expects to give and receive more or less equally. Famine, if it came, would affect everyone equally, and could not be relieved by individual charity. It is in line with this that the root רעב in texts set in the monarchic era almost without exception refers to a disaster affecting the community rather than to personal suffering: famine rather than hunger.

However, possibilities were emerging in the later monarchy which could lead to the destitution of an individual or nuclear family. This is suggested by Deuteronomy's emphasis on the *personae miserabiles*. The גר and the Levite would have fallen outside the circle of solidarity within which reciprocal relations could be assumed.[10] The parallel emphasis on widows and the fatherless suggests, however, a much narrower circle, confined to the stronger members of one בית אב, as Bendor suggests.[11] But I regard this radical restriction as unlikely in the village setting. It is much more likely in the developing urban sector sponsored by the steadily increasing power of the state, where the same sense of solidarity would not have existed in the community as a whole, and where there are clear signs of social stratification.[12] Here there would be some who could not rely on any regular source of income. Besides the widow and orphan, there were perhaps young male incomers from a countryside that could not support all the souls it produced. These would be the most likely candidates for destitution and hunger. The command in Deuteronomy to pay a wage labourer before the sun goes down (Deut. 24.14-15) is an index of the precarious livelihood of some in the cities of the late monarchy, probably, as well as later.

Some institutions might protect those exposed to the danger of destitution. The institution of patronage probably existed, giving people some security of livelihood in return for their support of the patron in the power negotiations of the elite.[13] The relationship of patron and client is, ideally, one of balanced reciprocity, where the return should be made at a level recognized as equivalent and in a limited period of time.[14]

It is of course not only the poor who are the objects of patronage. Mephibosheth eats 'at David's table' (2 Sam. 9.11), 450 prophets of Baal and 400 prophets of Asherah 'at Jezebel's table' (1 Kgs 18.19), 150 people every day 'at my [Nehemiah's] table' (Neh. 5.17-18). In each case the object of the provision is to reward the

10. Cf. Sahlins, *Economics*, 198–200.

11. Bendor, *Social Structure*, 183–96.

12. Janne J. Nurmi, *Die Ethik unter dem Druck des Alltags: Die Impulse der gesellschaftlichen Änderungen und Situation zu der sozialkritschen Prophetie in Juda im 8. Jh. V. Chr.* (Åbo: Åbo Akademis Förlag, 2004); Faust, *Archaeology*, 114–17.

13. Wolf, *Peasants*, 86–87; Ronald A. Simkins, 'Patronage and the Political Economy of Monarchic Israel', *Semeia* 87 (1999): 123–44; Houston, *Contending*, 44–48; William R. Domeris, *Touching the Heart of God: The Social Construction of Poverty among Biblical Peasants* (New York & London: T&T Clark, 2007), 80–94.

14. Sahlins, *Economics*, 194–95, 219–20.

recipients for their support and to ensure their loyalty. It is a prudent object for a ruler to bind influential people to their support, and they can do so through redistribution; it is one of its principal objects. Those who do not have access to the levers of redistribution may still be able to use wealth they have gained through redistribution or in other ways for a similar object, and the poor, because of their neediness, are the most likely to respond as required. The command in Deuteronomy to invite to the sacrificial feasts at Weeks and Booths 'the Levite who is within your gates, the גר, the fatherless child and the widow who is in your midst' (Deut. 16.11, cf. 14) may be an attempt to extend the 'generalized reciprocity' of the village to those who might fall outside it, especially in the urban setting; but it can easily be read as a theological validation of patronage.[15]

The permanent imbalance of power between patron and client means that an unscrupulous patron can easily manipulate the relationship, for example through loans, to bend the client to his will and to obtain labour service from his family or himself. Balanced reciprocity thus degenerates into the oddly-titled 'negative reciprocity', which is no reciprocity at all, but sheer exploitation, provoking the condemnations of an Amos or an Isaiah.[16] What the relationship does not lead to, however, is destitution. Labour power was valuable to the patron, and was worth a meal or two a day.

Moreover, the monarchy, despite its leading role in the development of a stratified society, was conceived to be an institution repressing such injustice. 'Justice and righteousness', משפט וצדקה, was the responsibility of the ruler (e.g. 2 Sam. 8.15, 1 Kgs 10.9, Isa. 9.7).[17] The king was expected to implement this responsibility by repressing the exploitation of the poor (Ps. 72.12-14) and by countering violent class relationships with violence against the oppressor through administrative and judicial means.

It is possible that the Israelite states also used their power of redistribution to assist the destitute. There are in many Israelite and Judaean cities large buildings near the gate where the small finds are of a domestic character rather than what one would expect in a public building.[18] Faust links this phenomenon with the

---

15. See Walter J. Houston, 'Rejoicing before the Lord: The Function of the Festal Gathering in Deuteronomy', in *Feasts and Festivals*, ed. Christopher Tuckett, Contributions to Biblical Exegesis and Theology, no. 53 (Leuven: Peeters, 2009).

16. Domeris, *Touching*, 94; see Sahlins, *Economics*, 195–96.

17. José Porfirio Miranda, *Marx and the Bible: A Critique of the Philosophy of Oppression* (London: SCM Press, 1977), 93; 107, nn. 35–38; Moshe Weinfeld, 'Justice and Righteousness' – משפט וצדקה – The Expression and its Meaning', in *Justice and Righteousness: Biblical Themes and Their Influence*, ed. Henning Graf Reventlow and Yair Hoffmann, JSOTS 137 (Sheffield: Sheffield Academic Press 1992), 228–46; Weinfeld, *Social Justice in Ancient Israel and in the Ancient Near East* (Jerusalem: The Magnes Press/Minneapolis: Fortress, 1995), 25–44.

18. Faust, *Archaeology*, 101–109 and literature mentioned on p. 101: Beersheba, Tirzah, Beth-shemesh, Mizpah, Hazor, Arad, etc.

frequent mention of the gate in connection with the poor (e.g. Amos 5.12), and suggests that these buildings were provided as accommodation for the homeless. Faust considers that the state only provided accommodation, and the residents had to rely on alms. However, it is not impossible that they also received basic rations, as the authorities would be doing the same for the city garrison. It may be therefore that in the socially divided cities a primitive welfare system reduced the need for personal alms.

5.3 *Deuteronomy*

It is clear already that Deuteronomy witnesses to an evolving urban culture where people were exposed to the danger of destitution in a way unheard of in the countryside. Nothing represented explicitly as almsgiving is mentioned in the code, although in 10.18-19 we find the reminder that 'Yhwh loves the גר and provides food and clothing, and you shall love the גר, since you were גרים in the land of Egypt'. But two passages in the code are relevant: the law of the third-year tithe in 14.28-9, and the immediately following seventh-year debt remission, specifically the exhortation in 15.7-11.

The third-year tithe provides for the storage of provisions for the needy, specified as the Levite, the גר, the widow and the fatherless. But this is not almsgiving, because it is to be done as a community, not as individuals. It is a redistributive institution rooted no doubt in the solidarity of the village, but to be applied also in the urban situation.

The following pericope, Deut. 15.1-11, although its main subject is another community institution, the seventh-year debt release, does address the positive responsibility of the individual. The patron is urged not to hesitate to lend to his needy client even when the year of release is approaching and the loan will be cancelled before it has been repaid (I have given reasons elsewhere to suppose that the remission is a cancellation rather than a suspension[19]). But in that case, the so-called loan will be effectively a gift. But to refuse to lend is implicitly seen as oppressive. The patron is thus forced to choose between committing injustice and sharing his bread with the hungry.

But what the text emphasizes is not that the disbursement is effectively gratuitous, but, implicitly, that the relationship is one of equality. The suppliant is in the gendered language of the text 'your brother', 'your poor and needy brother'. The community is seen in the image of a family.[20] So on the one hand, the transaction is characterized as a loan, not a gift, and on the other it is made a family affair. There

19. Houston, *Contending*, 181–82; cf. Gregory C. Chirichigno, *Debt-slavery in Israel and the Ancient Near East*, JSOTSup 141 (Sheffield: JSOT Press, 1993), 272–75.

20. Houston, *Contending*, 180–88; ' "Open Your Hand to Your Needy Brother": Ideology and Moral Formation in Deut. 15:1–18', in *The Bible in Ethics*, ed. John Rogerson, Margaret Davies and M. Daniel Carroll R., JSOTSup 207 (Sheffield: Sheffield Academic Press 1995), 296–314; cf. Lothar Perlitt, 'Ein einzig Volk von Brüdern', in *Kirche: Festschrift für Günther Bornkamm zum 75. Geburtstag*, ed. D. Lührmann and G. Strecker (Tübingen: Mohr, 1980), 27–52.

is a hidden contradiction here. We do not usually make loans to family members; in the tribal village we expect unconditional help, and in fact the debtor *is* getting a gift, if not an unconditional one. So why maintain the fiction of a loan? This is not too difficult to see: charity is humiliating – even now – for it underlines the inequality, the poverty, the low status of the recipient compared with the donor. If it is humiliating now, how much more so in a society saturated in the honour-shame complex? But as Graeber argues, even though as long as the debt subsists the debtor is subordinate to the creditor, once the debt is paid – or, might one add, once it is cancelled by higher authority (not by a gracious creditor) – a relationship of equality is restored.[21]

In fact Sahlins's classification of forms of exchange is inadequate to the analysis of charitable giving. Under the sobriquet of *noblesse oblige*, Sahlins classifies gift giving to the poor which expects no return under the heading of generalized reciprocity, the same heading as neighbourly help within the village.[22] But the power relationships are entirely different in the two cases. Intuitively this looks like a misfile, curiously similar to the deliberate ideological mystification of Deuteronomy 15. This is where Graeber's recent, entirely different analysis of 'the moral grounds of economic relations' becomes valuable.[23] He classifies them under three heads which do not correspond in any simple way to the Polanyi trio. They are 'communism', 'exchange' and 'hierarchy'. 'Charity' is a hierarchical relationship, one that, as Graeber points out, 'operates by a principle that is the very opposite of reciprocity'.[24] But how, in that case, can it be *justice*? As Graeber points out, 'reciprocity is our main way of imagining justice'.[25] How can it be justice unless, like Basil and John Chrysostom, we formulate it as the return to the poor of what belongs to them, or as a loan to God which God will duly return?

5.4 *Sixth Century and Later*

It is not any particular social structure or form of exchange that makes 'charity' in its simplest sense – the feeding of the hungry and the clothing of the naked – a necessity, but the breakdown of *all* social structures. The Assyrian and Babylonian invasions, the fall of the kingdoms, the deportation of elite groups and the institution of imperial rule, led to radical changes in the economy and society, in modes of oppression, and therefore in ideas of social justice.[26] In the

21. Graeber, *Debt*, 120–22.
22. Sahlins, *Economics*, 194.
23. Graeber, *Debt*, 90–126.
24. Graeber, *Debt*, 110.
25. Graber, *Debt*, 114.
26. Domeris, *Touching*, 128–50, discusses changes in the economy between the seventh and first centuries, and identifies the sixth century as the main watershed.

first place, the violence, devastation and disruption of the invasions in themselves must have created large numbers of hungry and homeless people. Ezekiel's 'four judgments, the sword, famine, wild beasts and pestilence' (Ezek. 14.21) are no figure of speech, but the reality in a land suffering major invasion. Secondly, the consequent collapse of social institutions and the entire infrastructure[27] meant that the old social structures of the rural community could not survive.[28] The משפחה disappears, eventually to be replaced by the new institution of the בית אבות, which probably originated among the deportees, and was less, or not at all, based on kinship.[29] Thirdly, the imperial powers imposed heavy taxes (Neh. 5.4, 14); indeed even before the annexations their demands for tribute had led to increased burdens on the cultivators (2 Kgs 15.19-20). The lack of co-operative institutions and the increased financial burdens meant that at least from the Persian period onwards the existence of the rural population would have been more precarious and more exposed to rapacious creditors, as Nehemiah 5 shows. Fourthly, the disappearance of the native monarchy and the beginning of imperial rule made it impossible to appeal to the king's responsibility of 'justice and righteousness'.[30]

Thus it should be no surprise that what is veiled in Deuteronomy is openly admitted in all later writings. In the prophetic literature it is precisely in the sixth century and after that we first hear of the obligation of private individuals to 'share their bread with the hungry'. Giving to the poor to relieve hunger is urged or praised in Ezekiel 18, for instance: it is a mark of the צדיק, as well as refraining from exploitative practices such as charging interest and retaining pledges, to 'give his bread to the hungry and to clothe the naked' (v. 7); similarly in Isaiah 58, the release of the oppressed (here perhaps persons in debt bondage) goes along with the exhortation which has provided my title:

[the fast that I desire]
Is it not to share your bread with the hungry, to take home the homeless poor,
when you see the naked, to cover them, and not to hide yourself from your own
flesh and blood? (Isa. 58.7)

27. Faust, *Judah in the Neo-Babylonian Period: The Archaeology of Desolation*, Archaeology and Biblical Studies, no. 18 (Atlanta: Society of Biblical Literature, 2012).

28. David Vanderhooft, 'The Israelite *Mishpaha* in the Priestly Writings, and Changing Valences in Israel's Kinship Terminology', in *Exploring the Long Durée: Essays in Honor of Lawrence E. Stager*, ed. J. David Schloen (Winona Lake, IN: Eisenbrauns, 2009), 219–35; Faust, *Judah*, 106–108.

29. See Daniel L. Smith, *The Religion of the Landless: A Sociology of the Babylonian Exile* (Bloomington, IN: Meyer-Stone Books, 1989), 93–126.

30. I argue that this accounts for the rarity of the expression in the Torah in 'Doing Justice: The Ideology, Theology and Distribution in the Hebrew Bible of משפט וצדקה', *ZAR* 22 (2017): 13–38 (32–38).

Compare Ps. 112.9a, and especially Job 31.16-20, where Job's oath of clearance asserts his generosity to the destitute: 'if I ate my piece alone, and the orphan did not share it' (v. 17).

In Job 29, on the other hand, Job's praise of his own justice (vv. 12–17) concentrates on his kinglike defence from exploitation of the poor, the widow, the orphan, the blind and the lame, in terms reminiscent of Psalm 72.[31] Nehemiah, similarly, can be seen acting in this way in Nehemiah 5, of course to his own advantage, pursuing his quarrel with the Judaean upper class by making them restore what they have gained from their peasant debtors. Texts from this period are still able to represent persons with power as actively delivering the poor from oppression.

In the period subsequent to the Hebrew Bible, however, this active defence of the vulnerable against injustice, whether by kings or patriarchs, tends to drop out of view, for native rulers able to act like Nehemiah no longer exist. At the same time a market economy is developing, and more of the country is absorbed into royal and other large estates, often owned by foreigners, with the cultivators reduced to tenants or sharecroppers. Neither of these developments was to the advantage of the peasants unable to compete with the power of the great estates, and the numbers of the desperately poor are likely to have increased.

So we reach the position sketched at the beginning of this essay, in which the connotations of צדקה are almost reduced to that of almsgiving: sharing one's bread with the hungry and clothing the naked are repeatedly mentioned, and in Tobit the burial of the dead. I say 'almost reduced': Ben Sira expects his students to exercise justice not only by giving alms, but also in their activity as judges by judging fairly for the poor (Sir. 4.7-10).[32]

5.5 Retrospect: The History of 'justice'

We have seen that in the monarchic period, the dual character of society, the royal urban sector and the communal rural sector, is paralleled by two coexisting concepts of social justice: the royal tradition of 'justice and righteousness' and the communal tradition appealed to in Deuteronomy.[33] The texts prescribing the

31. See Houston, *Contending*, 126–31.

32. Houston, 'The Scribe and His Class: Ben Sira on Rich and Poor', in *Writing the Bible: Scribes, Scribalism and Script*, ed. Philip R. Davies and Thomas Römer (Durham, UK: Acumen, 2013), 108–23 (115–16), following Pancratius C. Beentjes, '"Sei den Waisen wie ein Vater und den Witwen wie ein Gatte": ein kleiner Kommentar zu Ben Sira 4, 1–10', in *Der Einzelne und seine Gemeinschaft bei Ben Sira*, ed. Renate Egger-Wenzel and Ingrid Krammer, BZAW 270 (Berlin: de Gruyter, 1998), 51–64; *contra* Benjamin G. Wright III and Claudia V. Camp, '"Who Has Been Trusted by Gold and Found Perfect?" Ben Sira's Discourse of Wealth and Poverty', *Henoch* 23 (2001): 153–74 (161).

33. Cf. Nurmi, *Ethik*, 368–74; Stephen L. Cook, *The Social Roots of Biblical Yahwism*, Studies in Biblical Literature, no. 8 (Atlanta: Society of Biblical Literature, 2004), 143–80.

institutions of debt release and (possibly) third-year tithe, and also the jubilee in Leviticus, could be versions of royal administrative decrees, denuded of their enforcement mechanisms by the fall of the monarchy.[34] But, as we have seen, the ideological context in which they are presented is an attempt to recreate on a national scale the mutual support, between real or fictive kin in the pre-exilic village מִשְׁפָּחָה, which in Graeber's terms is 'communistic'.[35] On the other hand, in the royal ideology it is the king who is responsible for enforcing social justice, so that individual charity, however necessary in reality, does not need to be mentioned.

In the Persian period individual, hierarchical, non-reciprocal charity becomes firmly entrenched as a requirement of justice, even if other aspects are still important and rulers can still act as defenders of the poor.

In the Hellenistic period, צְדָקָה comes to be applied primarily to almsgiving. Ben Sira alludes to the Deuteronomic tradition of solidarity (Sir. 4.7-10; 29.10); the older traditions are not dead.[36] But by and large, almsgiving or works of mercy have become the main expression of justice.

5.6 Conclusion

Has justice then at the end of the process been reduced to 'charity', that is, a voluntary expression of benevolence within a hierarchical structure, or is almsgiving actually justice, that is, the discharge of a reciprocal obligation, a debt, to one's neighbour or to God? Whatever ideology writers of the Hellenistic and later periods apply to it, it cannot be said that any of them view it as voluntary. It is not presented as a matter of choice. It is an obligation, and the virtue of justice, so understood, consists in responding to human need.[37] For Ben Sira (29.1, 9, 11) it fulfils the commandments. It is an obligation, but of that (to us) paradoxical kind exemplified also by the Hebrew חֶסֶד, which refers to the discharge of obligations

Neither of these writers, however, recognizes the role of the monarchy in maintaining social justice, even as an ideological fantasy.

34. Stephen A. Kaufman, 'A Reconstruction of the Social Welfare Systems of Ancient Israel', in *In the Shelter of Elyon: Essays on Palestinian Life and Literature in Honor of G. W. Ahlström*, ed. W. Boyd Barrick and John R. Spencer, JSOTS 31 (Sheffield: JSOT Press, 1984), 277–86 (281); William S. Morrow, *Scribing the Center: Organization and Redaction in Deuteronomy 14:1–17:13*, SBLMS 49 (Atlanta: Scholars Press, 1995), 101; Walter J. Houston, 'The King's Preferential Option for the Poor: Rhetoric, Ideology and Ethics in Psalm 72', *BibInt* 7 (1999): 341–67, (357); Houston, *Contending*, 145–47, 181. Weinfeld, *Social Justice*, 157–68, attributes the utopian character of these texts to the literary rather than the historical context.

35. Graeber, *Debt*, 94–102.

36. Houston, 'The Scribe', 116–17.

37. Cf. Houston, *Contending*, 132–34.

incurred in a personal relationship, whether familial, covenantal or patronal: but how and when to discharge them is a personal choice.[38] Almsgiving is therefore understood as justice.

But it is surely a profoundly inadequate understanding of justice. In the first place, it is non-reciprocal and hierarchical. In the second place, it can only alleviate, not annul, the misery caused by injustice, even if it is said to restore what is owing to the poor because of injustice. To eliminate injustice, political structures are necessary, and they must be used in the interest of the poor (the royal ideology put into practice); or even better, the poor must take charge of their own destiny, as the liberation theologians have long argued, and so make real the Deuteronomic ideal of solidarity.

Bibliography

Anderson, Gary A. *Charity: The Place of the Poor in the Biblical Tradition*. New Haven/London: Yale, 2013.

Beentjes, Pancratius C. ' "Sei den Waisen wie ein Vater und den Witwen wie ein Gatte": ein kleiner Kommentar zu Ben Sira 4, 1–10'. In *Der Einzelne und seine Gemeinschaft bei Ben Sira*, edited by Renate Egger-Wenzel and Ingrid Krammer. BZAW 270; 51–64. Berlin: de Gruyter, 1998.

Bendor, S. *The Social Structure of Ancient Israel*. Jerusalem: Simor, 1996.

Chirichigno, Gregory C. *Debt-slavery in Israel and the Ancient Near East*. JSOTSup 141. Sheffield: JSOT Press, 1993.

Clark, Gordon R. *The Word* Hesed *in the Hebrew Bible*. JSOTS 157. Sheffield: JSOT Press, 1993.

Cook, Stephen L. *The Social Roots of Biblical Yahwism*. Studies in Biblical Literature, 8; 143–80. Atlanta: Society of Biblical Literature, 2004.

Domeris, William R. *Touching the Heart of God: The Social Construction of Poverty among Biblical Peasants*. New York & London: T&T Clark, 2007.

Faust, Avraham. *The Archaeology of Israelite Society in Iron Age II*. Winona Lake, IN: Eisenbrauns, 2012.

Faust, Avraham. *Judah in the Neo-Babylonian Period: The Archaeology of Desolation*. Archaeology and Biblical Studies 18. Atlanta: Society of Biblical Literature, 2012.

Graeber, David. *Debt, the First 5,000 Years*. Brooklyn: Melville House, 2011.

Houston, Walter J. ' "Open Your Hand to Your Needy Brother": Ideology and Moral Formation in Deut. 15:1–18'. In *The Bible in Ethics*, edited by John Rogerson, Margaret Davies and M. Daniel Carroll R. JSOTSup 207; 296–314. Sheffield: Sheffield Academic Press 1995.

Houston, Walter J. 'The King's Preferential Option for the Poor: Rhetoric, Ideology and Ethics in Psalm 72'. *BibInt* 7 (1999): 341–67.

Houston, Walter J. *Contending for Justice: Ideologies and Theologies of Social Justice in the Old Testament*. Rev. edn. London & New York: T&T Clark, 2008.

38. Gordon R. Clark, *The Word* Hesed *in the Hebrew Bible*, JSOTS 157 (Sheffield: JSOT Press, 1993); Houston, *Contending*, 45.

Houston, Walter J. 'Rejoicing before the Lord: The Function of the Festal Gathering in Deuteronomy'. In *Feasts and Festivals*, edited by Christopher Tuckett, Contributions to Biblical Exegesis and Theology, 53. Leuven: Peeters, 2009.

Houston, Walter J. 'The Scribe and His Class; Ben Sira on Rich and Poor'. In *Writing the Bible: Scribes, Scribalism and Script*, ed. Philip R. Davies and Thomas Römer, 108–23. Durham, UK: Acumen, 2013.

Houston, Walter J. 'Doing Justice: The Ideology, Theology and Distribution in the Hebrew Bible of משפט וצדקה', *ZAR* 22 (2017): 13–38.

Kaufman, Stephen A. 'A Reconstruction of the Social Welfare Systems of Ancient Israel'. In *In the Shelter of Elyon: Essays on Palestinian Life and Literature in Honor of G. W. Ahlström*, edited by W. Boyd Barrick and John R. Spencer. JSOTS 31; 277–86. Sheffield: JSOT Press, 1984.

Miranda, José Porfirio. *Marx and the Bible: A Critique of the Philosophy of Oppression*. London: SCM Press, 1977.

Morrow, William S. *Scribing the Center: Organization and Redaction in Deuteronomy 14:1–17:13*. SBLMS 49. Atlanta: Scholars Press, 1995.

Nurmi, Janne J. *Die Ethik unter dem Druck des Alltags: Die Impulse der gesellschaftlichen Änderungen und Situation zu der sozialkritschen Prophetie in Juda im 8. Jh. V. Chr.* Åbo: Åbo Akademis Förlag, 2004.

Perlitt, Lothar. 'Ein einzig Volk von Brüdern'. In *Kirche: Festschrift für Günther Bornkamm zum 75 Geburtstag*, edited by D. Lührmann and G. Strecker, 27–52. Tübingen: Mohr, 1980.

Polanyi, Karl. 'The Economy as Instituted Process'. In *Trade and Market in the Early Empires: Economies in History and Theory*, edited by K. Polanyi, Conrad M. Arensberg and Harry W. Pearson, 243–69. Glencoe, IL: Falcon's Wing, 1957.

Sahlins, Marshall. *Stone Age Economics*. London: Tavistock Publications, 1974.

Simkins, Ronald A. 'Patronage and the Political Economy of Monarchic Israel'. *Semeia* 87 (1999): 123–44.

Smith, Daniel L. *The Religion of the Landless: A Sociology of the Babylonian Exile*. Bloomington, IN: Meyer-Stone Books, 1989.

Vanderhooft, David. 'The Israelite *Mishpaha* in the Priestly Writings, and Changing Valences in Israel's Kinship Terminology'. In *Exploring the Long Durée: Essays in Honor of Lawrence E. Stager*, edited by J. David Schloen, 219–35. Winona Lake, IN: Eisenbrauns, 2009.

Weinfeld, Moshe. ' "Justice and Righteousness" – משפט וצדקה – The Expression and its Meaning'. In *Justice and Righteousness: Biblical Themes and Their Influence*, edited by Henning Graf Reventlow and Yair Hoffmann. JSOTS 137; 228–46. Sheffield: Sheffield Academic Press 1992.

Weinfeld, Moshe. *Social Justice in Ancient Israel and in the Ancient Near East*. Jerusalem: The Magnes Press/Minneapolis: Fortress, 1995.

Wolf, Eric R. *Peasants*. Foundations of Modern Anthropology Series. Englewood Cliffs, NJ: Prentice-Hall, 1966.

Wright, Benjamin G. III, and Claudia V. Camp. ' "Who Has Been Tested by Gold and Found Perfect?" Ben Sira's Discourse of Wealth and Poverty'. *Henoch* 23 (2001): 153–74.

Chapter 6

SPACE AND MEMORY IN
THE BOOK OF LEVITICUS*

Julia Rhyder

6.1 *Approaching Leviticus as Textualized Ritual*

In this essay, I employ social-scientific theories that conceptualize space as existing in physical, mental and symbolic fields simultaneously, and combine them with memory studies, in order to offer a new reading of how the authors of Leviticus construed Israel's cultic origins and what aims they were pursuing with this composition. One of the main trends in recent scholarship on Leviticus has been to emphasize the distinction between text and ritual, or more precisely between ritual text and ritual praxis.[1] For all their differences, earlier scholarly treatments of Leviticus tended to construe a fairly straightforward relationship between Leviticus rituals and Israelite cultic praxes, whether it was assumed that Leviticus was reflecting actual practices or projecting a cultic norm. However, this sort of construction seems quite problematic in light of ritual studies and ethnographic descriptions of rituals that highlight the significant gap that often characterizes the relationship between the rituals performed by a given group and the rituals described in the texts preserved by that group, as for instance in the Jains of Jaipur studied by Caroline Humphrey and James Laidlaw.[2] Even in those cases where there is evidence of a close connection between text and ritual, the relationship between the two remains quite complex, the textualization of ritual often leading

* This essay forms part of a larger research project currently underway at the University of Lausanne. I wish to extend my thanks to Christophe Nihan and Hervé Gonzalez, who were kind enough to read earlier drafts of this essay, and to George Brooke for his invitation to present an earlier version of this essay at a two-day colloquium held at the University of Manchester.

1. See especially James Watts, *Ritual and Rhetoric in Leviticus: From Sacrifice to Scripture* (Cambridge: Cambridge University Press, 2007); William Gilders, *Blood Ritual in the Hebrew Bible: Meaning and Power* (Baltimore: Johns Hopkins University Press, 2004).

2. Caroline Humphrey and James Laidlaw, *The Archetypical Actions of Ritual: A Theory of Ritual Illustrated by the Jains Rite of Worship* (Oxford: Clarendon Press, 1994).

to a 'written ideal quite alienated from what is in fact being done in common practice', as noted by Catherine Bell and others.[3]

The current essay takes place within this discussion and seeks to advance it via a twofold approach. First, the textualization of rituals in Leviticus is best analysed by resorting to spatiality theories; while there are many ways to approach the definition of rituals, it seems most helpful to analyse rituals first and foremost as constructing a certain type of space.[4] While spatiality and the Hebrew Bible has become a recent topic in scholarship,[5] there have been few attempts to analyse constructions of space in Leviticus. The main exception is probably the recent monograph by Mark George insofar as he has applied the theories of the French philosopher Henri Lefebvre to the priestly narratives about the wilderness sanctuary and how it functions as social space.[6] While this is in many ways a groundbreaking work in priestly studies, one critique that can be addressed to George is whether he sufficiently considers the difference between analysing the sort of empirical space studied by Lefebvre and others, and applying this approach to the textual spaces construed by the wilderness narratives in general, and Leviticus in particular.[7] In order to address this issue, we need to start from the observation that Leviticus describes the spaces of a cult which is not contemporary with those of its ancient readers. Its spaces are situated in a distant, foundational past. In other words, Leviticus is about establishing a certain memory of Israel's cult; and we need to take into account this specific construction of the past when we try to critically approach the spaces of Leviticus. In doing so, I will be able to build on the few past studies that have already sought to articulate space and memory studies, although to the best of my knowledge this is still seldom attempted in Hebrew Bible scholarship.[8]

---

3. Catherine Bell, *Ritual Theory, Ritual Practice* (Oxford: Oxford University Press, 1992), 137.

4. Jonathan Z. Smith, *To Take Place: Toward Theory in Ritual*, Chicago Studies in the History of Judaism (Chicago: University of Chicago Press, 1987).

5. See, e.g. James W. Flanagan, 'Ancient Perceptions of Space/Perceptions of Ancient Space', *Semeia* 87 (1999): 15–43; David M. Gunn and Paula M. McNutt, eds, *"Imagining" Biblical Worlds: Studies in Spatial, Social and Historical Constructs in Honor of James W. Flanagan*, JSOTSup 359 (Sheffield: Sheffield Academic Press, 2002); Alison Schofield, 'Re-Placing Priestly Space: The Wilderness as Heterotopia in the Dead Sea Scrolls', in *A Teacher for All Generations: Essays in Honor of James C. VanderKam*, eds. Eric F. Mason et al. (Leiden/Boston, Brill, 2012), 469–90; Mark George, ed., *Constructions of Space IV: Further Developments in Examining Ancient Israel's Social Space* (London: T&T Clark, 2013).

6. Mark George, *Israel's Tabernacle as Social Space* (Atlanta: Society of Biblical Literature, 2009).

7. This is perhaps most evident in the chapter 'Tabernacle Spatial Practice', in which George applies Lefebvre's first field of space ('physical space') to Exodus 25–40 (*Israel's Tabernacle*, 44–87).

8. See Simon Schama, *Landscape and Memory* (London: HarperCollins, 1995), and from a more philosophical perspective Gaston Bachelard, *The Poetics of Space*, trans. M.

6.2 *Critical Spatial Studies: What's in a Space?*

It can at first seem odd to speak of a space that exists only within a narrative, because we usually associate the word 'space' with physical locations within the tangible world. Yet, space has long been recognized in the social sciences as constituting not simply an empirical 'given' that is passively observed but also as the product of the dynamic interplay between sensory input, memory and imagination, as mediated by wider social and historical forces. Space was thus famously described by Lefebvre as a '*(social) product*'[9] that exists in physical, mental and symbolic fields simultaneously. Although the discussion has taken various avenues following Lefebvre's theoretical articulation some forty years ago, the proposed distinction between three dimensions of space has remained a valid insight for all subsequent studies of spaces.[10]

While the 'common-sense' dimension of space is the physical, material components that can be measured according to length, width, height and depth, in order for a physical location to achieve conceptual coherence it must also be invested with mental, and indeed symbolic, qualities. Mental space exists, for example, in the maps, blueprints and architectural plans that become virtual extensions of the sites they depict, as well as in the processes that demarcate certain areas where only limited or initiated persons may enter (e.g. designating a 'back-stage' or 'staff only' area). And yet, maps and plans cannot dictate how a space will then be understood according to broader, socially mediated meanings. Symbolic space is what transforms a physical structure and its mental dimensions into the spaces of lived experience, imbuing space with emotional qualities and subjective associations (such as when a 'house' becomes a 'home') in light of its position within broader, culturally determined categories of meaning and significance.

Jolas (Boston: Beacon, 1994). In the case of the Hebrew Bible, see Victor H. Matthews, 'Remembered Space in Biblical Narrative', in *Constructions of Space IV*, ed. George, 61–75. While James Watts's recent commentary (*Leviticus 1–10*, Historical Commentary on the Old Testament [Leuven: Peeters, 2013]) does not engage with space or memories studies per se, it does correctly perceive the imaginative potential of the spaces produced by the book of Leviticus, and the current essay is indebted to its insights.

9. Henri Lefebvre, *The Production of Space*, trans. D. Nicholson-Smith (Oxford: Blackwell, 1991), 26 (emphasis and parentheses original).

10. See, e.g. Yi-Fu Tuan, *Space and Place: The Perspective of Experience* (Minneapolis: University of Minnesota Press, 1977); Edward Soja, *Postmodern Geographies: The Reassertion of Space in Critical Theory* (London: Verso, 1989); Setha M. Low and D. Lawrence-Zúñinga, eds, *The Anthropology of Space and Place: Locating Culture* (Oxford: Blackwell, 2003). Although originally delivered as an unpublished lecture in 1967 (seven years before the publication of Lefebvre's *La production de l'espace*), Michel Foucault's 'Of Other Spaces', *Diacritics* 16/1 (1986): 22–27, became an instant classic when posthumously published in 1984 (French).

Crucially, the symbolic elements of a given space can exist beyond the life of a physical structure, creating what Marita Sturken calls an 'aesthetic of absence'.[11] Let us consider for a moment the city of New York. This is a space that exists not only as a city situated at a given longitude and latitude on the east coast of the United States, but also simultaneously in the film and Broadway sets that replicate its iconic streets, the numerous television shows that broadcast the city into our lounges, or the iconic photographs that depict the city in the immediate aftermath of 9/11. This mental and symbolic 'New York' exists in a diverse network of cultural media, which are themselves informed by and informing collective memories, and which have the potential to shape not only the city's mental and symbolic elements but also our perception of the city's *physicality* as well. Thus, when we perceive the New York skyline, we do not see only the buildings that make up the city in the present moment, but also – as per the example discussed by Sturken – the Twin Towers which are *no longer there*, such that the physical city appears at once as a combination of pre- and post-9/11 landscapes. This aesthetic of absence is fostered by commemorative rituals at the aptly named 'Ground Zero' that guide our expectations of what this space constitutes, so that we can no longer look at New York but through the lens that they provide. These media therefore have significant ideological potential, such that a photo of New York can, in fact, communicate a particular narrative of the legitimacy of Western military responses to 'terror' without making any overt political statement.

6.3 *Space and Memory*

With this more critical approach to spatiality in mind, we can return to Leviticus and observe not only how space is used by the authors to invest the narrative with authority but also to provide a particular, authoritative memory of Israel's cult. In keeping with the critical approach to spatiality advocated by Lefebvre and others, when I refer to 'space' in Leviticus I speak not only of the places mentioned in the narrative, such as Sinai or the אהל מועד but also the movement of social actors prescribed for the performance of rituals, the requirements for relegating unclean persons to locations away from the camp, the stipulation that certain calendric festivals constitute חג pilgrimages, and so on. Space is not a static category, but rather the dynamic outcome of human behaviour and social action – or as Edward Soja puts it, a category that is not only thought but also 'lived'[12] – such that the laws affecting the movement of social actors in space contribute just as much to

---

11. Marita Sturken, 'The Aesthetics of Absence: Rebuilding Ground Zero', *American Ethnologist*, 31, no. 3 (2004): 311–25.

12. Edward Soja, *Thirdspace: Journeys to Los Angeles and Other Real-and-Imagined Places* (Malden, MA: Blackwell, 1996), 67.

producing the imaginative space of Leviticus as do the places and structures that are explicitly named in the book.[13]

Although composed mainly of laws prescribing the performance of various rituals, Leviticus sets its legal material within the memory of the spaces associated with Israel's encampment at Mount Sinai. While mentioned rarely outside the Pentateuch,[14] Sinai was construed within these corpora as a privileged space associated with divine oracular revelation. (This would not have been a one-way street, however, since, as the text of Leviticus gained authority from being read and reread as the revelation of Israel's deity, so too would the space of Sinai have been affirmed as a significant site of divine revelation.) Interestingly, there is no indication in the Hebrew Bible – or, for that matter, in para- and post-biblical traditions – that Sinai is a place that should, or even could be revisited physically, even less become the object of a pilgrimage, as it would become in modern times.[15] The Sinai of Leviticus is primarily a *site of memory*, visited and revisited as part of broader processes of social reproduction, and intersecting with the other sites of memory defined by the book, such as the wilderness camp or the portable shrine.

As is frequently remarked by scholars working in the field of memory studies, memory is not simply a matter of distilling or deselecting events by individuals and communities in forming meaningful narratives about the past but also involves the construction of mental maps within which we locate and find meaning for our past, present and future experience.[16] The memories of the past that communities

13. While there is a question as to what extent we can describe space in Leviticus in isolation given that it shares with the second half of Exodus (chs 19–40) the same setting at Mount Sinai and the newly constructed wilderness sanctuary, the delineation of Leviticus as a discrete 'book', at least in the sense of a conceptual unit, seems warranted in light of the twofold ending of Leviticus 26 and 27, and also the super- and subscriptions that frame the book as a distinct revelation. See further, Thomas Römer, 'De la périphérie au centre. Les livres du Lévitique et des Nombres dans le débat actuel sur le Pentateuque', in *The Books of Leviticus and Numbers*, ed. Römer, BETL 215 (Leuven: Peeters, 2008), 3–34 (23); Christophe Nihan, 'The Priestly Laws of Numbers, the Holiness Legislation, and the Pentateuch', in *Torah and the Book of Numbers*, ed. C. Frevel et al. (Tübingen: Mohr Siebeck, 2013), 120–29.

14. Of its thirty-five occurrences in the Hebrew Bible, only four are located outside the Pentateuch. See Judg. 5.5; Ps. 68.9, 18; Neh. 9.13.

15. On this and related issues, see George J. Brooke et al., eds, *The Significance of Sinai: Traditions about Sinai and Divine Revelation in Judaism and Christianity*, Themes in Biblical Narrative, 12 (Leiden: Brill, 2008).

16. While the literature on social memory and sites of memory is vast, see esp. Jeffrey K. Olick et al., eds, *The Collective Memory Reader* (New York: Oxford University Press, 2011). On how such theories might be applied to the Hebrew Bible, see Diana V. Edelman and Ehud Ben Zvi, eds, *Remembering Biblical Figures in the Late Persian and Early Hellenistic Periods* (Oxford: Oxford University Press, 2013); Pernille Carstens et al., eds, *Cultural Memory in Biblical Exegesis*, Perspectives on Hebrew Scriptures and Its Contexts 17 (Piscataway, NJ: Gorgias Press, 2012).

preserve are those that provide a framework and narrative that affirm the norms and values of the present. It seems highly likely, then, that by embedding the laws of Leviticus within the memory of the divine establishment of Israel's cult at Sinai, the book's authors were not so much interested in describing tangible spaces of their own time as in fashioning a particular authoritative memory of the cultic spaces of the past. The text produces a set of remembered spaces which, by being strategically placed during Israel's sojourn in the wilderness, cannot be identified or even directly associated with any actual cultic space in Israel, be that in Jerusalem or elsewhere. Because of their imaginative potential, the spaces of the text can both resemble and differ from material reality; they represent space as it should be ideally configured and mentally mapped, but in a way that does not envisage a literal reproduction in any future setting. Such an ideal space would hold a representational power, providing a lens through which to view other, tangible and textual spaces, by guiding the reader's expectations as to what Israelite cultic space should constitute.

6.4 *Leviticus and the Spaces of Ancient Israel*

This complexity has not, in the main, been sufficiently appreciated by biblical scholars due to the persistence of a certain representation of how the book's textualized spaces related to empirical cultic spaces. While acknowledging that the spaces of Leviticus have been intentionally set in a distant past, scholars by and large treat them as complex analogues to specific cultic sites, such as especially central sites in Jerusalem, Bethel, Shechem or elsewhere. To be sure, the argument will vary depending on when the composition of Leviticus is dated, and whether the book is seen to describe existing cultic realities, prescribe what the cult should be, or a combination of both. But once scholars within this approach have determined the dating and the character or function of the book, they then peer through the text, as if through a window, into the material spaces themselves; a good illustration is provided by Israel Knohl's well-known argument that the virtual absence of music and prayer in Leviticus 1–16 would reflect the preference of priestly elites in the pre-Hezekian Jerusalem Temple for a silent cult.[17] Whether Leviticus is dated to the Neo-Assyrian or the Persian period, this approach perpetuates the view – dominant since the advent of biblical criticism – that Leviticus is a repository of the rituals and spatial arrangements of the Jerusalem temple, and so functioned like a priestly manual or handbook.[18] Even scholars dating the composition of

17. Israel Knohl, *The Sanctuary of Silence: The Priestly Torah and the Holiness School* (Minneapolis: Fortress Press, 1994).

18. A typical articulation of this classical position is that of J. R. Porter: '[Leviticus] is also in part a manual to instruct the priests in the correct performance of their liturgical duties, especially about their part in carrying out the increasingly elaborate ritual of sacrifice, but in other areas of the cultus, that is, the whole sphere of official public worship, too' (*Leviticus* [Cambridge: Cambridge University Press, 1976], 1).

Leviticus to the Neo-Babylonian period, and therefore at a time when there was allegedly no central sanctuary, tend to assume a fairly straightforward relation between the composition of Leviticus and cultic reality; in general, they postulate that the textual space represented in and by the book was produced as a response to the missing temple and was intended to work as a substitute of sorts.[19] For all their differences, these models have in common the assumption that the textual spaces of Leviticus have to mirror, in one way or another, empirical cultic spaces, whether existing or desired.

I certainly do not wish to deny that some of the materials preserved in Leviticus reflect actual cultic and ritual practices of ancient Israel; a good illustration of this is offered by the two silver plates found in Ketef Hinnom (KH 1 and 2), the second one of which in particular shows striking parallels with the 'priestly' blessing found in Num. 6.24-26.[20] Also, anthropological studies of rituals would lead us to expect a sufficient degree of continuity between the cultic realities described in Leviticus and the cultic experience of its audience, in order for the book to have left an impact on that audience. Moreover, the imitation of the Leviticus rituals is already prepared in the book itself, as is shown by specifications that certain laws be observed לדרתיכם, 'throughout your generations',[21] and some statutes and calendric festivals בכל מושבתיכם, 'in all your settlements'.[22] (Admittedly, the rationale behind the distribution of these formulae in Leviticus remains an issue, although one that can remain open in the limits of this essay; in my view it would be mistaken to assume that such formulae are operational only for the laws where they are explicitly mentioned.) But although the rituals of Leviticus, and together with them the spatiality of these rituals, could partly be reproduced by ancient audiences, the wilderness setting of these rituals would necessarily prevent any claim or attempt to integrally reproduce the complete set of spaces that are defined in and through the Leviticus rituals. While imitation of the Leviticus rituals would necessarily imply the reproduction of some aspects of the spatiality construed by the book, such imitation also left room for interpretation, and even adaptation, if these rituals were to be reconfigured beyond a wilderness context.

19. For this position see, e.g. George, *Israel's Tabernacle*, 191–94; Terence E. Fretheim, *Exodus* (Louisville, KY: John Knox Press, 1991), 264. A variant of this argument interprets Leviticus as a substitute for an existing temple whose cultic practice was considered problematic or illegitimate; see, e.g. Wesley J. Bergen, *Reading Ritual: Leviticus in Postmodern Culture*, JSOTSup 417 (London: T&T Clark, 2005), 1–12.

20. For the edition of the two silver plates see Gabriel Barkay et al., 'The Amulets from Ketef Hinnom: A New Edition and Evaluation', *BASOR* 334 (2004): 41–71. For the relation between KH 2 and Numbers 6, see, e.g. Angelika Berlejung, 'Ein Programm fürs Leben. Theologisches Wort und anthropologischer Ort der Silberamulette von Ketef Hinnom', *ZAW* 120, no. 2 (2008): 204–30.

21. See, e.g. Lev. 3.17; 10.9; 23.14, 21, 31, 41; as well as similar formulations in Lev. 7.36; 17.7.

22. Lev. 3.17; 7.26; 23.3, 14, 21, 31.

This is the situation we witness in the account of Neh. 8.13-18, which relates how the people of Jerusalem celebrated the feast of Sukkôt. This account, which is significantly missing from the Ezra A tradition and may well be a late work of fiction, is characterized by the repeated claim to follow the Torah of Moses (vv. 14-15a) in celebrating the feast, as is shown in particular by the clear connection between the gathering of branches and the building of booths with the prescription laid out in Lev. 23.39-43. Simultaneously, it is clear that the application of the law in Neh. 8.13-18 involves a different spatial configuration when compared to that of Leviticus, and that this new configuration impacts in significant ways on how the law is applied. Thus, whereas Lev. 23.40 commands the branches be used as instruments of "rejoicing" (שמחה), in Neh. 8.13-18 the branches are now used as a material for *constructing* the booths, which are then placed on the roofs of the houses. The ritual innovation, in this case, clearly reflects a change in spatial dynamics. While building on Leviticus 23, the account of Nehemiah 8 now articulates much more closely the collective dimension of the feast – already emphasized in Leviticus 23 through the remembrance of the exodus (Lev. 23.43) – with the sphere of the household (the booths on the roofs of individual houses) thereby adapting the feast to the urban context of Jerusalem in a way that was not (yet) possible in Leviticus 23.[23] Yet despite the spatial reconfiguration of the Sukkôt festival that takes place in Nehemiah 8, that account can still claim to be based upon, and even aligned with, the instructions found in the Torah of Moses, as is established at length at the beginning of the account.

6.5 *Visiting Imagined Spaces*

The previous comments raise the question of how the imaginative space produced by Leviticus functioned, and how ancient audiences of the book were invited to form certain mental images in order to map the symbolic space of the wilderness sanctuary. While this issue would require a much more systematic treatment than the present essay can afford, I suggest that one way in which ancient audiences were invited to enter the imaginative space of Leviticus was through the provision of detailed accounts of the ritual activities that were to take place in and around the wilderness sanctuary. Despite the vast majority of the content of Leviticus being about actions and spaces in which priestly activity is predominant, Moses is described from the beginning as being repeatedly instructed to relay Yhwh's commands to both the priestly and lay members of the community (see Lev. 1.2

---

23. Lev. 14.34 signals that houses were not considered part of the wilderness landscape, since the law concerning diseased houses must be projected into a future time period when the Israelites have settled in 'the land of Canaan'. Intriguingly, Lev. 23.39-43 does not command what material the booths are to consist of. By explaining that the branches are the material for constructing the booths, the account of Nehemiah 8 fills this gap. See on this Hannah K. Harrington, 'The Use of Leviticus in Ezra-Nehemiah', *JHS* 13, no. 3 (2013): 1–20.

and following);[24] and the book ends with explicit reference to the laws of Leviticus being given to the Israelites as a whole, and not just to the priests (Lev. 26.46; 27.34). This would seem odd if the book were to serve only as a priestly manual, as per the standard view mentioned above. The oft-repeated command to Moses to address the Israelites strongly suggests that the priestly authors wished a broader community of 'Israel' to visualize themselves as part of the text's intended audience, and thereby identify continuity between the בני ישראל of the wilderness generation and themselves. Even for those instructions that are said to be reserved for Aaron and his sons specifically, such as the instructions concerning sacrificial remains (Leviticus 6–7) and various types of skin-disease (Leviticus 13), the inclusion of these regulations within the book would have meant that non-priestly, as well as priestly, readers would have had access to them.

According to the text, then, the details of the various ritual and other cultic practices commanded at the wilderness sanctuary are to be publicly known, even when these practices can only be performed by the priests.[25] Leviticus 16 is especially illustrative in this regard, in that while it explicitly condemns entry into the holiest section of the wilderness sanctuary by any person other than the high priest at a given time of the year, it also simultaneously facilitates the imaginative entrance of a non-priestly audience by providing a concrete description of what this space constitutes and the actions whereby Aaron is permitted to enter it. To be sure, ancient audiences of Leviticus already had some access to the space of the inner sanctum via the description of the furniture in the account of the building of the wilderness sanctuary (see Exod. 25.10-40 and ch. 37 MT = 38 LXX). In Leviticus 16, however, the inner sanctum is no longer seen as a static space but as a fully operational one, through the lens of the ritual actions performed by the high priest inside the most private part of the sanctuary (cf. Lev. 16.13-17). The provision of such detailed description of Aaron's ritual actions meant that instead of 'following' Aaron only so far as the entrance to the inner sanctum and then being denied details of this most reserved of spaces, the reader 'follows' Aaron and imaginatively participates in the performance of the ritual with him. Whenever that ritual – or one similar to the description of Leviticus 16 – was performed in the Second Temple period, the members of the community who had to watch the high priest materially go into restricted space would nonetheless be able, through their familiarity with the text, to actively participate in the ritual by imaginatively entering another yet closely related space, namely, the inner sanctum of the wilderness sanctuary.

Mary Douglas rightly observed the lay access to the wilderness shrine afforded by Leviticus in her monograph *Leviticus as Literature*. Although she did not resort to any spatial theory, Douglas did rightly observe the importance of spatiality in the

---

24. Moses is commanded to repeat Yhwh's instructions to the entire community in Lev. 1.2; 4.2; 7.23, 29; 9.3; 10.11; 11.2; 12.2; 15.2; 17.2; 18.2; 19.2; 20.2; 22.18; 23.2, 10, 24, 34; 24.2, 15; 25.2; 27.2, 34, and is reported to have done so in Lev. 21.24; 23.44; 24.23.

25. As noted, in particular, by Watts, *Ritual and Rhetoric*, 193–217.

book. This led her, in particular, to argue that the structure of Leviticus somehow mirrors the spaces it describes, so that the whole book can be likened to a guided, virtual tour of the wilderness sanctuary.[26] Each chapter, she suggests, corresponds to a point within the tri-part wilderness shrine, so that as one reads the book, one imaginatively moves inwards from the outer court to the sanctuary and finally to the inner sanctum, and back again at the entrance of the court. There are, however, several problems in Douglas's attempt to map so closely the structure of the book and the spaces it describes. As already noted by some scholars, the structure she proposes is largely idiosyncratic, relying on highly subjective assessments of the themes of the various chapters of Leviticus and then construing which particular material point of the sanctuary this content would correlate to. One notable example is her reading of Leviticus 16, which she situates in her structure at the entrance of the tent of meeting although the text, as mentioned, is clearly speaking about access to the inner sanctum. Similar problems beset her reading of many other chapters, such as her idea that Leviticus 18, 19 and 20 would correspond to a pilgrimage in the outer sanctum, whereas the contents of these chapters have nothing to do with that specific space of the sanctuary.

Even if one does not follow Douglas's overall scheme, her observation is correct that a crucial component of the spatial dynamics of the book seems to be the imaginative availability of the wilderness spaces to a non-priestly as well as priestly audience. That is, the authors did not choose to keep the nature of these spaces a secret, but instead provided imaginative access to the sanctuary in its entirety. However, as can be seen from the example of the ritual of Leviticus 16, the spaces to which the Leviticus audience has access are thoroughly ritualized: in order to imaginatively visit those spaces the ancient readers of the book had to visualize the rituals performed in them. The imagination of space and the imagination of ritual go hand in hand in Leviticus to create the memory of a community whose members all have a vested stake in the sanctuary, whether they are priests or non-priests. It remains to be asked, though, what *purpose* such access to an imagined cultic space might have served from a social-historical perspective centred on the groups that produced the book and the ancient audiences that received it.

6.6 *Leviticus and Non-monarchic Space*

Undoubtedly, the imaginative space of Leviticus – the wilderness sanctuary, the rituals that are performed there, the priests that officiate in ritual, as well as purity, diet and criminal matters – contributes to a memory of Israel's past that is centred on the cult. As we have seen, the knowledge required for maintaining cultic space is remembered as having been disseminated throughout both priestly and non-priestly circles, such that the entire community is construed as having been oriented towards the cult and its rituals. By being able to visit and revisit

26. Mary Douglas, *Leviticus as Literature* (Oxford: Oxford University Press, 1999), 230.

the imagined cultic spaces of the past via reading and remembering the text, the audience of Leviticus would have internalized a particular mental image of cultic space in which the laws and rituals of that book were seen as essential. What is more, in situations when the ritual and legal requirements set out in Leviticus departed from what was in fact practised in the cults of ancient Israel, such internalized images would have encouraged an alignment of actual practice with that of the imagined space, and thus a conformity with the cultic vision set out by the authors of Leviticus. This is what we likely see, for instance, in the debate preserved in 4QMMT; however we reconstruct the context of this document, it is clear that alignment with what is 'written' in the Torah of Moses is considered to be determinant in defining right and proper conduct in ritual matters (e.g. 4Q396 fr. 1 2 iv 4–8 about the mating of different species of clean animals in reference to Lev. 19.19).[27]

As much as my discussion has hopefully demonstrated the limitations in trying to construe a linear, straightforward relation between Leviticus's imagined space and empirical cultic spaces, it would be wrong to simply disconnect the cultic space produced by Leviticus from actual cultic sites of ancient Israel. In order to define more precisely this relation, I would propose viewing Leviticus as a 'supplementary' space, coexistent with, but never simply identical to, empirical cultic spaces. In particular, the imaginative space of Leviticus would have clearly emphasized the significance of sanctuary space not only in the past but also in the present of ancient audiences, promoting an interest in and loyalty towards cultic centres. Incidentally, this concern to encourage commitment to cultic centres is explicitly voiced in two key passages of Leviticus itself, which somehow summarize the contents of the last section of the book, chs 17–26 (the so-called Holiness legislation) by commanding the Israelites to 'revere' (ירע), show loyalty towards, the sanctuary (Lev. 19.30; 26.2). This commitment or loyalty to cultic sites that characterizes the concept of space produced and promoted by Leviticus strongly supports the traditional view that the book was composed by priestly circles, associated with one of the major sanctuaries, despite the unique access to sacred space that the book provides for a non-priestly audience.

Such reverence for the cultic space of Leviticus is all the more significant when we consider that the wilderness sanctuary is presented as a centralized cultic site – in the sense that the בני ישראל achieve communal unity in and around this sanctuary – but, remarkably, without the patronage of a royal figure. Ancient Near Eastern building inscriptions invariably reserved an essential role for kings as instigators and patrons of the building programs of central cultic sites.[28] In the accounts preserved by these inscriptions, it is the king who receives the deity's

---

27. Elisha Qimron and Josh Strugnell, *Qumran Cave 4*, vol. V: *Miqṣat Maʿaśe Ha-Torah*, DJD X (Oxford: Clarendon, 1994).

28. See Victor (Avigdor) Hurowitz, *I Have Built You an Exalted House: Temple Building in the Bible in Light of Mesopotamian and Northwest Semitic Writings*, JSOTSup 115 (Sheffield: JSOT Press, 1992), esp. 38–39.

permission to build, records the building plan, gathers the materials for building and even presents himself as participating in the building work. Once constructed, the maintenance of the central temple and its sacrificial system relied on the king's patronage, such that the absence of a kingly figure in Leviticus and the narrative of Exodus 25–40 before it, could certainly not go unnoticed by ancient readers. Most significantly, a royal patron of sorts is even retained in several post-exilic texts of the Hebrew Bible that describe the building of centralized cultic space, whether explicitly (thus David and Solomon in 1–2 Chronicles) or in a more veiled way (e.g. the figure of the נשיא in Ezekiel 40–48, or צמח in Zech. 6.9-15), thereby suggesting that Leviticus, and the priestly literature more broadly, is making a deliberate point in producing a distinctive space from which the royal figure is omitted.

When this last observation is related to the overall argument of this essay, the lack of a royal figure or any royal space from the imaginative world of Leviticus seems to have been part of a priestly strategy of construing a memory of the cult as being sufficient in maintaining Israel's social cohesion. Royal functions in the construction of central cultic space are now shared in Leviticus between Yhwh, Moses and the people themselves, redistributing power in the creation of a thoroughly communal, social space.[29] In the memory of Israel's cultic origins, then, the priestly authors fashioned an imaginative central cultic space in which a king had *never* been necessary, but rather ritual law, cultic personnel and the laity's commitment to and intricate knowledge of cultic law, enabled Israel to function in agreement with its patron deity's will.

Bibliography

Bachelard, Gaston. *The Poetics of Space*, trans. M. Jolas. Boston: Beacon, 1994.

Barkay, Gabriel, et al. 'The Amulets from Ketef Hinnom: A New Edition and Evaluation'. *BASOR* 334 (2004): 41–71.

Bell, Catherine. *Ritual Theory, Ritual Practice*. Oxford: Oxford University Press, 1992.

Bergen, Wesley J. *Reading Ritual: Leviticus in Postmodern Culture*. JSOTSup 417. London: T&T Clark, 2005.

Berlejung, Angelika. 'Ein Programm fürs Leben. Theologisches Wort und anthropologischer Ort der Silberamulette von Ketef Hinnom'. *ZAW* 120, no. 2 (2008): 204–30.

Brooke, George J. et al., eds. *The Significance of Sinai: Traditions about Sinai and Divine Revelation in Judaism and Christianity*. Themes in Biblical Narrative, 12. Leiden: Brill, 2008.

29. This has been observed by George (*Israel's Tabernacle*, 162–67) concerning Exodus 25–40, and others concerning Leviticus specifically (see, e.g. Christophe Nihan, *From Priestly Torah to Pentateuch: A Study in the Composition of the Book of Leviticus* [Tübingen: Mohr Siebeck, 2007], 227–29; Baruch A. Levine, *In the Presence of the Lord: A Study of Cult and Some Cultic Terms in Ancient Israel* [Leiden: Brill, 1974], 27–52; Watts, *Leviticus 1–10*, 91–100).

Carstens, Pernille, et al., eds. *Cultural Memory in Biblical Exegesis*. Perspectives on Hebrew Scriptures and Its Contexts, 17. Piscataway, NJ: Gorgias Press, 2012.

Douglas, Mary. *Leviticus as Literature*. Oxford: Oxford University Press, 1999.

Edelman, Diana V., and Ehud Ben Zvi, eds. *Remembering Biblical Figures in the Late Persian and Early Hellenistic Periods*. Oxford: Oxford University Press, 2013.

Flanagan, James W. 'Ancient Perceptions of Space/Perceptions of Ancient Space'. *Semeia* 87 (1999): 15–43.

Foucault, Michel. 'Of Other Spaces'. *Diacritics* 16, no. 1 (1986): 22–27.

Fretheim, Terence E. *Exodus*. Louisville, KY: John Knox Press, 1991.

George, Mark. *Israel's Tabernacle as Social Space*. Atlanta: Society of Biblical Literature, 2009.

George, Mark, ed. *Constructions of Space IV: Further Developments in Examining Ancient Israel's Social Space*. London: T&T Clark, 2013.

Gilders, William. *Blood Ritual in the Hebrew Bible: Meaning and Power*. Baltimore: Johns Hopkins University Press, 2004.

Gunn, David M., and Paula M. McNutt, eds. *"Imagining" Biblical Worlds: Studies in Spatial, Social and Historical Constructs in Honor of James W. Flanagan*. JSOTSup 359. London: Sheffield Academic Press, 2002.

Harrington, Hannah K. 'The Use of Leviticus in Ezra-Nehemiah'. *JHS* 13, no. 3 (2013): 1–20.

Humphrey, Caroline, and James Laidlaw. *The Archetypical Actions of Ritual: A Theory of Ritual Illustrated by the Jains Rite of Worship*. Oxford: Clarendon Press, 1994.

Hurowitz, Victor Avigdor. *I Have Built You an Exalted House: Temple Building in the Bible in Light of Mesopotamian and Northwest Semitic Writings*. JSOTSup 115. Sheffield: JSOT Press, 1992.

Knohl, Israel. *The Sanctuary of Silence: The Priestly Torah and the Holiness School*. Minneapolis: Fortress Press, 1994.

Lefebvre, Henri. *The Production of Space*, trans. D. Nicholson-Smith. Oxford: Blackwell, 1991.

Levine, Baruch A. *In the Presence of the Lord: A Study of Cult and Some Cultic Terms in Ancient Israel*. Leiden: Brill, 1974.

Low, Setha M., and D. Lawrence-Zúñinga, eds. *The Anthropology of Space and Place: Locating Culture*. Oxford: Blackwell, 2003.

Matthews, Victor H. 'Remembered Space in Biblical Narrative'. In *Constructions of Space IV: Further Developments in Examining Ancient Israel's Social Space*, edited by. Mark K. George, 61–75. London: T&T Clark, 2013.

Nihan, Christophe. *From Priestly Torah to Pentateuch: A Study in the Composition of the Book of Leviticus*. Tübingen: Mohr Siebeck, 2007.

Nihan, Christophe. 'The Priestly Laws of Numbers, the Holiness Legislation, and the Pentateuch'. In *Torah and the Book of Numbers*, edited by C. Frevel et al., 120–29. Tübingen: Mohr Siebeck, 2013.

Olick, Jeffrey K., et al., eds. *The Collective Memory Reader*. New York: Oxford University Press, 2011.

Porter, J. R. *Leviticus*. Cambridge: Cambridge University Press, 1976.

Qimron, Elisha, and Josh Strugnell. *Qumran Cave 4*, vol. V: *Miqṣat Ma'aśe Ha-Torah*, DJD X. Oxford: Clarendon, 1994.

Römer, Thomas. 'De la périphérie au centre. Les livres du Lévitique et des Nombres dans le débat actuel sur le Pentateuque'. In *The Books of Leviticus and Numbers*, edited by Römer. BETL, 215; 3–34. Leuven: Peeters, 2008.

Schama, Simon. *Landscape and Memory*. London: HarperCollins, 1995.

Schofield, Alison. 'Re-Placing Priestly Space: The Wilderness as Heterotopia in the Dead Sea Scrolls'. In *A Teacher for All Generations: Essays in Honor of James C. VanderKam*, edited by Eric F. Mason et al., 469–90. Leiden/Boston, Brill, 2012.

Smith, Jonathan Z. *To Take Place: Toward Theory in Ritual*. Chicago Studies in the History of Judaism. Chicago: University of Chicago Press, 1987.

Soja, Edward. *Postmodern Geographies: The Reassertion of Space in Critical Theory*. London: Verso, 1989.

Soja, Edward. *Thirdspace: Journeys to Los Angeles and Other Real-and-Imagined Places*. Malden, MA: Blackwell, 1996.

Sturken, Marita. 'The Aesthetics of Absence: Rebuilding Ground Zero'. *American Ethnologist* 31, no. 3 (2004): 311–25.

Tuan, Yi-Fu. *Space and Place: The Perspective of Experience*. Minneapolis: University of Minnesota Press, 1977.

Watts, James. *Ritual and Rhetoric in Leviticus: From Sacrifice to Scripture*. Cambridge: Cambridge University Press, 2007.

Watts, James. *Leviticus 1–10*. Historical Commentary on the Old Testament. Leuven: Peeters, 2013.

Chapter 7

THE ZADOKITE AND LEVITE SCRIBAL CONFLICTS AND HEGEMONIC STRUGGLES

Jaeyoung Jeon

The understanding of ancient Israelite society and religion in the frame of social conflicts, especially in the Persian period, is largely indebted to Max Weber's groundbreaking study of ancient Judaism, *Das antike Judentum*.[1] This study extended its profound influence on biblical scholarship in the twentieth century, anticipating the so-called conflict tradition in Old Testament study.[2] Recent socio-historical studies of Persia's Yehud, however, have revealed that various groups and parties, such as priests, elders, prophetic groups and Levites, took part in the restoration, and that the social, religious, and political conflicts between the groups were probably much more complicated than Weber had imagined (e.g. the conflicts between upper and lower classes). These groups had different ideas and programmes on the restoration of the community, as well as diverse socio-economic statuses, and endeavoured to reinforce their programmes for the restored community at different levels of society. This essay starts by arguing that such efforts are profitably explained as processes of seeking hegemonic power and being able to counter other hegemonic powers in the process of restoring the community.

The idea of cultural hegemony is first used by Antonio Gramsci (1891–1937), an Italian Marxist theoretician and politician, to describe how the ruling class (bourgeoisie) maintains power by establishing its own world view as the cultural norm for all groups, including the proletariat.[3] According to Gramsci's theory, dominant groups or classes have hegemonic power when they 'propagate values

---

1. M. Weber, *Gesammelte Aufsätze zur Religionssoziologie. III. Das antike Judentum*, 7th edn (Tübingen: J. C. B. Mohr, 1983); English translation: M. Weber, *Ancient Judaism*, trans. and ed., H. H. Gerth and D. Martindale (New York: Free Press, 1967).

2. For a thorough elaboration of Max Weber's regency in Old Testament study, see A. Mayes, *The Old Testament in Sociological Perspective* (London: Marshall Pickering, 1989), esp. 36–77; and E. Otto, *Max Webers Studien des Antiken Judentums: Historische Grundlegung einer Theorie der Moderne* (Tübingen: Mohr Siebeck, 2011).

3. Gramsci's theory of hegemony has been presented in his series of writings from prison. For English translation, see A. Gramsci, *Selections from the Prison Notebooks*, ed. Q.

that reinforce their control over politics and the economy, through privileged access to social institutions' such as the media, schools and religious organizations.[4] Hegemonic power is therefore not merely economic domination by a ruling class or group, as previous Marxists had argued, but more ideological control in addition to economic and political dominance.

The Judahite community in the province of Yehud was a community without its own kingship, so a new type of political and religious leadership for the community was required. The biblical and extra-biblical sources from the period testify that diverse groups such as priests, aristocrats and elders of the family clans exercised the required leadership. Nevertheless, due to the strong control of the Persian government, the groups' authorities were not supported by military or administrative force; instead, they could only depend on cultural forces such as religious tradition/institutions, traditional social organizations (e.g. family clans) and religious ideologies. The type of authority and control they sought is therefore close to hegemony. In the following, I will apply Gramsci's theory of hegemonic power to the power struggles among the different groups, and interpret the biblical texts reflecting the struggles in terms of their scribal efforts for seeking hegemonic power as well as the ability to counter the hegemonic power.

7.1 *The Priests and Elders: Hegemonic Rivalry*

It has been well known that the provincial policy of the Persian Empire often made local temples the centres for local governance, politics, and even taxation. The Temple in Jerusalem, too, probably had a central role in the religious, social, and political realms of the community. Although the nature and limit of the priestly power and authority are still under debate, the priestly texts, especially in the Pentateuch, exhibit that the priestly group endeavoured to establish hegemony and control the temple and the community.[5] Gramsci describes a hegemonic group

Hoare and G. Smith (London: Lawrence & Wishhart, 1973); and more recently, A. Gramsci, *Prison Notebooks*, trans. J. A. Buttigieg (New York: Columbia University Press, 2011).

4. See M. Griffith, 'Hegemony', in *Encyclopedia of International Relations and Global Politics*, ed. M. Griffith (London: Routledge, 2013), 364.

5. The priests' growing influence in the late Persian or, more probably, the early Hellenistic Period has led some scholars to imagine 'theocracy', a total control of society by the priestly authority in Yehud. See R. Achenbach, *Die Vollendung der Tora: Studien zur Redaktionsgeschichte des Numeribuches im Kontext von Hexateuch und Pentateuch* (Wiesbaden: Otto Harrassowitz Verlag, 2003), 130. Similarly, VanderKam assumes the religious and political priority of the high priests in the Persian Period; see J. C. VanderKam, *From Joshua to Caiaphas: High Priests after the Exile* (Minneapolis: Fortress Press, Van Gorcum, 2004). Nevertheless, the notion of theocracy in this period should be treated with caution. Even though some biblical and extra-biblical texts indicate that there probably were such attempts, it is still uncertain how much their scribal expressions reflect the reality. For critical views on the status of the high priests in Yehud, see D. W. Rooke, *Zadok's Heirs: The*

that 'attempts to universalize their own interests' through an ideology that is in 'the interests of all'.[6] Similarly, the priestly group endeavoured to universalize their temple- and priest-centred ideology and world view through the priestly texts.[7] For instance, according to P, the proper worship in the tabernacle by the Aaronide priests is not only the concern of the priests, but also a critical issue for the very existence of the wilderness community. Especially, the structure of P from Genesis to Leviticus exhibits that the creation of the world is concluded by the building of the sanctuary of Yhwh. The sanctuary is the centre of the world, according to the priestly world view, and the Aaronide priests are the ones who make it function properly. The people of Israel or the temple community should therefore support and obey priestly rule. As such, P presents the religious, political and economic interests of the priests as the interests of the whole community, and the temple of Jerusalem probably functioned as a hegemonic institution for the priestly group during the Persian Period.

The significance of the temple in their pursuit of hegemonic power has probably led the priests to protect their exclusive prerogatives in temple service from other rival groups. The story of Korach in Numbers 16 can be a good example. Critics usually find two late priestly layers in the chapter, which are the earlier story of 250 chieftains of Israel and the later redaction of Korach with the Levites. According to the recent studies of Achenbach and others, including myself, the former contains a polemic against the challenge of the lay leaders to the priestly authority, whereas the latter is marked by a harsh polemic against the Levites.[8] In the earlier layer (vv. 2*, 3, 4, 6*, 7, 18, 35), 250 chieftains of Israel challenge the leadership of Moses and Aaron, which is vested in their exclusive holiness (v. 3). Yet their claim for equal holiness eventually turned out to be sinful, as demonstrated by their failure in the incense ordeal at the entrance of the tabernacle. Critics have recently argued that this story was composed by the Jerusalem temple priests in the mid- to

Role and Development of the High Priesthood in Ancient Israel (Oxford: Clarendon Press, 2000), 125–242; J. W. Cataldo, *Theocratic Yehud? Issues of Government in a Persian Period*, LHBOTS 498 (New York: T&T Clark, 2009), esp. 170–92. See also J. Jeon, 'The Zadokites in the Wilderness: The Rebellion of Korach (Num. 16) and the Zadokite Redaction', *ZAW* 127 (2015): 381–411. For recent discussion of the significance of temple Yehud in relation to Persian foreign policy, see K. -J. Lee, *The Authority and Authorization of Torah in the Persian Period* (Leuven: Peeters, 2011), esp. 203–12.

6. See Griffith, 'Hegemony', 346.

7. For such a priestly world view see, e.g. M. Haran, *Temples and Temple-Service in Ancient Israel: An Inquiry into the Character of Cult Phenomena and the Historical Setting of the Priestly School* (Oxford: Clarendon Press, 1978), 132–204.

8. In concurrence with the classical views, I find three layers in the chapter: the earliest, non-priestly stories of Dathan and Abiram (Num. 16.2*, 12-15, 25-26, 27b*, 28-32a, 33*); 250 chieftains (vv. 2*, 3, 4, 6*, 7, 18, 35) and the redactional layer of Korach and the Levites (1*, 5, 8-11, 16-17, 20-22, 24*, 33-34*). For a detailed discussion, see Achenbach, *Tora*, 37–123; and Jeon, 'Zadokites'.

late-Persian Period as a polemic against the lay elders of the community in order to establish or defend their exclusive priestly prerogatives in temple rituals as well as in the general leadership of the community;[9] more particularly, the story suggests that those priests known as the Zadokites[10] sought hegemony in the temple and thereby in the temple-centred community of Yehud through a struggle with the lay leadership of the community.[11] The struggle involved especially the exclusive priestly right for ritual performances such as incense offering, which had a growing significance in the temple service in the Second Temple Period.[12]

The opposition against which the Zadokites were polemicizing in this story was probably the group of lay leaders, which was also prominent in the community.[13] An ample number of biblical as well as extra-biblical sources testify to the elders' significant role in Yehud, as they represented and made decisions for the community, sometimes alongside the priests but often independently.[14] The elders seem to have co-supervised the temple with the priests, continuing to practice some temple rituals.[15] For instance, evidence of the elders' practice of incense offering in the Jerusalem temple is found in the late pre-exilic period (e.g. Ezek.

9. See, e.g. Rainer Albertz, *A History of Israelite Religion in the Old Testament Period, II: From the Exile to the Maccabees*, trans. J. Bowden (Louisville, KY: Westminster John Knox Press, 1994), 486–87; Achenbach, *Tora*, 54–66; and Jeon, 'Zadokites', 384–86, 395–400.

10. For the priesthood of the Jerusalem temple and the priestly genealogy in the Persian Period, see VanderKam, *From Joshua*, 43–111; cf. Rooke, *Zadok's Heirs*, 125–242.

11. For further information, see Jeon, 'Zadokites', 384–86.

12. For an exhaustive discussion about the significance of the incense offering, see P. Heger, *Development of Incense Cult in Israel* (Berlin: de Gruyter, 1997), 191–252.

13. For the significance of the lay leadership in Persia's Yehud, see e.g. O. Plöger, *Theokratie und Eschatologie* (Neukirchen: Neukirchener Verlag, 1959), 129–32; M. Smith, *Palestinian Parties and Politics That Shaped the Old Testament* (2nd corr. edn; London: SCM Press, 1987), 75–80; Albertz, *Israelite Religion*, 464–69. See also E. Gerstenberger, *Israel in the Persian Period* (Atlanta: SBL, 2011), 102–103; Achenbach, *Tora*, 54–66. The leadership of the elders is not a particular phenomenon in Persia's Yehud, but is also observable already in the exilic period among the exiles. It is apparent in Ezekiel, for instance, that the leadership of the exilic community was collectively exercised by a group of people designated as elders of Israel (זקני ישראל: Ezek. 14.1; 20.1, 3).

14. For instance, the mentions of the influential elders (חורים: in Neh. 2.16; 4.8, 13; 5.7; 7.5), elders of the Jews (שבי יהודיא: in Ezra 5.5, 9; 6.7, 8, 14) and the heads of families (ראשי האבות: in Ezra 2.68; 4.2, 3; 8.1; Neh. 8.13; 11.13, etc.). Especially in Ezra 5–6, the representatives of the community to the Persian delegates are the elders of the Jews (שבי יהודיא or שביא). Also, an Aramaic papyrus from Elephantine (for instance, A4.7:18-19//4.8:17-18) mentions Ostanes, the brother of Anani, and the other nobles of Jerusalem as the representatives of the community. For a more detailed discussion, see Jeon, 'Zadokites', 395–400.

15. See Jeon, 'Zadokites', 397–98.

8.7-13),[16] and there is no reason to assume that they ceased practising this custom in a temple rebuilt primarily by themselves. Such a context is the most probable one for the Zadokite priestly composition of Numbers 16.

Some scholars have suggested not only that a group of influential elders in the early Persian Period had their own program for the restoration derived from Deuteronomistic ideas but also that such affinity to the Deuteronomistic literature continued to manifest itself in their contributions to the Pentateuch.[17] These lay leaders seem to have had a broader concept of holiness and the idea of a general priesthood, as is well expressed in the idea of Israel as 'a priestly nation' (ממלכת כהנים) in the Deuteronomistic redaction passage of Exod. 19.5ff. (see also Deut. 7.6).[18] In addition, they are probably responsible for the Pentateuchal passages that elevate the status of the elders, such as the redactional addition of prophetic inspiration for the 70 elders (Num. 11.14-18, 24b-30) and their close approach to God on Mt. Sinai with the priests (Exod. 24.1, 9-11). The author of the present passage (Num. 16) also recognized the elders' familiarity with Deuteronomistic language and ideology so that the complaint of the chieftains is expressed, along with the Deuteronomistic expression לב לכם (v. 3), through the idea of a general holiness of the people: 'for the whole community, every one of them is holy' (Num. 16.3).[19]

In addition to an economically and politically dominant position, the elders also strove for hegemony by promoting their ideology in the interest of other classes.[20] They endeavoured to legitimate and perpetuate this ideology through their scribal efforts to complete and preserve the Deuteronomistic History, and to include Deuteronomy in the Pentateuch along with their own Pentateuchal compositions and redactions.[21] Their pursuit of hegemony is also visible in their polemic attack against the rival group, the Aaronide priests. For instance, the highly Deuteronomistic account of the Golden Calf (Exodus 32, esp. vv. 1-6, 15, 19-25), as has been well recognized, contains a harsh polemic against Aaron.[22]

16. The elders are blamed in that passage not for the incense offering by non-priestly personnel, but for idolatry. See also Achenbach, *Tora*, 82–90.

17. See, e.g. Smith, *Palestinian Parties*, 75–78; Albertz, *Israelite Religion*, 471–75.

18. See P. D. Hanson, *The Dawn of Apocalyptic: The Historical and Sociological Roots of Jewish Apocalyptic Eschatology*, rev. edn (Philadelphia: Fortress Press, 1983), 268; Albertz, *Israelite Religion*, 477–79.

19. See, e.g. Albertz, *Israelite Religion*, 487; Achenbach, *Tora*, 55–66.

20. For the Deuteronomistic groups and their interests in the peasant class, see e.g. Albertz, *Israelite Religion*, 471–80.

21. See Albertz, *Israelite Religion*, 471–80.

22. For a detailed history of the pertinent research, see J. Hahn, *Das 'Goldene Kalb': Die Jahwe-Verehrung bei Stierbildern in der Geschichte Israels*, 2nd edn (Bern: Peter Lang, 1987), 101–43; K. Schmid, 'Israel am Siani: Etappen der Forschungsgeschichte zu Ex 32–34 in seinen Kontexten', in *Gottes Volk Am Sinai: Untersuchungen Zu Ex 32–34 Und Dtn 9–10*, ed. M. Köckert and E. Blum, VWGTh, 18 (Gütersloh: Chr. Kaiser – Gütersloher Verlagshaus, 2001), 9–40. For a recent argument against the polemic nature of the chapter, see J. Watts, 'Aaron and the Golden Calf in the Rhetoric of the Pentateuch', *JBL* 130 (2011): 417–30.

According to the story, Aaron establishes the cult of the golden calf at Mt. Sinai/ Horeb, where the cult of the Mosaic Tabernacle originated. Especially through the well-known quotation in Exod. 32.8 of the account of Jeroboam's golden calves (1 Kgs 12.28), 'Behold your gods, O Israel, who brought you out of the land of Egypt', Aaron is portrayed in the image of Jeroboam, whose golden calf cult, according to the Deuteronomistic History, led the Northern Kingdom to its destruction.[23] The account, in effect, significantly undermines the appropriateness of Aaron as the high priest of the newly established Tabernacle cult. This story may therefore be read as a Deuteronomistic-oriented scribal attempt to undermine the Pentateuchal foundation of the exclusive priestly authority of the Aaronides.[24]

The damaged authority of Aaron in Exodus 32 probably provoked a scribal reaction from the priestly group. The account of Phinehas (Num. 25.6-15), which can be assigned to a post-priestly Zadokite redaction,[25] may be understood as the priestly response to the present polemic. According to the account, Phinehas and his descendants receive the covenant of eternal priesthood (v. 13) despite the already existing, secured priestly office of Aaron and his descendants. This seemingly redundant covenant, in effect, makes Phinehas a new Aaron, whose authority remains intact. Since Phinehas is a direct ancestor of Zadok, according to the late priestly genealogy (1 Chron. 6.4, 12, 35ff.), this story provides the Zadokites with a more secure historical ground for their exclusive priesthood.

7.2 *The Levites' Struggle for Counter-Hegemony in the Jerusalem Temple*

If the story of the 250 chieftains (Numbers 16) discussed above reflects the Zadokites' struggle for hegemony against the lay leaders, the final redaction of Korach and the Levites can be understood as a struggle against the Levites.[26] The Korach layer harshly blames Korach and the Levites for their claim of the

---

23. Exod. 32.4 replaces הנה with אלה. Noth regards it as a 'polemic twist', implying a plurality of gods in Jeroboam's royal sanctuaries. See M. Noth, *Exodus: A Commentary*, trans. J. S. Bowden (Philadelphia: Westminster Press, 1962), 248. See also B. S. Childs, *The Book of Exodus*, OTL (Philadelphia: Westminster Press, 1974), 566. Cf. M. Aberbach and L. Smolar, 'Aaron, Jeroboam and the Golden Calves', *JBL* 86 (1967): 129–40.

24. Some critics have recently argued that the description of the process of making the golden calf is based on the priestly account of building the tabernacle, and therefore the entire story is post-priestly. See H. Utzschneider, *Das Heiligtum und Das Gesetz: Studien zur Bedeutung der Sinaitischen Heiligtumstexte (Ex 25–40; Lev 8–9)*, OBO 77 (Göttingen: Vandenhoeck & Ruprecht, 1988), 86–87; E. Otto, 'Die nachpriesterschriftliche Pentateuchredaktion im Buch Exodus', in *Studies in the Book of Exodus: Redaction – Reception – Interpretation*, ed. M. Vervenne, BETL 76 (Leuven: Leuven University Press, 1996), 61–112, esp. 85.

25. See Jeon, 'The Zadokites', 403–406.

26. See Jeon, 'The Zadokites', 386–95.

priesthood, as it is highlighted in Moses's condemnation of the Levites (Num. 16.8-11): 'Hear now, you Levites! Is it too little for you that the God of Israel has separated you from the congregation of Israel . . . yet you seek the priesthood as well!' By means of redactional links to the previous layers, this layer poses two dreadful punishments on Korach and his congregation: namely, being consumed by fire (v. 35) and being swallowed by the earth (v. 32). This final layer therefore emphasizes the sinfulness of the Levites' claim for the priesthood and endeavours to defend exclusive priestly rights in the Temple service.

Korach is not a well-known figure in the Pentateuch, appearing only in late redactional passages (e.g. Exod. 6.21, 24; Num. 26.9; 27.3). In Chronicles, however, Korach is described as an ancestor of several influential Levitical clans responsible for the three main tasks of the Levites: singing, gatekeeping and ancillary temple service (1 Chron. 9.19, 31; 26.1, 19; 2 Chron. 20.19). Probably in consideration of such Levitical genealogy, the priestly (most likely Zadokite) scribe chose Korach as the main antagonist representing the Levites. R. Achenbach defines this redactional phase as theocratic revision, reflecting a powerful theocratic rule by the priestly group in the mid- to late-Persian Period.[27] I myself have defined the layer elsewhere as a Zadokite redaction through which the Zadokite priests in Jerusalem combat the growing power of the Levites.[28]

7.2.1 *The Growth of the Levites*

Have the Levites, then, really grown strong enough to threaten the priestly group during the mid- to late-Persian Period? In the historical memory of the early Persian Period reflected in Ezra, the Levites were a minor group not comparable to the priestly group in number. However, since Nehemiah empowered and supported the Levites as his supporting group in the temple,[29] the Levites' power and influence seem to have grown fast. For instance, the Levites, the singers and the gatekeepers, who appear as separate groups in Ezra and Nehemiah, seem to have been united in the course of time. Eventually in Chronicles, these three different groups of temple personnel are found as branches of the Levite tribal clan with well-established genealogies (e.g. 1 Chron. 9.14-34; 23; 24.20-31; 25–26). These 'united' Levites, mainly according to Chronicles, took control over temple administration (1 Chron. 26.20-28), sacrificial and liturgical processes (1 Chron. 23.28-32; 24.6; 25.1-8) and even the security of the temple (1 Chron. 26.1-19). Those accounts in Chronicles describe the Levites' roles in the Monarchic Period, yet they probably reflect some historical kernels regarding the Persian Period. Nehemiah's memoir mentions the role of the gatekeepers (e.g. Neh. 13.7) and his assignment to the Levites of the task of religious police of Jerusalem (Neh. 13.22).

---

27. See Achenbach, *Tora*, 55–66.

28. See Jeon, 'The Zadokites', 386–95.

29. See, e.g. K. Min, *The Levitical Authorship of Ezra-Nehemiah*, JSOTSup 409 (New York and London: T&T Clark, 2004), 116–37.

Also, many liturgical Psalms are attributed to the Levites such as the sons of Asap and Korach, supporting the Levites' function in liturgy. Joachim Schaper recently defined this dynamic change in the Temple as a 'Levitical reform' introduced in the mid- to late-Persian Period.[30]

7.2.2 Counter-Hegemony

If we accept this scenario, the growth of the Levites can be interpreted as the establishment of a counter to hegemonic power in the Temple against the dominant Zadokite priestly group. The formation of the 'united' Levites, first, can be an example of an 'alliance between different groups', a characteristic phenomenon in the pursuit of hegemonic power. When a group has hegemonic power, according to Gramsci, the group is allied to other subordinate groups, coordinated concretely with their general interests and the ideology that creates 'collective will' shared by the groups.[31] In our case, the Levites were allied with other groups of temple personnel such as the gatekeepers and singers as a family clan, through common political and economic interests as secondary temple personnel. Their collective will was to promote their status and extend their influence in the temple and the community.

7.2.3 Class Consciousness

In the process of the Levites' pursuit of counter-hegemony, the notion of the Levites as non-priestly temple personnel underwent a dynamic shift from 'false consciousness' to 'class-consciousness'. According to Gramsci, when a group becomes subordinate to a hegemonic group, it is often intellectually subordinate as well and adopts a conception of itself and the world that is not its own but is borrowed from the hegemonic group. Gramsci defines such a conception as false consciousness.[32] In that vein, the notion of the Levites as the secondary and subordinate group in temple service can be seen as false consciousness. This conception was not originated from the Levites themselves, but was imposed by the priestly group. Since Wellhausen, scholars have considered the origin of the Levites to be the priests in local shrines in the pre-exilic period who lost their positions during the reform of Josiah. The subordinate status of these local priests as the 'Levites' was later conceptualized and perpetuated in the exilic and post-exilic periods, most likely by the Zadokite priestly group in Jerusalem. For instance, the late redactional passage Ezek. 44.10-16 declares that the Levites were deprived of the priesthood for their service for *gilullim*; by contrast, the Zadokites

---

30. See J. Schaper, *Priester und Leviten im achamenidischen Juda: Studien zur Kult- und sozialgeschichte Israels in Persischer Zeit* (Tübingen: Mohr Siebeck, 2000), 226–68, 290–93.

31. See E. Laclau and C. Mouffe, *Hegemony and Socialist Strategy: Towards a Radical Democratic Politics*, 2nd edn (New York: Verso, 2001), 181–82.

32. See Gramsci, *Selections from the Prison Notebooks*, 326–27.

were loyal to Yhwh, and therefore they are exclusively legitimized for priestly service. The priestly passages in Numbers 3–4 represent a further development of this notion in providing the origin of the Levites' subordinate status and their detailed tasks. Finally, the Korach redaction mentioned above (Num. 16) excludes the Levites from any claim for priesthood.[33]

Such a concept of the Levites as second-class temple personnel seems to have eventually been accepted and internalized by the Levites during the Persian Period; but once the united Levites internalized this notion as their own identity, it seems to have begun to function as their class-consciousness.

According to Walter L. Adamson's study of Gramsci's Hegemony Theory, a subordinate group should first have class consciousness to effectively resist a hegemonic group. In class consciousness, the class is understood not only economically but also in terms of 'a common intellectual and moral awareness, a common culture'.[34] For the Levitical groups, this process took place along with their collective identity as Levites. That is to say, the Levite identity as the secondary temple personnel became the common ground for uniting all of the secondary workers such as singers and gatekeepers. After that, they further developed their self-consciousness as a significant tribal clan in the history of the religion of Israel, as is presented in Levitical literature such as Chronicles and the Levitical Psalms (e.g. Neh. 9.4-38).

7.2.4 *Organic Intellectuals*

The critical self-consciousness of a group is always a creation of intellectual elites and is essential to achieve counter-hegemony.[35] Gramsci defines the elites who are responsible for this task as 'organic intellectuals'. They elaborate and spread the group's ideologies against the current dominant ideology formulated by 'traditional intellectuals', who are the intellectuals from the hegemonic group.[36] In our case, the Levitical scribes functioned as a sort of organic group of intellectuals who created the Levites' self-awareness as an autonomous group, and developed and spread their ideology. The Zadokite scribes, on the other hand, might be understood in this frame as the traditional intellectuals against whom the Levitical scribes had to struggle. For Gramsci, formulating consciousness as an autonomous group against the hegemonic group is a critical element for the development 'from a subaltern group to a hegemonic and dominant group'.[37]

---

33. The degradation was probably not admitted by the Levites at the beginning, so that the lowest number of the Levites participated in the return (Ezra 2.36-40; Neh. 7.39-43). See Schaper, *Priester*, 127.

34. See W. L. Adamson, *Hegemony and Revolution: A Study of Antonio Gramsci's Political and Cultural Theory* (Berkeley: University of California Press, 1983), 171.

35. See Laclau and Mouffe, *Hegemony*, 171.

36. See Laclau and Mouffe, *Hegemony*, 187.

37. See Gramsci, *Prison Notebooks*, 55.

Another example of the Levite intellectuals' creation of self-consciousness is the alternative consecration account of the Levites in the Pentateuch. The priestly account of the consecration of the Levites is provided in Num. 3.5-10, where the Levites are given to Aaron for serving him (v. 6). In the story of the Golden Calf, however, a non-priestly account of the consecration of the Levites is presented (Exod. 32.26-30), in which the Levites violently execute the punishment of the people for Moses and are consecrated to Yhwh as a reward. The passage conveys a message that when Aaron and the people trespassed against Yhwh, only the Levites were faithful to him, and therefore the Levites are morally superior even to the Aaronides. The term used for the consecration of the Levites, מלא + יד (Exod. 32.29), can be understood in this context as a polemical use of the typical term in P for the consecration of the Aaronide priests (Exod. 29.9; Lev. 8.33; 16.32).

Other features in this passage regarding the Levites are the descriptions of the Levites as an organized armed unit and as slaughterers of the people 'from gate to gate' (v. 27). These descriptions remind us of the gatekeepers of the Jerusalem Temple (and of the city [Neh. 11.19; 13.22]), who were probably the only organized armed force in Jerusalem except the Persian troops. This passage is an isolated redactional insertion, and often has been unsuccessfully assigned to one of the classical sources such as J or E; in more recent redactional models, the entire chapter is being dated as post-priestly without reaching a consensus on the nature of the current passage.[38] In any case, the passage's Levitical concern and the anti-Aaronide sentiment has long been recognized.[39] Noth, for instance, understands the passage as the claim of the Levites to priestly privileges against the priesthood of the royal sanctuaries.[40] Noth's contextualization of the passage in the early Monarchic Period is no longer tenable; this isolated block may rightly be assigned to a Levite intellectual (scribe) in the Persian Period.[41]

Another example of the Levite intellectuals' creation of self-consciousness is the alternative origin of the Levitical office in Chronicles. The priestly Tetrateuch, especially from Exodus to Numbers, contains the history and regulations of the Mosaic tabernacle cult, where the Levites have secondary and inferior status. The Chronicler, however, introduces a new cultic system for the Jerusalem temple founded by King David in which the Levites occupy almost all the significant positions. The Chronicler omits the entire history of Moses from the history of Israel, such as the stories of Exodus, Wilderness and Sinai (1 Chron. 1–9), and

38. See above, n. 22.

39. See, e.g. A. H. J. Gunneweg, *Leviten Und Priester: Hauptlinien Der Traditionsbildung Und Geschichte Des Israelitisch-Jüdischen Kultpersonals* (Göttingen: Vandenhoeck und Ruprecht, 1965), 29–38; Noth, *Exodus*, 250. Childs, *The Book of Exodus*, 561.

40. See Noth, *Exodus*, 250.

41. For a further discussion about the Levitical contribution to the Pentateuch in the Persian Period, see J. Jeon, 'The Visit of Jethro (Exodus 18): Its Composition and Levitical Reworking', *JBL* 136 (2017): 289–306.

jumps from the patriarchs directly to King David. Moses, or the law of Moses, are mentioned only in very limited cases; also, the Mosaic Tabernacle is mentioned only sporadically, mostly in connection to the Levitical functions (1 Chron. 9.19, 23; 23.26; 2 Chron. 24.6) and the building of the temple (1 Chron. 16.39; 17.5; 21.29). A truly meaningful history of the religion of Israel, for the Chronicler, begins with King David in 1 Chronicles 10. David initiates a new cult in Jerusalem with the ark and the Levites, while the old Mosaic tabernacle is placed in a high place at Gibeon (1 Chron. 16.39). King David gives detailed plans for the temple and the system of clergies with divine inspiration (1 Chron. 28.11ff.), just as Moses did for the Tabernacle in the priestly Tetrateuch.[42] For the Chronicler, as von Rad pointed out, King David is a new Moses and the Jerusalem Temple is the new legitimate cultic place that replaces the old priestly tabernacle.[43] In Chronicles, therefore, David and his cultic regulations are consistently referred to as the source of legitimation for the Levitical temple service, whereas mentioning Moses or the Torah of Moses is deliberately kept to a minimum: Moses is mentioned 21 times in total, whereas David is mentioned 227 times.

According to the Chronicler, the Levites are the most important figures in the Jerusalem Temple and even in the Kingdom, in contrast to the priestly Tetrateuch. They control Temple administration and sacrifices at the outer altar, and are responsible for liturgy and security (1 Chron. 15; 16; 23–26). The priests are responsible only for the inner sanctum. In the royal court as well, they are administrators (1 Chron. 23.33ff.), judges (1 Chron. 26.29ff.), warriors (1 Chron. 26.30ff.), scribes (1 Chron. 24.6), teachers (2 Chron. 17.7f.) and even prophets (1 Chron. 25.5). The description of such a highly exalted status for the Levites represents a well-developed self-awareness of the Levites as a class or group.

Along with the ambitious cultic programme for the Levites, the Chronicler responds to Zadokite scribalism as well. The account of the Levites in the Northern Kingdom (2 Chron. 11.13-17), for instance, claims that the Northern Levites fled from Jeroboam, opposing his cult of the golden calves, and led the pious worshippers of Yhwh to Jerusalem for proper sacrifice. These Levites continued to stay in Jerusalem, supporting the Davidic Dynasty. These accounts may be a response to the Zadokite criticism of the Levites in Ezekiel 44, mentioned above, which condemns the Levites for serving at idolatrous altars in Israel. According to the corrected history in 2 Chronicles 11 and 34, the Levites had always been faithful to Yhwh and the Jerusalem Temple, and therefore the Zadokites' accusation is groundless. This can be an example of how the 'organic' Levite elites resisted the 'traditional' Zadokite elites through their scribal activity.

42. See, e.g., S. Japhet, *I and II Chronicles: A Commentary* (Louisville: Westminster John Knox Press, 1993), 493–94.

43. See G. von Rad, *Das Geschichtsbild des chronistischen Werkes* (Stuttgart: Kohlhammer, 1930), 80–119.

7.2.5 War of Position

When a group endeavours to establish counter-hegemony against the dominant hegemonic group, the former challenges the mechanism of ideological domination. Gramsci defines such cultural and ideological struggles as a 'war of position', which is distinguished from a 'war of manoeuvre' involving physical strife. The Chronicler's attempt to honour and authorize the Levites in the temple service accompanies, at some points, a de-authorization of the dominant priestly group; this can be understood as the 'war of position' from the Levite side. In Chronicles, the leaders of the priests are accused of defiling the temple, leading to its destruction (2 Chron. 36.14). Moreover, Zadok, ancestor of the Zadokites, is portrayed as originally a priest of a high place at Gibeon with the Mosaic Tabernacle, which was eventually abandoned by David (1 Chron. 16.39; 21.28–22.1). Although the Tabernacle was there, there was no ark in it; the ark was with the Levites when they initiated worship in Jerusalem together with David (1 Chron. 16; 2 Chron. 1.4).

In addition, the Zadokites' exclusive priestly rights are denied in Chronicles. In the chronicler's sacrificial system, not only Eliezer's descendants, the Zadokites, but also Abiathar's family, the descendants of Aaron's son Ithamar, have legitimate priesthood in Jerusalem (1 Chron. 24.1-19). The two families serve in the sanctum in turn, but the order of their service is controlled by Shemaiah (שמעיה), a Levite scribe (1 Chron. 24.6). The account of Solomon's dismissal of Abiathar from his office (1 Kgs 2.26ff.) is, of course, omitted in Chronicles. In this system, therefore, the Zadokites' claim for exclusive priesthood becomes completely unfounded.

7.3 Conclusion

In this essay, I have endeavoured to show that the scribal conflicts between the priests and Levites reflected in the Pentateuch, Ezekiel and Chronicles can be effectively explained by Gramsci's theory of hegemony. If we understand the priestly text as hegemonic and Chronicles as counter-hegemonic, this perspective invites us to read Chronicles in close relationship with the Pentateuch. Application of modern theory to an ancient time, however, requires due caution in order to avoid possible anachronism. The theory of hegemonic power by Gramsci originated in his observation of the political situation in early twentieth-century Europe, especially the conflict between the bourgeoisie and the proletariat. The historical context of Persian Yehud was probably quite different. The province was ruled by Persian governors; therefore, the degree of autonomy of the people and, consequently, the hegemony of a certain group were probably limited within the narrow realms of society. Furthermore, the lack of historical sources for this period precludes a precise reconstruction of the socio-historical situation of the time. It is consequently uncertain whether the Levites really achieved hegemonic power in the temple at a certain point. The focus should therefore remain on their scribal efforts reflected in the ambitious description of their origin and history.

It should also be considered that along with conflicts and opposition, the various groups in Persia's Yehud cooperated with each other in building the community. For instance, while the Levites had to contend with the priestly group for higher status, the two groups were colleagues in temple service and had to work together and compromise with each other.[44] Similarly, the priests and elders probably cooperated with each other consistently on various issues.[45] They were not enemies, but parts of the community, just like the diverse and conflicting voices incorporated into one Torah. A comprehensive description of the aspects of cooperation and alliance between them would require separate research entirely devoted to the subject. For the moment, the struggles of different groups for hegemony in the temple and community can be understood as significant elements that dynamically affected both the society of Persian Yehud and the formation of biblical texts.

Bibliography

Aberbach, M., and L. Smolar. 'Aaron, Jeroboam and the Golden Calves'. *JBL* 86 (1967): 129–40.

Achenbach, R. *Die Vollendung der Tora: Studien zur Redaktionsgeschichte des Numeribuches im Kontext von Hexateuch und Pentateuch*. Wiesbaden: Otto Harrassowitz Verlag, 2003.

Adamson, W. L. *Hegemony and Revolution: A Study of Antonio Gramsci's Political and Cultural Theory*. Berkeley: University of California Press, 1983.

Albertz, Rainer. *A History of Israelite Religion in the Old Testament Period, I: From the Beginnings to the End of the Monarchy*, trans. Bowden. Louisville: Westminster John Knox Press, 1994.

Albertz, Rainer. *A History of Israelite Religion in the Old Testament Period, II: From the Exile to the Maccabees*, trans. J. Bowden. Louisville: Westminster John Knox Press, 1994.

Cataldo, J. W. *Theocratic Yehud?: Issues of Government in a Persian Period*. LHBOTS 498. New York: T&T Clark, 2009.

Childs, B. S. *The Book of Exodus*, OTL. Philadelphia: Westminster Press, 1974.

Gerstenberger, E. *Israel in the Persian Period*. Atlanta: Scholars Press, 2011.

Gramsci, A. *Selections from the Prison Notebooks*, edited by Q. Hoare and G. Smith. London: Lawrence & Wishhart, 1973.

Gramsci, A. *Prison Notebooks*, trans. J. A. Buttigieg. New York: Columbia University Press, 2011.

Griffith, M. 'Hegemony'. In *Encyclopedia of International Relations and Global Politics*, edited by M. Griffith, 364. London: Routledge, 2013.

Gunneweg, A. H. J. *Leviten Und Priester: Hauptlinien Der Traditionsbildung Und Geschichte Des Israelitisch-Jüdischen Kultpersonals*, 29–38. Göttingen: Vandenhoeck und Ruprecht, 1965.

44. See, e.g. the episode of the failed incense offering by King Uzziah (2 Chron. 26.16-21) in which the exclusive priestly right for incense offering is declared (esp. v. 18). The Levite scribe (Chronicler) admits the priestly right, which the Zadokite scribes strongly claimed in Numbers 16.

45. The priests and elders probably constituted a collective political body in the mid- to late-Persian Period.

Hahn, J. *Das 'Goldene Kalb': Die Jahwe-Verehrung bei Stierbildern in der Geschichte Israels*, 2nd edn, 101–43. Bern: Peter Lang, 1987.

Hanson, P. D. *The Dawn of Apocalyptic: The Historical and Sociological Roots of Jewish Apocalyptic Eschatology*. Rev. edn. Philadelphia: Fortress Press, 1983.

Haran, M. *Temples and Temple-Service in Ancient Israel: An Inquiry into the Character of Cult Phenomena and the Historical Setting of the Priestly School*. Oxford: Clarendon Press, 1978.

Heger, P. *Development of Incense Cult in Israel*. Berlin: de Gruyter, 1997.

Japhet, S. *I and II Chronicles: A Commentary*. Louisville: Westminster John Knox Press, 1993.

Jeon, J. 'The Visit of Jethro (Exodus 18): Its Composition and Levitical Reworking', *JBL* 136 (2017): 289–306.

Jeon, J. 'The Zadokites in the Wilderness: The Rebellion of Korach (Num 16) and the Zadokite Redaction'. *ZAW* 127 (2015): 381–411.

Laclau, E., and C. Mouffe. *Hegemony and Socialist Strategy: Towards a Radical Democratic Politics*. 2nd edn. New York: Verso, 2001.

Lee, K.-J. *The Authority and Authorization of Torah in the Persian Period*. Leuven: Peeters, 2011.

Mayes, A. *The Old Testament in Sociological Perspective*. London: Marshall Pickering, 1989.

Min, K. *The Levitical Authorship of Ezra-Nehemiah*. JSOTSup 409. New York and London: T&T Clark, 2004.

Nihan, C. *From Priestly Torah to Pentateuch*. Tübingen: Mohr Siebeck, 2007.

Noth, M. *Exodus: A Commentary*, trans. J. S. Bowden. Philadelphia: Westminster Press, 1962.

Otto, E. 'Die nachpriesterschriftliche Pentateuchredaktion im Buch Exodus'. In *Studies in the Book of Exodus: Redaction – Reception – Interpretation*, edited by M. Vervenne. BETL 76; 61–112. Leuven: Leuven University Press, 1996.

Otto, E. *Max Webers Studien des Antiken Judentums: Historische Grundlegung einer Theorie der Moderne*. Tübingen: Mohr Siebeck, 2011.

Plöger, O. *Theokratie und Eschatologie*. Neukirchen: Neukirchener Verlag, 1959.

Rooke, D. W. *Zadok's Heirs: The Role and Development of the High Priesthood in Ancient Israel*. Oxford: Clarendon Press, 2000.

Schaper, J. *Priester und Leviten im achamenidischen Juda: Studien zur Kult- und sozialgeschichte Israels in Persischer Zeit*. Tübingen: Mohr Siebeck, 2000.

Schmid, K. 'Israel am Siani: Etappen der Forschungsgeschichte zu Ex 32–34 in seinen Kontexten', In *Gottes Volk Am Sinai: Untersuchungen Zu Ex 32–34 Und Dtn 9–10*, edited by M. Köckert and E. Blum. VWGTh 18; 9–40. Gütersloh: Chr. Kaiser – Gütersloher Verlagshaus, 2001.

Smith, M. *Palestinian Parties and Politics That Shaped the Old Testament*. 2nd edn. London: SCM Press, 1987.

Utzschneider, H. *Das Heiligtum und Das Gesetz: Studien zur Bedeutung der Sinaitischen Heiligtumstexte (Ex 25–40; Lev 8–9)*. OBO 77. Göttingen: Vandenhoeck & Ruprecht, 1988.

Vanderkam, J. C. *From Joshua to Caiaphas: High Priests after the Exile*. Minneapolis: Fortress Press; Van Gorcum, 2004.

von Rad, G. *Das Geschichtsbild des chronistischen Werkes* (Stuttgart: Kohlhammer, 1930).

Watts, J. 'Aaron and the Golden Calf in the Rhetoric of the Pentateuch', *JBL* 130 (2011): 417–30.

Weber, M. *Ancient Judaism*, trans. and ed., H. H. Gerth and D. Martindale. New York: Free Press, 1967.

Weber, M. *Gesammelte Aufsätze zur Religionssoziologie, III. Das antike Judentum*, 7th edn. Tübingen: Mohr, 1983.

Chapter 8

THE CONCEPT OF UTOPIA AND THE PSALM OF HABAKKUK: AN ALTERNATIVE READING

Chen Bergot

8.1 *Introduction*

The Book of Habakkuk is a prophetic book in its own right in the corpus of the Twelve.[1] It is the only prophetic text in the Hebrew Bible where it is possible to find a psalm attributed to a prophet by means of a superscription. This peculiarity raises many questions with regard to the redaction history of the book and the insertion of the psalm (Habakkuk 3) within the remaining prophetic collection (Habakkuk 1–2).

There are two schools of thought within current scholarship. The first holds that the prophetic collection and the psalm were composed at the same time. The second considers the psalm to be a stand-alone composition added to the prophetic material at a later stage.[2] Both positions highlight the complex redaction history

1. I would like to express my sincere thanks to my colleague Luc Bulundwe for his comments, corrections and proofreading.

2. For authors who view the psalm as an autonomous composition, see especially T. Hiebert, *God of My Victory: The Ancient Hymn in Habakkuk 3*, HSM 38 (Atlanta: Scholars Press, 1986); T. Lescow, 'Die Komposition der Bücher Nahum und Habakuk', *BN* 77 (1995): 59–85; J. Nogalski, *Redactional Processes in the Book of the Twelve*, BZAW 218 (Berlin: W. de Gruyter, 1993); L. Perlitt, *Die Propheten Nahum, Habakuk, Zephanja*, ATD 25, 1 (Göttingen: Vandenhoeck & Ruprecht, 2004); K. Seybold, *Nahum, Habakuk, Zephanja*, Zürcher Bibelkommentare AT 24. 2 (Zürich: Theologischer Verlag, 1991). On the rest of the state of research see especially F. I. Andersen, *Habakkuk: A New Translation with Introduction and Commentary*, AB 25 (New York: Doubleday, 2001); D. Cleaver-Bartholomew, 'An Alternative Approach to Hab 1,2–2,20', *SJOT* 17 (2003): 206–25; O. Dangl, 'Habakkuk in Recent Research', *CRBS* 9 (2001): 131–68; M. H. Floyd, 'Prophecy and Writing in Habakkuk 2,1-5', *ZAW* 105 (1994): 462–81 ; R. D. Haak, *Habakkuk*, VTSup 44 (Leiden: E. J. Brill, 1992); B. Huwyler, 'Habakuk und seine Psalmen', in *Prophetie und Psalmen:Festschrift für Klaus Seybold zum 65. Geburtstag*, AOAT 280 (Münster: Ugarit-Verlag, 2001), 231–59; G. T. M. Prinsloo, 'Life for the Righteous, Doom for the Wicked: Reading Habakkuk from a Wisdom Perspective', *Skrif en kerk* 21 (2000): 621–40; G. T. M. Prinsloo, 'Reading Habakkuk 3 in

of this original prophetic book, yet their disagreement raises the question: How to interpret the psalm attributed to the prophet Habakkuk in the context of the prophetic collection of the MT and the LXX?[3]

The prophetic collection and the psalm seem to fit within different temporalities and problematics, and bring about different realities. While the prophetic collection describes the terrestrial sufferings of a community subjugated by different enemies (רָשָׁע, the 'wicked', and הַכַּשְׂדִּים, 'the Chaldeans'), the psalm seems to describe an idealized alternative reality in which Yhwh retakes power and saves His people (3.13, יָצָאתָ לְיֵשַׁע עַמֶּךָ), of which the prophet Habakkuk is the representative figure. How does one interpret this literary transition between the prophetic collection and the psalm, underlined by the use of two distinct genres, which is the peculiarity of the Book of Habakkuk? This interpretative question further leads one to reflect upon the literary function of the psalm and how it would be read towards the end of the Persian era or even at the beginning of the Hellenistic period.[4]

The possibility that the psalm could be describing an alternative reality to the one described in the prophetic collection is at the heart of my interest in using the concept of utopia in the present inquiry. The concept of utopia encompasses many social realities; but more than anything it seeks to put in place, in writing, an alternative reality far better than the one experienced by the producers and

---

the Light of Ancient Unit Delimiters', *HTS* 69 (2013): no. 1975, 11 pages; M. A. Sweeney, 'Structure, Genre, and Intent in the Book of Habakkuk', *VT* 41 (1991): 63–83; M. E. Thompson, 'Prayer Oracle and Theophany: The Book of Habakkuk', *TynBul* 44 (1993): 33–53; M. Witte, 'Orakel und Gebete im Buch Habakuk', in *Orakel und Gebete: Interdisziplinäre Studien zur Sprache der Religion in Ägypten, Vorderasien und Griechenland in hellenistischer Zeit*, ed. M. Witte and J. F. Diehl, FAT 2; 38 (Tübingen: Mohr Siebeck, 2009), 67–91; J. Wöhrle, *Der Abschluss des Zwölfprophetenbuches: Buchübergreifende Redaktionsprozesse in den Späten Sammlungen*, BZAW 389 (Berlin: W. de Gruyter, 2008), 291–334.

3. At the turn of our era, three traditions of reading the book of Habakkuk have circulated: (1) the witnesses who have kept the prophetic collection and the psalm, such as the Masoretic tradition, the LXX, the Naḥal Ḥever's manuscript (first century CE), and the Murabbaʿât (second century BCE.), (2) the Pesher of Habakkuk at Qumran (second century BCE), without the psalm, and (3) the Barberini Greek version (second century CE) of the psalm of Habakkuk alone. On the Barberini version, see especially E. M. Good, 'The Barberini Greek Version of Habakkuk III', *VT* 9 (1959): 29. See also C. Dogniez, 'La Version Barberini: Éléments pour une étude littéraire d'un autre texte Grec d'Habacuc 3', in *Die Septuaginta – Entstehung, Sprache, Geschichte*, ed. Kreuzer et al., WUNT 286 (Tübingen: Mohr Siebeck, 2012), 295–310.

4. With regard to the text of the LXX, the dating of the Greek translation of the Twelve is still debatable. It spreads between the middle of the third century BCE and the beginning of the first century BCE. On this matter, see H. -J. Fabry, 'The Reception of Nahum and Habakkuk in the Septuagint and Qumran', in *Emanuel: Studies in Hebrew Bible, Septuagint, and Dead Sea Scrolls in Honor of Emanuel Tov*, ed. S. M. Paul et al., VTSup 94 (Leiden: Brill, 2003), 241–56.

recipients of the text. The analytical potential of the concept of utopia might be relevant for rethinking both the literary and editorial coherence between the prophetic collection (Habakkuk 1–2) and the psalm (Habakkuk 3), and whether the psalm in particular can be read as a description of an intervention by Yhwh contributing to an alternative reality better than that experienced by the 'I' in Habakkuk 1–2.

8.2 *The Concept of Utopia*

Utopia is a complex concept which refers to many literary and social realities.[5] When one speaks of 'utopia', any or all of the following three manifestations can be envisaged: (1) a literary genre, (2) an ideology and, (3) a social movement that produces utopias.[6] Those three realities do not constitute three autonomous empirical fields but instead evolve in a constant dialectic relation. In fact, utopia can be conceptualized in the first place as born out of the reality of a text (excluding for now the oral component of the phenomenon), while needing at the same time both an ideology associated with the origin of the representation and a setting to generate it.

Utopian representations are therefore manifold and varied, and they correspond to diverse literary logics. Texts said to be utopian are not necessarily characterized by their form but first and foremost by the reality they create. The literary genre

---

5. The state of research on the concept of utopia is vast and complex. Important references in the area of Old Testament studies include E. Ben Zvi, ed., *Utopia and Dystopia in Prophetic Literature*, Publications of the Finnish Exegetical Society, no. 92 (Helsinki: The Finnish Exegetical Society; Göttingen: Vandenhoeck & Ruprecht, 2006). See also K. Berge, 'Literacy, Utopia and Memory: Is There a Public Teaching in Deuteronomy?', *Journal of Hebrew Scriptures* 12, no. 3 (2012): 1–19; M. J. Boda, 'In Conversation with Steven Schweitzer, *Reading Utopia in Chronicles* (LHBOTS, 442; London: T & T Clark International, 2007)', *Journal of Hebrew Scriptures* 9 (2009): 1–19; J. Cataldo, 'Whispered Utopia: Dreams, Agendas, and Theocratic Aspirations in Yehud', *SJOT* 24 (2010): 53–70; J. Ferguson, *Utopias of the Classical World*, Aspects of Greek and Roman Life (London: Thames and Hudson, 1975); S. J. Schweitzer, *Reading Utopia in Chronicles*, LHBOTS (New York and London: T&T Clark, 2007). On the concept of utopia, see R. Levitas, *The Concept of Utopia* (New York and London: P. Allan, 1990); F. E. Manuel, ed., *Utopias and Utopian Thought*, Beacon Paperback, no. 251 (Boston: Beacon Press, 1967); L. T. Sargent, 'The Three Faces of Utopianism Revisited', *Utopian Studies* 5 (1994): 1–37; L. T. Sargent, 'Authority & Utopia: Utopianism in Political Thought', *Polity* 14 (1982): 565–84; R. Schaer, ed., *Utopia: The Search for the Ideal Society in the Western World* (New York: The New York Public Library; Oxford: Oxford University Press, 2000).

6. S. J. Schweitzer, 'Utopia and Utopian Literary Theory: Some Preliminary Observations', in *Utopia and Dystopia in Prophetic Literature*, ed. E. Ben Zvi (Helsinki: Finnish Exegetical Society; Göttingen: Vandenhoeck & Ruprecht, 2006), 13.

associated with the representation is not a determinative factor.[7] Utopian discourse is not, moreover, set within a precise temporality; uncertainty about the 'when?' is an important formal characteristic of utopian discourse,[8] which can be situated in the present, the past or the future.[9]

The issue of localizing utopian description, however, is more complex. The etymology of the term *ou-topia* meaning literally 'no-place' or 'nowhere', connotes a place difficult to identify. However, utopian texts from classical antiquity show a willingness to locate these descriptions on the map of the ancient Greek world, as illustrated by Plato's description of *Atlantis*.[10] Thus, most texts containing descriptions of utopia seem to be set in a geographical area, even if the given area does not correspond precisely to any tangible reality. Such descriptions are set in a *topos* to be found between reality and fiction.[11] Utopia therefore exists primarily in the space provided by the text;[12] but beyond considerations of place and time, the most defining characteristic of a utopia is the ambiguous relationship between the reality of the text and the now in which the text is placed.

A utopian description is characterized by the form of reality proposed to the readers as an alternative reality better[13] than that of the text's author or community. This better reality takes the form of an ideal society or, beyond the concept of society, an ideal state or disposition preferable to the current experience. Similarly, according to Ben Zvi, 'the terms utopia and utopian . . . do not simply refer to constructions of circumstances that stand in time and/or space separate from, and are simply "better" than the present but to imagined circumstances whose main attribute is that they fulfil the horizon of the best imaginable state of affairs within a particular community or sets of communities and, as a result, are perceived by them as unrealizable within their usual course of events'.[14] This definition will be preferred in the discussion below.

---

7. E. Ben Zvi, 'Utopias, Multiple Utopias, and Why Utopias at All? The Social Roles of Utopian Visions in Prophetic Books within Their Historical Context', in *Utopia and Dystopia in Prophetic Literature*, ed. E. Ben Zvi (Helsinki: Finnish Exegetical Society; Göttingen: Vandenhoeck & Ruprecht, 2006), 55.

8. There are divergent opinions on this position. See especially Schweitzer's argument, *Reading Utopia in Chronicles*, 21–23 ; and Sargent, 'The Three Faces', 5.

9. Schweitzer, 'Utopia and Utopian Literary Theory', 22; F. Vieira, 'The Concept of Utopia', in *The Cambridge Companion to Utopian Literature*, ed. G. Claeys (Cambridge University Press, 2010), 9.

10. Ferguson, *Utopias of the Classical World*, 122–23; Schweitzer, 'Utopia and Utopian Literary Theory', 21.

11. Vieira, 'The Concept of Utopia', 8.

12. Schweitzer, *Reading Utopia in Chronicles*, 15.

13. Cf. Schweitzer, 'Utopia and Utopian Literary Theory', 16, who speaks of 'a better alternative reality'.

14. Ben Zvi, 'Utopias', 56.

In theory, utopian discourse could describe an ideal state as taking place in the progression of present time in the world of the text, taking due consideration of the models of representation for the targeted audience, but with external conditions constituting an obstacle. The realization of the described ideal is compromised by sociopolitical factors that must be challenged.[15] In that type of context, utopian descriptions reveal specific ideological or political tensions out of which an author constructs an alternative reality, which then overcomes the shortcomings experienced; that type of representation can therefore be read as a form of social critique.[16] By virtue of making real an alternative reality in the space created by the text, a utopian text becomes an important channel of hope for the group[17] which, typically from a social position of subordination,[18] produces and receives the text and, through its reading, is empowered to experience the alternative reality.

A utopian description is therefore determined by several specific characteristics. It describes an ideal state closer to a possibility than to a certainty. At the same time, a utopian description finds its source in a reality determined by a specific context, even though its form could lead to the rejection of the present time and of history.[19]

8.3 *Prophetic Collection and Psalm: Which Dialectic Relationship?*

The present analysis proposes an approach to the Book of Habakkuk, and more particularly the psalm that concludes it, which uses the theoretical concept of utopia. At first sight, however, the content of the psalm does not seem to subscribe to the specific criteria of the concept.

The theophany described in the hymn is generally read and interpreted as an eschatological representation of a divine intervention, foretold by the prophet, which takes place in a distant future far removed from the 'I' of the text. If that reading of the psalm is upheld, the divine intervention described in the psalm is not in a dialectic relation with the prophetic collection or the present of the reader. However, different aspects of the text could challenge this eschatological reading of Habakkuk's psalm; and there is a residual ambivalence about how the psalm should be read because of its *Sitz im Buch*.[20] Two literary clues in particular might lead us to read the psalm within the continuity of the prophetic collection and in the present tense of the prophetic figure as either a consequence of or an alternative to the events described, and thus not necessarily as an event set in an

---

15. Schweitzer, 'Utopia and Utopian Literary Theory', 19.

16. Schweitzer, *Reading Utopia in Chronicles*, 18; Ben Zvi, 'Utopias', 56–57.

17. Ben Zvi, 'Utopias', 57–59.

18. A. Touraine, 'Society as Utopia', in *Utopia*, ed. R. Schaer, 18–31 (26).

19. Vieira, 'The Concept of Utopia', 9; Sargent, 'Authority and Utopia', 581.

20. On this issue, see G. T. M. Prinsloo, 'Reading Habakkuk as a Literary Unit: Exploring the Possibilities', *Old Testament Essays* 12 (1999): 515–35.

undetermined future. The description of a utopia that might exist in the present of the reader would differ from an eschatology, which would be more likely to fit within the future of the text's recipient.[21]

The first element that calls for a rethinking of the temporality of the divine intervention in the psalm is the prophetic figure whose name (חֲבַקּוּק) and title (הַנָּבִיא) appear in the title of the prophetic collection (1.1) as well as in the title of the psalm (3.1). The prophetic figure runs through the composition as a whole and makes it possible to combine the two literary units of the book. The mention of the prophet's name in the title of the psalm makes it possible, from a literary point of view, to connect the divine intervention both with the prophetic collection and to the events told by the prophets with regard to the sending of the Chaldeans. In other words, the prophetic figure functions as a key for reading the divine intervention (cf. 3.16b), which thus sustains a dialectic relationship with the prophetic collection and the temporality of the prophet.

The second clue that supports a joint reading of the two units of the book of Habakkuk is the concluding verse of the prophetic collection וַיהוָה בְּהֵיכַל קָדְשׁוֹ הַס מִפָּנָיו כָּל־הָאָרֶץ ('Yhwh is in his holy temple. Let all the earth be silent before him', 2.20). This verse is decisive for the interpretation of the psalm because it combines both textual units.[22] First, the conjunction ו before Yhwh can be translated as 'but' because of the problematic of idolatry that comes before. Habakkuk 2.20 thus functions as the conclusion to the five doom oracles (2.5-19) while simultaneously being linked to the psalm. The formulation בְּהֵיכַל קָדְשׁוֹ associated with Yhwh is in effect only found in psalms and hymns.[23] The order to be silent that closes the prophetic collection, הַס מִפָּנָיו כָּל־הָאָרֶץ, seems equally intended to prepare for the reading of the theophanic psalm. The same injunction is also found in Zeph. 1.7 and Zech. 2.17, where in both instances the injunction to be silent is followed by an event that vindicates the order. In the context of Zephaniah, the order is followed by a divine intervention which takes the form of a sacrifice. In the context of Zechariah, it is followed by a manifestation of Yhwh and His being on the move. In both cases the order to be silent given by the prophet acts as a prelude to a divine act of redemption. Thus, in the context of the book of Habakkuk, the injunction to silence that closes the prophetic collection – without the direct complement in v. 20 – also serves as a prelude to Yhwh's act of being on the move described in the psalm.

An ambivalence thence becomes apparent on the most appropriate way of reading both the composition of Habakkuk as a whole and the psalm in particular within its literary context. More specifically, when the literary evidence just summarized is used to establish a connection between the psalm and the circumstances of the Babylonian invasion as well as the oracles of doom uttered by the prophet, the timing of Yhwh's intervention no longer seems to be set in an

21. Schweitzer, *Reading Utopia in Chronicles*, 15–16.
22. Prinsloo, 'Life for the Righteous', 628.
23. Jon. 2.5, 8; Mic. 1.2; Psalm 5; 11; 79; 138.

uncertain future but rather in something akin to an alternative present to that of the prophet and, by extension, with the use of the prophetic 'I', to that of the readers. However, if the psalm of Habakkuk seems to construct an alternative reality, does it necessarily imply a utopian reading?

8.4 *The Psalm of Habakkuk and the Concept of Utopia*

A first reading of the book of Habakkuk leads one to notice that the narrative is constructed within abstract temporal and spatial dimensions. In the first place, the two titles (1.1; 3.1) that dictate the reading of the book do not provide any indication for the dating of a specific reign or regarding the biography of the prophet. Across the 56 verses of the book as a whole, the only indication which makes it possible to situate Habakkuk's text is the reference to Yhwh's punitive sending of the Chaldeans in 1.6. The final redaction of the text presumes that the reader had sufficient knowledge of the Chaldeans' role as well as the historical and ideological impact of their invasion.

The spatial location of the prophetic figure and the place where events take place are similarly uncertain. Judah and Jerusalem are never mentioned. The prophet's location must be deduced by using knowledge available in other prophetic books as well as the events surrounding the coming of the Chaldeans. Once again, it is the reader's presumed knowledge that allows for the deduction of the Jerusalem-centred position of this description.

The uncertainty around the narrative's temporality continues into the psalm, which contains neither a temporal marker nor the mention of any specific enemy. The only element of continuity between the prophetic collection and the hymn is, as we have seen, the prophetic figure that appears only in the title of the psalm and the 'I' of the text (3.2, 16, 18-19). The additional formal element that the psalm contributes to the temporality of the divine intervention is the interchangeable use of the *yiqtol* and of the *qatal* to describe divine action.[24] The successive use of those two tenses is evident both in v. 3 and in v. 6.[25] The consequent ambiguity makes it difficult to situate the divine intervention in the timeline of the prophetic 'I' and leads one to read the psalm's temporal context of reference as a form of gnomic present.

---

24. Andersen, *Habakkuk*, 263–64; Hiebert, *God of My Victory*, 77–79.

25. E.g., in v. 3, the verb that announces the arrival of Yhwh is in *yiqtol* יָבוֹא, which might situate the divine intervention either in the present or in a future close to the time of the prophetic figurehead. Yet the same announcement is supported in the rest of the verse by a series of statements in *qatal* that enunciate several general truths on the greatness of Yhwh and which point to processes in the present and the future. The ambiguity extends to the rest of the hymn, as in the beginning of v. 6 where a *qatal* is used for the first active verb in relation to the action of Yhwh.

Beyond the temporal and spatial aspects of the text, uncertainty persists with regard to the identity of the addressees of the prophet's initial denunciation.[26] What is he denouncing in 1.2-4? Injustices that are somehow related to the invasion of the Chaldeans, or social injustice that developed over time within the community? The latter suggestion seems the more plausible since the sending of the Chaldeans is only mentioned in 1.6, introduced by the formula כִּי־הִנְנִי. In keeping with classic models of prophetic literature, the shortcomings within the community (1.4) would thus be the reason for Yhwh's decision to send a ruthless enemy as the instrument of his wrath, in order to restore moral order in the community. Therefore, the collection's opening serves as a social critique clearly articulated by the prophetic figure.

The assumed injustice is, as just noted, denounced by the prophetic figure, who cannot accept this situation of suffering (1.12-17). Proceeding from that critique, the text seems to establish a contrast between the fate of the wicked (רָשָׁע), represented by the Chaldeans, and the fate of the just (צַדִּיק), represented by the prophetic figure. This alternation continues into the remainder of the prophetic collection with the assertion וְצַדִּיק בֶּאֱמוּנָתוֹ יִחְיֶה ('The just will live by their faithfulness', 2.4), in contrast to the 'proud' (2.5), whose fate is, in a way, described in the five oracles of doom (2.6-19). These 'proud', in fact, could be associated with the 'wicked' of the five oracles and as such could describe members of the community just as well as they do the Chaldeans.[27] Strikingly, apart from the assertion in 2.4, the fate set aside for the 'just' victims of the injustices enunciated in the prophet's initial lamentation in 1.2-4 is never mentioned in the prophetic collection; the first two chapters of the book are exclusively dedicated to denouncing the wrongs of the wicked and announcing his demise (see the five oracles of doom in 2.5-19). Therefore, it is ch. 3 that would fulfil the programmatic function of constructing an alternative reality better than the one described in the first two chapters.

All the failures described in the book's first chapter are resolved in the psalm (ch. 3) thanks to the divine intervention of Yhwh who in a constructed set-up re-establishes a situation of justice and salvation for the prophet (3.13a, 18) by destroying the unnamed enemy seen as the cause of the social injustices. Various elements of the text make it possible to consider the prophet

---

26. Sweeney, 'Structure, Genre, and Intent in the Book of Habakkuk', 66–67, 77; Prinsloo, 'Reading Habakkuk as a Literary Unit', 520–21.

27. Achenbach raises the hypothesis of a rewriting of the oracles of doom in ch. 2 during the Achaemenid period. According to him, the principles of wisdom in Ancient Israelite law were rewritten and developed from the perspective of international justice, thus bringing Babylon to mind; see Achenbach, 'The Transformation of Measures for Social Justice into Measures for International Law in the Book of Habakkuk', *Zeitschrift für Altorientalische und Biblische Rechtsgeschichte* 18 (2012): 263–78. See also Wöhrle, *Der Abschluss des Zwölfprophetenbuches*, 291–311 who sees two distinct important steps (the "Fromme-Frevler-Schicht" and the "Babylonier-Schicht") in the assumed redactional history of the book of Habakkuk.

as the representative of the community of the 'just', a role made particularly evident by the use of pronouns. While the prophetic 'I' is the main voice of the psalm, it is noticeable in two passages that it is no longer the prophet who takes centre stage but rather the people: in 3.13, יָצָאתָ לְיֵשַׁע עַמֶּךָ ('you go forth for the salvation of your people'), the people include the prophet, as confirmed in the words of 3.18, אָגִילָה בֵּאלֹהֵי יִשְׁעִי ('I rejoice because of the God of my salvation'). The second clue for the prophet's inclusion within the community he represents is in verse 16b where a pronoun in the first person plural is found next to the verb 'attack/invade': אָנוּחַ לְיוֹם צָרָה לַעֲלוֹת לְעַם יְגוּדֶנּוּ 'I will find rest when the day of distress will befall the people who invade *us*'. In this latter instance, the prophet and the community are gathered together.

The psalm of Habakkuk would therefore develop an alternative reality that describes an ideal. This ideal takes the form of a military intervention by Yhwh which brings about the deliverance of part of the community, namely the 'just' for whom the prophet speaks. That same group, who consider themselves to be the oppressed 'just', opposes the רָשָׁע ('wicked') – note the opposition in 3.13 between עַמֶּךָ and מְבֵּית רָשָׁע – whose identity remains hidden and should not be hastily considered to be only the Chaldeans.[28] The text never clearly establishes a parallel between the רָשָׁע and the Chaldeans of ch. 1 v. 6; indeed, the ambiguity surrounding the antagonists' identity runs through the entirety of the work. The five oracles of doom, for instance, have this ambiguity as their foundation; they can be read either as a condemnation of one part of the community – if one reads only the introductory verse of every oracle in the third person – or against Babylon if the body of the text is read in the second person.[29] The text's ambiguity on the identity of רָשָׁע, the 'wicked', may in fact be deliberate. Is it the ultimate fate of the Babylonians that would interest a readership in the Persian era, or that of the 'wicked'? The issue of justice within the community seems to concern the readership more directly than the fate of Babylon, which they know to have fallen. Therefore, the announcement of the fall of Babylon could symbolize the fate reserved for the רָשָׁע, the 'wicked', and would give legitimacy to the authority of the prophet while equally fulfilling a didactic function.

From the perspective of experienced injustice, be it internal to the community, external or both, the psalm stages a detailed divine intervention and its impact upon the 'enemy' as well as the 'wicked'. This alternative reality could resolve the cognitive dissonance[30] of the two first chapters, which stems from the contradiction between the representation of Yhwh as a creating (1.12) and mighty (1.14) God, and that of the people as living in a bad and unjust environment of which Babylon – an incarnation of evil and lawlessness – is the figurehead. In this alternative reality, Yhwh is portrayed as the mighty warrior who can restore world order. The description of Yhwh's intervention is in opposition to the rise of evil

---

28. Prinsloo, 'Life for the Righteous', 637.
29. Achenbach, 'The Transformation of Measures', 269–70.
30. On this issue, see Ben Zvi, 'Utopias', 63, 82–83.

and the enemy (3.16), and results in the deliverance of the 'just', embodied by the prophetic figure Habakkuk. The internal logic of the narrative seeks to prove that just as Babylon had fallen (a historical fact known to the Persian-era readership), the perpetrators of social injustice will similarly be punished. In the meantime, the psalm proposes a better alternative reality marked by the deliverance of the suffering people; in that reality, the 'wicked' are destroyed and a new state can be established instead of the desolation that surrounds the prophet (3.17). Verse 17, which describes the agrarian desolation that confronts the prophet, highlights the difference between the tragic situation in which the prophet and his people find themselves, and the ideal situation that would result from Yhwh's intervention. Therefore, the book of Habakkuk could be credited with a didactic goal of seeking to illustrate the principle and logic of Yhwh's justice by bringing to life a better alternative reality in the psalm through its recitation.

8.5 *Conclusion*

The divine intervention described in the psalm could be qualified as an alternative reality from the perspective of Habakkuk 1–2 for the following reasons. First of all, the intervention takes place in a deliberately ambiguous time and spatial location; it is located *ou-topia*, that is to say independently of any reality experienced by the reader. The only reality of this ideal representation, a theophany, exists in the text where it takes place and, by extension, given the text's literary form, in the voice of those who recite the psalm. By carefully describing the divine intervention expected in the initial lament of the prophet (1.2-4), who becomes the voice of the suffering 'just', the psalm constructs a detailed alternative reality better than oppression by the 'wicked' whoever that might be. In this alternative reality of the psalm, the identity of the 'wicked' – who fall in the face of the divine attack (3.13) – is deliberately unspecified, offering to the reader the freedom to make this open reality their own, given the reality they are faced with.

The hymnic genre of Habakkuk 3 itself has potential to contribute to the process of materializing an alternative reality that may have been brought to life at the time of reading. The hymnic components present in the psalm – the title in v. 1, the subtitle in v. 19b, the musical accompaniment in v. 19b and *selah* in vv. 3, 9, and 13 – are in themselves certainly not evidence of a liturgical use of the psalm; but they could fulfil a liturgical function in the narrative. The shape of the psalm could make it possible to locate the prophet and his community along with the readers within a form of scriptural liturgy at the time of its reading.

That kind of representation could therefore contribute to a form of social cohesion both by offering a space for expression and by raising in the reader, through the process of reading, the hope of identifying themselves with the prophet and the community of the 'just' that he represents. Through reading and praying the psalm, its readership would share an ultimate alternative reality, salvation as a result of divine manifestation, a reality disclosed by the authority of the prophet Habakkuk and, through his prophetic voice, by Yhwh himself. Through the voice of the prophetic 'I', therefore, and in a moment of prayer, the reader's community could actualize its own experience of this better alternative reality.

Bibliography

Achenbach. 'The Transformation of Measures for Social Justice into Measures for International Law in the Book of Habakkuk'. *Zeitschrift für Altorientalische und Biblische Rechtsgeschichte* 18 (2012): 263–78.

Andersen, F. I. *Habakkuk: A New Translation with Introduction and Commentary*. AB 25. New York: Doubleday, 2001.

Berge, K. 'Literacy, Utopia and Memory: Is There a Public Teaching in Deuteronomy?'. *Journal of Hebrew Scriptures*, 12, no. 3 (2012): 1–19.

Boda, M. J., et al. 'In Conversation with Steven Schweitzer, *Reading Utopia in Chronicles* (LHBOTS, 442; London: T&T Clark International, 2007)', *Journal of Hebrew Scriptures* 9 (2009): 1–19.

Cataldo, J. 'Whispered Utopia: Dreams, Agendas, and Theocratic Aspirations in Yehud'. *SJOT* 24 (2010): 53–70.

Claeys, G., ed. *The Cambridge Companion to Utopian Literature*. Cambridge: Cambridge University Press, 2010.

Cleaver-Bartholomew, D. 'An Alternative Approach to Hab 1,2–2,20'. *SJOT* 17 (2003): 206–25.

Dangl, O. 'Habakkuk in Recent Research'. *CRBS* 9 (2001): 131–68.

Dogniez, C. 'La Version Barberini: Éléments pour une étude littéraire d'un autre texte Grec d'Habacuc 3'. In *Die Septuaginta – Entstehung, Sprache, Geschichte*, edited by S. Kreuzer et al., WUNT 286; 295–310. Tübingen: Mohr Siebeck, 2012.

Fabry, H. J. 'The Reception of Nahum and Habakkuk in the Septuagint and Qumran'. In *Emanuel: Studies in Hebrew Bible, Septuagint, and Dead Sea Scrolls in Honor of Emanuel Tov*, edited by S. M. Paul et al., VTSup 94; 241–56. Leiden: Brill, 2003.

Ferguson, J. *Utopias of the Classical World*. Aspects of Greek and Roman Life. London: Thames and Hudson, 1975.

Floyd, M. H. 'Prophecy and Writing in Habakkuk 2,1–5'. *ZAW* 105 (1994): 462–81.

Good, E. M. 'The Barberini Greek Version of Habakkuk III'. *VT* 9 (1959): 29.

Haak, R. D. *Habakkuk*. VTSup 44. Leiden; New York: E. J. Brill, 1992.

Hiebert, T. *God of My Victory: The Ancient Hymn in 'Habakkuk 3'*. HSM 38. Atlanta: Scholars Press, 1986.

Huwyler, B. 'Habakuk und seine Psalmen'. In *Prophetie und Psalmen: Festschrift für Klaus Seybold zum 65. Geburtstag*. AOAT 280; 231–59. Münster: Ugarit-Verlag, 20019.

Lescow, T. 'Die Komposition der Bücher Nahum und Habakuk'. *BN* 77 (1995): 59–85.

Levitas, R. *The Concept of Utopia*. London: P. Allan, 1990.

Manuel, F. E.,ed. *Utopias and Utopian Thought*. Beacon Paperback, 251. Boston: Beacon Press, 1967.

Nogalski, J. *Redactional Processes in the Book of the Twelve*. BZAW 218. Berlin and New York: W. de Gruyter, 1993.

Perlitt, L. *Die Propheten Nahum, Habakuk, Zephanja*. ATD 25/1. Göttingen: Vandenhoeck & Ruprecht, 2004.

Prinsloo, G. T. M. 'Reading Habakkuk as a Literary Unit: Exploring the Possibilities'. *OTE* 12 (1999): 515–35.

Prinsloo, G. T. M. 'Life for the Righteous, Doom for the Wicked: Reading Habakkuk from
    a Wisdom Perspective'. *Skrif en kerk* 21 (2000), 621–40.
Prinsloo, G. T. M. 'Reading Habakkuk 3 in the Light of Ancient Unit Delimiters'. *HTS
    Teologiese Studies* 69, no. 1 (2013): Art. no. 1975, 11 pages. http://dx.doi.org/10.4102/
    hts.v69i1.1975.
Sargent, L. T. 'Authority & Utopia: Utopianism in Political Thought'. *Polity* 14
    (1982): 565–84.
Sargent, L. T. 'The Three Faces of Utopianism Revisited'. *Utopian Studies* 5 (1994): 1–37.
Schaer, R., ed. *Utopia: The Search for the Ideal Society in the Western World.* New York;
    Oxford: The New York Public Library; Oxford University Press, 2000.
Schweitzer, S. J. 'Utopia and Utopian Literary Theory: Some Preliminary Observations'.
    In *Utopia and Dystopia in Prophetic Literature*, edited by E. Ben Zvi, 13–26. Helsinki;
    Göttingen: Finnish Exegetical Society; Vandenhoeck & Ruprecht, 2006.
Schweitzer, S. J. *Reading Utopia in Chronicles.* Library of Hebrew Bible/Old Testament
    Studies. New York; London: T&T Clark, 2007.
Seybold, K. *Nahum, Habakuk, Zephanja.* Zürcher Bibelkommentare. AT 24,2.
    Zürich: Theologischer Verlag, 1991.
Sweeney, M. A. 'Structure, Genre, and Intent in the Book of Habakkuk'. *VT* 41
    (1991): 63–83.
Thompson, M. E. 'Prayer Oracle and Theophany: The Book of Habakkuk'. *TynBul* 44
    (1993): 33–53.
Touraine, A. 'Society as Utopia'. In *Utopia*, edited by R. Schaer, 18–31.
Vieira, F. 'The Concept of Utopia'. In *The Cambridge Companion to Utopian Literature*,
    edited by G. Claeys (Cambridge University Press, 2010).
Witte, M. 'Orakel und Gebete im Buch Habakuk'. In *Orakel und Gebete: interdisziplinäre
    Studien zur Sprache der Religion in Ägypten, Vorderasien und Griechenland in
    hellenistischer Zeit*, edited by M. Witte and J. F. Diehl. FAT 67–91. Tübingen: Mohr
    Siebeck, 2009.
Wöhrle, Jakob. *Der Abschluss des Zwölfprophetenbuches: Buchübergreifende
    Redaktionsprozesse in den Späten Sammlungen.* BZAW 389. Berlin: W. de
    Gruyter, 2008.
Zvi, E. Ben, ed. *Utopia and Dystopia in Prophetic Literature.* Publications of the
    Finnish Exegetical Society, 92. Helsinki: Göttingen: The Finnish Exegetical Society;
    Vandenhoeck & Ruprecht, 2006.
Zvi, E. Ben. 'Utopias, Multiple Utopias, and Why Utopias at All? The Social Roles of
    Utopian Visions in Prophetic Books within Their Historical Context'. In *Utopia
    and Dystopia in Prophetic Literature*, edited by Ehud Ben Zvi, 55–85. Helsinki;
    Göttingen: Finnish Exegetical Society; Vandenhoeck & Ruprecht, 2006.

Part II

SOCIAL-SCIENTIFIC PERSPECTIVES ON THE DEAD SEA
SCROLLS AND EARLY CHRISTIAN LITERATURE

Chapter 9

THE SOCIAL SCIENCES AND THE DEAD SEA SCROLLS

George J. Brooke

The complete, or nearly complete, publication of all the scrolls and scroll fragments from the wilderness of Judea, especially the eleven caves at and near Qumran, has heralded a new era in the study of the Dead Sea Scrolls. For those scrolls from the Qumran caves, the availability of such a large range of information has resulted in the fragmentation of the scholarly study of the scrolls so that there are several sub-disciplines with their own sets of expertise, such as language studies, literary studies, historical studies and so on – and each of those specialisms has generated sub-specialisms. Alongside such scholarly specialization it has become all the more urgent that some kind of synthesis should be offered to permit a diachronic survey of the materials from the caves and the people responsible for them. Such a survey would also need to take into account the wider contemporary cultural context.

The aim of this study is to argue that such a synthesis can only be securely accomplished if it is undertaken not just through the application of the set standards of ancient historiography and textual analysis but also with the assistance of the full range of the social sciences. This essay will survey swiftly some of the applications of the study of the social sciences to the study of the Dead Sea Scrolls. From this survey I hope to draw out some conclusions about the positive and negative effects of the use of the social sciences, so that the historical synthesis of all the material from the eleven Qumran caves might be described and assessed within a methodological framework that is fully aware of its limitations as well as its advantages.

Many modern universities have faculties, schools or departments where the social sciences are studied and applied. The make-up of such collected academic disciplines varies from institution to institution, though commonly five sub-disciplines are normally found among the social sciences: sociology, anthropology, psychology, politics and economics. Commonly others are included or those five sub-disciplines are further subdivided in various ways.[1]

---

1. At the University of Manchester, for historical reasons, Philosophy is included in the School of Social Sciences along with Social Statistics (indicating the quantitative approach

Let us consider briefly the five core social sciences, recalling that they often have substantial overlapping concerns.

9.1 *Sociology*

A recent search for 'sociology' in the titles of articles and books as entered on the Orion Bibliography database produces just a dozen titles since 1996, three written by David Chalcraft and one by Philip Davies,[2] contributors to the colloquium of which the present volume is a result. But enter the word 'sect' and nearly three hundred results appear and the term 'social' produces nearly one hundred entries. Such data are problematic because included, for example, are multiple reviews of books, any one of which might have the relevant term in its title. Nevertheless, it is possible to discern a couple of points. First, the serious use of sociology as a discipline for the study of the scrolls from the Qumran caves has been somewhat limited. It seems to be the case, not surprisingly, that a very particular concern of the sociology of religion, namely sectarianism, has cornered the market. Second, it is noteworthy that many studies are aware of the need for taking into account the social dimension or social settings of the texts being analysed, even if they do not always engage very profoundly with any particular aspect of social theory. It seems as if social history is still largely written on the basis of traditional historiographical assumptions, rather than in relation to any specialist social scientific model.

So what more might be said? First, it is important to note that in some respects the scrolls from the eleven caves at and near Qumran have provided students of the ancient world with the best historical test case that they could have for the assessment of the insights of the recent study of religious sects, at least if 'sect' is defined quite broadly. To have a location that was clearly inhabited and capable of archaeological investigation, as well as classical authors who seem to describe the same movement, even with one of them (Pliny the Elder) possibly describing the very location of Qumran itself, together with the fragmentary scrolls themselves,

---

to social science), whereas Psychology is to be found as a School in the Faculty of Medical and Human Sciences.

2. David J. Chalcraft, 'The Development of Weber's Sociology of Sects: Encouraging a New Fascination' and 'Towards a Weberian Sociology of the Qumran Sects', both in *Sectarianism in Early Judaism: Sociological Advances*, ed. David J. Chalcraft, Bible World (London: Equinox, 2007), 26–51 and 74–105 respectively; Chalcraft, 'Is a Historical Comparative Sociology of (Ancient Jewish) Sects Possible?' in *Sects and Sectarianism in Jewish History*, ed. Sacha Stern, IJS Studies in Judaica 12 (Leiden: Brill, 2011), 235–86. Philip R. Davies, 'Sects from Texts: On the Problems of Doing a Sociology of the Qumran Literature', in *New Directions in Qumran Studies: Proceedings of the Bristol Colloquium on the Dead Sea Scrolls, 8–10 September 2003*, ed. Jonathan G. Campbell, W. John Lyons and Lloyd K. Pietersen, LSTS 52 (London: T&T Clark International, 2005), 26–42.

seems too good to be true. Indeed some scholars have thought it too good to be true and have tried to disconnect the site from the scrolls,[3] while others are still very uncertain about associating the collectors of the scrolls with some subgroup of the Essenes as described by the classical authors.[4] However, if the scrolls are accepted as an integral part of the archaeological finds from the Qumran site and its immediate environs, then the likelihood of interpreting them apart is greatly reduced. And if the Essenes are recognized as a pluriform movement, then it is somewhat unnecessary to insist on a straightforward or consistent overlapping of the evidence from the scrolls and that from the classical authors.[5]

Second, one possible way of proceeding with the application of the sociology of sectarianism to the Qumran group and the scrolls it collected is through comparative analysis with other groups that might be understood as having some similar characteristics. The major example of such an approach is the study by Eyal Regev.[6] Regev has attempted to present a cross-cultural survey which makes comparisons in antiquity between the groups behind the sectarian scrolls, the traditions preserved in 1 Enoch, the reform movement represented by the Book of Jubilees, and introversionist Essenism; then Regev also makes comparisons with more recent movements, notably the Anabaptists, the Mennonites, the Hutterites, the Amish, the Puritans, the Quakers and the Shakers. The basis of the comparison is Regev's preliminary conclusion that the Qumran group are a type of introversionist sect and so it is with similarly defined introversionist groups that he makes his comparisons. Whether further historical study of the scrolls and the movement that collected them will support a preliminary definition of the movement as introvertionist waits to be seen; increasingly it is becoming clear that the Qumran subgroup was part of a wider movement which more often than not seems to have been engaged with the world around it whether in terms of calendars or medicine or communal organization or commentary on authoritative scriptures. There is a cultural pluralism about the evidence that strongly suggests that any sociological model will need considerable nuance when applied to the movement as a whole or its constituent parts.

3. See, e.g. Yitzhak Magen and Yuval Peleg, *The Qumran Excavations 1993–2004 Preliminary Report* (Jerusalem: Israel Antiquities Authority, 2007).

4. See, e.g. Martin Goodman, 'The Qumran Sectarians and the Temple in Jerusalem', in *The Dead Sea Scrolls: Texts and Context*, ed. Charlotte Hempel, STDJ 90 (Leiden: Brill, 2010), 263–73; Steve Mason, 'The Historical Problem of the Essenes', in *Celebrating the Dead Sea Scrolls: A Canadian Collection*, ed. Peter W. Flint, Jean Duhaime and Kyung S. Baek, SBLEJL 30 (Atlanta: SBL, 2011), 201–51.

5. On the logic of the various arguments see Edna Ullmann-Margalit, *Out of the Cave: A Philosophical Inquiry into the Dead Sea Scrolls Research* (Cambridge: Harvard University Press, 2006).

6. Eyal Regev, *Sectarianism in Qumran: A Cross-Cultural Perspective*, Religion and Society, 45 (Berlin: de Gruyter, 2007).

And in this area a third matter has arisen which has been helpfully addressed by several scholars. This matter is a concern for trying to appreciate the terminology of the texts with much greater subtlety than scholars of a generation ago.[7] Part of the need for the refinement of the use of the terminology has arisen because the archaeologists of the Qumran site have become increasingly convinced that little or nothing of sectarian habitation belongs to the time before the second quarter of the first century BCE. If compositions such as the Rule of the Community belong to the end of the second or beginning of the first century BCE, then the group that is referred to as the *yaḥad* in the Rule cannot be precisely co-terminous with the Qumran community.[8] Furthermore, there has to be much more subtlety about whether those who did eventually occupy the Qumran site were central or marginal in the movement of which they were a part.[9]

Fourth, it is indeed the plural character of the evidence that makes the application of any one sociological theory or model difficult, but which also opens up the possibility for the enhanced understanding of what is actually taking place diachronically. This has resulted in the recognition that Bryan Wilson's typological categories of sectarian identity should not be reified but refined as models of thinking, as he himself also refined them during his career, through application to specific texts and the groups that possibly lay behind them. What has begun to emerge is the discerning of multiple identities within the movement associated with the sectarian compositions. I have argued for this in the founding stages of the movement variously associated with the so-called Teacher.[10] Others, especially Jutta Jokiranta, have argued for it at other stages in the life of the movement.[11]

---

7. An early exception is the oft-cited study by Carol Newsom, '"Sectually Explicit" Literature from Qumran', in *The Hebrew Bible and Its Interpreters*, ed. William H. Propp, Baruch Halpern and David Noel Freedman, Biblical and Judaic Studies from the University of California, San Diego 1 (Winona Lake: Eisenbrauns, 1990), 167–87.

8. See, e.g. John J. Collins, *Beyond the Qumran Community: The Sectarian Movement of the Dead Sea Scrolls* (Grand Rapids: Eerdmans, 2010).

9. See the helpful contributions by Alison Schofield, *From Qumran to the Yaḥad: A New Paradigm of Textual Development for the Community Rule*, STDJ 77 (Leiden: Brill, 2009).

10. George J. Brooke, 'The "Apocalyptic" Community, the Matrix of the Teacher and Rewriting Scripture', in *Authoritative Scriptures in Ancient Judaism*, ed. Mladen Popović, JSJSup 141 (Leiden: Brill, 2010), 37–53.

11. Jutta Jokiranta, 'Sociological Approaches to Qumran Sectarianism', in *The Oxford Handbook of the Dead Sea Scrolls*, ed. Timothy H. Lim and John J. Collins (Oxford: Oxford University Press, 2010), 200–31; Jokiranta, *Social Identity and Sectarianism in the Qumran Movement*, STDJ 105 (Leiden: Brill, 2013). Jokiranta's bibliographies are particularly useful resources and her own studies are insightful initial attempts at the responsible application of various sociological theories to these ancient texts; see especially her warnings in '"Sectarianism" of the Qumran "Sect": Sociological Notes', *Revue de Qumrân* 20/78 (2001): 223–40.

Fifth, in fact the discussion of the groups behind the so-called sectarian compositions has moved beyond the consideration of the sociology of sectarianism towards the description of the identities of the groups behind the scrolls, sometimes through the application of various identity theories.[12] There is not room to cover them all here. By way of example there are some initial and not altogether convincing applications of sociolinguistics to discern in-group ideology.[13] Others have wondered about deviance theory to explain why someone might join a minority group.[14] Some have suggested the usefulness of labelling theory for how the self and other are constructed.[15] Perhaps more significantly there has been a move to uncover the status, value and purpose of the textually constructed individual, perhaps not surprisingly often beginning the discussion with the 'I' of the Hodayot, the Thanksgiving Hymns. Carol Newsom has led the way by reflecting on the social implications of rhetorical criticism to talk of the self, a discussion she has more recently set in the wider context of Second Temple times.[16] Angela Kim Harkins has reconsidered the religious experience of the hymnists, a matter that has overlaps with the concerns of anthropology and psychology.[17] Trine Hasselbalch has used

12. A start was made in this direction in Florentino García Martínez and Mladen Popović, eds, *Defining Identities: We, You, and the Other in the Dead Sea Scrolls: Proceedings of the Fifth Meeting of the IOQS in Groningen*, STDJ 70 (Leiden: Brill, 2008).

13. See William M. Schniedewind, 'Qumran Hebrew as an Antilanguage', *JBL* 118 (1999): 235–52; Schniedewind, 'Linguistic Ideology in Qumran Hebrew', in *Diggers at the Well: Proceedings of a Third International Symposium on the Hebrew of the Dead Sea Scrolls and Ben Sira*, ed. Takamitsu Muraoka and John F. Elwolde, STDJ 36 (Leiden: Brill, 2000), 245–55. Cf. Gary A. Rendsburg, 'Qumran Hebrew (With a Trial Cut [1QS])', in *The Dead Sea Scrolls at 60: Scholarly Contributions of New York University Faculty and Alumni*, ed. Lawrence H. Schiffman and Shani Tzoref, STDJ 89 (Leiden: Brill, 2010), 217–46.

14. George J. Brooke, 'Justifying Deviance: The Place of Scripture in Converting to a Qumran Self-Understanding', in *Reading the Present in the Qumran Library: The Perception of the Contemporary by Means of Scriptural Interpretation*, ed. Kristin De Troyer and Armin Lange, SBL Symposium Series 30 (Atlanta: SBL, 2005), 73–87; Lloyd K. Pietersen, ' "False Teaching, Lying Tongues and Deceitful Lips" (4Q169 frgs 3-4 2.8)', in *New Directions in Qumran Studies: Proceedings of the Bristol Colloquium on the Dead Sea Scrolls, 8-10 September 2003*, ed. Jonathan G. Campbell, W. John Lyons and Lloyd K. Pietersen, LSTS 52 (London: T&T Clark International, 2005), 166–81.

15. Matthew A. Collins, *The Use of Sobriquets in the Qumran Dead Sea Scrolls*, LSTS 67 (London: T&T Clark, 2009), esp. 197–201.

16. Carol A. Newsom, *The Self as Symbolic Space: Constructing Identity and Community at Qumran*, STDJ 52 (Leiden: Brill, 2004); Newsom, 'Models of the Moral Self: Hebrew Bible and Second Temple Judaism', *JBL* 131 (2012): 5–25.

17. Angela Kim Harkins, *Reading with an "I" to the Heavens: Looking at the Qumran Hodayot through the Lens of Visionary Traditions*, Ekstasis 3 (Berlin: de Gruyter, 2012).

sociolinguistics to identify the hybrid nature of the individual constructed by the Hodayot.[18]

9.2 Anthropology[19]

Some study was undertaken relatively early on in the history of Qumran research on the anthropological categories that might be used in the sectarian compositions, reflecting a particular way of looking at what it was to be human from the sectarian perspective.[20] Most of the further discussion of such anthropology has been undertaken from a theological perspective, commonly as part of the history of ideas rather than as a matter of cultural anthropology. This has often been directed at assisting in the better understanding of the anthropology of New Testament writers.[21] Nevertheless, there have been some particular insights for the texts from Qumran in their own right, such as the analysis of physiognomy.[22]

More recently, four aspects of anthropology have come to the fore in Qumran studies. The first is a growing industry concerned with gender that is slowly changing direction. What has been a somewhat tardy reflection of second wave

---

18. Trine Bjørnung Hasselbalch, *Meaning and Context in the Thanskgiving Hymns: Linguistic and Rhetorical Perspectives on a Collection of Prayers from Qumran*, SBLEJL 42 (Atlanta: SBL Press, 2015).

19. The kind of specifically religious topics that might be covered here are listed by Fiona Bowie, *The Anthropology of Religion: An Introduction* (Oxford: Blackwell Publishers, 2000): the body, boundaries and identity, gender, environment, ritual and rite, shamanism and witchcraft.

20. E.g., Hermann Lichtenberger, *Studien zum Menschenbild in Texten der Qumrangemeinde*, SUNT 15 (Göttingen: Vandenhoeck & Ruprecht, 1980).

21. See, e.g. Friedrich Avemarie, 'Image of God and Image of Christ: Developments in Pauline and Ancient Jewish Anthropology', in *The Dead Sea Scrolls and Pauline Literature*, ed. Jean-Sébastien Rey, STDJ 102 (Leiden: Brill, 2014), 209–35; George H. van Kooten, *Paul's Anthropology in Context: The Image of God, Assimilation to God, and Tripartite Man in Ancient Judaism, Ancient Philosophy and Early Christianity*, WUNT 232 (Tübingen: Mohr Siebeck, 2008); Jörg Frey, 'Flesh and Spirit in the Palestinian Jewish Sapiential Tradition and in the Qumran Texts: An Inquiry into the Background of Pauline Usage', in *The Wisdom Texts from Qumran and the Development of Sapiential Thought*, ed. Charlotte Hempel, Armin Lange and Hermann Lichtenberger, BETL 159 (Leuven: Peeters/University Press, 2002), 367–404.

22. See, e.g. Mladen Popović, *Reading the Human Body: Physiognomics and Astrology in the Dead Sea Scrolls and Hellenistic-Early Roman Period Judaism*, STDJ 67 (Leiden: Brill, 2007). It is a pity that Johanna H. W. Dorman, *The Blemished Body: Deformity and Disability in the Qumran Scrolls* (Groningen: Groningen University Press, 2007), barely uses any modern sociological or anthropological theory as she describes the various texts concerned with her topic.

feminism in Dead Sea Scroll studies, the study of women and their roles in antiquity,[23] is moving towards a more inclusive gender studies approach in which issues concerning both women and men are taken seriously, such as the masculine concern with perfection and the way in which purity issues affect both men and women.[24]

The second aspect belongs to the realm of cultural anthropology and involves the study of rite and ritual.[25] After some insightful comments by Rob Kugler,[26] Russell Arnold has most intensively applied the insights of Catherine Bell[27] to the Qumran liturgical texts.[28] John Collins has also underlined the place of liturgy. He has considered whether the insights of Frits Staal might be applied to the Qumran materials.[29] Staal argued for the 'Meaninglessness of Ritual', by which he meant that ritual is activity governed by rules: 'What is essential in the ceremony is the precise and faultless execution, in accordance with rules, of numerous rites and recitations'.[30] Participants might assign meaning to such ceremonies occasionally,

23. See the helpful survey and bibliography in Tal Ilan, 'Women in Qumran and the Dead Sea Scrolls', in *The Oxford Handbook of the Dead Sea Scrolls*, ed. Timothy H. Lim and John J. Collins (Oxford: Oxford University Press, 2010), 123–47.

24. And there might even be a move beyond 'patriarchy': see Carol Myers, 'Was Ancient Israel a Patriarchal Society?', *JBL* 133 (2014): 8–27. On a concern with gender that prioritizes masculinist approaches, see Jessica M. Keady, *Vulnerability and Valour: A Gendered Analysis of Everyday Life in the Dead Sea Scrolls Communities*, LSTS 91 (London: Bloomsbury T&T Clark, 2017).

25. There is room in the study of the Dead Sea Scrolls for an introductory survey work such as Richard E. DeMaris, *The New Testament in its Ritual World* (Abingdon: Routledge, 2008), on entry rites and exit rites.

26. Robert A. Kugler, 'Making All Experience Religious: The Hegemony of Ritual at Qumran', *JSJ* 33 (2002): 131–52.

27. See Catherine M. Bell, *Ritual Theory, Ritual Practice* (New York: Oxford University Press, 1992); Bell, *Ritual: Perspectives and Dimensions* (New York: Oxford University Press, 1997). Yet to be applied to the Dead Sea Scrolls in any detailed way are the significant categories of Roy A Rappaport, *Ritual and Religion in the Making of Humanity*, Cambridge Studies in Social and Cultural Anthropology (Cambridge: Cambridge University Press, 1999).

28. Russell C. D. Arnold, *The Social Role of Liturgy in the Religion of the Qumran Community*, STDJ 60 (Leiden: Brill, 2006); Arnold, 'The Dead Sea Scrolls, Qumran and Ritual Studies', in *The Dead Sea Scrolls in Context: Integrating the Dead Sea Scrolls in the Study of Ancient Texts, Languages and Cultures*, ed. Armin Lange, Emanuel Tov and Matthias Weigold, VTSup 140 (Leiden: Brill, 2011), 547–62.

29. John J. Collins, 'Prayer and the Meaning of Ritual in the Dead Sea Scrolls', in *Prayer and Poetry in the Dead Sea Scrolls and Related Literature: Essays in Honor of Eileen Schuller on the Occasion of Her 65th Birthday*, ed. Jeremy Penner, Ken M. Penner and Cecilia Wassen, STDJ 98 (Leiden: Brill, 2012), 69–85.

30. Frits Staal, 'The Meaninglessness of Ritual', *Numen* 26 (1979): 2–22.

but such attempts at meaning are not a necessary dimension of ritual. In his assessment of the rituals described in the Dead Sea Scrolls Collins finds Staal's proposal lacking. For Collins, ritual in the communities of the scrolls 'constituted a *habitus*, an enactment of the world as it ought to be, characterized by obedience to what was believed to be divine law, as interpreted and amplified by the priestly leaders of the community, and by purity, which entailed separating from the outside world. It ensured community cohesion, by requiring that members eat together, bless together, and take counsel together. At the same time it implemented the hierarchical structure of the community. The common prayers, with texts standardized in writing, were part of this process, and articulate aspects of its meaning. They contributed to the sanctification of the whole life of the *yaḥad*, but it was that whole life, rather than any specific rituals or prayers, that was thought to be the effective replacement of the temple cult'.[31]

A significant corollary of the study of liturgy and prayer in the Dead Sea Scrolls has been the attention paid to the liturgical context of the production and performative use of texts. Some extremely valuable observations on the material culture of prayer texts have been made by Daniel Falk.[32] In addition, in relation to the prayer texts themselves, some significant study has been undertaken on the scripturalization of prayer, that is, on how the practice of prayer is an ongoing reflection of how authoritative texts are internalized and have their authority endorsed, even being reworked in the process.[33] The very use of scripture can be understood as being the source for the system of symbols that are distinctively and variously applied in the forming of community identity.[34]

Third, also of interest are the signs that the concept of liminality might be of significance for the better understanding of the groups reflected in the compositions from the Qumran caves.[35] It has become apparent that it is no longer

---

31. Collins, 'Prayer and the Meaning of Ritual in the Dead Sea Scrolls', 84–85.

32. Daniel K. Falk, 'Material Aspects of Prayer Manuscripts at Qumran', in *Literature or Liturgy? Early Christian Hymns and Prayers in their Literary and Liturgical Context in Antiquity*, ed. Clemens Leonhard and Hermut Löhr, WUNT 2/363 (Tübingen: Mohr Siebeck, 2014), 33–88. While there has been extensive description of the physical remains of the scrolls and their writing, as in the work of Emanuel Tov, *Scribal Practices and Approaches Reflected in the Texts Found in the Judean Desert*, STDJ 54 (Leiden: Brill, 2004), there has yet to be careful description of the physical remains in terms of material culture, namely how the use of texts effected their production.

33. See Judith H. Newman, *Praying by the Book: The Scripturalization of Prayer in Second Temple Judaism*, SBLEJL 14 (Atlanta: Scholars Press, 1999).

34. Note the use of the insights of Clifford Geertz on religion as a set of symbols by Maxine L. Grossman, 'Cultivating Identity: Textual Virtuosity and "Insider" Status', in *Defining Identities: We, You, and the Other in the Dead Sea Scrolls: Proceedings of the Fifth Meeting of the IOQS in Groningen*, ed. Florentino García Martínez and Mladen Popović, STDJ 70 (Leiden: Brill, 2008), 1–11.

35. The concept was developed by Arnold van Gennep, *Les rites de passage* (Paris: Nourry, 1908) to describe the central moments of rituals through which an initiate moved from

obvious how the location of the sectarian movement should be conceptualized. It has been commonly assumed that the community at Qumran in particular had taken itself away from mainline society and imposed upon itself a marginalization that withdrawal from the temple made significant. Although there have been scholarly voices that have tried to claim just the opposite for the movement,[36] the social and geographical location of the movement and its subgroups is now understood in more complex ways.[37] Liminality is an overarching category that can also cope with matters of assimilation and acculturation.

Liminality has both spatial and temporal dimensions.[38] Victor Turner concluded from his ethnographic work that the concept of liminality was helpful in describing a temporary state for relatively small groups in which normal social structures are set aside. In a brief study I have proposed that the sectarians used their understanding of prophecy to suggest how they might move through their temporary state of exile and wilderness towards a hopeful reoccupation of Jerusalem.[39] Indeed, although there is a problem in giving the location of Qumran too much significance, nevertheless it is possible to consider the site as itself liminal, just within the land and yet still looking at Mount Nebo and its Moses who did not enter.[40]

Fourth, all three items discussed so far impinge especially on the discussion of purity and impurity, ritual and otherwise. No summary discussion of such issues in the Dead Sea Scrolls is possible nowadays without reference to the work of Mary Douglas.[41] Not only did her work influence fundamentally the presentation

---

separation and 'death' to postliminal rites of incorporation, or new being. Victor Turner, *The Forest of Symbols: Aspects of Ndembu Ritual* (Ithaca: Cornell University Press, 1967), applied the concept beyond ritual.

36. Most famously Hartmut Stegemann, 'The Qumran Essenes: Local Members of the Main Jewish Union in Late Second Temple Times', in *The Madrid Qumran Congress: Proceedings of the International Congress on the Dead Sea Scrolls, Madrid 18–21 March 1991*, ed. J. Trebolle Barrera and L. Vegas Montaner, STDJ 11 (Leiden: Brill/Madrid: Universidad Complutense, 1993), 83–166.

37. See, e.g. Alison Schofield, 'Between Center and Periphery: The *Yaḥad* in Context', *DSD* 16 (2009): 330–50.

38. Being on the boundaries between heaven and earth, especially in times of communal prayer could also be analysed through various notions of liminality or the liminoid.

39. George J. Brooke, 'The Place of Prophecy in Coming out of Exile: The Case of the Dead Sea Scrolls', in *Scripture in Transition: Essays on Septuagint, Hebrew Bible, and Dead Sea Scrolls in Honour of Raija Sollamo*, ed. Anssi Voitila and Jutta Jokiranta, JSJSup 126 (Leiden: Brill, 2008), 535–50.

40. Cf. George J. Brooke, 'Moses in the Dead Sea Scrolls: Looking at Mount Nebo from Qumran', in *La Construction de la figure de Moïse/The Construction of the Figure of Moses*, ed. Thomas Römer; Supplément à *Transeuphratène* 13 (Paris: Gabalda, 2007), 209–21.

41. Mary Douglas, *Purity and Danger: An Analysis of the Concepts of Pollution and Taboo* (London: Routledge and Kegan Paul, 1966).

of matters of purity in ancient Israel,[42] but her particular study of scriptural dietary laws lies behind much modern discussion of early Jewish meal practice. The institutional and wider cultural role of food as depicted in the Dead Sea Scrolls has yet to be investigated fully. Purity is not exclusively a priestly concern, but it is not surprising that in a movement where priestly interests are strongly represented, having everything in its right state in its right place runs through much of the halakhic material extant in the collection. The hierarchy envisaged in the eschatological meal described in the Rule of the Congregation (1QSa) is in part a reflection of ensuring that everything and everybody is rightly ordered and placed.

9.3 *Psychology*

In a brief survey of this kind it is only possible to make some broad general observations about the place of psychology in the study of the Dead Sea Scrolls. For the most part the concerns of psychology and especially of social psychology have played little explicit role in the appreciation of the content of the scrolls or of the communities and individuals behind them. To some extent this is not surprising since the place of the individual, the dominant concern of psychology and especially of psychoanalysis, in late Second Temple Judaism in Palestine was certainly somewhat other than it is in Western society today. It is also not surprising since the sub-discipline of Psychological Biblical Studies is a relative newcomer, feeling its own way: 'psychological biblical criticism is not a method. It is a way of reading the biblical text that is sensitive to the psychological factors that may be at play'.[43] Not surprisingly this kind of approach tries to reconstruct what people might have done either through regular habit or at some key moments; it glimpses 'the interaction of psychological factors, especially unconscious factors, in shaping both internal and external behavior',[44] inasmuch as those can be discerned in the close reading of texts and the imaginatively controlled recreation of their social environments. In all this, as Walter Brueggemann has noted, 'there is a danger, in

---

42. See, e.g. Jonathan Klawans, 'Purity in the Dead Sea Scrolls', in *The Oxford Handbook of the Dead Sea Scrolls*, 377–402. Klawans describes the influence of Douglas on both Jacob Neusner and Jacob Milgrom.

43. D. Andrew Kille, 'Psychology and Biblical Studies', in *The New Interpreter's Dictionary of the Bible, Me–R, Volume 4*, ed. Karen D. Sakenfeld et al. (Nashville: Abingdon Press, 2009), 684–85 (684). On the numerous possibilities of reading strategies opened up by psychological sensitivity to scriptural (and other) texts see the wide range of essays in Harold J. Ellens and Wayne G. Rollins, eds, *Psychology and the Bible: A New Way to Read the Scriptures*, 4 vols (Westport: Praeger, 2004).

44. The concise definition of psychodynamics provided by D. Andrew Kille and Wayne G. Rollins, eds, *Psychological Insight into the Bible: Texts and Readings* (Grand Rapids: Eerdmans, 2007), 271.

the eclectic enterprise of psychological criticism, to impose a psychological theory on the text in a way that overrides the specificity of the text itself and distorts the text in order to serve the theory that an interpreter may advocate'.[45]

There have been some attempts at considering the mindset of the community member. In general these have depended upon reading between the lines and locating any discernible world view within the theological parameters implied by the texts themselves, especially the sectarian ones. For example, some have given attention to the individual's engagement with the life of the movement. In a notable study on how someone might pragmatically negotiate between determinism and free will, Philip Alexander has rehearsed the problem of living in such tension but noted that it rarely impinges on an individual's everyday choices.[46] Or again, the self-understanding of a community member has been considered through the study of the term *ndb*, indicating that members thought of themselves as freely engaging with their obligations as community members.[47] In a more focussed manner the mystical experience of community members has been discerned, though usually in traditional theological terms rather than in relation to the study of the frame of mind or emotional intelligence of the community member.[48]

Among the most significant attempts at psychological profiling are the works of two scholars. Carol Newsom has moved beyond her application of Marxist-based literary theory to self-understanding in the sectarian scrolls,[49] and she has begun to engage with how best to understand individual religious experience and self-motivation.[50] Angela Kim Harkins has focussed on 'creating an embodied

45. Walter Brueggemann, 'Psychological Criticism: Exploring the Self in the Text', in *Method Matters: Essays on the Interpretation of the Hebrew Bible in Honor of David L. Petersen*, ed. J. M. LeMon and Kent H. Richards; SBL Resources for Biblical Study 56 (Atlanta: SBL, 2009), 213–32 (215).

46. Philip S. Alexander, 'Predestination and Free Will in the Theology of the Dead Sea Scrolls', in *Divine and Human Agency in Paul and His Cultural Environment*, ed. John M. G. Barclay and Simon J. Gathercole, LNTS 335 (London: T&T Clark, 2006), 27–49.

47. Devorah Dimant, 'The Volunteers in the Rule of the Community: A Biblical Notion in Sectarian Garb', *RevQ* 23/2 (2007): 233–45; reprinted in Dimant, *History, Ideology and Bible Interpretation in the Dead Sea Scrolls*, FAT 90 (Tübingen: Mohr Siebeck, 2014), 289–300.

48. The insights of Thomas Kazen, *Emotions in Biblical Law: A Cognitive Science Approach*, Hebrew Bible Monographs 36 (Sheffield: Sheffield Phoenix Press, 2011), have yet to be applied to the Scrolls.

49. Newsom, *The Self as Symbolic Space*.

50. Newsom, 'Models of the Moral Self', 5–25; Newsom, 'Religious Experience in the Dead Sea Scrolls: Two Case Studies', in *Experientia Volume 2: Linking Texts and Experience*, ed. Colleen Shantz and Rodney A. Werline, SBLEJL 35 (Atlanta: SBL, 2012), 205–21; Newsom, 'Flesh, Spirit, and the Indigenous Psychology of the Hodayot', in *Prayer and Poetry in the Dead Sea Scrolls and Related Literature: Essays in Honor of Eileen Schuller on the Occasion of Her 65th Birthday*, ed. Jeremy Penner, Ken M. Penner and Cecilia Wassen, STDJ 98 (Leiden: Brill, 2012), 339–54.

subjectivity for religious experience' and has combined several methodologies, mixing some insights from ritual studies, the study of the place of emotions and spatial theory (movement from first space to third space with attention to the insights of neuropsychology) in order to appreciate better how the performance of texts from the Hodayot (especially in its arrangement as in 4Q428) is reflective of visionary experience and entry into the heavens, made apparent through the textualization of exegetical frames of reference.[51]

In a more limited fashion I myself have tried to apply a basic Freudian model to the understanding of various textual features of the pesharim in order to try to illuminate the affective significance of the texts. Members of a Jewish movement dominated by priestly concerns and looking towards Jerusalem must have had to cope with the loss of regular participation in temple worship, loss which was probably both spiritually challenging and the source of a sense of grief not unlike that expressed in the book of Lamentations.[52] Guided by Hugh Pyper's psychodynamic analysis of Lamentations,[53] I have attempted to outline the triangular aspect of the silent God, the abused mother (Jerusalem and its Temple) and the self-justifying sons (the community members) as reflected especially in the pesharim.[54] The question remains concerning what kind of mental state was most suitable for community membership.

In addition to such approaches, the widespread interest in memory, which has a psychological dimension to it, also deserves a mention. In fact, not much has been written on the role of memory within the sectarian movement behind some of the scrolls, but there are notable items by Loren Stuckenbruck who highlights how the Teacher was remembered, even memorialized, and by Ben Wold who engages with the vocabulary of remembering in the scrolls.[55] As for the role of memory in the production and transmission of texts, whether sectarian or not, some tentative comments are made in an essay of mine which

---

51. Harkins, *Reading with an "I" to the Heavens*.

52. On the Durkheimian question 'Why do things move people?' in relation to the temple in Jerusalem see the study by Stephen C. Barton, 'Why Do Things Move People? The Jerusalem Temple as Emotional Repository', *JSNT* 37 (2015): 351–80; the insights in the study could readily be transferred to the study of the scrolls.

53. Hugh S. Pyper, *An Unsuitable Book: The Bible as Scandalous Text* (Sheffield: Sheffield Phoenix Press, 2005), 89–101.

54. George J. Brooke, *Reading the Dead Sea Scrolls: Essays in Method*, SBLEJL 39 (Atlanta, GA: SBL, 2013), 151–73.

55. Loren T. Stuckenbruck, 'The Teacher of Righteousness Remembered: From Fragmentary Sources to Collective Memory in the Dead Sea Scrolls', in *Memory in the Bible and Antiquity: The Fifth Durham-Tübingen Research Symposium (Durham, September 2004)*, ed. Stephen Barton, Loren T. Stuckenbruck and Benjamin G. Wold, WUNT 212 (Tübingen: Mohr Siebeck, 2007), 75–94; Benjamin G. Wold, 'Memory in the Dead Sea Scrolls: Exodus, Creation and Cosmos', in *Memory in the Bible and Antiquity*, 47–74.

tries to juxtapose the workings of any individual memory with those of cultural or collective memory.[56]

9.4 *Politics*

The politics of the scrolls have generally been described and discussed in terms of political history rather than political theory. That history has either been concerned with the relationship of the wider movement behind the collection of the scrolls and the Hasmoneans, Herodians and Romans, or concerned with the characteristics of the various elite groups present in late Second Temple period Judean Judaism. For the former, it is often noted that there is little explicit mention of the political leaders of the time and that the most that can be done is a sketch of a series of figures or incidents as those can be gleaned or discerned between the lines of various fragmentary compositions.[57] Such political history tends to focus on the history of elite leaders and those around them. For the latter, the political character of the movement behind the various sectarian compositions has most often been considered in relation to the widespread institution of voluntary associations in Hellenistic antiquity.[58]

Beyond the role of the historical model of the voluntary association, it is regularly pointed out that the communities of several of the sectarian compositions are institutionally strictly hierarchical. This is most well known from the Rule of the Congregation (1QSa) where the particular roles suitable to each age group are laid out and the eschatological meal is described with all members in their ranked order.

Political matters might also include the following. First, the construction of institutions can belong with the sociologists, but the standard models for community organization in the Scrolls are largely political: the twelve tribes

---

56. George J. Brooke, 'Memory, Cultural Memory and Rewriting Scripture', in *Rewritten Bible after Fifty Years: Texts, Terms, or Techniques? A Last Dialogue with Geza Vermes*, ed. József Zsellengér, JSJSup 166 (Leiden: Brill, 2014), 119–36; reprinted in Brooke, *Reading the Dead Sea Scrolls*, 51–65.

57. Such sketches are provided, e.g. by Hanan Eshel, *The Dead Sea Scrolls and the Hasmonean State*, Studies in the Dead Sea Scrolls and Related Literature (Grand Rapids: Eerdmans; Jerusalem: Yad Ben-Zvi Press, 2008).

58. Among the secondary literature, the studies most commonly referred to are Moshe Weinfeld, *The Organizational Pattern and the Penal Code of the Qumran Sect*, NTOA 2 (Göttingen: Vandenhoeck & Ruprecht; Fribourg: Éditions Universitaires, 1986); and Matthias Klinghardt, 'The Manual of Discipline in the Light of Statutes of Hellenistic Associations', in *Methods of Investigation of the Dead Sea Scrolls and the Khirbet Qumran Site: Present Realities and Future Prospects*, ed. Michael O. Wise, Norman Golb, John J. Collins and Dennis G. Pardee; Annals of the New York Academy of Sciences 722 (New York: The New York Academy of Sciences, 1994), 251–70.

(Temple Scroll), Israel at Sinai (*yaḥad*; Exod. 19.8), the priesthood (Sons of Zadok) and the military (1000s, 100s, 50s, 10s); fictive kinship models are present only in a limited way (notably in the use of the term 'brother'), though there is one mention of Fathers and Mothers (4Q270 7 i,13–14). Second, there is the nature of kingship; this was evidently much debated in the Hellenistic period and the scrolls have things to say about this political institution which limit its human actualization (cf. the so-called Law of the King in the Temple Scroll: 11Q19 56–59), and that seem to transfer the notion of sovereignty almost entirely to God, such as is apparent in the Songs of the Sabbath Sacrifice, with hints of the messianic representation of that divine sovereignty, as in Eschatological Commentary A (4Q174). Third, there are matters to do with resistance, both violent and non-violent.[59] Some aspects of violence are as much a matter of social anthropology as they are of politics.[60]

In addition, the dominant features of the ethnic construction of politics in the eastern Hellenistic Mediterranean of the three centuries before the fall of the Jerusalem temple in 70 CE had to do with (1) the make-up and identity of the ethnos, (2) the mother city of that ethnos and its institutions, together with the delimitation of the wider region governed from that polis, (3) the practice of a particular cult and (4) a set of behavioural features which non-members could recognize as marks of identity; for the Judean ethnos those would include circumcision, certain dietary practices and the observance of the Sabbath. It is clear that the non-scriptural scrolls, both sectarian and non-sectarian compositions, have things to say on all four political matters. Put briefly, the sectarian ethnic construction was especially exclusive, restricted to the sons of Shem (over against the descendants of Japhet or Ham) or understood as restricted to Israel narrowly defined in sectarian terms. The city at the centre of attention was Jerusalem; even if some members of the sectarian movement had withdrawn from the city, their aspiration was to return there with divine favour – Jerusalem is the place name most common in the scrolls.[61] The cult and its priesthood are the focus of

59. See Loren L. Johns, 'Identity and Resistance: The Varieties of Competing Models in Early Judaism', in *Qumran Studies: New Approaches, New Questions*, ed. Michael T. Davis and Brent A. Strawn (Grand Rapids: Eerdmans, 2007), 254–77. Apocalypticism can be discussed under this heading.

60. See, e.g. Alex P. Jassen, 'Violent Imaginaries and Practical Violence in the *War Scroll*', in *The* War Scroll, *Violence, War and Peace in the Dead Sea Scrolls and Related Literature: Essays in Honour of Martin G. Abegg, Jr. on the Occasion of His 65th Birthday*, ed. Kipp Davis, Dorothy M. Peters, Kyung S. Baek and Peter W. Flint, STDJ 115 (Leiden: Brill, 2016), 175–203; Jassen works with the insights of Ingo W. Schröder and Bettina E. Schmidt, 'Introduction: Violent Imaginaries and Violent Practices', in *Anthropology of Violence and Conflict*, ed. Bettina E. Schmidt and Ingo W. Schröder (London: Routledge, 2001), 1–24.

61. See George J. Brooke, 'Moving Mountains: From Sinai to Jerusalem', in *The Significance of Sinai: Traditions about Divine Revelation in Judaism and Christianity*, ed. George J. Brooke, Hindy Najman and Loren T. Stuckenbruck, TBN 12 (Leiden: Brill, 2008), 73–89.

several key sectarian compositions, such as Miqsat Ma'aseh ha-Torah which sets out various halakhic decisions concerning the city, the cult and its priests. And among the standard ethnic marks of behaviour, more than one composition has concern for the keeping of the Sabbath in a strict fashion. Nevertheless, despite the presence of all those features, what they have to say has not yet been discussed and analysed in any thoroughgoing way in the light of modern political theories as applied to other ancient political systems.

9.5 *Economics*

The Damascus Document boldly claims that alongside profanation of the temple and fornication 'wealth' is one of the three nets of Belial. The application of the discipline of economics to the better understanding of what is taking place in the communities behind the sectarian scrolls has been very limited.[62] In her very lengthy study of wealth, the definitive resource to consult as a starting point, Catherine Murphy has argued that the sectarian symbolic world of radical covenant fidelity makes every economic transaction an application of Torah.[63] She has described her method as socio-historical; it does not depend on any kind of modelling based upon economic theory as might be applicable to the kind of local agrarian subsistence present in the Levant at the time with many also experiencing in good times the networks of trade that were well established for various goods, both luxury and everyday.

Three matters can be briefly stated. First, there has been some attempt at reconstructing those small groups where poverty in any local context might be addressed, particularly through some application of common ownership, at least in terms of usufruct. Here much has depended upon word study and historical imagination, not least in relation to the classical reports in the writings of Philo and Josephus on the Essenes. Chief among such commentators has been Brian Capper.[64] In several different studies Capper has been concerned to describe and

---

62. It would be good to see, e.g. the application of the ideas on 'Ancient Economy' provided by John Stambaugh and David Balch, *The Social World of the First Christians* (London: SPCK, 1986), 63–81; or reflection on debt as in Douglas E. Oakman, 'Jesus and Agrarian Palestine: The Factor of Debt', in *The Social World of the New Testament: Insights and Models*, ed. Jerome H. Neyrey and Eric C. Stewart (Peabody: Hendrickson, 2008), 63–82.

63. Catherine M. Murphy, *Wealth in the Dead Sea Scrolls and in the Qumran Community*, STDJ 40 (Leiden: Brill, 2002).

64. See, e.g. Brian J. Capper, 'The Palestinian Cultural Context of the Earliest Christian Community of Goods', in *The Book of Acts in Its Palestinian Setting*, ed. Richard J. Bauckham; the Book of Acts in its First Century Setting 4 (Grand Rapids: Eerdmans, 1995), 323–56; Capper, 'Essene Community Houses and Jesus' Early Community', in *Jesus and Archaeology*, ed. James H. Charlesworth (Grand Rapids: Eerdmans, 2006), 472–502; Capper, 'Jesus, Biblical Covenant, and the Essene New Covenant of Ancient Judaea: On the Origins of the Early Christian Familial Economic Covenant', *Qumran Chronicle* 19/1–2 (2011): 1–30.

reconstruct how some kind of system of shared goods might actually have worked, especially across networks of small communities based around small groups of families. Capper has offered many feasible ideas and in some ways offers indirect explanation for why someone might wish to join a system of mutual support, but the evidence upon which he bases his reconstructions is notoriously difficult to pin down.

Second, the identity of the 'poor' in several texts, notably Instruction and the Commentary on Psalms A, has been a matter of wide discussion.[65] For example, the discussion by Benjamin Wright of the categories of rich and poor in Instruction concludes that the designation was not just for literary effect, but reflects actual poverty.[66] For Wright, much of the economic teaching in Instruction is based in harsh social realities and is aimed at trying to assist the impoverished student of wisdom from falling further into abject poverty or even risking indentured servitude. But Wright also wonders whether the designation 'poor' and the extensive concern with poverty in a work like Instruction offers an ideal to be upheld. Such seems to be reflected in a passage he cites: 'Do not esteem yourself highly in your poverty when you are anyway a pauper, lest you bring into contempt your own way of life' (4Q416 2 ii 20–21). The student is not to bring the life of poverty into disrepute. For Eibert Tichelaar, however, the teaching on poverty in Instruction is addressed to those who might possibly one day find themselves in poverty but are probably not at the moment when they receive instruction, and might never be.[67]

Third, there are a few examples of the application of some precise aspects of economic theory to the study of the Scrolls. One intriguing instance is Alex Jassen's attempt to appreciate the dynamics of spoken violence in the sectarian Scrolls through the use of 'scarce resources theory' (Thomas Malthus) as applied to religion by Hector Avalos.[68]

65. It is a pity that Gary A. Anderson's book, *Charity: The Place of the Poor in the Biblical Tradition* (New Haven: Yale University Press, 2013), which offers many insights about attitudes to poverty in the Second Temple period and beyond, is more about those with substance to share; it actually says nothing about the topic of the poor as depicted in the Dead Sea Scrolls.

66. Benjamin G. Wright III, 'The Categories of Rich and Poor in the Qumran Sapiential Literature', in *Sapiential Perspectives: Wisdom Literature in Light of the Dead Sea Scrolls. Proceedings of the Sixth International Symposium of the Orion Center for the Study of the Dead Sea Scrolls and Associated Literature, 20–22 May, 2001*, ed. John J. Collins, Gregory E. Sterling and Ruth A. Clements, STDJ 51 (Leiden: Brill, 2004), 101–23.

67. Eibert J. C. Tigchelaar, 'The Addressees of 4QInstruction', in *Sapiential, Liturgical and Poetical Texts from Qumran: Proceedings of the Third Meeting of the International Organization for Qumran Studies*, ed. Daniel K. Falk, Florentino García Martínez and Eileen M. Schuller, STDJ 35 (Leiden: Brill, 2000), 62–75.

68. Alex P. Jassen, 'The Dead Sea Scrolls and Violence: Sectarian Formation and Eschatological Imagination', *Biblical Interpretation* 17 (2009): 12–44; working with Hector Avalos, *Fighting Words: The Origins of Religious Violence* (Amherst: Prometheus, 2005).

9.6 *Conclusion*

There is much more that could be pointed out and noted. Overall, the application of the social sciences to the study of the Dead Sea Scrolls has been very selective and rather piecemeal. Only a few scholars have shown themselves to be experts, and they have contributed greatly. Where does this all too brief overview lead us? What have the social sciences as organized under five traditional categories offered to the better appreciation of the Dead Sea Scrolls? In most respects the answers are obvious, but they are worth stating briefly both to encourage modern readers of ancient texts to become more aware of what the social sciences can contribute but also to warn against any naïve use and abuse of the social sciences.

Positively, first and foremost, the social sciences offer students of the Dead Sea Scrolls numerous sets of questions and varieties of models to apply for the better understanding of the texts and the communities behind them. At their best such questions and models assist in the avoidance of unjustified or false reconstructions. In the hands of those who have studied them in their own right, the social scientific models cannot be used to fill gaps in the evidence that scholars yearn to fill, but to provide some coherence where it often seems out of reach. Second, the social sciences offer etic categories that enable the modern reader to engage empathetically with materials that often seem distant and inaccessible; the social sciences encourage the translation of the ancient world. At their best the social sciences reflect aspects of common humanity contextualized in multiple places and manners. When carefully applied they can indicate both what is in common with and what different from the experiences of others. Third, the social sciences do not model only what is contained in the observable moment but they also take into account change and development, place and transition; sensitivity in such things is much needed to aid in the understanding of the vagaries of textual transmission and the varieties of group formation and types of leadership in the movement behind the scrolls. All scholars of the Dead Sea Scrolls need the help of the social sciences and in many instances, as indicated in this study, they have been used creatively and insightfully; they have provoked new readings of ancient texts and new understandings of ancient situations. A few of the social sciences have dominated the discussion, especially the sociology of sectariansim; as a result, there is room for many more studies that take seriously the theoretical insights of the full range of the social sciences.

Negatively, first, the social sciences are based, for the most part, on recent or contemporary observations. The application of such modern theorized observations to the past and to a different cultural landscape risks anachronism and unsuitable analogy. Second, in addition, the general tendency in the social sciences is an assumption of universal human experience, so the particular is acknowledged as part of a wider whole, before being fully understood in its own terms. Without due care, the emphasis in the application of any social scientific theory is to highlight similarities and downplay differences. Third, this tendency towards universal concerns sometimes seems to result in overgeneralisation, so that the subtleties of individual compositions and their very specific wordings are sometimes lost; there is yet room for the textual exegete. Fourth, the social science concern towards generalisation sometimes seems to underplay the significance of specific historical circumstances and contexts; there is yet room for the historian and for the controlled historical imagination.

Bibliography

Alexander, Philip S. 'Predestination and Free Will in the Theology of the Dead Sea Scrolls'. In *Divine and Human Agency in Paul and His Cultural Environment*, edited by John M. G. Barclay and Simon J. Gathercole. LNTS 335; 27–49. London: T&T Clark, 2006.

Anderson, Gary A. *Charity: The Place of the Poor in the Biblical Tradition*. New Haven: Yale University Press, 2013.

Arnold, Russell C. D. *The Social Role of Liturgy in the Religion of the Qumran Community*. STDJ 60. Leiden: Brill, 2006.

Arnold, Russell C. D. 'The Dead Sea Scrolls, Qumran and Ritual Studies'. In *The Dead Sea Scrolls in Context: Integrating the Dead Sea Scrolls in the Study of Ancient Texts, Languages and Cultures*, edited by Armin Lange, Emanuel Tov and Matthias Weigold. VTSup 140; 547–62. Leiden: Brill, 2011.

Avalos, Hector. *Fighting Words: The Origins of Religious Violence*. Amherst: Prometheus, 2005.

Avemarie, Friedrich. 'Image of God and Image of Christ: Developments in Pauline and Ancient Jewish Anthropology'. In *The Dead Sea Scrolls and Pauline Literature*, edited by Jean-Sébastien Rey. STDJ 102; 209–35. Leiden: Brill, 2014.

Barton, Stephen C. 'Why Do Things Move People? The Jerusalem Temple as Emotional Repository'. JSNT 37 (2015): 351–80.

Bell, Catherine M. *Ritual Theory, Ritual Practice*. New York: Oxford University Press, 1992.

Bell, Catherine M. *Ritual: Perspectives and Dimensions*. New York: Oxford University Press, 1997.

Bowie, Fiona. *The Anthropology of Religion: An Introduction*. Oxford: Blackwell Publishers, 2000.

Brooke, George J. 'Justifying Deviance: The Place of Scripture in Converting to a Qumran Self-Understanding'. In *Reading the Present in the Qumran Library: The Perception of the Contemporary by Means of Scriptural Interpretation*, edited by Kristin De Troyer and Armin Lange. SBL Symposium Series 30; 73–87. Atlanta: SBL, 2005.

Brooke, George J. 'Moses in the Dead Sea Scrolls: Looking at Mount Nebo from Qumran'. In *La Construction de la figure de Moïse/The Construction of the Figure of Moses*, edited by Thomas Römer. Supplément à *Transeuphratène* 13; 209–21. Paris: Gabalda, 2007.

Brooke, George J. 'The Place of Prophecy in Coming out of Exile: The Case of the Dead Sea Scrolls'. In *Scripture in Transition: Essays on Septuagint, Hebrew Bible, and Dead Sea Scrolls in Honour of Raija Sollamo*, edited by Anssi Voitila and Jutta Jokiranta. JSJSup 126; 535–50. Leiden: Brill, 2008.

Brooke, George J. 'Moving Mountains: From Sinai to Jerusalem'. In *The Significance of Sinai: Traditions about Divine Revelation in Judaism and Christianity*, edited by George J. Brooke, Hindy Najman and Loren T. Stuckenbruck. TBN 12; 73–89. Leiden: Brill, 2008.

Brooke, George J. 'The "Apocalyptic" Community, the Matrix of the Teacher and Rewriting Scripture'. In *Authoritative Scriptures in Ancient Judaism*, edited by Mladen Popović. JSJSup 141; 37–53. Leiden: Brill, 2010.

Brooke, George J. 'Memory, Cultural Memory and Rewriting Scripture'. In *Reading the Dead Sea Scrolls: Essays in Method*; SBLEJL 39; 51–65. Atlanta: SBL, 2013.

Brooke, George J. *Reading the Dead Sea Scrolls: Essays in Method*. SBLEJL 39. Atlanta: SBL, 2013.

Brooke, George J. 'Memory, Cultural Memory and Rewriting Scripture'. In *Rewritten Bible after Fifty Years: Texts, Terms, or Techniques? A Last Dialogue with Geza Vermes*, edited by József Zsellengér. JSJSup 166; 119–36. Leiden: Brill, 2014.

Brueggemann, Walter. 'Psychological Criticism: Exploring the Self in the Text'. In *Method Matters: Essays on the Interpretation of the Hebrew Bible in Honor of David L. Petersen*, edited by J. M. LeMon and Kent H. Richards. SBL Resources for Biblical Study 56; 213–32. Atlanta: SBL, 2009.

Capper, Brian J. 'The Palestinian Cultural Context of the Earliest Christian Community of Goods'. In *The Book of Acts in Its Palestinian Setting*, edited by Richard J. Bauckham. the Book of Acts in its First Century Setting 4; 323–56. Grand Rapids: Eerdmans, 1995.

Capper, Brian J. 'Essene Community Houses and Jesus' Early Community'. In *Jesus and Archaeology*, edited by James H. Charlesworth; 472–502. Grand Rapids: Eerdmans, 2006.

Capper, Brian J. 'Jesus, Biblical Covenant, and the Essene New Covenant of Ancient Judaea: On the Origins of the Early Christian Familial Economic Covenant'. *Qumran Chronicle* 19/1–2 (2011): 1–30.

Chalcraft, David J. 'The Development of Weber's Sociology of Sects: Encouraging a New Fascination'. In *Sectarianism in Early Judaism: Sociological Advances*, edited by David J. Chalcraft. Bible World; 26–51. London: Equinox, 2007.

Chalcraft, David J. 'Towards a Weberian Sociology of the Qumran Sects'. In *Sectarianism in Early Judaism: Sociological Advances*, edited by David J. Chalcraft. Bible World, 74–105. London: Equinox, 2007.

Chalcraft, David J. 'Is a Historical Comparative Sociology of (Ancient Jewish) Sects Possible?' In *Sects and Sectarianism in Jewish History*, edited by Sacha Stern. IJS Studies in Judaica 12; 235–86. Leiden: Brill, 2011.

Collins, John J. *Beyond the Qumran Community: The Sectarian Movement of the Dead Sea Scrolls*. Grand Rapids: Eerdmans, 2010.

Collins, John J. 'Prayer and the Meaning of Ritual in the Dead Sea Scrolls'. In *Prayer and Poetry in the Dead Sea Scrolls and Related Literature: Essays in Honor of Eileen Schuller on the Occasion of Her 65th Birthday*, edited by Jeremy Penner, Ken M. Penner and Cecilia Wassen. STDJ 98; 69–85. Leiden: Brill, 2012.

Collins, Matthew A. *The Use of Sobriquets in the Qumran Dead Sea Scrolls*. LSTS 67. London: T&T Clark, 2009.

Davies, Philip R. 'Sects from Texts: On the Problems of Doing a Sociology of the Qumran Literature'. In *New Directions in Qumran Studies: Proceedings of the Bristol Colloquium on the Dead Sea Scrolls, 8–10 September 2003*, edited by Jonathan G. Campbell, W. John Lyons and Lloyd K. Pietersen. LSTS 52; 26–42. London: T&T Clark International, 2005.

DeMaris, Richard E. *The New Testament in its Ritual World*. Abingdon: Routledge, 2008.

Dimant, Devorah. 'The Volunteers in the Rule of the Community: A Biblical Notion in Sectarian Garb'. *RevQ* 23/2 (2007): 233–45.

Dimant, Devorah. 'The Volunteers in the Rule of the Community: A Biblical Notion in Sectarian Garb'. In *History, Ideology and Bible Interpretation in the Dead Sea Scrolls*. FAT 90; 289–300. Tübingen: Mohr Siebeck, 2014.

Dorman, Johanna H. W. *The Blemished Body: Deformity and Disability in the Qumran Scrolls*. Groningen: Groningen University Press, 2007.

Douglas, Mary. *Purity and Danger: An Analysis of the Concepts of Pollution and Taboo*. London: Routledge and Kegan Paul, 1966.

Ellens, Harold J., and Wayne G. Rollins, eds. *Psychology and the Bible: A New Way to Read the Scriptures*. 4 vols. Westport: Praeger, 2004.

Eshel, Hanan. *The Dead Sea Scrolls and the Hasmonean State*. Studies in the Dead Sea Scrolls and Related Literature. Grand Rapids: Eerdmans; Jerusalem: Yad Ben-Zvi Press, 2008.

Falk, Daniel K. 'Material Aspects of Prayer Manuscripts at Qumran'. In *Literature or Liturgy? Early Christian Hymns and Prayers in their Literary and Liturgical Context in Antiquity*, edited by Clemens Leonhard and Hermut Löhr. WUNT 2/363; 33–88. Tübingen: Mohr Siebeck, 2014.

Frey, Jörg. 'Flesh and Spirit in the Palestinian Jewish Sapiential Tradition and in the Qumran Texts: An Inquiry into the Background of Pauline Usage'. In *The Wisdom Texts from Qumran and the Development of Sapiential Thought*, edited by Charlotte Hempel, Armin Lange and Hermann Lichtenberger. BETL 159; 367–404. Leuven: Peeters/ University Press, 2002.

García Martínez, Florentino, and Mladen Popović, eds. *Defining Identities: We, You, and the Other in the Dead Sea Scrolls. Proceedings of the Fifth Meeting of the IOQS in Groningen*. STDJ 70. Leiden: Brill, 2008.

Goodman, Martin. 'The Qumran Sectarians and the Temple in Jerusalem'. In *The Dead Sea Scrolls: Texts and Context*, edited by Charlotte Hempel. STDJ 90; 263–73. Leiden: Brill, 2010.

Grossman, Maxine L. 'Cultivating Identity: Textual Virtuosity and "Insider" Status'. In *Defining Identities: We, You, and the Other in the Dead Sea Scrolls: Proceedings of the Fifth Meeting of the IOQS in Groningen*, edited by Florentino García Martínez and Mladen Popović. STDJ 70; 1–11. Leiden: Brill, 2008.

Harkins, Angela Kim. *Reading with an "I" to the Heavens: Looking at the Qumran Hodayot through the Lens of Visionary Traditions*. Ekstasis, 3. Berlin: de Gruyter, 2012.

Hasselbalch, Trine Bjørnung. *Meaning and Context in the Thanskgiving Hymns: Linguistic and Rhetorical Perspectives on a Collection of Prayers from Qumran*. SBLEJL 42. Atlanta: SBL Press, 2015.

Ilan, Tal. 'Women in Qumran and the Dead Sea Scrolls'. In *The Oxford Handbook of the Dead Sea Scrolls*, edited by Timothy H. Lim and John J. Collins, 123–47. Oxford: Oxford University Press, 2010.

Jassen, Alex P. 'The Dead Sea Scrolls and Violence: Sectarian Formation and Eschatological Imagination'. *Biblical Interpretation* 17 (2009): 12–44.

Jassen, Alex P. 'Violent Imaginaries and Practical Violence in the *War Scroll*'. In *The War Scroll, Violence, War and Peace in the Dead Sea Scrolls and Related Literature: Essays in Honour of Martin G. Abegg, Jr. on the Occasion of His 65th Birthday*, edited by Kipp Davis, Dorothy M. Peters, Kyung S. Baek and Peter W. Flint. STDJ 115; 175–203. Leiden: Brill, 2016.

Johns, Loren L. 'Identity and Resistance: The Varieties of Competing Models in Early Judaism'. In *Qumran Studies: New Approaches, New Questions*, edited by Michael T. Davis and Brent A. Strawn, 254–77. Grand Rapids: Eerdmans, 2007.

Jokiranta, Jutta. ' "Sectarianism" of the Qumran "Sect": Sociological Notes'. *Revue de Qumrân* 20/78 (2001): 223–40.

Jokiranta, Jutta. 'Sociological Approaches to Qumran Sectarianism'. In *The Oxford Handbook of the Dead Sea Scrolls*, edited by Timothy H. Lim and John J. Collins; 200–31. Oxford: Oxford University Press, 2010.

Jokiranta, Jutta. *Social Identity and Sectarianism in the Qumran Movement*. STDJ 105. Leiden: Brill, 2013.

Kazen, Thomas. *Emotions in Biblical Law: A Cognitive Science Approach*. Hebrew Bible Monographs 36. Sheffield: Sheffield Phoenix Press, 2011.

Keady, Jessica M. *Vulnerability and Valour: A Gendered Analysis of Everyday Life in the Dead Sea Scrolls Communities*. LSTS 91. London: Bloomsbury T&T Clark, 2017.

Kille, D. Andrew, and Wayne G. Rollins, eds. *Psychological Insight into the Bible: Texts and Readings*. Grand Rapids: Eerdmans, 2007.

Kille, D. Andrew. 'Psychology and Biblical Studies'. In *The New Interpreter's Dictionary of the Bible, Me–R, Volume 4*, edited by Karen D. Sakenfeld et al., 684–85. Nashville: Abingdon Press, 2009.

Klawans, Jonathan. 'Purity in the Dead Sea Scrolls'. In *The Oxford Handbook of the Dead Sea Scrolls*, edited by Timothy H. Lim and John J. Collins; 377–402. Oxford: Oxford University Press, 2010.

Klinghardt, Matthias. 'The Manual of Discipline in the Light of Statutes of Hellenistic Associations'. In *Methods of Investigation of the Dead Sea Scrolls and the Khirbet Qumran Site: Present Realities and Future Prospects*, edited by Michael O. Wise, Norman Golb, John J. Collins, and Dennis G. Pardee; Annals of the New York Academy of Sciences 722; 251–70. New York: The New York Academy of Sciences, 1994.

Kugler, Robert A. 'Making All Experience Religious: The Hegemony of Ritual at Qumran'. *Journal for the Study of Judaism* 33 (2002): 131–52.

Lichtenberger, Hermann. *Studien zum Menschenbild in Texten der Qumrangemeinde*. SUNT 15. Göttingen: Vandenhoeck & Ruprecht, 1980.

Magen, Yitzhak, and Yuval Peleg. *The Qumran Excavations 1993–2004 Preliminary Report*. Jerusalem: Israel Antiquities Authority, 2007.

Mason, Steve. 'The Historical Problem of the Essenes'. In *Celebrating the Dead Sea Scrolls: A Canadian Collection*, edited by Peter W. Flint, Jean Duhaime and Kyung S. Baek. SBLEJL 30; 201–51. Atlanta: SBL, 2011.

Murphy, Catherine M. *Wealth in the Dead Sea Scrolls and in the Qumran Community*. STDJ 40. Leiden: Brill, 2002.

Myers, Carol. 'Was Ancient Israel a Patriarchal Society?' *JBL* 133 (2014): 8–27.

Newman, Judith H. *Praying by the Book: The Scripturalization of Prayer in Second Temple Judaism*. SBLEJL 14. Atlanta: Scholars Press, 1999.

Newsom, Carol. ' "Sectually Explicit" Literature from Qumran'. In *The Hebrew Bible and Its Interpreters*, edited by William H. Propp, Baruch Halpern and David Noel Freedman; Biblical and Judaic Studies from the University of California, San Diego 1; 167–87. Winona Lake: Eisenbrauns, 1990.

Newsom, Carol A. *The Self as Symbolic Space: Constructing Identity and Community at Qumran*. STDJ 52. Leiden: Brill, 2004.

Newsom, Carol A. 'Flesh, Spirit, and the Indigenous Psychology of the Hodayot'. In *Prayer and Poetry in the Dead Sea Scrolls and Related Literature: Essays in Honor of Eileen Schuller on the Occasion of Her 65th Birthday*, ed. Jeremy Penner, Ken M. Penner and Cecilia Wassen. STDJ 98; 339–354. Leiden: Brill, 2012.

Newsom, Carol A. 'Models of the Moral Self: Hebrew Bible and Second Temple Judaism'. *JBL* 131 (2012): 5–25.

Newsom, Carol A. 'Religious Experience in the Dead Sea Scrolls: Two Case Studies'. In *Experientia Volume 2: Linking Texts and Experience*, edited by Colleen Shantz and Rodney A. Werline. SBLEJL 35; 205–221. Atlanta: SBL, 2012.

Oakman, Douglas E. 'Jesus and Agrarian Palestine: The Factor of Debt'. In *The Social World of the New Testament: Insights and Models*, ed. Jerome H. Neyrey and Eric C. Stewart, 63–82. Peabody: Hendrickson, 2008.

Pietersen, Lloyd K. ' "False Teaching, Lying Tongues and Deceitful Lips" (4Q169 frgs 3–4 2.8)'. In *New Directions in Qumran Studies: Proceedings of the Bristol Colloquium on the Dead Sea Scrolls, 8–10 September 2003*, edited by Jonathan G. Campbell, W. John Lyons and Lloyd K. Pietersen; LSTS 52; 166–81. London: T&T Clark International, 2005.

Popović, Mladen. *Reading the Human Body: Physiognomics and Astrology in the Dead Sea Scrolls and Hellenistic-Early Roman Period Judaism*. STDJ 67. Leiden: Brill, 2007.

Pyper, Hugh S. *An Unsuitable Book: The Bible as Scandalous Text*. Sheffield: Sheffield Phoenix Press, 2005.

Rappaport, Roy A. *Ritual and Religion in the Making of Humanity*. Cambridge Studies in Social and Cultural Anthropology. Cambridge: Cambridge University Press, 1999.

Regev, Eyal. *Sectarianism in Qumran: A Cross-Cultural Perspective*. Religion and Society, 45. Berlin: de Gruyter, 2007.

Rendsburg, Gary A. 'Qumran Hebrew (With a Trial Cut [1QS])'. In *The Dead Sea Scrolls at 60: Scholarly Contributions of New York University Faculty and Alumni*, edited by Lawrence H. Schiffman and Shani Tzoref. STDJ 89; 217–46. Leiden: Brill, 2010.

Schniedewind, William M. 'Qumran Hebrew as an Antilanguage'. *JBL* 118 (1999): 235–52.

Schniedewind, William M. 'Linguistic Ideology in Qumran Hebrew'. In *Diggers at the Well: Proceedings of a Third International Symposium on the Hebrew of the Dead Sea Scrolls and Ben Sira*, edited by Takamitsu Muraoka and John F. Elwolde. STDJ 36; 245–255. Leiden: Brill, 2000.

Schofield, Alison. 'Between Center and Periphery: The Yaḥad in Context'. *Dead Sea Discoveries* 16 (2009): 330–50.

Schofield, Alison. *From Qumran to the Yaḥad: A New Paradigm of Textual Development for the Community Rule*. STDJ 77. Leiden: Brill, 2009.

Schröder, Ingo W., and Bettina E. Schmidt. 'Introduction: Violent Imaginaries and Violent Practices'. In *Anthropology of Violence and Conflict*, edited by Bettina E. Schmidt and Ingo W. Schröder; 1–24. London: Routledge, 2001.

Staal, Frits. 'The Meaninglessness of Ritual'. *Numen* 26 (1979): 2–22.

Stambaugh, John, and David Balch. *The Social World of the First Christians*. London: SPCK, 1986.

Stegemann, Hartmut. 'The Qumran Essenes: Local Members of the Main Jewish Union in Late Second Temple Times'. In *The Madrid Qumran Congress: Proceedings of the International Congress on the Dead Sea Scrolls, Madrid 18–21 March 1991*, edited by J. Trebolle Barrera and L. Vegas Montaner. STDJ 11; 83–166. Leiden: Brill/ Madrid: Universidad Complutense, 1993.

Stuckenbruck, Loren T. 'The Teacher of Righteousness Remembered: From Fragmentary Sources to Collective Memory in the Dead Sea Scrolls'. In *Memory in the Bible and Antiquity: The Fifth Durham-Tübingen Research Symposium (Durham, September 2004)*, edited by Stephen Barton, Loren T. Stuckenbruck and Benjamin G. Wold. WUNT 212; 75–94. Tübingen: Mohr Siebeck, 2007.

Tigchelaar, Eibert J. C. 'The Addressees of 4QInstruction'. In *Sapiential, Liturgical and Poetical Texts from Qumran: Proceedings of the Third Meeting of the International Organization for Qumran Studies*, ed. Daniel K. Falk, Florentino García Martínez and Eileen M. Schuller. STDJ 35; 62–75. Leiden: Brill, 2000.

Tov, Emanuel. *Scribal Practices and Approaches Reflected in the Texts Found in the Judean Desert*. STDJ 54. Leiden: Brill, 2004.

Turner, Victor. *The Forest of Symbols: Aspects of Ndembu Ritual*. Ithaca: Cornell University Press, 1967.

Ullmann-Margalit, Edna. *Out of the Cave: A Philosophical Inquiry into the Dead Sea Scrolls Research*. Cambridge: Harvard University Press, 2006.

Van Gennep, Arnold. *Les rites de passage*. Paris: Nourry, 1908.

Van Kooten, George H. *Paul's Anthropology in Context: The Image of God, Assimilation to God, and Tripartite Man in Ancient Judaism, Ancient Philosophy and Early Christianity*. WUNT 232. Tübingen: Mohr Siebeck, 2008.

Weinfeld, Moshe. *The Organizational Pattern and the Penal Code of the Qumran Sect*. NTOA 2. Göttingen: Vandenhoeck & Ruprecht; Fribourg: Éditions Universitaires, 1986.

Wold, Benjamin G. 'Memory in the Dead Sea Scrolls: Exodus, Creation and Cosmos'. In *Memory in the Bible and Antiquity*, 47–74. Tübingen: Mohr Siebeck, 2007.

Wright, Benjamin G. III, 'The Categories of Rich and Poor in the Qumran Sapiential Literature'. In *Sapiential Perspectives: Wisdom Literature in Light of the Dead Sea Scrolls. Proceedings of the Sixth International Symposium of the Orion Center for the Study of the Dead Sea Scrolls and Associated Literature, 20–22 May, 2001*, ed. John J. Collins, Gregory E. Sterling and Ruth A. Clements. STDJ 51; 101–23. Leiden: Brill, 2004.

Chapter 10

REVIEWING PURITY AND IMPURITY FROM A
GENDERED PERSPECTIVE: THE WAR SCROLL (1QM)
AS A CASE STUDY*

Jessica M. Keady

To date, scholars who have discussed issues of purity and impurity in the Dead Sea Scrolls (e.g. Hannah Harrington and Jonathan Klawans)[1] have constructed ancient Jewish purity systems with a focus on priestly traditions and the relationships between purity and sin within the relevant texts. Although such discussions are important to understanding purity and impurity in Second Temple Judaism, these scholarly discussions usually have to be qualified because everyday life among ordinary Dead Sea Scrolls communities would not necessarily have reflected the systematic and rigid ideals found in the texts. An intriguing question therefore arises: What were the everyday social effects that purity and impurity would have brought to the Dead Sea Scrolls communities and the physical and social positions that ordinary men would have been expected to adopt?

Ian Werrett has recently argued that alternative methodological approaches, such as feminist and social-scientific perspectives, should be used to further the understanding of the purity texts available from Qumran and illuminate the world view of the wider communities.[2] Masculinity studies, for instance, has proved to be a highly valuable contribution to contemporary gender studies, one which encompasses both the deconstruction of specific kinds of gendering as well as a reconsideration of gender itself as a given source of power. Although

---

* The present essay is a revised version of material presented in my monograph, *Vulnerability and Valour: A Gendered Analysis of Everyday Life in the Dead Sea Scrolls Communities*, LSTS 91 (London: Bloomsbury, 2017).

1. See, e.g. Hannah K. Harrington, *The Purity Texts*, Companion to the Qumran Scrolls, 5 (London: T&T Clark, 2004); and Jonathan Klawans, *Impurity and Sin in Ancient Judaism* (Oxford: Oxford University Press, 2000).

2. Ian Werrett, 'The Evolution of Purity at Qumran', in *Purity and the Forming of Religious Traditions*, ed. Christopher Frevel and Christopher Nihan, DHR 3 (Leiden: E. J. Brill, 2013), 518.

there are publications on the literary depiction of women in the Dead Sea Scrolls,[3] there has not yet been an in-depth discussion of the relationship between gender and purity at Qumran. There is a need not only to problematize gender, but also to acknowledge that gender is inclusive of males, as well as females. The term 'gendered' within the present chapter relates to the categorization of 'men' and 'women' and to the social implications such binaries have within society. A gendered analysis cannot be regarded as relating only to women or the feminine but instead will also include discussion of masculine roles and productions.[4] There are risks in imposing modern methodologies onto ancient texts but I am in agreement with Maria Wyke who, in her understanding of gender in antiquity, argues that 'ancient bodies' continue to be the sites on which discussions of modern sexualities and genders can be discussed, confronted and assessed.[5]

The present essay therefore will use theoretical insights from contemporary Masculinity studies to uncover the everyday, ordinary male Qumranian, the vulnerable positions he occupies while impure, and the significance of those positions from a religious, personal and familial perspective. As the nexus of purity and impurity is paramount throughout these texts, I will take as a frame for understanding and exploration the War Texts, specifically 1QM and 4Q491–497, and I will shape my arguments around three distinct but overlapping fields of study. First, I will discuss masculinities and the War Texts (1QM and 4Q491–497) in relation to ideology, war and behaviour in order to uncover the dynamic natures of masculinity and purity. Next, I will review impurity and disability in the War Texts (1QM and 4Q491–497) and the interrelations therein between hierarchy, purity and masculinity. Finally, I will be determining whether an interdisciplinary gendered approach can enhance understanding about how everyday life for ordinary members of the Dead Sea Scrolls communities may have been experienced by males when they did not fit the ideal pure form.

3. See Cecilia Wassen, *Women in the Damascus Document* (Atlanta: SBL, 2005); Eileen Schuller, 'Women in the Dead Sea Scrolls: Research in the Past Decade and Future Directions', in *The Dead Sea Scrolls and Contemporary Culture: Proceedings of the International Conference held at the Israel Museum, Jerusalem July 6-8, 2008*, ed. Adolfo D. Roitman et al., STDJ 93 (Leiden: E. J. Brill, 2011), 571–88; Maxine L. Grossman, 'Reading for Gender in the Damascus Document', *DSD* 11 (2004): 212–39; Melissa Aubin, ' "She is the beginning of all ways of perversity": Femininity and Metaphor in 4Q1842', *Women in Judaism: A Multidisciplinary Journal* 2 (2001): 1–23.

4. Virginia Burrus, 'Mapping as Metamorphosis: Initial Reflections on Gender and Ancient Religious Discourse', in *Mapping Gender in Ancient Religious Discourse*, ed. Todd Penner and Caroline Vander Stichele (Leiden: Boston, 2007), 3.

5. Maria Wyke, 'Introduction', in *Parchments of Gender. Deciphering the Bodies of Antiquity*, ed. Maria Wyke (Oxford: Clarendon Press, 1998), 1.

10.1 *Masculinities and the War Texts (1QM and 4Q491–497)*

The War Texts (1QM and 4Q491–497) is the name given to a group of Dead Sea Scrolls depicting preparations for the eschatological battle between the 'Sons of Light' (led by God) and the 'Sons of Darkness' (led by Belial). These early Jewish sectarian manuscripts were discovered near the archaeological site of Khirbet Qumran on the northwestern shore of the Dead Sea, and range in date from the second century BCE to the middle of the first century CE. Since the first discovery of the War Texts (1QM and 4Q491–497) in Cave I in 1947 there have been over 90 parchments and more than 360 papyrus fragments identified as relating to 1QM from Cave IV, either as actual copies of the Scroll or containing material closely related to it.[6] The War Texts (1QM and 4Q491–497) form an intriguing body of ancient texts, since outside of the Dead Sea Scrolls there are no known literary parallels or equivalents in Second Temple literature. This highlights both their importance and the unique nature of the sectarian material. To date, much has been written about the formation of the War Texts from an exegetical perspective, but mainly with a focus on the genre of the texts and their location within Second Temple Judaism. As a consequence, the socio-historical placement and influence of these texts has been neglected. That neglect becomes even more salient when we consider that men in the Dead Sea Scrolls communities were to be always 'perfect ones of spirit and flesh' (1QM VII, 5) – and nothing less.

As a bridge to understanding contextual depiction, Mary Douglas's classic text *Purity and Danger* has become one of the most influential books on the topic of bodies and symbolic boundaries. Douglas classifies bodily functions as a symbol of society and argues that where there is dirt there is a system and, as such, dirt is never an isolated event. As Douglas herself describes it, 'dirt is the by-product of a systematic ordering and classification of matter, in so far as ordering involves rejecting inappropriate elements'.[7] Although Douglas does not refer to the Dead Sea Scrolls in her analysis of the body, for her the Bible is a key source, especially Leviticus 15 and the symbolic attachments Douglas describes as relating to bodily impurities. However, as Christian Frevel and Christophe Nihan have explored in their study on the formation of purity in the Ancient Mediterranean World, Douglas's work has been subjected to criticism on account of the abstraction that is implied in her writings.[8] Drawing on the abstract ideals that Douglas creates, I agree with Simon Coleman when he argues that much of the work on the body in anthropology takes us beyond Douglas's useful 'but curiously disembodied'

---

6. Brian Schultz, *Conquering the World. The War Scroll (1QM) Reconsidered*, STDJ 76 (Leiden: E. J. Brill, 2009), 16.

7. Mary Douglas, *Purity and Danger: An Analysis of the Concepts of Pollution and Taboo* (London: Routledge, 1966), 43.

8. Christopher Frevel and Christopher Nihan, 'Introduction', in *Purity and the Forming of Religious Traditions in the Ancient Mediterranean World and Ancient Judaism*, ed. Christopher Frevel and Christopher Nihan, DHR 3 (Leiden: E. J. Brill, 2013), 6.

depiction of the body as a symbol of society, and into the realm of gender analysis and Masculinity Studies.[9]

In order to understand purity from an interdisciplinary, gendered perspective, it is important to move beyond Douglas's symbolic work on the body. Interpreting the War Texts (1QM and 4Q491–497) requires exploration of what cultural and religious 'norms' may have underpinned the roles, rules, restrictions and expectations of men in their everyday lives and how the diverse purity issues that existed between the sexes were presented, constructed and, more importantly, lived. As David Clines argues in his landmark essay on masculinity and King David, the construction of masculinities in the portrayal of David 'reflects the cultural norms of men of the author's time'.[10] The same point is applicable to the War Texts (1QM and 4Q491–497), whose eschatological constructions of purity (1QM VII), warfare (1QM IX) and ranking (1QM VII, 1–4) reflect the ways the Dead Sea Scrolls communities symbolically perceived their involvement in everyday life.

In the limited literature that exists on masculinity and the Second Temple period (between 530 BCE to 70 CE), biblical scholars have sought insight from the field of Classics, which has a wealth of comparative material on Greek and Roman masculine ideals from an ancient perspective. For example, Joseph Roisman in his discussion of the rhetoric of manhood in the Attic orators, which consist of speeches from elite male citizens dating from the fifth to the second century BCE, defined masculinity as a cultural construct which defines a man's responsibilities and beliefs within a structured setting.[11] Roisman's discussion of the Attic orators and masculinity has value at many points for comparative analysis of the Scrolls, and of the *War Scroll* in particular. Of special interest is Roisman's claim that 'Athenian concepts of manhood are indicative of larger systems of community morality'.[12]

Similarly David Morgan, who discusses modern theories relating to war and masculinity, argues that the masculine characteristics constructed, acted and reproduced in war and the military are some of the most explicit in a community and wider society.[13] In order to understand the military life and the way it can be understood in gendered terms, Morgan proposes looking at the constructions of

9. Simon Coleman, 'Recent Development in the Anthropology of Religion', in *The New Blackwell Companion to the Sociology of Religion*, ed. Bryan S. Turner (Oxford: Wiley-Blackwell, 2010), 117.

10. David J. A. Clines, *Interested Parties. The Ideology of Writers and Readers of the Hebrew Bible* (Sheffield: Sheffield Academic Press, 1995), 215.

11. Joseph Roisman, *The Rhetoric of Manhood. Masculinity in the Attic Orators* (Berkeley: University of California Press, 2005), 2.

12. Roisman, *The Rhetoric of Manhood*, 7.

13. David H. J. Morgan, 'Theater of War. Combat, the Military and Masculinities', in *Theorizing Masculinities*, ed. Harry Brod and Michael Kaufman (London: SAGE Publications, 1994), 165.

the masculine body in texts that discuss war, ideology and behaviour.[14] Indeed, as mentioned above, the War Texts (1QM and 4Q491–497) start with a juxtaposition of those who belong to the Sons of Righteousness and those who do not: 'the Sons of Light and the lot of darkness, shall fight each other' (1QM I, 11); and the Sons of Light are to be 'volunteers for war, perfect ones of spirit and flesh' (1QM VII, 5). Such depictions of perfection, light, spirit and flesh illustrate the masculine ideology of the Dead Sea Scrolls communities and especially the male characteristics and bodily traits needed in war. The War Texts (1QM and 4Q491–497) outline how a man should react in the appointed time of vengeance: he is to be 'strong and brave' (1QM XV, 7) and he is not to be 'terrified, alarmed or trembling' (1QM XVII, 7–8). Indeed, in these writings even the horses are described in masculine terms, as they are to be 'male horses, swift of foot, soft of mouth, long of breath' (1QM VI, 12); and those riding them shall be 'men of worth' (1QM VI, 12).

Viewed through a Foucauldian lens, these ordinary male bodies have been controlled and regulated through movements, time and everyday activities. Thereby the body can become invested with relations of power; bodies have potential to become, more specifically, obedient 'docile bodies'.[15] In a Jewish context, these male bodies are pure, masculinized and ready to do God's work (1QM XIV, 12). Masculine ideologies of the body allow the body to become an object of social power and thus amenable to being controlled, identified and reproduced. The idealized males in the War Texts (1QM and 4Q491–497) are represented as pure and ready to provoke violence among others; they are to avoid tarring their purity and becoming defiled since they will then not be able to fight. Any exposure to impurity would directly affect masculine behaviour(s). The portrayals of the men outlined in the War Texts (1QM and 4Q491–497) represent the ideal: the ideal ages (1QM VI, 14-VII, 1), the ideal fight (1QM VI, 12), the ideal qualities (1QM VI, 16–17) and ideal purity (1QM VII, 3–7). Despite the ideal, however, reality is at play since the men reading the manuscripts are projecting their own beliefs about what masculinity ought to look like and represent; and essential to those beliefs – and to their social performance in terms of bravery, strength and honour – is the presence of purity.

As Andrea Cornwall and Nancy Lindisfarne have argued from an ethnographic perspective, masculinity can be understood as the 'essence of a person', one that can be measured, possessed or lost.[16] Significantly, Cornwall and Lindisfarne's notions of measurement, possession and instability have potential to illuminate not only masculinity but also aspects of purity and impurity. For example, similar to masculinity, purity is also dynamic, unstable and ever-changing. Just as a member

14. David Morgan, 'Theater of War', 167.

15. Michel Foucault, *Discipline and Punish: The Birth of the Prison* (trans. Alan Sheridan; London: Alley Lane, 1977), 77.

16. Andrea Cornwall and Nancy Lindisfarne, 'Dislocating Masculinity: Gender, Power and Anthropology', in *Dislocating Masculinity: Comparative Ethnographies*, ed. Andrea Cornwall and Nancy Lindisfarne (London and New York: Routledge, 1994), 11.

of the Dead Sea Scrolls communities can change and enhance his purity, he can also enhance his masculinity. Although men and women may exhibit various masculinities and femininities throughout their everyday lives, their ideologies have the potential to disguise the variety and instabilities in ways that allow people to *think* they are consistently acting as a man or as a woman.[17]

10.2 *Impurity and Disability in the War Texts (1QM and 4Q491–497)*

David Braddock and Susan Parish, in their institutional history of disability studies, argue that people with disabilities in the Hebrew Bible were classified alongside prostitutes and menstruating women and as such, judged to be unclean.[18] Saul Olyan also discusses menstruation and parturition as 'representations of non-defective physical disabilities' in his discussion of disability in the Hebrew Bible.[19] The risk of impurity that women carry may be why they are restricted from entering the men's camps when they have gone to war: 'No young boy or woman shall enter their camps when they leave Jerusalem to go to battle until their return' (1QM VII, 3–4). From a gendered perspective, it is significant that it is not just the female who is restricted from entering the men's camps since a man who 'is not purified from a (bodily) discharge' (1QM VII, 6) is also not to enter battle. Such an uncontrolled bodily emission may, in the parlance of contemporary discourse, be the consequence of a nocturnal 'wet dream'.

As David Morgan has argued in relation to modern day society, such exclusion not only defines who 'does what', but ultimately who 'is what' within a community.[20] The work of Morgan, in his most recent discussion of vision and embodiment, draws on how communal relations are created and maintained through different types of looks, shy glances, averted glances and strict stares, all of which reveal and command both authority and weakness within a community.[21] Morgan's work has relevance to considerations of purity and gender in the War Texts (1QM and 4Q491–497), and his discussion of shame has special poignancy since it is through shame that hierarchy is created within a community and distinctions made between 'good and evil', 'powerful and weak', 'pure and impure'.[22] Thomas Hentrich has drawn on modern disability studies and applied this work to the

---

17. David Buchbinder, *Studying Men and Masculinities* (London: Routledge, 2013), 38.

18. See David L. Braddock and Susan L. Parish, 'An Institutional History of Disability', in *Handbook of Disability Studies*, ed. Gary L. Abrecht et al. (London: Sage, 2001), 11–68.

19. Saul M. Olyan, *Disability in the Hebrew Bible: Interpreting Mental and Physical Differences* (Cambridge: Cambridge University Press, 2008), 59.

20. David Morgan, *The Embodied Eye: Religious Visual Culture and the Social Life of Feeling* (Berkeley: University of California Press, 2012), 3.

21. Ibid., 3.

22. Ibid., 3.

Bible to show how the gender of a person has importance secondary only to their disability.[23] The impurity of those described in 1QM VII, 4–5 are based on male bodily blemishes and physical disabilities; the men are described as 'lame', 'blind', 'crippled', 'blemished' and 'unclean'. Their male bodies have become impure in the eyes of both God and the wider communities. It is the male body that has become impure and this affects the male ideology and impacts upon the societal structure to which they belong.

Donn Welton views the various gendered bodies discussed in Leviticus, such as the menstrually impure body (Lev. 15.29), sexual bodies (Lev. 15.18) and medically ill bodies (e.g. those afflicted with leprosy), as having the effect of singling out the body and turning it into an object of attention.[24] According to Welton, in biblical texts attention is focused specifically upon the body only where there has been a breakdown in the 'rhythms of everyday life'.[25] In the case of the War Texts (1QM and 4Q491–497), the breakdown in the rhythms of everyday life is defined in terms of the impure/pure dichotomy, since purity determines whether a man belonging to one of the communities is able to go to war (1QM VII, 4–5) and thus prove his masculinity. But what if a man was unable to go to war due to purity issues? How would he have been positioned by others within Dead Seas Scrolls communities and, more specifically, those closest to him, including his family?

Roismann, in his discussion of men in the military in Athens, has shown that all able-bodied men could be called to military service whereas women, children and the disabled were excluded. The Athenian military was therefore constituted by an exclusive group of males. A very similar phenomenon can be seen in the communities implied by the War Texts (1QM and 4Q491–497), whose impure males were unable to go to war and thus likely to be ascribed low social status both by women and by other men (see, e.g. 1QM VII, 7). The extent and social consequences are difficult to exaggerate. In the Jewish contexts implied by the War Texts, the randomness and uncontrollability of male blemishes and seminal emissions make the male body a constant source of potential pollution to himself, his wife and his wider community. Despite the value attached to social order in hierarchical communities, males can be embodied in ways that result in instability and disorder. Wyke has argued that the 'male body is permanently troubled'.[26] At Qumran, the male body can be seen as permanently troubled especially in relation to the laws of purity.

23. Thomas Hentrich, 'Masculinity and Disability in the Bible', in *'This' Abled Body: Rethinking Disabilities in Biblical Studies*, ed. Hector Avalos et al. (Atlanta: SBL, 2007), 73.

24. Donn Welton, 'Biblical Bodies', in *Body and Flesh: A Philosophical Reader*, ed. Donn Welton (Oxford: Wiley-Blackwell, 1998), 232.

25. Welton, 'Biblical Bodies', 247.

26. Wyke, 'Introduction', 4.

10.3 *The Next Step: Dead Sea Scrolls Scholarship, Purity and Gender*

The present chapter has suggested some ways in which experiences of gender may have paralleled or even influenced understandings of purity and impurity in the communities of the Dead Sea Scrolls. Although there would have been discrepancies between the ancient literary sources and the daily experiences of men and women's lives, the texts provide insights into the constructions of femininity and masculinity that Jewish women and men would have been likely to adhere to. Studying ancient texts should not distract us from attempting to reconstruct the people, communities and social situations behind the manuscripts. By using gendered and everyday methodologies that discuss the male in an eschatological setting, it is possible to engender ancient Judaism through a modern lens that makes the people behind the War Texts (1QM and 4Q491–497) more visible and embodied, rather than systemic and passive. In order to enhance understanding of the purity rules in those texts, the present chapter has highlighted both the vulnerability of the prevailing scholarly abstractions about purity, and the interpretative potential of putting the problematic impure male at the centre of quests for the ideologies of gender and masculinity in the ancient communities of the Dead Sea Scrolls.

So, where next? A potentially very fruitful conversation between the War Texts (1QM and 4Q491–497), Masculinity studies and issues of pure and impure in the daily life of the ordinary male in the Dead Sea Scrolls communities might be facilitated by Rom Harré and Van Langenhove's Positioning Theory.[27] Currently used by social scientists (especially social psychologists) to understand gender and identities as interactional phenomena that help to maintain relationships and other aspects of daily life, Positioning Theory has roots in conflict studies and takes a special interest in understanding how 'sides' (positions) are taken and then enacted within a system of social action. Positioning Theory is therefore interested in establishing the precise relationships both between language and thought, and between language and action, and it views narrative as playing an especially important role in the representation of 'lived meaning'. Viewing the War Texts (1QM and 4Q491–497) from this standpoint might allow previously unnoticed stories and storylines to emerge which could then be analysed as narrative discourse and thus be used to position various types of members of the Dead Sea Scrolls communities, including the ordinary types of males discussed in the present chapter. Such analysis is largely untried in scholarship on the scrolls and, at least partly for that reason, is worthy of consideration as one possible way of advancing critical understanding of the present topic.

10.4 *Summary*

The present essay has focused on the purity texts of the Dead Sea Scrolls, especially the War Texts (1QM and 4Q491–497). These early Jewish texts focus on preparations for an eschatological battle between the forces of good and evil. An interdisciplinary

27. Rom Harré and Van Langenhove, *Positioning Theory* (London: Blackwell, 1999).

conversation between three areas of Dead Sea Scrolls scholarship – the War Texts, Masculinity Studies and systems of purity in Mediterranean antiquity – has been developed in order to understand better the everyday life of the Dead Sea Scrolls communities. As a result, both the interplay between masculinity, purity and impurity, and especially the vulnerabilities implicit in the workings of purity/ impurity among the males in the communities, have been understood in a fresh way that invites further exploration and critical response.

Bibliography

Aubin, M. ' "She is the beginning of all ways of perversity": Femininity and Metaphor in 4Q1842'. *Women in Judaism: A Multidisciplinary Journal* 2 (2001): 1–23.

Braddock, David L., and Susan L. Parish. 'An Institutional History of Disability'. In *Handbook of Disability Studies*, edited by Gary L. Albrecht, Katherine D. Seelman and Michael Bury, 11–68. London: SAGE, 2001.

Buchbinder, D. *Studying Men and Masculinities.* London/New York: Routledge, 2013.

Burrus, V. 'Mapping as Metamorphosis: Initial Reflections on Gender and Ancient Religious Discourse'. In *Mapping Gender in Ancient Religious Discourse*, edited by Todd Penner and Caroline Vander Stichele, 1–11. Leiden: Boston, 2007.

Clines, D. J. A. *Interested Parties. The Ideology of Writers and Readers of the Hebrew Bible.* Sheffield: Sheffield Academic Press, 1995.

Coleman, S. 'Recent Development in the Anthropology of Religion'. In *The New Blackwell Companion to the Sociology of Religion*, edited by Bryan S. Turner, 103–21. Oxford: Wiley-Blackwell, 2010.

Cornwall, A., and N. Lindisfarne. 'Dislocating Masculinity: Gender, Power and Anthropology'. In *Dislocating Masculinity. Comparative Ethnographies*, edited by A. Cornwall and N. Lindisfarne, 11–47. London and New York: Routledge, 1994.

Douglas, M. *Purity and Danger. An Analysis of the Concepts of Pollution and Taboo.* London: Routledge, 1966.

Foucault, Michel. *Discipline and Punish: The Birth of the Prison*, trans. Alan Sheridan. London: Alley Lane, 1977.

Frevel, C., and C. Nihan. 'Introduction'. In *Purity and the Forming of Religious Traditions in the Ancient Mediterranean World and Ancient Judaism*, edited by C. Frevel and C. Nihan. DHR 3; 1–47. Leiden: E. J. Brill, 2013.

Grossman, M. L. 'Reading for Gender in the Damascus Document'. *DSD* 11 (2004): 212–39.

Harré, R., and V. Langenhove. *Positioning Theory.* London: Blackwell, 1999.

Harrington, H. K. *The Purity Texts.* Companion to the Qumran Scrolls, 5. London: T. & T. Clark, 2004.

Hentrich, T. 'Masculinity and Disability in the Bible'. In *'This Abled Body: Rethinking Disabilities in Biblical Studies*, edited by Hector Avalos et al., 73–91. Atlanta: SBL, 2007.

Keady, Jessica M. *Vulnerability and Valour: A Gendered Analysis of Everyday Life in the Dead Sea Scrolls Communities*, LSTS 91. London: Bloomsbury, 2017.

Klawans, J. *Impurity and Sin in Ancient Judaism.* Oxford: Oxford University Press, 2000.

Morgan, D. *The Embodied Eye: Religious Visual Culture and the Social Life of Feeling.* Berkeley: University of California Press, 2012.

Morgan, D. H. J. 'Theater of War: Combat, the Military and Masculinities'. In *Theorizing Masculinities*, edited by Harry Brod and Michael Kaufman, 165–83. London: Sage, 1994.

Olyan, S. M. *Disability in the Hebrew Bible: Interpreting Mental and Physical Differences.*
    Cambridge: Cambridge University Press, 2008.
Roisman, J. *The Rhetoric of Manhood. Masculinity in the Attic Orators.* Berkeley: University
    of California Press, 2005.
Schuller, E. 'Women in the Dead Sea Scrolls: Research in the Past Decade and Future
    Directions'. In *The Dead Sea Scrolls and Contemporary Culture: Proceedings of the
    International Conference held at the Israel Museum, Jerusalem July 6–8, 2008*, edited by
    Adolfo D. Roitman et al. STDJ 93; 571–88. Leiden: E. J. Brill, 2011.
Schultz, B. *Conquering the World. The War Scroll (1QM) Reconsidered.* STDJ 76. Leiden:
    E. J. Brill, 2009.
Wassen, C. *Women in the Damascus Document.* Academia Biblica, 21. Atlanta: SBL, 2005.
Welton, D. 'Biblical Bodies'. In *Body and Flesh: A Philosophical Reader*, edited by Donn
    Welton, 229–58. Oxford: Blackwell, 1998.
Werrett, I. C. 'The Evolution of Purity at Qumran'. In *Purity and the Forming of Religious
    Traditions*, edited by C. Frevel and C. Nihan. DHR 3; 493–518. Leiden: E. J. Brill, 2013.
Wyke, M. 'Introduction'. In *Parchments of Gender: Deciphering the Bodies of Antiquity*,
    edited by Maria Wyke, 1–11. Oxford: Clarendon Press, 1998.

Chapter 11

THE TEACHER OF RIGHTEOUSNESS FROM THE PERSPECTIVE OF THE SOCIOLOGY OF ORGANIZATIONS

David Hamidović

Serious study of the manuscripts from Qumran entered a second age at the end of the 1990s. All of the manuscripts discovered between 1947 and 1956 are now known, at least in the form of photographs, as a result of the so-called liberation of the manuscripts in 1991. Since that date, access to the manuscripts has been facilitated almost continuously by the publication of new editions in paper and electronic formats that are more and more user-friendly. The knowledge of the whole corpus preserved in the eleven caves has paved the way for new synthetic and thematic studies; and among the new orientations of those studies, the sociological approach has established itself as particularly creative and fruitful.

In sociological readings of the scrolls, studies by David J. Chalcraft and Jutta Jokiranta have been especially influential. In their work the main concern is neither the description of religious belief or practice nor identifying the best name for the established circle of *Khirbet* Qumran associated with the manuscripts; instead, the issue is to conceptualize the relation of that circle to others and thereby define its identity and that of its members chiefly in terms of relation. Due in part to the influence of that approach, the appropriateness of calling the Essenes a 'sect' has been widely discussed the last few years.[1] It is worth recalling that questioning

---

1. See P. R. Davies, 'The "Damascus Sect" and Judaism', in *Sects and Scrolls: Essays on Qumran and Related Topics*, ed. P. R. Davies (Atlanta: Scholars Press, 1996), 70–84, esp. 82–83; J. Jokiranta, ' "Sectarianism" of the Qumran "Sect": Sociological Notes', *RevQ* 78 (2001): 223–39; D. J. Chalcraft, 'Introduction: Sectarianism in Early Judaism: Sociological Advances? Some Critical Sociological Reflections', in *Sectarianism in Early Judaism: Sociological Advances*, ed. D. J. Chalcraft (London: Equinox, 2007), 2–23; D. J. Chalcraft, 'Towards a Weberian Sociology of the Qumran Sects', in *Sectarianism in Early Judaism*, 74–105; C. Wassen and J. Jokiranta, 'Groups in Tension: Sectarianism in the *Damascus Document* and the *Community Rule*', in *Sectarianism in Early Judaism*, 205–45; J. J. Collins, *Beyond the Qumran Community: The Sectarian Movement of the Dead Sea Scrolls* (Grand Rapids: Eerdmans, 2009), 74; D. J. Chalcraft, 'Is a Historical Comparative Sociology

on an Essene identity in relation to the other Jews and more widely with regard to the Essenes' contemporaries is part of the approach to the study of social identities and the theories of social categorization which developed in the social sciences since the 1970s.

Studies of social identity and theories of social categorization involve the use of different scales: most notably, a collective scale corresponding to concepts of social identity, and an individual scale pertaining to personal identity. Social identity is a part of an individual's self-concept which derives from the knowledge of a person's membership of a social group (or groups) alongside the emotional significance attached to that membership. Studies of Qumran have tended to focus upon the collective scale, but Jokiranta reminds us that collective identity is underpinned by real individuals. Understanding the link between the two scales therefore becomes necessary for understanding the Qumran community and the significance of belonging to it;[2] and thus social psychology is called upon to explain how individual members of the community understand their collective identity and how that identity is shared by other individuals in the group. The pertinent relations moreover cannot be considered without a step-by-step contextual analysis; for the perception of one's own identity in terms of belonging to a group can vary over time, according to an evolution in the perception of oneself and others, but also according to the context. For example, the Essenes cannot define themselves collectively as a group, and individually as belonging to that group, solely on the basis of believing that the Jerusalem Temple is unclean, a belief attested several times in the Qumran texts.[3] The preservation of the group's internal cohesion, and thus also of group membership, presumes other foundations; and among those foundations is the experiential progression from joining the community and becoming a member, to becoming increasingly integrated into the group. Those same processes, moreover, simultaneously set the group apart from other groups and individuals in its milieu. The group's identification with the 'rest of Israel'[4] and with the 'poor',[5] for instance, as well as its members' understanding that they

---

of (Ancient Jewish) Sects Possible?', in *Sects and Sectarianism in Jewish History*, ed. S. Stern, IJS Studies in Judaica 12 (Leiden: E. J. Brill, 2011), 233–86.

2. J. Jokiranta, *Social Identity and Sectarianism in the Qumran Movement*, STDJ 105 (Leiden: E. J. Brill, 2013), 17–109.

3. See, e.g. CD 4.18; 6.12.

4. CD 1.4; 2.6-13; 1QM 13.8; 14.8-9; 1QH^a 14.8; 4Q185 1-2 ii 2; 4Q393 3.7

5. The economic definition of the poor (*'ani*) and of the wretched one (*'ebyon*) – see, e.g. Ezek. 16.49; 22.29 – is transformed by the Essenes into a reference to themselves; cf. CD 6.16.21; 14.14; 19.9; 1QH^a 10.34; 11.26; 13.18-20; 1QpHab 12.3.6.10; 1QM 11.9.13; 13.12-14; 4Q171 I 9; II 10 ('congregation of poor'). Similar are Mt. 5.3; Lk. 6.20. On the origins of the analysed pattern, see J. Un-Sok Ro, *Die sogenannte 'Armen frömmigkeit' im nachexilischen Israel*, BZAW 322 (Berlin-New York: W. de Gruyter, 2002); and more recently, D. Hamidović, 'The Divine Economy of the Poor in the Qumran Texts', in *'Retribution' in Jewish and Christian Writings: A Concept in Debate*, ed. D. Hamidović, M. Silvestrini and A. Thromas, forthcoming.

are living in an eschatological time,[6] contributes to a strengthening of the group's cohesion.

In the analysis below, my own reading of the Qumran texts is based on studies in the sociology of organizations. For purposes of the present study, therefore, I am not interested in debates about the validity or usefulness of terms such as 'sect', 'sectarianism' or the French word 'sectarisme' for characterizing the community at Qumran; nor is it my aim to rehearse the scholarly appropriation of M. Weber, B. Wilson, R. Stark and W. S. Bainbridge concerning the sociology of 'sectarianism',[7] notwithstanding the weighty influence of their theories in discussions of everything from Essene collective identity within Judaism and the world of Eastern Mediterranean Sea, to understanding the sociology of religious groups in ancient Judaism.

11.1 *The Limits of Intellectual 'Braconnage' (Poaching)*

The application of modern and postmodern approaches and concepts to ancient texts calls for a series of precautions to avoid inappropriate usage of scientific terms without a solid research basis. In that regard, the excessive use of concepts whose definition and methodological implications have not been probed is especially noteworthy. The current trend in scientific research of inflating the significance or value of concepts by adding the word 'studies' to them is a case in point.[8] By

---

6. D. Hamidović, 'L'eschatologie essénienne dans la littérature apocalyptique: temporalités et limites chronologiques', *REJ* 169 (2010): 37–55.

7. M. Weber, *The Methodology of the Social Sciences*, trans. E. A. Shils and H. A. Finch (Glencoe, IL: The Free Press, 1949), 90; Weber, *The Protestant Ethic and the Spirit of Capitalism*, trans. P. Baehr and G. C. Wells (London: Penguin, 2002); Weber, 'Voluntary Associational Life (Vereinswesen)', *Max Weber Studies* 2 (2002): 199–209; B. Wilson, 'An Analysis of Sect Development', in *Patterns of Sectarianism: Organization and Ideology in Social and Religious Movements*, ed. B. Wilson (London: Heinemann, 1967), 22–45; Wilson, *Religious Sects: A Sociological Study* (London: McGraw-Hill, 1970); Wilson, *Magic and the Millennium: A Sociological Study of Religious Movements of Protest among Tribal and Third-World Peoples* (London: Heinemann, 1973); Wilson, *Religion in Sociological Perspective* (Oxford: Oxford University Press, 1982); Wilson, *The Social Dimension of Sectarianism: Sects and New Religious Movements in Contemporary Society* (Oxford: Clarendon Press, 1990); and R. Stark and W. S. Bainbridge, *The Future of Religion: Secularization, Revival and Cult Formation* (Berkeley: University of California, 1985); Stark and Bainbridge, *A Theory of Religion* (New Jersey: Rutgers University Press, 1987).

8. On problems surrounding the use of 'certain social-scientific buzzwords', see D. J. Chalcraft, 'Is Sociology Also Among the Social Sciences? Some Personal Reflections on Sociological Approaches in Biblical Studies', in *Anthropology and the Bible: Critical Perspectives*, ed. E. Pfoh, Biblical Intersections, no. 3 (Piscataway, NJ: Gorgias Press, 2010), 37–75, esp. 46 n.16.

contrast, the present analysis intends to adhere to well-established approaches in the social sciences and the humanities. The sociological approach adopted below will be employed to understand the continuities and discontinuities of life forms born during and after modernity. The sociological approach differs from the historical approach in terms of the objects and the periods of time under consideration. While history can employ other methods and concepts to engage with modern and postmodern life forms and periods, it is not limited to those objects and periods. Since the nineteenth century, and more particularly since the 1960s and 1970s, biblical studies have used both approaches. However, some differences have been noted between Hebrew Bible and New Testament scholars. The latter have often spoken of 'socio-scientific' approaches or the social sciences in general, whereas the former have been more likely to refer more specifically to sociology, anthropology or social history. Epistemologists are now acknowledging that the use of the compound adjective 'socio-scientific' creates confusion within these different approaches. In addition, another compound adjective has often been used, namely 'socio-historical'.[9] Supporters of the first expression gave to the word 'scientific' the meaning of an explicit use of models and theories. It was generally assumed that the data gathered in this way was as anachronistic as the concepts used.[10] The proponents of the second expression understand themselves as historians of the social. They criticize the application of models in the research. John H. Elliott[11] argued that the so-called socio-scientific work goes beyond social history in its development of social imagination, and he emphasized that the purpose of the social sciences is to study models of human behaviour, understood to be 'tolerably' *predictable, certain and stable*. Similarly, he added that a study is called 'sociological' provided that it submits a hypothesis pertaining to a relation between social phenomena, and leading to the gathering of facts for the explanation of the given social relations and phenomena.[12]

As a historian of antiquity, and with the preceding definitions and distinctions in mind, I want to make use of the sociology of organizations. I will use that approach in the conviction that a historian of the social (or another speciality) ought to explain their own subjective setting, and that the historian whose subject matter is a collective object ought to make explicit their understanding of the 'social'[13] and be aware of the benefits and limits of this complementarity

9. D. B. Martin, 'Social-Scientific Criticism', in *To Each Its Own Meaning: An Introduction to Biblical Criticisms and Their Application*, ed. S. L. McKenzie and S. R. Haynes (Louisville: Westminster John Knox, 1999), 125–41, esp. 129.

10. J. H. Elliott, *What is Social-Scientific Criticism?* Guides to Biblical Scholarship, New Testament Series (Minneapolis: Augsburg Fortress, 1993), 7.

11. Ibid., 13–14.

12. J. H. Elliott, 'From Social Description to Social-Scientific Criticism: The History of a Society of Biblical Literature Section 1973–2005', *BTB* 38 (2008): 26–36.

13. S. Delamarter, 'Sociological Models for Understanding the Scribal Practices in the Biblical Dead Sea Scrolls', in *Rediscovering the Dead Sea Scrolls: An Assessment of Old and New Approaches and Methods*, ed. M. L. Grossman (Grand Rapids: Eerdmans, 2010), 186.

with sociology.[14] Mobilizing the sociology of organizations and applying it to the Qumran texts in order to grasp the conceptual system which governed the Qumran community is surely an instance of emic 'braconnage' or poaching, one whose emic character does not necessitate ignoring etic perspectives which provide insight into the world view of those who are writing the texts. A deliberate application of modern concepts formulated by sociologists whose research has focussed upon organizations is justified by the Qumran texts themselves in so far as they include concepts that members of the community held about their own organization.

11.2 *The Road to Hell Is Paved with Good Intentions, or the Sociology of Organizations*

A seminal work in the sociology of organizations is Michel Crozier and Erhard Friedberg's *L'acteur et le système*, first published in 1977.[15] According to Crozier and Friedberg, after making a number of observations during their teaching, they identified a need to outline 'un mode de raisonnement particulier',[16] instead of the mere description of a 'bonne organisation'[17] as that notion is understood in marketing and human relations today. The two sociologists present their propositions concerning problems in the study of organizations as well as the solutions humans have provided in order to 'assurer et développer leur coopération en vue de buts communs'.[18] Crozier and Friedberg view their reflections in this area as having relevance beyond the framework of companies and administrations since they are equally pertinent to decision-making in industrial relations and local political-administrative systems. The main purpose of Crozier and Friedberg's undertaking is to examine the 'problème du changement';[19] and for purposes of the present inquiry, one of their most important conclusions is that 'ce mode de raisonnement ne vise pas tant les organisations, comme objet social spécifique, que l'action organisée des hommes'.[20]

The characterization of 'action organisée' between the agent and the system – that is, the realization that the agent exists as such because they act in the system,

---

14. L. L. Grabbe, *Ancient Israel: What Do We Know and How Do We Know It?* (London: T&T Clark, 2007), 4–5, highlights that theories in the social sciences are not to be taken as facts but rather as suggestions to be evaluated and analogies to be compared.

15. M. Crozier and E. Friedberg, *L'acteur et le système: Les contraintes de l'action collective* (Paris: Editions du Seuil, 1977), who partly rely upon the pioneer work of J. G. March and H. A. Simon, *Organizations* (New York: Wiley, 1958).

16. Crozier and Friedberg, *L'acteur et le système*, 9.

17. Ibid., 10.

18. Ibid.

19. Ibid.

20. Ibid.

and that the system exists because the agents are acting and supporting it – is the topic of the book. The main purpose is to explain that, contrary to common opinion, organizational issues and resulting collective actions do not correspond to 'natural' factors arising more or less automatically from human interactions.[21] The relationship between the agents and the system consists of the specific actions of agents, more or less autonomous, which foster mutual cooperation and the achievement of common goals, despite personal divergence. Such achievements should not be conceived either as predetermined in every situation or as being adapted to a given context, but rather as contingent solutions, as 'largely indeterminate and thus arbitrary'.[22] Since they have the purpose of integrating divergent or contradictory behaviours, a simple structure is needed to provide a framework for interpersonal relations: the organization. The name is born out of custom, history or belief. The organization circumscribes and defines the agents' liberty and their capacity to act.

Crozier and Friedberg, focussing upon constraints within the organization, highlight 'counter-intuitive' or 'perverse effects'[23] which are collective in nature and deemed aberrant by most people even though they are the result of multiple, personal, independent, carefully considered choices and rational decisions. Thus, they put into opposition the common orientations and personal intuitions. Organization would not be necessary if the agents were not motivated by personal interest and had complete trust in each other in the pursuit of common interests. Since those conditions are not achieved but contrary to fact, organizations ideally guarantee a principle of relation between agents for the purpose of achieving common goals. That principle, in turn, becomes more and more autonomous and structures itself into a genuine instituted organization.

Collective action is thus closely linked to organization. In and of itself, the organization is not the solution to the problems encountered in the course of collective action, but a means to the end of control and regulation. This brings to mind the impulse of political men and women to create commissions to solve new issues but whose effects leave those issues largely untouched.

Nevertheless, organization generates counter-intuitive effects. Agents act rationally with respect to the common goals but are trapped by the means, the frameworks given to them to make cooperation possible. While it is true that the agents can and do change the means, the agents cannot do without them if they are to initiate change. Organizational analysis thus becomes a prerequisite for a new way of thinking about collective action to emerge. An apt comparison would be the practice in the field of medicine where the functioning of an artificial device is studied in order to better understand the human body. Organization thus is not natural but rather a 'problème à expliquer'.[24]

21. Ibid., 15.
22. Ibid., 16.
23. Ibid.
24. Ibid., 21.

11.3 *The Arrival of the Teacher of Righteousness in the Community After Twenty Years of Erring*

The Qumran community, the *yaḥad*, and perhaps even the Essene movement as a whole, can be analysed according to the principles above in order to conceptualize the link between collective action and common goals on the one hand and personal strategies on the other. According to those same principles, no individual actor would accept being considered only as an agent for the achievement of the organization's goals; instead, every agent develops a personal strategy[25] to align his own goals and desires with the collective objective. On that understanding, a personal action contributing to a collective objective conforms to a 'rationalité limitée',[26] a *modus vivendi* between the personal and the collective which determines individual action towards a collective goal. In other words, even if the organization is a structure made for rationalization, it has a limit: the liberty of each individual.

From that standpoint, it is interesting to consider the action attributed to the Teacher of Righteousness within the Qumran community. In order to achieve their objectives, an individual agent is required to use resources that are readily available and to adapt them to his own interest.[27] Do the Qumran texts bear some written traces of resources which the Teacher of Righteousness mobilized and adapted? Studies of the Qumran manuscripts, and especially scholarship informed by sociology, have emphasized the collective dimension at the heart of the community's self-definition and its relationship with others. I suggest that a complementary element should be introduced, namely the individual dimension. Do the Qumran texts allow us to get close to one or more of the Teacher of Righteousness's individual strategies in the community, beyond the memories held about him by others? To answer these questions, I suggest that the arrival of the Teacher of Righteousness[28] in the community be studied with the aid

---

25. 'Derrière les humeurs et les réactions affectives il est en effet possible à l'analyste de découvrir des régularités, qui n'ont de sens que par rapport à une stratégie. Celle-ci n'est donc rien d'autre que le fondement inféré ex post des régularités de comportements observés empiriquement. Il s'en suit qu'une telle "stratégie" n'est nullement synonyme de volonté, pas plus qu'elle n'est nécessairement consciente' (ibid., 48).

26. Ibid., 46.

27. J. Jokiranta, 'Qumran: The Prototypical Teacher in the Qumran Pesharim: A Social-Identity Approach', in *Ancient Israel: The Old Testament in Its Social Contexts*, ed. P. F. Esler (Minneapolis: Augsburg Fortress, 2006), 254–63, esp. 254, understands the Teacher in the *pesharim* as 'an ideal member who captures some essential characteristics of the group's identity'.

28. The Teacher of Righteousness is rarely quoted in the manuscripts from Qumran and is only mentioned in the *Damascus Document* and the *pesharim*, namely *Pesher* Habakkuk (1QpHab), *Pesher* Micah (1Q14), *Pesher* Psalms^a (4Q171), *Pesher* Psalms^b (4Q173); see the list of occurrences in M. A. Knibb, 'The Teacher of Righteousness – A Messianic Title?', in *A Tribute to Geza Vermes: Essays on Jewish and Christian Literature and History*, ed. P. R. Davies and R. T. White (Sheffield: JSOT, 1990), 51–52.

of principles of strategic analysis, along with help from literary analysis for purposes of removing the text's rhetorical layer. The writing of texts in antiquity was never impartial, not least because it often represented a collective interest. The texts often describe an action or relate a collective interest. Therefore the redaction and copy of texts can constitute the resources of the Qumran community.

The beginning of the *Damascus Document*, CD A 1.3-11, depicts the arrival of the Teacher of Righteousness. It describes the collective purpose by means of historiosophy, wisdom presented in the style of historical narrative. The passage includes an element that could be linked to the personal strategy of the Teacher:

> **3** Because they left him in their unfaithfulness, he hid his face to Israel and to his sanctuary **4** and he delivered them to the sword. Yet, in memory of the forefathers' Covenant,[29] he left a rest **5** to Israel and did not hand them over to annihilation. And at the end of a wrath of three hundred **6** and ninety years, after he had handed them over into the hand of Nebuchadnezzar, king of Babylon, **7** he visited them and made grow out of Israel and of Aaron a root of planting for taking possession **8** of his land and to fatten with the fertility of his soil. And they understood their fault and recognized that **9** they (were) guilty; and they were like the blind ones, like those who grope (to find) a way **10** (during) twenty years. And God considered their deeds, because they had searched for him with a perfect heart. **11** Thus he raised a Teacher of Righteousness[30] for them, in order to guide them into the path of his heart.

As is now well known, numbers in this sort of text have sometimes been read literally in order to deduce the date of the founding of the Essene movement. Most scholars have understood that the movement could have been founded 390 years after the taking of Jerusalem by Nebuchadnezzar in 587/586 BCE, and thus in 197/196 BCE. The twenty years of uncertainty, moreover, has been used to date the Teacher's arrival at *c.* 177/176 BCE.[31] Other scholars, however, have noted that

---

29. Literally, 'the Covenant of the first ones'. The passage recalls the foundation of the Essene group in the framework of the history of Israel. The 'first ones' are not the first ones to enter into the Covenant as in CD A 3.10, or the founding ones of the Essene movement in CD A 4.6-10, but rather are the patriarchs.

30. The title *moreh (ha-)ṣedeq* can also be translated to read 'legitimate Teacher' or 'authentic Teacher'. His personal name is never mentioned in the manuscripts. Considering that the other roles of the community are not nominative, does this mean that multiple persons successively discharged the functions of Teacher of Righteousness?

31. The hypothesis of J. Murphy O'Connor, 'The Damascus Document Revisited', *RB* 92, no. 2 (1985): 223–46, is famous: the Teacher of Righteousness would have come from 'Damascus', a coded name for Babylon where exiled Jews had been living for several centuries; see also P. R. Davies, 'The Prehistory of the Qumran Community', in *The Dead Sea Scrolls: Forty Years of Research*, ed. D. Dimant and U. Rappaport, STDJ 10 (Leiden: E. J. Brill, 1992), 116–25. But the hypothesis has been refuted by H. Stegemann, *Die Essener, Qumran, Johannes der Täufer und Jesus: Ein Sachbuch*, 3rd edn (Freiburg: Herder, 1994),

such numbers ought to be understood according to their symbolic value.[32] The symbolic time of 390 years, for instance, matches an exegesis of Ezek. 4.5: Ezekiel's symbolic number for the sin of the house of Israel is 390 days, a day for each year. In the next verse, forty days are added to figuratively represent the impiety of the house of Judah, the sum of those numbers being 430, a symbolic number recalling the 430 years of the Israelites' enslavement in Egypt according to Exod. 12.40. The symbolic reading does not produce a specific date for the foundation of the Essene movement; but in that regard, it may not be entirely neutral or insignificant, for it may correspond to a more general time-frame when the Essene group appeared, around the beginning of the second century BCE, a dating that continues to command wide approval among scholars working on the Qumran manuscripts.[33]

Still, one can ask why the Teacher of Righteousness' presence at the head of the group is not overtly mentioned at the very beginning of the movement. Questions of the text's historical validity are not the issue, for as an example of historiosophy the text presents the origins of the movement for didactic or even devotional purposes. Accordingly, and in keeping with traditions of religious movements' foundational narratives, it would have been easier to simply present the Teacher as the movement's initiator, without alluding to the addition of a period of twenty years. As with other time periods mentioned in the story,[34] the symbolic reading remains a possibility – the twenty years probably indicates half a generation – but it remains difficult to find a biblical text to which the twenty years is clearly an

234, 280, though Stegemann also admitted that the Essenes had picked up some concepts cherished by the exiled Jews in Babylonia. Stegemann envisages a Palestinian Jew belonging to the movement of the pious, or *Ḥasidim*, described in *1 Macc.* 2.42 (198–213); but it should not be overlooked that the Maccabees sought refuge on the eastern side of the Jordan, and thus outside the area of Jerusalem; see also *1 Macc.* 7.13-18, where 60 'pious' who came to negotiate the permission to worship in the Temple of Jerusalem were executed by the High priest Alcimus.

32. For different counting and discussions, see A. Laato, 'The Chronology in the *Damascus Document* at Qumran', *RevQ* 15 (1992): 605–607; F. M. Schweitzer, 'The Teacher of Righteousness', in *Mogilany 1989: Papers on the Dead Sea Scrolls Offered in Memory of Jean Carmignac, II: The Teacher of Righteousness*, ed. Z. J. Kapera (Krakow: The Enigma Press, 1991), 92; H. Ulfgard, 'The Teacher of Righteousness, the History of the Qumran Community, and Our Understanding of the Jesus Movement: Texts, Theories and Trajectories', in *Qumran Between the Old and New Testaments*, ed. F. H. Geyer and T. L. Thomson (Sheffield: Sheffield Academic Press, 1998), 316–18. No chronology, however, truly explains the period of twenty years.

33. For example, J. C. VanderKam, *The Dead Sea Scrolls Today* (Grand Rapids: Eerdmans, 1994), 100.

34. M. A. Knibb, 'Teacher of Righteousness', in *Encyclopedia of the Dead Sea Scrolls*, vol. 2 (Oxford: Oxford University Press, 2000), 919, writes: ' "twenty" looks like a round figure [and] would adjust the chronology of the appearance of the Teacher of Righteousness to around the middle of the second century BCE.'

allusion. CD A 1.9-10 is certainly reminiscent of Isa. 59.10, just before the mention of twenty years in the former; but the absence of any specific time period in the Isaianic passage is significant. The arrival of the Teacher after the movement had been in existence for twenty years is puzzling when the other temporal references noted above are considered.

As the symbolic reading therefore remains difficult to understand, we should be alert to the presence of any historical detail that might be a vestige or relic of the Essene movement's beginnings.[35] To use an expression cherished by New Testament scholars, this type of detail could be identified by applying the criterion of 'ecclesiastical embarrassment'.[36] Foundational stories of religious movements always represent their founder as an idealized figure.[37] To my knowledge, there

35. In the same perspective, G. J. Brooke, 'The "Apocalyptic" Community, the Matrix of the Teacher and Rewriting Scripture', in *Authoritative Scriptures in Ancient Judaism*, ed. M. Popović, Supplements to the Journal for the Study of Judaism, no. 141 (Leiden: E. J. Brill, 2010), 45, envisages the adding of twenty years as the sign of a calculation corresponding to the contemporary time of the editor.

36. See J. P. Meier, *A Marginal Jew: Rethinking the Historical Jesus* (New York: Doubleday, 1991), 168–71, and the French translation in Jean-Bernard Degorce and Charles Ehlinger, *Un certain Juif Jésus. Les données de l'histoire*, vol. 1, Lectio Divina (Paris: Cerf, 2009), 102–105. S. E. Porter, *The Criteria for Authenticity in Historical-Jesus: Previous Discussion and New Proposals*, JSNTSup 191 (Sheffield: Sheffield Academic Press, 2000), 162, speaks of a 'movement against the redactional tendency'; G. Thiessen and D. Winter, *The Quest for the Plausible Jesus: The Question of Criteria* (Louisville: Westminster John Knox, 2002). B. F. Meyer, *The Aims of Jesus* (London: SCM, 2002), speaks of a 'contradiction' criterion. Meier quotes the theologian E. Schillebeeckx who does not seem to have used this expression. The weaknesses of these criticisms are demonstrated by F. Bermejo-Rubio, 'Changing Methods, Disturbing Material: Should the Criterion of Embarrassment Be Dismissed in Jesus Research?', *REJ* 175 (2016): 1–25.

37. The quasi-contemporary example of Jesus of Nazareth, according to the memory, or memories, made about him in the New Testament and other Christian writings, is a relevant anthropological point of comparison. However, the notion of charisma applied to Jesus (see, e.g. M. Weber, *Economie et société* [Paris: Plon, 1971], 577; and more generally, J. Wach, *Sociologie de la religion* [Paris: Payot, 1955], 302–303; P. Bourdieu, 'Genèse et structure du champ religieux', *Revue française de sociologie* 12 [1971]: 295–334; J. -L. Evard, *La religion perverse: Essai sur le charisme* [Paris: Éditions du Rocher, 2008]; B. Thériault and J. Duhaime, ed., *Les charismes* [special issue], *Théologiques* 17, 1 [2009] and to the Teacher of Righteousness (see H. Ulfgard, 'The Teacher of Righteousness', 334–35, 345) seems too wide and vague in its definition for the texts regarding both figures. See A. Dupont-Sommer, *Aperçus préliminaires sur les manuscrits de la mer Morte* (Paris: Maisonneuve, 1950), 121; J. Carmignac, *Le Docteur de Justice et Jésus-Christ* (Paris: Editions de l'Orante, 1957); H. Stegemann, 'The "Teacher of Righteousness" and Jesus: Two Types of Religious Leadership in Judaism at the Turn of the Era', in *Jewish Civilization in the Hellenistic-Roman Period*, ed. S. Talmon, JSPSup 10 (Sheffield: Sheffield Academic Press, 1991), 196–213.

is not a single instance where the alleged founder of a religious movement is not actually present at the inception of the given group. In the present narrative, the arrival of the Teacher of Righteousness almost twenty years after the movement's foundation has the potential to instil doubts in the faithful both about the origins of their movement and about the foundational role of the Teacher. The detail regarding the twenty years is even more curious when we consider that the *Pesher Psalms*[a], 4Q171 III 15-17 seems to give a different version of the story in the course of interpreting Ps. 37.23-24:

> **15** His interpretation is about the priest, the Teacher of [Righteousness whom]
> **16** God [cho]se for standing/pillar [. . .] he settled him for founding (*lebanot*) the congregation [of his elected ones of truth] for him **17** [and] enforcing his [voi]ce, in truth.

In this excerpt, the Teacher of Righteousness is explicitly identified as the community's founder chosen by God. That legitimation collides with the story of CD A 1. If the variant in 4Q171 III 15-17 were historical, it should have been easy for the editors of CD A 1 historiosophy to hush the detail of the twenty years before the Teacher's arrival and to locate him instead at the origin of the movement. However, as that is not the case, the Teacher's arrival can be inferred to have taken place only after a time of 'fault' and blindness.

The inference just drawn, when situated in the movement's history, might strengthen the hypothesis that the Essene movement was born from a scission in an earlier group, a conflict identified by some scholars with the separation of the Essenes and the Pharisees.[38] Representing one version of that perspective, P. R. Davies has argued that the division within the movement was caused by the arrival of the Teacher.[39] H. Lapin, in stark contrast to Davies, has proposed that CD A 1 as a whole presents an internally devised fiction intended to create an identity for

---

38. See D. Hamidović, *L'Écrit de Damas*, Collection de la Revue des Études Juives, no. 51 (Louvain: Peeters, 2011), 48. The discussion about whether the Teacher's arrival in the existing movement created a split within it is ongoing; the group led by the Teacher could correspond to the Essenes and this would place him in the role of the community's founding figure. See F. García Martínez, 'Qumran Origins and Early History: A Groningen Hypothesis', *Folia Orientalia* 25 (1988): 113–36; F. García Martínez and A. S. van der Woude, 'A "Groningen" Hypothesis of Qumran Origins and Early History', *RevQ* 14, no. 4 (1990): 521–41; F. García Martínez, 'The Origins of the Essene Movement and of the Qumran Sect', in *The People of the Dead Sea Scrolls: Their Writings, Beliefs and Practices*, ed. F. García Martínez and Julio Trebolle Barrera (Leiden: E. J. Brill, 1995), 77–96. It seems to me that the rhetorical layers in the text and their verbosity do not make it possible to settle the debate.

39. P. R. Davies, *The Damascus Covenant: An Interpretation of the 'Damascus Document'*, JSOTSup 25 (Sheffield: Sheffield Academic Press, 1983); Davies, 'Communities at Qumran and the Case of the Missing "Teacher"', *RevQ* 15 (1991): 275–86; Davies, 'The Teacher of Righteousness and the End of Days', in *Sects and Scrolls: Essays on Qumran and Related*

the community.[40] According to Lapin, the detail about the twenty years does not correspond to historical reality but only to a time period added with a view to establishing a founding figure for the movement; from the same perspective, the Teacher would have been added to CD A 1 to create a past for the alleged founder. And from yet another angle, M. O. Wise has developed a historicising interpretation of the detail in an effort to date the founding of the movement.[41]

Between the minimalist hypothesis[42] of seeing the Teacher of Righteousness as a purely fictional figure and the maximalist proposition[43] that sees him as

Topics, ed. P. R. Davies (Atlanta: Scholars, 1996), 89–94; Davies, 'Between Text and Archaeology', *DSD* 18 (2011): 332–36.

40. H. Lapin, 'Dead Sea Scrolls and the Historiography of Ancient Judaism', in *Rediscovering the Dead Sea Scrolls*, ed. M. L. Grossman, 124.

41. M. O. Wise, 'Dating the Teacher of Righteousness and the Floruit of his Movement', *JBL* 122 (2003): 53–87. Wise envisages that the length of the Persian period is perceived by some Jews according to the time of 490 years registered in Dan. 9.24-27, after a rereading of Jeremiah's prophecy in Jer. 25.11-12; 29.10 announcing Jerusalem's liberation 70 years after its capture by the Babylonians.

42. See H. Lapin, 'Dead Sea Scrolls', 124.

43. See R. de Vaux, *Les institutions de l'Ancien Testament*, vol. 2 (Paris: Éditions du Cerf, 1960), 267; J. Murphy O'Connor, 'Teacher of Righteousness', in *ABD*, vol. 6, 340–41; O'Connor, 'The Essenes and their History', *RB* 81 (1974): 215–44; H. Burgmann, *Vorgeschichte und Frühgeschichte der essenischen Gemeinden von Qumrân und Damaskus*, ANTJ 7 (Frankfurt am Main: Lang, 1987), 189–228; O. Betz and R. Riesner, *Jesus, Qumran and the Vatican: Clarifications* (London: SCM, 1994), 47–48; Stegemann, *Die Essener*, 205–12; VanderKam, *The Dead Sea Scrolls Today*, 103–104; E. Puech, 'Le grand prêtre Simon (III) fils d'Onias III, le Maître de Justice?', in *Antikes Judentum und frühes Christentum*, ed. H. Stegemann (Berlin: W. de Gruyter, 1999), 137–58. Although the movement's proto-history is not considered in such a detailed manner by the proponents of the so-called Groningen Hypothesis as in the studies referenced here, that school none the less asserts that the Teacher's arrival in the middle of the second century BCE, during the pontificate of Jonathan and Simon Maccabeus, was the cause of a split inside the preexisting movement; see F. García Martínez, 'Qumran Origins and Early History', 113–36; F. García Martínez and A. S. van der Woude, 'A "Groningen" Hypothesis of the Qumran Origins and Early History', 521–41; F. García Martínez, 'The Origins of the Essene Movement and of the Qumran Sect', 77–96. The hypothesis of the priest in chief, the priests' *sagan*, the second after the High priest, who would have taken over the High priest's office *in absentia* after Alcimus's death, see J. H. Ulrichsen, 'Menighetsforståelsen i Qumrantekstene', *NTT* 83 (1982): 156. Furthermore, the role of the 'impious priest' – whether it is a unique person or a sobriquet for designating several opponents over a larger period – does not seem to have a great role in the founding of the Essene movement; on that subject, the first attempts at historical contextualization – A. Dupont-Sommer, *The Jewish Sect of Qumran and the Essenes*, London, 1955; J. P. M. van der Ploeg, *The Excavations at Qumran*, London, 1958 – possess abiding value.

an anonymous High priest (possibly despoiled of his position in the Temple of Jerusalem[44]), it seems to me that we have to return to the CD A 1 text and its function. The literary genre of historiosophy suggests that the historical facts have been mediatized to fulfil a function whose nature and audience we will need to investigate. The readers and hearers of the *Damascus Document* undoubtedly include Essenes; but for purposes of a more nuanced contextualization, it is worth mentioning H. Lapin's argument that believers needed to know the history of their group, and particularly the history of their group's founder, needs which would give meaning and relevance to a narration of the Teacher's history in accordance with conventions operative at the turn of our era. That same argument, however, collides with the aforementioned twenty-years motif, which does not cast the Teacher in the role of founder, in the strictest sense of the term, but rather as one who takes over a preexisting group; thus, if the goal of this story was to fortify belief in a founding figure, it fails in its objective. When historiosophy as a genre comes face to face with the chronology of the movement's beginning, the outcome does not agree with the hypothesis of a merely fictional figure, constructed after the fact either to satisfy the questions of insiders or to conform with contemporary foundational narratives of religious movements.[45]

Considering the historiosophy, the audience, and the implications of the 'embarrassment' criterion for the twenty-years motif, I suggest that the function of the foundational story is to provide a model of community membership for non-Essene Jews.[46] The Teacher's late arrival – probably at the age of reason or even maturity, to judge by his role in leading the believers out of error – could serve as an *exemplum*, a model to be followed by Jews who enter the movement after its founding; and a similar paradigmatic function can be discerned in the portrayal of the movement's beginnings, marked as they are by the group's passage through confusion before attaining to the observation of God's ways. From that same account of beginnings, one can infer that the first believers were in error since they find God's ways only when the Teacher arrives. The idea that twenty years passed before the Teacher's arrival therefore implies that anyone can be in error at any given moment in their lives; but it also suggests the possibility of repentance and joining the Essene movement.

The reading just proposed is strengthened, moreover, by two other mentions of the Teacher in the *Damascus Document*, especially if one ignores the reference to his death in CD B 19.35–20.1. The passage in CD B 20.27-32 develops further

---

44. Puech, 'Le grand prêtre Simon (III)', 137–58, named him 'Simon III, son of Onias III'.

45. See, for example, the narratives of Jesus's childhood and the beginning of his public ministry.

46. The discovery of two copies of the *Damascus Document* in the Old-Kairo Karaite synagogue at the end of the nineteenth century should be mentioned. The thesis of a fortuitous discovery of the text by some Karaites seems irrelevant to me; see D. Hamidović, 'Qumran Texts in Jewish and Christian Traditions', forthcoming.

the paradigmatic value of the Teacher's arrival and its relevance for attracting new adepts:

> **27** But all those who kept tied to these laws,[47] go[in]g **28** and coming in accordance with the *Torah*, (who) have listened to the voice of the Teacher and have confessed themselves in front of God (saying): "We have sinned, **29** we have been impious, just us as well as our fathers, when we were walking against the prescriptions of the Covenant. Righteous[ness] **30** and truth (are constituting) your laws for us" (1QS 1.25-26; Ps. 106.6; Dan. 9.5); and (who) did not raised their hands against his holy prescriptions, his righteous law[s] **31** and his true testimonies; (who) got instructed into the first laws by which **32** the men of the community have been judged;[48] (who) heard the voice (of) the Teacher of Righteousness and have not rejected **33** the prescriptions of righteousness when hearing them.

The Teacher is the one who issued the 'first laws', the first authentic interpretation of the *Torah*, according to CD B 20.8-9.[49] That excerpt shows the Teacher's function in regard to new members joining the group. Their situation prior to membership is compared to a time of sin and impiety, since they confess their faults after having listened to 'the Teacher's voice'. In this way, the Teacher as a spokesperson is a conduit for this new membership; he has the ability to convince Jews to follow the right way. The reference to confession of sins is quite close to a passage from the *Rule of the Community*, 1QS 1.25-26, which describes part of the ceremony for entry into the Covenant and thus also into the community.[50] According to the *Damascus Document* the Teacher therefore fulfils a specific goal of the community, namely, that of convincing other Jews to join the group.

In that same collective project, the Teacher functions like an official matchmaker between Jews in general and the Essene community, a function he can fulfil because he has received the revelation of the first laws. F. García

---

47. 4Q267 3.4-5 before the *vacat* adds: '[. . . those who kept tie]d to the Covenant[. . .]'.

48. The adjective 'unique', *yhyd*, can allude both to the Teacher of Righteousness and to the community, *yahad*.

49. The Teacher of Righteousness extracted out of the *Torah* the first hidden laws which the Essenes have to follow. They are waiting for another at the end of times, cf. CD A 6.10-11; 1QS 9.10-11; Testament of Judah 24.3. This is why the distinction between the function of ascertaining the validity of the interpretations and the function of teaching the law assigned to the Teacher seem exaggerated to me, as if the movement's teaching is not presented as coming from the Teacher; see S. Fraade, *Legal Fictions: Studies of Law and Narrative in the Discursive Worlds of Ancient Jewish Sectarians and Sages*, Supplements to the Journal for the Study of Judaism, no. 147 (Leiden: E. J. Brill, 2011), 43, concerning 4QMMT.

50. The ceremony celebrating the entry into the Covenant never quotes the Teacher but does quote the priests and the Levites. One cannot deduce the room left for the Teacher in the community described in 1QS from the argument *a silentio*.

Martínez understands the same passage as proof that the Teacher did not have a monopoly over the interpretation of the laws and that the community could likewise deliver interpretations: the Teacher's voice 'was "institutionalized" within the groups that took their inspiration from this figure and became the channel of continuous revelation at the end of times'.[51] In light of the explicit references to the Teacher, such an understanding of the passage seems well founded to me, because it distinguishes between the Teacher of Righteousness as a person in his own right and the memory of him preserved in the Qumran text via the concept of 'voice'.

García Martínez goes on to emphasize the memory aspects of the Teacher in the Essene community. Collective memory not only constitutes a type of 'continuous revelation' but also relies on the function assigned to the Teacher, who serves as the example to be followed by Jews who are not already Essenes. For that same reason, however, and despite the similarity between the inferred setting and the beginning of the document, a difference is to be observed between the Teacher as a historical figure at the movement's beginnings, and the collective memory of the Teacher. The latter facilitates a continuous interpretation of the law by members who have a full say in the community. In fact, the interpretation can no longer be made by the Teacher since he is dead; instead it is delivered through the 'Teacher's voice', an authentication device of the henceforth collective interpretation of the laws. By contrast, at the time of his physical life, the Teacher is not a founding figure but rather a leader in the group. After his death, his leadership is maintained by the concept of the 'Teacher's voice', which has the advantages of providing a felt sense of continuity for the Essene project and minimizing the historical shift (implied by 1QS 6.9-10) in the community's leadership towards a more collective form of authority.[52] In line with the first part of the *Damascus Document*, the Teacher's story also discloses to the Jews the only avenue of repentance open to them: namely, adherence to the Essene movement.[53]

Most probably, the effort to present the Teacher as a coherent figure through the writing of memory finds both its apogee and its summary in 4Q171 III 15–17, where the Teacher's role as group founder is made explicit and clear. Besides the goals of instituting continuity in the transmission of the divine revelation and most

---

51. F. García Martínez, 'Beyond the Sectarian Divide: The "Voice of the Teacher" as an Authority-Conferring Strategy in Some Qumran Texts', in *The Dead Sea Scrolls: Transmission of Traditions and Production of Texts*, ed. S. Metso, H. Najman and E. Schüller, STDJ 92 (Leiden: E. J. Brill, 2010), 227–34. Also Ulfgard, 'The Teacher of Righteousness', 318.

52. See D. Hamidović, 'Living *Serakhim*: Process of Authority in the *Community Rule*', in *The Process of Authority: The Dynamics in Transmission and Reception of Canonical Texts*, ed. J. Dušek and J. Roskovec (Berlin: W. de Gruyter, 2016), 61–90.

53. Brooke, 'The "Apocalyptic" Community', 45; and Brooke, 'Justifying Deviance: The Place of Scripture in Converting to a Qumran Self-Understanding', in *Reading the Present in the Qumran Library: The Perception of the Contemporary by Means of Scriptural Interpretation*, ed. K. de Troyer and A. Lange (Atlanta: SBL, 2005), 73–87, where the author uses the notion of conversion. See also D. Hamidović, *L'Écrit de Damas*, xi.

likely insuring the survival of the group after the Teacher's death, the rhetorical and memorial features of this passage stand in contrast to CD A 1 in regard to the place of the Teacher in his movement. The so-called Groningen hypothesis, that the founder of the community was recognized at his arrival by the preexisting group because he caused a split in it,[54] does not do justice either to the relevant thematic context in CD A 1 or to the comparative evidence in CD B 19–20. The historical figure of the Teacher in the latter context, where he is portrayed not as the founder of the Essene movement but rather as a leader whose joining of the preexisting group after a defective life constitutes the model that every Jew should follow, ought to be compared with the memorial figure of the Teacher, a figure that ensures continuity of revelation and interpretation in a context of new members joining the group. The two figures are not irreconcilable, for the contexts and functions of the stories are the same: attracting new members. And that means the Teacher's memory, supported by his 'voice', has a historical basis, especially if the common context of expression is given due consideration. A radical separation of the memory from history would be tantamount to negating the existence of the memory itself, since there cannot be a memory without some historical grounding for it (unless one opts for myths, which offer an alternative basis to historical facts).

Regarding the implications of the 'embarrassment' criterion for understanding the motif of the twenty-year period, the Qumran texts deal with the memory of the Teacher rather than with myth. More precisely the two faces of the Teacher, which seem to be interrelated, illustrate among other things his versatility in the Qumran texts, a quality nicely encapsulated by George J. Brooke's description of him as a 'multi-tasker'.[55] Beyond this plurality of functions attributed to the Teacher in the texts, a multitude of intertwined memories need to be recognized which presuppose diverse foundations but are in every case literary and theological in nature. The question of the historical basis for any of these memories has been debated at length, ever since research on the Qumran texts began to cross the boundaries between literary and theological analysis on the one hand and questions of historical context and reference on the other. Historians of antiquity currently working on the Qumran texts have pinpointed the methodological pitfall in that enterprise and are increasingly concluding that the texts only preserve the Teacher's memory or memories, whose historical basis is not accessible through our extant sources.[56] I concur with that view apart from the following caveat: to my

54. García Martínez, 'Qumran Origins and Early History', 113–36; García Martínez and van der Woude, 'A "Groningen" Hypothesis of Qumran Origins and Early History', 521–41; García Martínez, 'The Origins of the Essene Movement and of the Qumran Sect', 77–96.

55. Brooke, 'The "Apocalyptic" Community', 37–53, esp. 46 and 50, rightly notes that only the person of the Teacher endorses the roles of priest, a new Moses and the agent of revelation of the Law, the prophetic commentator, the poet and the wise.

56. On the question whether the Teacher of Righteousness is the author of the main Qumran texts, such as 4QMMT, see E. Qimron and J. Strugnell, ed., *Qumran Cave 4: V: Miqṣat Maʿase ha-Torah*, DJD 10 (Oxford: Oxford University Press, 1994), 119–21. On 1QS, see J. Murphy O'Connor, 'La genèse littéraire de la *Règle de la Communauté*,

knowledge, the reference that situates the Teacher's arrival twenty years after the birth of the movement has not yet been interpreted symbolically with reference to Jewish texts earlier than the second century BCE.

11.4 *The Teacher's Basis of Power in the Community*

The foregoing analysis of history and social memory can be integrated into the conceptual framework of the sociology of organizations in ways that might illuminate the personal strategy of the Teacher beyond the community's historiosophic narrative in CD A 1. In the narrative of CD A 1, the brief presentation of the Teacher's arrival into the preexisting community provides no explicit account for his power inside the community; on the contrary, and as argued above in my interpretation of the twenty-years motif, only the Teacher's value as a role model for other Jews is put forward. To be sure, being raised up as an example entails having a form of responsibility within the group; but in itself, it neither assumes nor implies an ascription of power, whereas the historiosophic discourse at the beginning of the *Damascus Document* specifies that the Teacher delivers the first interpretations of the divine revelation and therefore holds a position of leadership within the Essene movement.

In order to identify the Teacher's personal strategy at the time of his arrival into the group, the reference to the twenty-year period must be given further attention.[57] The Teacher's role as an example to which new members should

RB 76 (1969): 531; partly, Schweitzer, 'The Teacher of Righteousness', 59. On the *Temple Scroll*: Y. Yadin, *The Temple Scroll: The Hidden Law of the Dead Sea Sect* (London: Random House, 1985), 85, 195–96, 226–28; B. Z. Wacholder, *The Dawn of Qumran: The Sectarian Torah and the Teacher of Righteousness* (Cincinnati: Hebrew Union College Press, 1983), 202–12; Schweitzer, 'The Teacher of Righteousness', 55–57, 95. On the *pesharim*: J. A. Fitzmyer, *Responses to 101 Questions on the Dead Sea Scrolls* (New York: Paulist, 1992), 33–34. And on the *Hodayot*, especially the so-called Teacher's hymns: G. Jeremias, *Der Lehrer der Gerechtigkeit* (Göttingen: Vandenhoeck & Ruprecht, 1963), 171–77; J. Becker, *Das Heil Gottes: Heils- und Sündenbegriffe in den Qumrantexten und im Neuen Testament*, SUNT 3 (Göttingen: Vandenhoeck & Ruprecht, 1963), 53; and Schweitzer, 'The Teacher of Righteousness', 66–73. One must also recognize the distinction between the Teacher as a historical figure and the memorial figure of the Teacher. The present research has proceeded in accordance with the embarrassment criterion, but on that basis no passage in the texts seems eligible. That is why only the memory or memories made of the Teacher can be alleged; in that vein, see S. Holm-Nielsen, *Hodayot: Psalms from Qumran*, Acta theological danica, no. 2 (Aarhus: Universtitetsvørlaget, 1960); P. R. Callaway, *The History of the Qumran Community: An Investigation*, JSPSup 3 (Sheffield: JSOT Press, 1988), 185–97.

57. The mention of the Teacher's death at the beginning of CD B 20 probably means that at least the B recension of CD was written after his death; and that may be the case for the work as a whole. It is also possible that his death might have been anticipated.

conform implies a strongly horizontal quality in the community's structure, with members being on an equal footing after their integration into the group. That idea, however, is not repeated elsewhere in the story, an absence which could entail that the memory of the Teacher had acquired greater importance than the initial personal strategy of the Teacher, who either had died by the time these passages were written or, if he was still alive, had devised other strategies more important than his initial one even though his original aim of attracting new members remained. Either way, by the time of that stage in the writing/editing, the Teacher is no longer the model to be followed but rather the sole authoritative interpreter of the *Torah*.

The consequent mutation in the personal strategy is apparent in the text when the allusive formulation of the initial strategy and the more explicit passage about subsequent strategy are compared. By the time of the latter context, a clear distinction between the Teacher and the members is established, with the community being represented in terms of its vertical dimension, and the Teacher being at its pinnacle. Such a development illustrates the idea that an agent's strategy cannot be conceived outside the context from which it draws its rationale, or outside the given memory, beyond the level of its producers' rhetorical interests.[58]

Contrary to common opinion, as Crozier and Friedberg explain, real power does not exist simply because there is some hierarchical position within an organization. In their view, 'a source of uncertainty [that defines the zone of power] only exists and finds meaning through the investment of agents who seize it in the pursuit of their strategies. Yet, the "objective" existence [i.e., of power] does not tell us anything about the will or more simply the capacity of the agents to truly seize and use the opportunity that it represents.'[59] Power only exists, in other words, through the working of individual strategies.

As for the Teacher of Righteousness, his power cannot be based exclusively on his status as role model, whereby he initially creates, more or less consciously, a resemblance or analogy between himself and new members of the community. By contrast, the Teacher's subsequent personal strategy – be it memorial, historical or neither – corresponds to one of the four sources of power discussed by Crozier and Friedberg,[60] namely, the demonstration of a skill or professional

---

58. As noted by D. J. Chalcraft, 'Is Sociology Also Among the Social Sciences?', 63, the application of the sociological approach to texts does not pay enough attention either to the function of texts or to text-centred communities.

59. Crozier and Friedberg, *L'acteur et le système*, 71–72: 'une source d'incertitude [qui définit la zone de pouvoir] n'existe et ne prend sa signification dans les processus organisationnels qu'à travers son investissement par les acteurs qui s'en saisissent pour la poursuite de leurs stratégies. Or, l'existence "objective" ne nous dit rien sur la volonté ou plus simplement sur la capacité des acteurs de véritablement saisir et utiliser l'opportunité qu'elle constitue.'

60. Ibid., 85.

specialization difficult to replace within the organization.[61] Thus, the presentation of the Teacher of Righteousness in CD A 1 not as the group's founder but merely as an exemplary and thus leading figure reveals the initial fragility of his position and of his expectations in the group he just joined. Indeed, from a historiosophic perspective, and in order to assert the Teacher's power and his leadership in the group, it would have been easy to establish him as the community's founding figure right away, and thus to omit any reference to the twenty-year period preceding his joining of the group. For that reason, I see the detail about the twenty years as an 'embarrassment' for the Teacher's leadership, and thus as a historical fact.

It is of course impossible to know whether the Teacher of Righteousness himself realized the fragility of his leadership at the outset of his encounter with the group and from there proceeded only gradually to develop a personal strategy for strengthening his power within the movement. An alternative possibility is that from the very beginning he had planned to be the group's interpreter of divine words but initially masked that intention, before proclaiming his role as interpreter and revealer, by presenting himself as the model for other Jews who would join the movement. And still another possibility is that the memory of the Teacher's role as interpreter and 'revealer' was constructed after his death, by group members who survived him.

The present essay has introduced the sociology of organizations as a reading strategy for understanding select aspects of the Qumran community and, more precisely, attempted to explain the position of leadership assumed by the Teacher of Righteousness within the community according to the *Damascus Document*. That same attempt, moreover, opens up a number of research avenues which remain unexplored; the *Pesher* Habakkuk, for instance, with its interpretation of the struggle between the Teacher of Righteousness and the Wicked Priest,[62] could be read according to the second source of power treated by Crozier and Friedberg,[63] namely, uncertainties originating from the organization and its environment. The Teacher of Righteousness can furthermore be understood as a 'secant marginal'[64] because of his multiple affiliations, both with the community and with the priesthood. Crozier and Friedberg's third source of power, linked as it is to the way in which an organization shapes the flow of communication both between its subgroups and between its members,[65] could be used to illuminate

---

61. We could have extended the reflection on the grounding of this power by looking at the roles assigned to the *mevaqqer*, the community's inspector, according to the *Damascus Document*, and at their evolution.

62. P. Wallendorf, *Rättfärdighetens Lärare: En exegetisk undersökning* (Helsinfors: Aarhus Stiftsbogtryck, 1964), 80, 134, insists on the conflictual picture of the Teacher in all the preserved occurrences; he deduced the figure's characteristics.

63. Crozier and Friedberg, *L'acteur et le système*, 85–86.

64. See H. Jamous, *Contribution à une sociologie de la décision: la réforme des études médicales et des structures hospitalières* (Paris: Centre national de la recherche scientifique, 1968), 344–70.

65. Crozier and Friedberg, *L'acteur et le système*, 86–87.

the relationships between the Teacher, the *maskil* and the *mevaqqer*;[66] while their fourth source of power, involving knowledge of organizational rules,[67] offers space and tools for analysing the writing, rewriting and interpretation of the *serakhim* within the community.[68] Those are only a few of the reading trajectories suggested by the sociology of organizations which could sharpen our understanding of particular passages or specific figures in positions of leadership within the community, beyond an exclusively rhetorical type of analysis.

Bibliography

Becker, J. *Das Heil Gottes: Heils- und Sündenbegriffe in den Qumrantexten und im Neuen Testament*. SUNT 3. Göttingen: Vandenhoeck & Ruprecht, 1963.

Bermejo-Rubio, F. 'Changing Methods, Disturbing Material: Should the Criterion of Embarrassment Be Dismissed in Jesus Research?' *REJ* 175 (2016): 1–25.

Betz, O., and R. Riesner. *Jesus, Qumran and the Vatican: Clarifications*. London: SCM, 1994.

Bourdieu, P. 'Genèse et structure du champ religieux'. *Revue française de sociologie* 12 (1971): 295–334.

Brooke, G. J. 'Justifying Deviance: The Place of Scripture in Converting to a Qumran Self-Understanding'. In *Reading the Present in the Qumran Library: The Perception of the Contemporary by Means of Scriptural Interpretation*, edited by K. de Troyer and A. Lange, 73–87. Atlanta: SBL, 2005.

Brooke, G. J. 'The "Apocalyptic" Community, the Matrix of the Teacher and Rewriting Scripture'. In *Authoritative Scriptures in Ancient Judaism*, edited by M. Popović; JSJSup. 141; 37–53. Leiden: E. J. Brill, 2010.

Burgmann, H. *Vorgeschichte und Frühgeschichte der essenischen Gemeinden von Qumrân und Damaskus*. ANTJ 7. Frankfurt am Main: Lang, 1987.

Callaway, P. R. *The History of the Qumran Community: An Investigation*. JSPSup 3. Sheffield: JSOT Press, 1988.

Carmignac, J. *Le Docteur de Justice et Jésus-Christ*. Paris: Editions de l'Orante, 1957.

Chalcraft, D. J. 'Introduction: Sectarianism in Early Judaism: Sociological Advances? Some Critical Sociological Reflections'. In *Sectarianism in Early Judaism: Sociological Advances*, edited by D. J. Chalcraft, 2–23. London: Equinox, 2007.

Chalcraft, D. J. 'Towards a Weberian Sociology of the Qumran Sects'. In *Sectarianism in Early Judaism*, 74–105. London: Equinox, 2007.

Chalcraft, D. J. 'Is Sociology Also Among the Social Sciences? Some Personal Reflections on Sociological Approaches in Biblical Studies'. In *Anthropology and the Bible: Critical Perspectives*, edited by E. Pfoh, Biblical Intersections, no. 3; 37–75. Piscataway, NJ: Gorgias Press, 2010.

---

66. M. Goff, *Discerning Wisdom: The Sapiential Literature of the Dead Sea Scrolls*, VTSup 116 (Leiden: E. J. Brill, 2007), 6.

67. Crozier and Friedberg, *L'acteur et le système*, 88–89.

68. See recently Hamidović, 'Living *Serakhim*', 61–90.

Chalcraft, D. J. 'Is a Historical Comparative Sociology of (Ancient Jewish) Sects Possible?'. In *Sects and Sectarianism in Jewish History*, edited by S. Stern; IJS Studies in Judaica, no. 12; 233–86. Leiden: E. J. Brill, 2011.

Collins, J. J. *Beyond the Qumran Community: The Sectarian Movement of the Dead Sea Scrolls*. Grand Rapids: Eerdmans, 2009.

Crozier, M., and E. Friedberg. *L'acteur et le système: Les contraintes de l'action collective*. Paris: Éditions du Seuil, 1977.

Davies, P. R. *The Damascus Covenant: An Interpretation of the 'Damascus Document'*. JSOTSup 25. Sheffield: Sheffield Academic Press, 1983.

Davies, P. R. 'Communities at Qumran and the Case of the Missing "Teacher"'. *RevQ* 15 (1991): 275–86.

Davies, P. R. 'The Prehistory of the Qumran Community'. In *The Dead Sea Scrolls: Forty Years of Research*, edited by D. Dimant and U. Rappaport. STDJ 10; 116–25. Leiden: E. J. Brill, 1992.

Davies, P. R. 'The Teacher of Righteousness and the End of Days'. In *Sects and Scrolls: Essays on Qumran and Related Topics*, edited by P. R. Davies, 89–94. Atlanta: Scholars, 1996.

Davies, P. R. 'The "Damascus Sect" and Judaism'. In *Sects and Scrolls: Essays on Qumran and Related Topics*, edited by P. R. Davies, 70–84. Atlanta: Scholars Press, 1996.

Davies, P. R. 'Between Text and Archaeology'. *Dead Sea Discoveries* 18 (2011): 332–36.

Degorce, Jean-Bernard, and Charles Ehlinger. *Un certain Juif Jésus. Les données de l'histoire*, vol. 1, Lectio Divina. Paris: Cerf, 2009.

Delamarter, S. 'Sociological Models for Understanding the Scribal Practices in the Biblical Dead Sea Scrolls'. In *Rediscovering the Dead Sea Scrolls: An Assessment of Old and New Approaches and Methods*, edited by M. L. Grossman, 182–97. Grand Rapids: Eerdmans, 2010.

De Vaux, Roland. *Les institutions de l'Ancien Testament*, vol. 2. Paris: Éditions du Cerf, 1960.

Dupont-Sommer, A. *Aperçus préliminaires sur les manuscrits de la mer Morte*. Paris: Maisonneuve, 1950.

Dupont-Sommer, A. *The Jewish Sect of Qumran and the Essenes*. London: MacMillan, 1955.

Elliott, J. H. *What is Social-Scientific Criticism?* Guides to Biblical Scholarship, New Testament Series, 7. Minneapolis: Augsburg Fortress, 1993.

Elliott, J. H. 'From Social Description to Social-Scientific Criticism: The History of a Society of Biblical Literature Section 1973–2005'. *BTB* 38 (2008): 26–36.

Evard, J. -L. *La religion perverse: Essai sur le charisma*. Paris: Éditions du Rocher, 2008.

Fitzmyer, J. A. *Responses to 101 Questions on the Dead Sea Scrolls*. New York: Paulist, 1992.

Fraade, S. *Legal Fictions: Studies of Law and Narrative in the Discursive Worlds of Ancient Jewish Sectarians and Sages*. Supplements to the Journal for the Study of Judaism, no. 147. Leiden: E. J. Brill, 2011.

García Martínez, F. 'Qumran Origins and Early History: A Groningen Hypothesis'. *Folia Orientalia* 25 (1988): 113–36.

García Martínez, F., and A. S. van der Woude. 'A "Groningen" Hypothesis of Qumran Origins and Early History'. *RevQ* 14 (1990): 521–41.

García Martínez, F. 'The Origins of the Essene Movement and of the Qumran Sect'. In *The People of the Dead Sea Scrolls: Their Writings, Beliefs and Practices*, edited by F. García Martínez and Julio Trebolle Barrera, 77–96. Leiden: E. J. Brill, 1995.

García Martínez, F. 'Beyond the Sectarian Divide: The "Voice of the Teacher" as
    an Authority-Conferring Strategy in Some Qumran Texts'. In *The Dead Sea
    Scrolls: Transmission of Traditions and Production of Texts*, edited by. S. Metso, H.
    Najman and E. Schüller. STDJ 92; 227–34. Leiden: E. J. Brill, 2010.
Goff, M. *Discerning Wisdom: The Sapiential Literature of the Dead Sea Scrolls*, VTSup 116.
    Leiden: E. J. Brill, 2007.
Grabbe, L. L. *Ancient Israel: What Do We Know and How Do We Know It?* London: T&T
    Clark, 2007.
Hamidović, D. 'L'eschatologie essénienne dans la littérature apocalyptique: temporalités et
    limites chronologiques'. *REJ* 169 (2010): 37–55.
Hamidović, D. *L'Écrit de Damas*. Collection de la Revue des Études Juives, no. 51.
    Louvain: Peeters, 2011.
Hamidović, D. 'Living *Serakhim*: Process of Authority in the *Community Rule*'. In *The
    Process of Authority: The Dynamics in Transmission and Reception of Canonical Texts*,
    edited by J. Dušek and J. Roskovec, 61–90. Berlin: W. de Gruyter, 2016.
Hamidović, D. 'The Divine Economy of the Poor in the Qumran Texts'. In *'Retribution'
    in Jewish and Christian Writings: A Concept in Debate*, edited by D. Hamidović,
    M. Silvestrini and A. Thromas. Forthcoming.
Hamidović, D. 'Qumran Texts in Jewish and Christian Traditions'. Forthcoming.
Holm-Nielsen, S. *Hodayot: Psalms from Qumran*. Acta theological danica,
    no. 2. Aarhus: Universtitetsvørlaget, 1960.
Jamous, H. *Contribution à une sociologie de la décision: la réforme des études médicales et
    des structures hospitalières*. Paris: Centre national de la recherche scientifique, 1968.
Jeremias, G. *Der Lehrer der Gerechtigkeit*. Göttingen: Vandenhoeck & Ruprecht, 1963.
Jokiranta, J. ' "Sectarianism" of the Qumran "Sect": Sociological Notes'. *RevQ* 78
    (2001): 223–39.
Jokiranta, J. 'Qumran: The Prototypical Teacher in the Qumran Pesharim: A
    Social-Identity Approach'. In *Ancient Israel: The Old Testament in Its Social Contexts*,
    edited by P. F. Esler, 254–63. Minneapolis: Augsburg Fortress, 2006.
Jokiranta, J. *Social Identity and Sectarianism in the Qumran Movement*, STDJ 105.
    Leiden: E. J. Brill, 2013.
Knibb, M. A. 'The Teacher of Righteousness – A Messianic Title?'. In *A Tribute to Geza
    Vermes: Essays on Jewish and Christian Literature and History*, edited by P. R. Davies
    and R. T. White, 51–65. Sheffield: JSOT, 1990.
Knibb, M. A. 'Teacher of Righteousness'. In *Encyclopedia of the Dead Sea Scrolls*, vol. 2,
    918–21. Oxford: Oxford University Press, 2000.
Laato, A. 'The Chronology in the *Damascus Document* at Qumran'. *RevQ* 15 (1992):
    605–607.
Lapin, H. 'Dead Sea Scrolls and the Historiography of Ancient Judaism'. In *Rediscovering
    the Dead Sea Scrolls: An Assessment of Old and New Approaches and Methods*, edited by
    M. L. Grossman, 108–127. Grand Rapids: Eerdmans, 2010.
March, J. G., and H. A. Simon. *Organizations*. New York: Wiley, 1958.
Martin, D. B. 'Social-Scientific Criticism'. In *To Each Its Own Meaning: An Introduction to
    Biblical Criticisms and Their Application*, edited by S. L. McKenzie and S. R. Haynes,
    125–141. Louisville: Westminster John Knox, 1999.
Meier, J. P. *A Marginal Jew: Rethinking the Historical Jesus*. New York: Doubleday, 1991.
Meyer, B. F. *The Aims of Jesus*. London: SCM, 2002.
O'Connor, J. Murphy. 'La genèse littéraire de la *Règle de la Communauté*'. *RB* 76
    (1969): 528–49.

O'Connor, J. Murphy. 'The Essenes and their History'. *RB* 81 (1974): 215–44.

O'Connor, J. Murphy. 'The Damascus Document Revisited'. *RB* 92, no. 2 (1985): 223–46.

O'Connor, J. Murphy. 'Teacher of Righteousness'. In *ABD*, VI, 340–41. New York, 1992.

Porter, S. E. *The Criteria for Authenticity in Historical-Jesus: Previous Discussion and New Proposals*. JSNTSup 191; 162. Sheffield: Sheffield Academic Press, 2000.

Puech, E. 'Le grand prêtre Simon (III) fils d'Onias III, le Maître de Justice?' In *Antikes Judentum und frühes Christentum*, edited by H. Stegemann, 137–58. Berlin: W. de Gruyter, 1999.

Qimron, E., and J. Strugnell, eds. *Qumran Cave 4: V: Miqṣat Maʿase ha-Torah*. DJD 10. Oxford: Oxford University Press, 1994.

Ro, J. Un-Sok. *Die sogenannte 'Armen frömmigkeit' im nachexilischen Israel*. BZAW 322. Berlin-New York: W. de Gruyter, 2002.

Schweitzer, F. M. 'The Teacher of Righteousness'. In *Mogilany 1989: Papers on the Dead Sea Scrolls Offered in Memory of Jean Carmignac, II: The Teacher of Righteousness*, edited by Z. J. Kapera, 53–97. Krakow: The Enigma Press, 1991.

Stark, R., and W. S. Bainbridge. *The Future of Religion: Secularization, Revival and Cult Formation*. Berkeley: University of California, 1985.

Stark, R., and W. S. Bainbridge. *A Theory of Religion*. New Jersey: Rutgers University Press, 1987.

Stegemann, H. 'The "Teacher of Righteousness" and Jesus: Two Types of Religious Leadership in Judaism at the Turn of the Era'. In *Jewish Civilization in the Hellenistic-Roman Period*, edited by S. Talmon. JSPSup 10; 196–213. Sheffield: Sheffield Academic Press, 1991.

Stegemann, H. *Die Essener, Qumran, Johannes der Täufer und Jesus: Ein Sachbuch*, 3rd ed. Freiburg: Herder, 1994.

Thériault, B., and J. Duhaime, ed. *Les charismes*. Special issue, *Théologiques* 17, no. 1 (2009).

Thiessen, G., and D. Winter. *The Quest for the Plausible Jesus: The Question of Criteria*. Louisville: Westminster John Knox, 2002.

Ulfgard, H. 'The Teacher of Righteousness, the History of the Qumran Community, and Our Understanding of the Jesus Movement: Texts, Theories and Trajectories'. In *Qumran Between the Old and New Testaments*, edited by F. H. Geyer and T. L. Thomson, 310–46. Sheffield: Sheffield Academic Press, 1998.

Ulrichsen, J. H. 'Menighetsforståelsen i Qumrantekstene'. *NTT* 83 (1982): 156.

VanderKam, J. C. *The Dead Sea Scrolls Today*. Grand Rapids: Eerdmans, 1994.

Van der Ploeg, J. P. M. *The Excavations at Qumran*. London: Catholic Book Club, 1958.

Wach, J. *Sociologie de la religion*. Paris: Payot, 1955.

Wacholder, B. Z. *The Dawn of Qumran: The Sectarian Torah and the Teacher of Righteousness*. Cincinnati: Hebrew Union College Press, 1983.

Wallendorf, P. *Rättfärdighetens Lärare: En exegetisk undersökning*. Helsinfors: Aarhus Stiftsbogtryck, 1964.

Wassen, C., and J. Jokiranta. 'Groups in Tension: Sectarianism in the *Damascus Document* and the *Community Rule*'. In *Sectarianism in Early Judaism*, 205–45. London: Equinox, 2007.

Weber, M. *The Methodology of the Social Sciences*, trans. E. A. Shils and H. A. Finch. Glencoe, IL: The Free Press, 1949.

Weber, M. *Economie et société*. Paris: Plon, 1971.

Weber, M. *The Protestant Ethic and the Spirit of Capitalism*, trans. P. Baehr and G. C. Wells. London: Penguin, 2002.

Weber, M. 'Voluntary Associational Life (Vereinswesen)'. *Max Weber Studies* 2 (2002): 199–209.

Wilson, B. 'An Analysis of Sect Development'. In *Patterns of Sectarianism: Organization and Ideology in Social and Religious Movements*, edited by B. Wilson, 22–45. London: Heinemann, 1967.

Wilson, B. *Religious Sects: A Sociological Study*. London: McGraw-Hill, 1970.

Wilson, B. *Magic and the Millennium: A Sociological Study of Religious Movements of Protest among Tribal and Third-World Peoples*. London: Heinemann, 1973.

Wilson, B. *Religion in Sociological Perspective*. Oxford: Oxford University Press, 1982.

Wilson, B. *The Social Dimension of Sectarianism: Sects and New Religious Movements in Contemporary Society*. Oxford: Clarendon Press, 1990.

Wise, M. O. 'Dating the Teacher of Righteousness and the Floruit of his Movement'. *JBL* 122 (2003): 53–87.

Yadin, Y. *The Temple Scroll: The Hidden Law of the Dead Sea Sect*. London: Random House, 1985.

Chapter 12

SAVING FACE IN GALATIA: ΕΥ̓ΠΡΟΣΩΠΈΩ AND CONCERN FOR HONOUR IN THE ARGUMENT OF PAUL'S LETTER

David S. Harvey

12.1 *Introduction*

It is those who want to make a good showing (εὐπροσωπῆσαι) in the flesh that try to compel you to be circumcised – only that they may not be persecuted for the cross of Christ. Even the circumcised do not themselves obey the law, but they want you to be circumcised so that they may boast (καυχήσωντα) about your flesh. (Gal. 6.12-13, NRSV)

H. D. Betz's claim that the postscript to Galatians (6.11-18) is the 'hermeneutical key' to its interpretation has been largely accepted by recent interpreters.[1] Curiously, despite this, the readings of these verses have rarely attempted to impact wider interpretation of the letter and its situation. Some of this may be due to the seminal position Galatians holds within the development of Christian theology, a position that apparently predisposes interpreters to expect a theological conclusion. Clearly there are theological issues present in the postscript, although many of the prominent 'Galatian' terms are notably absent (e.g. δικαιοσύνη, πίστις, and πνεῦμα); however, Paul's primary focus is directed towards an accusation as to the motives of the agitators, an accusation that he frames not theologically but socially.[2] The agitators, so Paul accuses, despite their attempts to appear otherwise, are not interested in issues of the law, but are self-motivated by the desire 'to make

---

1. H. D. Betz, *Galatians* (Philadelphia: Fortress Press, 1979), 313; cf. R. N. Longenecker, *Galatians* (Dallas: Word, 1990), 288–89; J. L. Martyn, *Galatians* (New York: Doubleday, 1997); and J. A. D. Weima, *Neglected Endings: The Significance of the Pauline Letter Closings* (Sheffield: JSOT, 1994), 160.

2. This position on the accusation of 6.12 is noted by M. D. Nanos, *The Irony of Galatians: Paul's Letter in First-Century Context* (Minneapolis: Fortress Press, 2002), 217; and J. K. Hardin, *Galatians and the Imperial Cult: A Critical Analysis of the First-Century*

a good face' (εὐπροσωπῆσαι). This use of language should, I will argue, alert us to the presence of honour concern in the crisis in Galatia.

12.2 Modelling Honour for Paul's World

Competition for honour, understood as an 'energetically claimed and fiercely defended' public social value that shaped the social-stratification of the Mediterranean world into which Christianity emerged,[3] has been increasingly identified by scholars as a pivotal component in almost every social interaction in Paul's cultural context.[4] Scholarly debate cautioning exegetes against careless anachronistic assumptions regarding the competition for honour, particularly when using social-scientific models developed in modern contexts, has been both fierce and thorough, drawing in perspectives from the fields of New Testament, classics and anthropology alike, and is still without consensus.[5] The ancient sources, however, do support the notion that the 'communal consciousness' of Paul's world was preoccupied with honour.[6] Cicero, for instance, said: 'By nature we yearn and hunger for honour, and once we have glimpsed, as it were, some part of its radiance, there is nothing we are not prepared to bear and suffer in

Social Context of Paul's Letter (Tübingen: Mohr Siebeck, 2008), 87. Hardin (86 n. 6) also defends the use of the term 'agitators'.

3. J. M. G. Barclay, 'Grace and the Countercultural Reckoning of Worth: Community Construction in Galatians 5–6', in *Galatians and Christian Theology: Justification, the Gospel and Ethics in Paul's Letter*, ed. M. W. Elliott et al. (Grand Rapids: Baker, 2014), 306–17 (311).

4. The bibliography is growing rapidly; see, e.g. P. F. Esler, *Modelling Early Christianity: Social-Scientific Studies of the New Testament in Its Context* (London: Routledge, 1995); and, for this essay, Esler, *Galatians* (London: Routledge, 1998). These support the work of Esler's colleagues within the *Context Group*, esp. B. J. Malina, *The New Testament World: Insights from Cultural Anthropology* (Louisville: Westminster John Knox, 2001). The origins of this approach is often traced to the collection of essays in J. G. Peristiany, ed. *Honour and Shame: The Values of Mediterranean Society* (London: Weidenfeld and Nicholson, 1965) and more recently J. G. Peristiany and J. A. Pitt-Rivers, *Honour and Grace in Anthropology* (Cambridge: Cambridge University Press, 1992).

5. Cf. F. G. Downing, ' "Honor" among Exegetes', *CBQ* 61 (1999): 53–73; L. J. Lawrence, *An Ethnography of the Gospel of Matthew: A Critical Assessment of the Use of the Honour and Shame Model in New Testament Studies* (Tübingen: Mohr Siebeck, 2003); Z. A. Crook, 'Honor, Shame and Social Status Revisited', *JBL* 128, no. 3 (2009): 591–611; D. Cairns, 'Honour and Shame: Modern Controversies and Ancient Values', 53, no. 1 (2011): 23–41; and D. D. Gilmore, ed., *Honor and Shame and the Unity of the Mediterranean* (Washington, DC: American Anthropological Association, 1987).

6. P. Garnsey and R. P. Saller, *The Roman Empire: Economy, Society and Culture* (London: Duckworth, 1987), 117.

order to secure it' (Cicero, *Tusc.* 2.24.58). Cicero further recognized that a great citizen would seek an equality of freedom for all but only their own prominence in honour (*principem dignitate, Phil.* 1.34). Horace saw the elite and non-elite as 'bound in chains to her [Glory's] resplendent chariot' (*Sat.* 2.6.23–24), while Dio Chrysostom held that society's motivation originated from 'the struggle for reputation' (ὁ περὶ τῆς δόξης ἀγών, *Or.* 66.18). Honour was, to quote Jon Lendon, the 'filter through which the world was viewed.'[7]

Alvin Gouldner noted in the 1960s that the Judaeo-Christian tradition has tempered our awareness of the conflict that characterized this ancient culture.[8] 'Rank must be preserved', said Cicero (*Pro Cnaeo Plancio* 15); therefore he recommended being 'acutely sensitive' to any encroachment on one's honour so that one might 'overturn and wreck' any challenger (*Sull.* 46).[9] Contest was at the heart of this mechanism of social mobility because honour was derived from comparison. The constant attempt to improve one's position on a supposed scale and, in doing so, demean the status of another describes both the mercurial nature of honour and the agonistic nature of ancient society.[10] As C. A. Barton observes, 'Even the smallest challenge was important in Roman life. The Roman, Horace tells us, will fight over anything: whether the hair of goats can be called wool; whether Castor or Dolichos is more cunning; whether the road built by Appius or that built by Minucius is better for a journey to Brundisium (*Epistulae* 1.18.15, 19–20).'[11] While competition brought out the heroic in some, it also had, in the event of the breakdown of social bonds, the ability to become destructive. Ripostes invariably followed challenges in a continual sequence until one party was left unable to respond, often due to the strength and devastating level of social retaliation.[12] The public nature of the quest for honour regularly roused the strongest of emotions – resentment, envy and pride.[13]

---

7. J. E. Lendon, *Empire of Honour* (Oxford: Clarendon, 1997), 35.

8. A. W. Gouldner, *Enter Plato: Classical Greece and the Origins of Social Theory* (London: Routledge, 1967), 41. The term 'conflict' is much debated in social sciences. Most references are vague, but Dahrendorf is helpful: 'A conflict consists of "contests, competitions, disputes, and tensions, as well as . . . manifest clashes between social forces."' Cf. D. Duling, *A Marginal Scribe: Studies in the Gospel of Matthew in a Social-Scientific Perspective* (Eugene: Wipf and Stock, 2011), 154.

9. On the acute sensitivity required by honour, see especially C. A. Barton, *Roman Honor: The Fire in the Bones* (Berkeley: University of California Press, 2001), 35.

10. Lendon, *Empire*, 90, cf. Barton, *Roman Honor*, 62, Gouldner, *Enter Plato*, 45–46.

11. Barton, *Roman Honor*, 47; 'The provisional and contested nature of reality . . . infused all Roman ways of thinking' (69).

12. P. Bourdieu, 'The Sentiment of Honour in Kabyle Society', in *Honour and Shame: The Values of Mediterranean Society*, ed. J. G. Peristiany (London: Weidenfeld and Nicholson, 1965), 191–242.

13. Barclay, 'Grace and the Countercultural Reckoning of Worth', 312.

'Honour was', as Lendon argues, 'mediated through the perceptions of others'.[14] It was a social prestige earned and validated in a public sphere. Dio Chrysostom reflected:

> You see what hardships these athletic competitors (τοὺς ἀγωνιστὰς) endure while training, spending money, and finally often even choosing to die in the very midst of the games. Why is it? If we were to abolish the crown for the sake of which they strive (φιλοτιμέομαι), and the inscription which will commemorate their victory at the Olympian or the Pythian games, do you think that they would endure for even one day the heat of the sun, not to mention all the other unpleasant and arduous things which attach to their occupation? . . . For all men set great store by the outward tokens of high achievement, and not one man in a thousand is willing to agree that what he regards as a noble deed shall have been done for himself alone and that no other man shall have knowledge of it.[15]

Those who were honoured, moreover, validated the content of honourable behaviour. As Elizabeth Forbis notes, whether with literary *exempla virtutis* or monumental tributes, what was praised brought admiration but was also designed to bring emulation.[16] The honour competition called its adherents to strive for an agreed definition of 'better', the result being that honour was, by nature, exclusive and hierarchic; 'if everyone attains equal honour then there is no honour for anyone'.[17] Difference, therefore, as that which separated honourable from dishonourable, was fundamental to the importance of honour as a social value and helps to explain the competitive fierceness with which honourable statuses were defended. Boasting and self-promotion, with their inherent accentuation of difference, functioned in this context as tools of 'socially acceptable self-aggrandizement'.[18]

12.3 *Εὐπροσωπέω as Concern for Honour*

The cultural background sketched above highlights a widely overlooked feature of Gal. 6.12-13 that, I want to argue here, becomes key to reading Paul's objection to the agitators. Difficult to find is the commentator who makes more than passing reference to the opening verb in 6.12 (i.e. εὐπροσωπέω), despite the fact that the wish to εὐπροσωπῆσαι is Paul's direct complaint against the agitators

14. Lendon, *Empire*, 37, 37 n. 31.

15. Dio Chrysostom *Orationes* 31.21–22. For fuller discussion see C. P. Jones, *The Roman World of Dio Chrysostom* (Cambridge: Harvard University Press, 1978), 71, 136.

16. E. Forbis, *Municipal Virtues in the Roman Empire: The Evidence of Italian Honorary Inscriptions* (Stuttgart: Teubner, 1996), 12, 103.

17. M. I. Finley, *The World of Odysseus* (London: Pimlico, 1999), 118.

18. M. T. Finney, *Honour and Conflict in the Ancient World: 1 Corinthians in Its Greco-Roman Social Setting* (London: T&T Clark, 2012), 16.

in the Galatian *ekklesia*.[19] While there is much compacted into these few verses to occupy a scholar, where the verb is mentioned at all the tendency is to do little more than observe its rarity (it is a *hapax legomenon*), note its supposed meaning (e.g. 'to put on a good show'[20]) and, in more recent work, show general awareness of Bruce Winter's proposal regarding the legal usage of the word.[21] Any possible social nuance, if considered at all, is not considered particularly significant to the context.[22]

This lack of attention seems to have largely convinced the field that taking εὐπροσωπέω seriously is unnecessary. However, Winter's exploration of εὐπροσωπέω suggests that there is still digging to be done. Building on an argument that the word has a quasi-legal nuance connected to Latin ideas of *persona*, he suggests that the verb signifies a process of 'wishing to secure a good legal status'.[23] On that basis he builds an elaborate thesis to locate the opponents in Galatians as local Jewish-Christians attempting to avoid persecution from the imperial cult. Against Winter's thesis, the present inquiry considers it unnecessary to look as far afield as Winter does from traditional scholarly opinion on the origins of the opponents;[24] but just as importantly, the texts he offers in defence of his thesis fail to show conclusively the alleged usage of εὐπροσωπέω as a legal term – rather, they describe the social context around a legislative situation.[25]

This is due to εὐπροσωπέω more generally carrying a social rather than a legal nuance. (To be sure, a legal situation is still a social situation).[26] It is the language of the honour conflict – success in the honour competition establishes reputation, or 'good face'. The face was the seat of honour in Paul's social world (cf. Cicero, *Mil.* 30.82). It was one's mask, one's reputation, and hence the location

---

19. Curiously, J. B. Lightfoot, *St. Paul's Epistle to the Galatians* (London: Macmillan, 1884) is a rare exception, although he does not explicitly note the honour dynamics.

20. *TDNT*, vol. 6, 769–70.

21. B. W. Winter, *Seek the Welfare of the City: Christians as Benefactors and Citizens* (Grand Rapids: Eerdmans, 1994), 138; see also the improved argument in B. W. Winter, 'The Imperial Cult and Early Christianity in Roman Galatia (Acts xiii 13–50 and Galatians vi 11–18)', in *Actes du 1er Congrès international sur Antioche de Pisidie*, ed. T. Drew-Bear, M. Tashalan and C.M. Thomas (Lyon: Université Lumière-Lyon, 2002), 67–76.

22. E.g. Betz, *Galatians*, 313; and J. D. G. Dunn, *Galatians* (London: A&C Black, 1993), 336. Hardin does notice that εὐπροσωπέω is essential to Paul's primary accusation in these verse; see Hardin, *Galatians and the Imperial Cult*, 87.

23. Winter, 'The Imperial Cult', 73–74.

24. Longenecker, *Galatians*, xciv.

25. Aristotle, *Pol.* 1263b.15; Lucian, *Merc. cond.* 3; *Merc. cond.* 11; *J.Tr* 14; Plutarch, *De cohibenda ira* 458F; *P. Teb* 19.12, Demosthenes, *De cor.* 149.

26. Hardin notices this but persists with a legal reading, albeit a more nuanced one; see Hardin, *Galatians and the Imperial Cult*, 91. Similar is A. V. Prokhorov, 'Taking the Jews out of the Equation: Galatians 6.12–17 as a Summons to Cease Evading Persecution', *JSNT* 36 (2013): 172–88 (177–78).

of honour competition.[27] According to Barton, a provocative face could frame a contest and draw a line in the sand.[28] In Plutarch's *De cohibenda ira* there is a typical face-related honour exchange when Antigonus responds to an attempt to demean him with the retort μὴν ἐδόκουν εὐπρόσωπος εἶναι (*lit.*, 'I thought I seemed to have a good face', 458F), which he says prior to a retort that destroys the social status of the challengers.

The importance of the face to honour was such that court cases had to allow a moratorium on honour just so that litigation could happen, otherwise a wrongly timed blush could prove overly costly for either prosecution or defence.[29] While the faces of the shamed were scratched from their statues, conversely, those who could look at terror and keep face were the brave and heroes of society, a fact not lost on Lucan who notices that the face-obscuring nature of a Roman military helmet protects the honour of its wearer: 'The soldier in civil war, his face hidden behind a helmet, was shameless' (Lucan, *Bellum civile* 4.706). This naturally affected society; the 'honour sensitive' went through life studying the faces of peers: 'from a glance of the eyes, a raising or lowering of the brows, a groan, a laugh', so they might regulate conduct.[30] Social propriety and general peace are often thought to have been maintained, in Rome, by an ever-present fear of 'losing face'.[31] Jewish texts, although questionable in terms of their impact on Galatia, reflect similar perspectives, suggesting the prevalence of concern for face across Paul's world.[32]

Essentially, face functions as a gloss for someone's claim to honourable social standing, a metaphorical representation of their public-facing side of life.[33]

27. The term 'face' originally carried the meaning of 'mask' but by the time of the early first century it was used to describe the status of a person. Its Latin equivalent was *persona*. Cf. M. Nédoncelle, 'Prosopon et Persona dans L'antiquté', *RSR* 22 (1948): 277–99 (299); and V. H. T. Nguyen, *Christian Identity in Corinth: A Comparative Study of 2 Corinthians, Epictetus and Valerius Maximus* (Tübingen: Mohr Siebeck, 2008), 16.

28. Barton, *Roman Honor*, 57.

29. Cf. J. M. Kelly, *Studies in the Civil Judicature of the Roman Republic* (Oxford: Clarendon Press, 1976), 93–111.

30. Lendon, *Empire*, 39.

31. Barton, *Roman Honor*, 18, 35.

32. See, e.g. Gen. 17.3; Exod. 33.11; Ps. 27.6; 1QH 4.5; 2 En. 44.2. Stephen Barton notes, with some irony, that the ubiquity of face concern even in the twenty-first century is such that a common site for people to present their own constructed 'claims' to status is aptly called 'Facebook'; see Stephen Barton, 'The Metaphor of Face in Paul', in *Conception, Reception, and the Spirit: Essays in Honor of Andrew T. Lincoln*, ed. J. G. McConville and L. K. Pietersen (Eugene: Cascade, 2015), 136–53 (152).

33. S. Ting-Toomey, 'Face and Facework: An Introduction', in *The Challenge of Facework: Cross-Cultural and Interpersonal Issues*, ed. S. Ting-Toomey (Albany: State University of New York Press, 1994), 1–14 (3). On honour glosses, cf. M. Herzfeld, ' "As in Your Own House": Hospitality, Ethnography, and the Stereotype of Mediterranean Society', in *Honor and Shame and the Unity of the Mediterranean*, ed. D. D. Gilmore (Washington, DC: American Anthropological Association, 1987), 75–89 (75).

Face represents the level of honour you can 'get away with'. Those interested in facework note that having 'good face' requires the simultaneous act of gaining public approval as 'good for the group' while attempting to improve one's honour standing in relation to those within that group.[34] In Oprisko's words, 'Face fulfills the need for a process of socially valuing individuals as they wish to appear and of appearing as one would like to be valued.'[35] Face, within a model of honour, relates to public conduct in the presence of those from whom one seeks to be valued and respected.[36]

12.4 *Concern for Face in Galatians*

Returning to Galatians with a simple honour model of face, the synonymity between the boast in the flesh (6.13) and the establishing of a 'good face' in the flesh (6.12) is revealed and easily understood as the language of honour competition. Curiously, though, Paul critiques a very normal feature of honour – seeking to improve your social status or 'saving face' is the 'bread and butter' of competitive life in a limited good society.[37] Paul's complaint against 'face saving' is not just a generic critique of honour, the type of which we sometimes encounter in his contemporary world. For, first, Paul challenges the opponents themselves by accusing them of actually only being concerned to improve their own social standing by circumcising the Galatians. Paul exposes that an honour game is actually at play rather than the many theological issues that are masquerading as the real problem. Second, Paul implies a wider theological critique of honour via the double repetition of σάρξ in 6.12-13 and the juxtaposition of the agitators' attempts of self-preservation/self-promotion and his own value-neutralizing boast in the cross.

If we can bear in mind that the hubristic behaviour typical of ancient groups was motivated to improve social standing by *emphasizing* and *accentuating* difference between community members, then we can continue to further track the importance of this reading of εὐπροσωπέω to Galatians. Two texts present themselves as worthy of consideration – 1.22 and 2.6.

---

34. For 'face' and 'facework', see the pioneering work of E. Goffman, 'On Face-Work: An Analysis of Ritual Elements in Social Interaction', in *Interaction Ritual*, ed. E. Goffman (New York: Doubleday, 1967), 5–45; and the helpful introductions from Ting-Toomey, 'Face and Facework', and C. MacMartin, L.A. Wood and R. O. Kroger, 'Facework', in *The New Handbook of Language and Social Psychology*, ed. W. P. Robinson and H. Giles (Chichester: Wiley, 2001), 221–37.

35. R. L. Oprisko, *Honor: A Phenomenology* (New York: Routledge, 2012), 79.

36. F. H. Stewart, *Honor* (Chicago: University of Chicago Press, 1994), 54.

37. A. D. Clarke, *Secular and Christian Leadership in Corinth: A Socio-Historical and Exegetical Study of 1 Corinthians 1–6* (Leiden: Brill, 1993), 96. Criticizing honour is not unknown, or even rare, but that it needed to be done suggests just how normal the concern for honour was in mainstream society.

First, in regard to Gal. 1.22, Paul has just defined his previous life using honour terminology – προέκοπτω and συνηλικιώτης (1.14) very much being the language of peer competition.[38] This is, however, in marked contrast with his new life in which Christ and not social status has set him apart (1.15-17), resulting in glory, not for himself but rather for God. Paul presents himself as unconcerned about increasing his own social standing to the extent that he is comfortable being ἀγνοούμενος τῷ προσώπῳ (*lit.* unknown by face, 1.22).

This disregard for perceived social standing increases into the following chapter where we find a second 'face' reference. When Paul journeys to Jerusalem his disregard for status allows for private meetings (2.2) – away from the court of public opinion – the non-circumcision of Titus (2.3) and a controversial admission that the purported pillar-status of Peter, James and John is only τῶν δοκούντων ('seemingly', 2.2, 6). The key passage of interest, however, is 2.6, where a connection with 6.12 is to be seen whose importance is missed by most commentators. The issue of πρόσωπον is on the table when Paul explains that his own disregard for honour is a result of God not being concerned about human status, a reality presented aptly in the clause, 'God does not take face' (2.6). It is interesting that, despite the clear presence of face and distinction language in the passage, the issue is not explored by scholars. The opponents' attempt to defend a boastworthy distinction is not only criticized in 2.6, alongside descriptions of those with status in Jerusalem as τῶν δοκούντων, but the argument then leads into a discussion of the irrelevance of differentiating between Jew and gentile due to Christ's crucifixion (2.15-21).

12.4.1 *Face-Rejecting Theology*

The discussion above should suffice to show the subtle but crucial position of εὐπροσωπέω in 6.12 to the force of Galatians as a whole – Paul is closing the letter with a brilliant rhetorical stab at the agitators' purported status-improving motivation. It is not simply that they wish to impose a tenet of Torah to which Paul objects, but rather that their very motivation of achieving 'good face' is entirely incongruent with their God who, in 2.6, does not 'take face' (The face-saving behaviour of the agitators, it is worth noting, can now be seen as a salient aspect of the parallel with the Antioch encounter.) By exposing their continued honour-based motivation, with only a single word Paul has made the agitators God's opponents – they have rejected the status-levelling implication of the cross, expressed explicitly at 3.26-28 and further in the concept of the 'oneness' of God (3.20). While these troublemakers are pursuing the God-opposed 'good face' of status improvement and differentiation,[39] Paul himself recommends an unusual glory perfectly in keeping with his epistle's theology, a boast in the cross

---

38. R. Jewett, 'Paul, Shame, and Honor', in *Paul in the Greco-Roman World*, ed. J. P. Sampley (Harrisburg: Trinity, 2003), 551–74 (558).

39. Kahl is one of the few who sees εὐπροσωπέω as important here, yet merely superficial. Significantly, she does note that the challenge from the agitators is to abandon the murky

(καυχᾶσθαι) – an imitation of Christ in dying to the world, and apparently also to its values (6.14-15; cf. 2.19-20).[40] The new creation, this status-ignoring diversity, would entirely fail as a project even if something as apparently simple as 'concern for face', or more broadly, the valuing of any flesh-based status, re-conquered its nascent adherents – which is why neither of the statuses mentioned in 6.15 has worth (cf. 5.6).[41]

12.4.2 *Anti-Εὐπροσωπέω Ethics*

The reading just defended has implications for the so-called ethical section of Galatians. While scholarship has struggled to see how Gal. 5.13-6.10 connects to the rest of the epistle and relates to the crisis in Galatia, a face-aware reading can attempt a response to both.[42] In this argument the 'ethics' of Galatians are intentionally positioned to establish a community that rejects the competition for all public claims to honour. Such claims highlight and value differentiated status thus contradicting the efficacy of the cross, which should be the Galatians' only 'boast', and place trust in a value system that is categorically not valued by God. A more thorough exploration is possible, but for now I note that these verses continually focus on a rejection of self-seeking or self-improving behaviour and the conflict that accompanies it (5.15); they promote a servitude in love (5.13) that opposes fleshly behaviour by encouraging those who would normally have 'lost face' (6.1). A further reminder about concern for personal status, using the same vocabulary as that in ch. 2 for those who were 'seemingly' pillars, appears in the midst of a passage encouraging mutual support and warning against pride and 'one-upmanship' (6.1-5).[43] Meanwhile, competitive behaviour is further shackled by the instruction to 'bear each others' burdens'.[44] This is ethical advice

identity in Christ for clear and traditional categories of 'us and them'. B. Kahl, *Galatians Re-Imagined* (Minneapolis: Fortress, 2010), 226.

40. The social irony of this is loud – the cross degrades status for the Romans *and* for the Gospel, only the subject of degradation is very different.

41. DeBoer approaches the εὐπροσωπέω problem nearly identically to Martyn (*Galatians*, 561), i.e. he connects the boasting to the 'good face' but does not consider it. The only addition is that he allows for the connection of the 'good face' to the agitators' unawareness of the change of regimes (3.25), and thus to their lives being oriented to flesh not Spirit; M. de Boer, *Galatians* (Louisville: Westminster John Knox, 2011), 398.

42. Cf. J. M. G. Barclay, *Obeying the Truth: Paul's Ethics in Galatians* (Vancouver: Regent College, 2005), 9–26, which is a good survey of the issue in scholarship up until the early 1980s; a more recent survey is in T. A. Wilson, *The Curse of the Law and the Crisis in Galatia: Reassessing the Purpose of Galatians* (Tübingen: Mohr Siebeck, 2007), 1–16.

43. Perhaps aware of the need of sober judgement of oneself before God, at 6.4 Paul does allow boasting in self-assessment, but only privately, effectively neutering the possiblity of the boast growing into community conflict once more.

44. Burden-bearing is normally slave work (6.2) – in 1 Cor. 9.19-21 ἔννομος Χρισφτοῦ is to be a slave to all. This would suggest that the 'law of Christ' is a Christian hospitality law,

192   *Scripture as Social Discourse*

specifically tailored to ensure that the Galatian churches will reject the status-obsession that typified contemporary associations; hence the instructions at 5.26 – avoid κενόδοξοι (false-*glory*), and abandon conflict and envy – that is, reject the competition for honour.

12.5 *A Brief Postscript on Honour Models*

Using a model of honour does need eternal vigilance, as T. F. Carney warned about models generally several years ago, and they are not perfect solutions to recreate the context of the text.[45] However, they can, despite the opposition that comes their way when used on NT texts, serve as helpful heuristic devices that place us closer to the world of the text.[46] In regard to the topic of the present study the few studies that have focused on Paul's use of εὐπροσωπέω in 6.12 are forced either to offer some vague platitude or to construct an overly elaborate thesis that does not particularly impinge on the argument of the epistle. Conversely, asking questions of an honour nature seems almost effortlessly to illuminate interpretative options that better explain the passage and the letter. There is sufficient evidential language in 6.11-18 to avoid the trite accusations of 'finding what you set out to find' that are often unfairly levelled against models, and to suggest that a model of honour has 'goodness of fit' to attempt a reading of Galatians.[47]

That said, however, the Galatians epistle also warns against an overly shallow understanding of honour. Paul's rejection of εὐπροσωπέω, theologically and ethically, provides 'grist for the mill of "abduction"' – the process of using models to read texts and then the texts to modify the models.[48] Too often contemporary (and questionably understood) models have been applied so naively that the response, 'It's a heuristic process', is not a sufficient defence. While I agree that a Geertzian 'thick description' is difficult to generate from a two millennia distance, I think that those applying honour models to NT texts would do well to always consider the 'third context' – namely the surrounding cultures' texts that provide

where the care for others cannot become an unbearable burden for the weak since it turns, like the enslavement of 5.13, on the mutuality of ἀλλήλοις. Cf. Barclay, *Obeying*, 131; and C. H. Dodd, 'Ennomos Christou', in *More New Testament Studies* (Manchester: Manchester University Press, 1968), 134–48.

45. T. F. Carney, *The Shape of the Past: Models and Antiquity* (Lawrence: Coronado, 1975), 36–37; cf. R. L. Rohrbaugh, 'Models and Muddles: Discussions of the Social Facets Seminar', *Foundations and Facets Forum* 3, no. 2 (1987), 23–33 (32).

46. See footnote 5 above.

47. Cf. D. G. Horrell, 'Models and Methods in Social-Scientific Interpretation: A Response to Philip Esler', *JSNT* 78 (2000): 83–105.

48. S. Kirkpatrick, *Competing for Honor: A Social-Scientific Reading of Daniel 1–6* (Leiden: Brill, 2005), 31.

an abundance of data on the centrality of honour in daily life.[49] Many studies do this, but too many have divorced their honour models from the actual cultural context, thereby missing, among other things, the various attempts by different sources to reject, challenge, or critique – as I am suggesting Paul does – the obsession with social standing commonly held among those alive around the time of the New Testament.[50]

My worry is, however, that 'honour' is becoming a cant word among biblical social sciences. Like Gerald Downing, I worry that it could become so imprecisely banded about that it becomes essentially meaningless, or its use becomes so technically fraught that only the bravest dare use it, and few would understand them.[51] What I hope to have shown in the present essay is that when sufficient evidence of 'goodness of fit' encourages the use of a model, with appropriate glosses (in this case, concerning εὐπροσωπέω and honour), the degree to which a model can expose the 'problems of partial awareness' justifies its continued use as a methodology, at least in explorations of the Epistle to the Galatians if not more widely.[52]

Bibliography

Barclay, J. M. G. *Obeying the Truth: Paul's Ethics in Galatians.* Vancouver: Regent College, 2005.

Barclay, J. M. G. 'Grace and the Countercultural Reckoning of Worth: Community Construction in Galatians 5–6'. In *Galatians and Christian Theology: Justification, the Gospel and Ethics in Paul's Letter*, edited by M. W. Elliott et al., 306–17. Grand Rapids: Baker, 2014.

Barton, C. A. *Roman Honor: The Fire in the Bones.* Berkeley: University of California Press, 2001.

Barton, S. C. 'The Metaphor of Face in Paul'. In *Conception, Reception, and the Spirit: Essays in Honor of Andrew T. Lincoln*, edited by J. G. McConville and L. K. Pietersen, 136–53. Eugene: Cascade, 2015.

Betz, H. D. *Galatians.* Philadelphia: Fortress Press, 1979.

Bourdieu, P. 'The Sentiment of Honour in Kabyle Society'. In *Honour and Shame: The Values of Mediterranean Society*, edited by J. G. Peristiany, 191–242. London: Weidenfeld and Nicholson, 1965.

---

49. P. F. Esler, *Ancient Israel: The Old Testament in Its Social Context* (London: SCM Press, 2005), 13.

50. I think that this problem originates in Malina, *New Testament World*. See the helpful observations in Downing, '"Honor" among Exegetes', 64, regarding the various criticisms of honour by those of a Cynic persuasion; cf. P. F. Craffert, 'An Exercise in the Critical Use of Models: The "Goodness of Fit" of Wilson's Sect Model', in *Social Scientific Models for Interpreting the Bible*, ed. J. J. Pilch (Atlanta: SBL, 2001), 21–46.

51. Downing, '"Honor" among Exegetes', 68.

52. Carney, *Shape*, 12.

Cairns, D. 'Honour and Shame: Modern Controversies and Ancient Values'. *Critical Quarterly* 53, no. 1 (2011): 23–41.

Carney, T. F. *The Shape of the Past: Models and Antiquity.* Lawrence: Coronado, 1975.

Clarke, A. D. *Secular and Christian Leadership in Corinth: A Socio-Historical and Exegetical Study of 1 Corinthians 1–6.* Leiden: Brill, 1993.

Craffert, P. F. 'An Exercise in the Critical Use of Models: The "Goodness of Fit" of Wilson's Sect Model'. In *Social Scientific Models for Interpreting the Bible*, edited by J. J. Pilch, 21–46. Atlanta: SBL, 2001.

Crook, Z. A. 'Honor, Shame and Social Status Revisited'. *JBL* 128, no. 3 (2009): 591–611.

De Boer, M. *Galatians.* NTL. Louisville: Westminster John Knox, 2011.

Dodd, C. H. 'Ennomos Christou'. In *More New Testament Studies*, 134–48. Manchester: Manchester University Press, 1968.

Downing, F. G. '"Honor" among Exegetes'. *CBQ* 61 (1999): 53–73.

Duling, D. *A Marginal Scribe: Studies in the Gospel of Matthew in a Social-Scientific Perspective.* Eugene: Wipf and Stock, 2011.

Dunn, J. D. G. *Galatians.* BNTC. London: A&C Black, 1993.

Esler, P. F. *Modelling Early Christianity: Social-Scientific Studies of the New Testament in Its Context.* London: Routledge, 1995.

Esler, P. F. *Galatians.* London: Routledge, 1998.

Esler, P. F. *Ancient Israel: The Old Testament in Its Social Context.* London: SCM Press, 2005.

Finley, M. I. *The World of Odysseus.* London: Pimlico, 1999.

Finney, M. T. *Honour and Conflict in the Ancient World: 1 Corinthians in Its Greco-Roman Social Setting.* London: T&T Clark, 2012.

Forbis, E. *Municipal Virtues in the Roman Empire: The Evidence of Italian Honorary Inscriptions.* Stuttgart: Teubner, 1996.

Garnsey, P., and R. P. Saller. *The Roman Empire: Economy, Society and Culture.* London: Duckworth, 1987.

Gilmore, D. D., ed. *Honor and Shame and the Unity of the Mediterranean.* Washington, DC: American Anthropological Association, 1987.

Goffman, E. 'On Face-Work: An Analysis of Ritual Elements in Social Interaction'. In *Interaction Ritual*, edited by E. Goffman, 5–45. New York: Doubleday, 1967.

Gouldner, A. W. *Enter Plato: Classical Greece and the Origins of Social Theory.* London: Routledge, 1967.

Hardin, J. K. *Galatians and the Imperial Cult: A Critical Analysis of the First-Century Social Context of Paul's Letter.* Tübingen: Mohr Siebeck, 2008.

Herzfeld, M. '"As in Your Own House": Hospitality, Ethnography, and the Stereotype of Mediterranean Society'. In *Honor and Shame and the Unity of the Mediterranean*, edited by D. D. Gilmore, 75–89. Washington, DC: American Anthropological Association, 1987.

Horrell, D. G. 'Models and Methods in Social-Scientific Interpretation: A Response to Philip Esler'. *JSNT* 78 (2000): 83–105.

Jewett, R. 'Paul, Shame, and Honor'. In *Paul in the Greco-Roman World*, edited by J. P. Sampley, 551–74. Harrisburg: Trinity, 2003.

Jones, C. P. *The Roman World of Dio Chrysostom.* Cambridge: Harvard University Press, 1978.

Kahl, B. *Galatians Re-Imagined.* Minneapolis: Fortress, 2010.

Kelly, J. M. *Studies in the Civil Judicature of the Roman Republic.* Oxford: Clarendon Press, 1976.

Kirkpatrick, S. *Competing for Honor: A Social-Scientific Reading of Daniel 1–6.* Leiden: Brill, 2005.

Lawrence, L. J. *An Ethnography of the Gospel of Matthew: A Critical Assessment of the Use of the Honour and Shame Model in New Testament Studies.* Tübingen: Mohr Siebeck, 2003.

Lendon, J. E. *Empire of Honour.* Oxford: Clarendon, 1997.

Lightfoot, J. B. *St. Paul's Epistle to the Galatians.* London: Macmillan, 1884.

Longenecker, R. N. *Galatians.* WBC. Dallas: Word, 1990.

MacMartin, C., L. A. Wood and R. O. Kroger. 'Facework'. In *The New Handbook of Language and Social Psychology,* edited by. W. P. Robinson and H. Giles, 221–37. Chichester: Wiley, 2001.

Malina, B. J. *The New Testament World: Insights from Cultural Anthropology.* 3rd edn. Louisville: Westminster John Knox, 2001.

Martyn, J. L. *Galatians.* New York: Doubleday, 1997.

Nanos, M. D. *The Irony of Galatians: Paul's Letter in First-Century Context.* Minneapolis: Fortress Press, 2002.

Nédoncelle, M. 'Prosopon et Persona dans l'antiqué'. *RSR* 22 (1948): 277–99.

Nguyen, V. H. T. *Christian Identity in Corinth: A Comparative Study of 2 Corinthians, Epictetus and Valerius Maximus.* Tübingen: Mohr Siebeck, 2008.

Oprisko, R. L. *Honor: A Phenomenology.* New York: Routledge, 2012.

Peristiany, J. G., ed. *Honour and Shame: The Values of Mediterranean Society.* London: Weidenfeld and Nicholson, 1965.

Peristiany, J. G., and J. A. Pitt-Rivers. *Honour and Grace in Anthropology.* Cambridge: Cambridge University Press, 1992.

Prokhorov, A. V. 'Taking the Jews out of the Equation: Galatians 6.12–17 as a Summons to Cease Evading Persecution'. *JSNT* 36 (2013): 172–88.

Rohrbaugh, R. L. 'Models and Muddles: Discussions of the Social Facets Seminar'. *Forum* 3, no. 2 (1987): 23–33.

Stewart, F. H. *Honor.* Chicago: University of Chicago Press, 1994.

Ting-Toomey, S. 'Face and Facework: An Introduction'. In *The Challenge of Facework: Cross-Cultural and Interpersonal Issues,* edited by S. Ting-Toomey, 1–14. Albany: State University of New York Press, 1994.

Weima, J. A. D. *Neglected Endings: The Significance of the Pauline Letter Closings.* Sheffield: JSOT, 1994.

Wilson, T.A. *The Curse of the Law and the Crisis in Galatia: Reassessing the Purpose of Galatians.* Tübingen: Mohr Siebeck, 2007.

Winter, B. W. *Seek the Welfare of the City: Christians as Benefactors and Citizens.* Grand Rapids: Eerdmans, 1994.

Winter, B. W. 'The Imperial Cult and Early Christianity in Roman Galatia (Acts xiii 13–50 and Galatians vi 11–18)'. In *Actes Du 1er Congress International Sur Antioche De Pisidie,* edited by T. Drew-Bear, M. Tashalan and C.M. Thomas; 67–76. Lyon: Université Lumière-Lyon, 2002.

Chapter 13

THE USE OF SOCIAL MODELS IN BIBLICAL STUDIES: PHILIPPIANS 1.27–2.5 AS A CASE STUDY

Peter Oakes

13.1 *Models and their Uses*

I would define a 'model', in fairly general terms, as *a simplified representation of a world, or of some aspect of it*.[1] For scholarship, I would elaborate the definition slightly to say that a 'model' is *a simplified representation designed for carrying out an analytical task*. A 'social model' is *a model of a society or some aspect of it*. A 'social-scientific model' is *a model constructed on the basis of social-scientific study*.

Human beings always need to use models. We only cope with walking down the street because we have a simplified mental representation of society. We see society in two categories: a set of named individuals who are family, friends, acquaintances, or particular people in public view or otherwise known of indirectly; then a number of groups such as 'authority figures', 'people carrying knives', 'people in general'. From our experience of repeated patterns of behaviour, or from reports, we assign expected behaviour to the various groups. As we walk along the road we provisionally identify people as belonging to one of our standard groups and we react to them accordingly. We know that, in reality, people are individuals. That puts us slightly on our guard for unexpected behaviour. However, the effective way to get from one end of the road to the other is to act on the assumptions in our model of people's typical behaviour.

Model use of this kind draws on our experience that people's behaviour tends to be as it has been before. However, modelling does not, in itself, assume a deterministic view of behaviour. The police officer in the street might come across and kick you. This will usually change your view of the police. Among the models that we use to make sense of the world are ones that specifically deal with change. For example, Anthony Giddens and others point out that we all reshape language

---

1. This definition is close to that of Bruce J. Malina, *The New Testament World: Insights from Cultural Anthropology* (Atlanta: John Knox/London: SCM, 1981), 17. It is, of course, not entirely general. There are other senses of the term, such as, 'a person to be imitated'.

Scripture as Social Discourse

in the act of using it.[2] Most of us do not have that idea in our everyday model of the world: it is not usually significant. However, our models do tend to include the idea of language as changing when it is used by people who have particularly great leverage in the linguistic system,[3] such as certain figures in the media. Use and transformation of language are among the social processes that we recognize in the models by which we live – and by which we do academic work.

If I reflect on how, some years back, I went about interpreting Polycarp's letter to the Philippians, I realize that I did so by thinking about what the text means within a simplified picture – a social model – of the second-century world. Polycarp sits in Smyrna. With him is a group of elders. Together they lead an undifferentiated and uncharacterized group called the church at Smyrna. Across the Aegean is a group called the church at Philippi. They are characterized in various ways. They have deacons and elders, but no bishop. They have probably had members martyred. They have trouble with an elder called Valens and maybe with some teaching that Polycarp views as heresy. The third specific set of players in this world are Ignatius and his fellow martyrs, who have recently passed through Philippi. Ignatius has written letters expressing strong views on the importance of bishops. Finally, the rest of the world is broadly divided into three groups: other Christian communities, Roman authorities, and non-Christians in general. My model of this world thus consists of three individuals (Polycarp, Ignatius and Valens) and six groups. This gives me a manageable number of factors to bring into play to interpret the letter. The result of the interplay of these factors and the text is that I arrive at an interpretation that has two main elements. I see Polycarp's letter as cautiously written in a way that handles the complications caused by it being a letter from a bishop to a church without a bishop, in a context where Ignatius has made episcopacy a big issue. I also see the letter as an encouragement for the Philippians to stand firm in the suffering, or fear of suffering, that has come about in the aftermath of the journey of Ignatius and the other martyrs through the town.[4]

My model is a gross simplification of the second-century world. However, it is only by making a significant simplification that we can reduce the context to few enough factors to make interpretation possible. Other readers of Polycarp have reached different interpretations of the letter. One reason for this is that effectively they have worked with different models of the second-century world. For example,

---

2. Anthony Giddens, *New Rules of Sociological Method: A Positive Critique of Interpretative Sociologies* (London: Hutchinson, 1976), 128; David G. Horrell, *The Social Ethos of the Corinthian Correspondence: Interests and Ideology from 1 Corinthians to 1 Clement* (Edinburgh: T&T Clark, 1996), 49.

3. Cf. Giddens, *New Rules*, 110; Horrell, *Social Ethos*, 50.

4. Peter Oakes, 'Leadership and Suffering in the Letters of Polycarp and Paul to the Philippians', *The New Testament and the Apostolic Fathers* 2: *Trajectories through the New Testament and the Apostolic Fathers*, ed. Andrew Gregory and Christopher Tuckett (Oxford: Oxford University Press, 2005), 353–73.

Peter Meinhold gives a prominent place to the development and interplay of various orthodox and 'heretical' groups.[5]

Models are not inherently social-scientific. For example, the standard scholarly model of the layout and functioning of a Roman military camp is a generalization from archaeological study, combined with descriptions of Roman camps by Polybius and others.[6] In fact, as in this example, models frequently cut across disciplines. The model of the development of the Roman colony of Philippi, arrived at in *Philippians: From People to Letter*, drew on archaeology, history and sociology.[7] The inherent interdisciplinarity of most of our models is a vital point for us to recognize and build on. If we think carefully about which simplifications we are making, in all the disciplines that are required for a particular interpretative task, then we can hope to manage the complexity that we face, in a way that handles the task as well as we possibly can.

Notice also that the aim of my work on Polycarp was not to verify my model of second-century life. It was to interpret Polycarp's style and themes. The text could verify, falsify or reshape the model but the model was a tool, not the aim of my study. The models that I have described were not provisional models of the results that I was expecting. Of course, as my research progressed, I began to make observations. I then constructed models to organize my thinking about the observations. For example, I began to envisage a structure of Polycarp's letter. A diagram of the structure of a text is a model: it simplifies the text to help us make progress in understanding it. Also, as my study went on, I began to get ideas about what my interpretative results might be. However, my results were not models. They were statements: Polycarp's main theme is . . . ; Polycarp's letter has a particular style because . . . . Some studies do yield results that are expressed as models, but this one did not.

All of us use models when we interpret text. When scientists carry out experiments they hold all the variables constant except the ones in which they are interested. When other scholars think about an issue they do so by creating a simplified picture of the world. By simplifying to the relevant factors we are able to make analytical progress. Otherwise we get bogged down.

13.2 *Resistance to, and Advantages of, Use of Models*

This essay approaches talking about models in a more basic way than is generally the case in the often heated scholarly debates about the issue. In particular, there is dispute about the definition of the term, with some scholars wanting to include

5. For example, P. Meinhold, 'Polykarpos', *PW* 21:2, 1686–87.

6. Lawrence Keppie, *The Making of the Roman Army: From Republic to Empire*, paperback edn (London: Batsford, 1998), 36–75; Polybius 6.27–32.

7. Peter Oakes, *Philippians: From People to Letter*, SNTSMS 110 (Cambridge: Cambridge University Press, 2001, 2007), 14–16, 34–35, 46.

a wider range of academic tools under the term than do others. For example, John Elliott would see the term 'models' as including frames of reference that are constructed for research, whereas David Horrell would not.[8] This means that the two of them can sometimes be doing the same kind of academic activity but, while Elliott thinks he is using a model, Horrell thinks he is not.

I would argue that Horrell uses Giddens's theory of structuration to generate a model in order to use it for interpretation. According to what one could call the structuration model, the world consists of actions, actors and a symbolic order. The symbolic order is 'produced' and 'reproduced' in actions by actors, and is transformed by the actions. The symbolic order has only a virtual existence, which makes this a very subtle and difficult model to make interpretative use of. However, Horrell goes on to make the model easier to use by making the symbolic order a player in his system. He writes, 'The symbolic order shapes the lives of the believers, yet at the same time is reproduced (and transformed) by members of the Christian community.'[9] This means that the symbolic order shapes actions[10] which, in turn, shape the symbolic order. This is what scientists would call a 'feedback model': A affects B which affects A. This kind of loop is the basis of all electronic control systems. The Giddens-Horrell structuration model also has a second loop. As well as influencing actions, the symbolic order sustains power relations. Power relations feed back into the system by controlling the strength of the influence that the actions of any particular actor have on the symbolic order.[11]

This is an example of a kind of model that represents a theory, in this case the theory of structuration. Horrell creates a simplified view of the world that he then uses as a research framework for interpretation of the Corinthian correspondence. He looks for examples of elements of his model in the letters and, by noting how they fit the pattern in various contrasting ways, he can see how the texts differ from each other in, for example, the extent to which each supports the power structures of Graeco-Roman society.[12]

As noted above, Horrell does not call a research framework a model. He has three powerful reasons for not doing so. First, people who use models often work in ways that do not suit Horrell's work, or that of many Biblical interpreters.

8. John Elliott, *Social Scientific Criticism of the New Testament* (London: SPCK/ Minneapolis: Fortress, 1995/1993), 63; David G. Horrell, 'Models and Methods in Social-Scientific Interpretation: A Response to Philip Esler', *JSNT* 78 (2000): 83–105, here p. 93; Horrell, *Social Ethos*, 11–12.

9. Horrell, *Social Ethos*, 55. In the paragraph in question, the symbolic order appears to gain an increasingly substantial existence as Horrell works to elucidate his idea for his reader. I suspect that this is because readers think in terms of models, so elucidation is generally a case of striving towards finding a more straightforward model to present to the reader.

10. Horrell includes texts under the category of social actions (*Social Ethos*, 52).

11. Horrell, *Social Ethos*, 50.

12. Horrell, *Social Ethos*, 55–57, 281–84.

Social models work on the basis of repeated behaviour. Horrell is interested in change of behaviour. Emphasis on repeated behaviour often has academic roots in deterministic assumptions, and sometimes in the search for 'social laws'. Emphasis on repeated behaviour plays down local and individual variation. Second, users of models have often produced research whose main conclusion seems to be the verification of the model. More seriously, sometimes the use of models at the outset of research can effectively assume results and hence distort the study.[13] Third, Horrell wants to define 'model' in a way that fits what he sees as the most common usage by social scientists. This leads him to take a 'model' as being a way of summarizing the results of empirical research.[14] When Esler responds by arguing that the term is far wider than this,[15] Horrell replies that Esler makes the term so wide as to be vacuous.[16]

In fact, some of the complexity in discussions about models stems from the ambiguity with which the term has sometimes been discussed, even by those advocating their use. In arguing against Horrell's critique of models, Esler begins by citing the use of 'model' by many scholars as a fairly general term. Then he argues that in Biblical studies it now refers to a specific social-scientific approach. However, by the next page Esler is back to asserting that modelling is unavoidable.[17] Similarly, in Esler's subsequent exchange with Horrell he rashly concedes that he should 'cease dignifying as (albeit implicit) "models"' the common anachronistic 'North Atlantic' interpretative assumptions.[18] To say that these are not even implicit models is incompatible with arguing that modelling is unavoidable. Similarly, in one of the best short introductions to models, in John Elliott's *Social Scientific Criticism of the New Testament*,[19] he moves between various uses of the word 'model', from model trains to abstract social models. The moves are fairly clear to the reader. However, the word 'model', without qualification, does end up getting used in several different ways which really relate to the definitions of particular types of model.

The ambiguity in discussion of the term allows Horrell to write in lexically confusing ways such as the phrase, 'models in the strict sense'.[20] There should

13. Horrell, *Social Ethos*, 13–26; 'Models and Methods', 84–94. The last point is especially the concern expressed by Stanley Barrett (*Anthropology: A Student's Guide to Theory and Method* [Toronto: University of Toronto Press, 1996]), 216, quoted by Horrell, 'Models and Methods', 90.

14. Horrell, *Social Ethos*, 17–18, 24; 'Models and Methods', 93–94.

15. Philip F. Esler, review of Horrell, *Social Ethos*, in *JTS* 49, no. 1 (1998): 253–60, here pp. 254–56. His point is wider than the quotes picked up by Horrell.

16. Horrell, 'Models and Methods', 85.

17. Esler, Review of Horrell, 254–55.

18. Philip F. Esler, 'Models in New Testament Interpretation: A Reply to David Horrell', *JSNT* 78 (2000): 107–113, here p. 109.

19. Elliott, *Social Scientific Criticism*, 40–48.

20. Horrell, 'Models and Methods', 86.

be no 'strict' or 'loose' sense. We should talk either about 'models' or about particular types of model. What Horrell dislikes are particular types of models or particular uses of them. The ambiguity of discourse leads him from this into distancing himself from models as a whole. The only way to lexical orderliness is first to have a general discussion about models, and their uses and abuses. Then, having discussed the rights or wrongs of using models in interpretation, we can move on to consider the use of particular types of models, such as cross-cultural, social-scientific ones. If we agree that we all use models, then we can move to discussing whether some kinds of models are better than others.

The issue of models is important. As Biblical interpreters we need to find the right route through the complexity of contextual study. A key answer lies in thinking about the choices we make in simplifying the world in order to carry out interpretation. Horrell is, in fact, a scholar who thinks carefully about the simplifications that he makes. The problem is that many other scholars do not appear to register the (often interdisciplinary) complexity of the task they are undertaking and therefore do not consciously choose their simplifications to fit the task.

Furthermore, because interpretative use of models fits with how our brain works, they provide the natural route to academic interpretation. We model. We interpret in the light of our models. That is how we live. The effective way to interpret is consciously to construct a relevant, simplified representation of the world, then to interpret the text in relation to that model. That is what we will do anyway, but unreflectively, hence inaccurately, if we try to use any other approach, whether it be dependence on theory or whether we think we are simply interpreting the text in relation to the real world in all its complexity.

Another advantage of using models is that it helps us in explaining things. Since our brains function in terms of models, it is easiest to communicate by presenting models. A further advantage is, ironically, that thinking in terms of models should actually help us to avoid problems such as determinism and relativism. For example, the sociology of knowledge talks about 'social construction of reality' when, in fact, it would be clearer if it expressed this as 'social construction of models of reality'. A further advantage is that modelling involves recognizing, and usually owning up to, the simplifications we are making. This is potentially embarrassing but it allows for critique, whereas in many scholars' work the simplifications are difficult to unearth and pin down. A sixth advantage is that conscious modelling is often very creative. The range of work in, for instance, the 1991 Context Group collection, *The Social World of Luke-Acts*, is testimony to that.[21]

A final advantage is that talking about modelling links us in to the universal range of academic study, from science to art. It does not mean that we are turning theology into a matter of, say, scientific determinism. It just means that theologians, like scientists, are faced by potentially unmanageable complexity and have to draw

---

21. Jerome H. Neyrey, ed., *The Social World of Luke-Acts: Models for Interpretation* (Peabody: Hendrickson, 1991).

pictures in order to stay sane. Our simplifying activity is, in principle, the same activity as scientists and mathematicians engage in in representing the world. Nils Bohr's model of the atom, or a mathematical model of traffic flow on the M6, is a simplified representation of the world, as is Richard Rohrbaugh's model of the pre-industrial city in *The Social World of Luke-Acts*.

The final section of the essay offers an example of how social models can offer a fruitful way into biblical study.

13.3 *A Brief Case Study, Philippians 1.27–2.5*

Philippians: From People to Letter argued for a population model of the town and of the Christian community that might be expected in such a town. The method was to model the social development of the town up to the period when Paul wrote.[22] The resultant model of the social make-up of the town was then 'slanted' to take account of the varying degrees to which particular social groups would be likely to have been socially accessible to Paul and, by extension, to the early Christians who he reached.[23] The slanted model of the social composition of the Christian community was tested against various pieces of data from Philippians, Acts 16 and elsewhere in the NT. It turned out to fit this data rather better than most commentators' suggestions for the nature of Paul's audience.[24]

The social categories that were used to frame the model were derived from relationship to the agricultural means of production that were basic to the town's economy. The categories were: 'elite' (those owning the land); 'colonist farmers' (descendents of Roman colonists, farming the land either as owners of small plots or as tenants); 'service groups' (those providing goods or services to the elite, to farmers, or to each other); 'poor' (those unable to access sufficient produce to live viably); 'slaves'. These are not the categories that I would use now but they worked reasonably well in relation to the types of evidence available to model the development of the colony. The resulting model of the church at Philippi was as follows:

Service groups 43%; slaves 16%; colonist farmers 15%; poor 25%; elite 1%.

Ethnic analysis of these groups led to seeing this model as containing 36 per cent Roman citizens and 64 per cent non-citizens, mainly Greeks.[25]

Some readers of the book have reported points such as that Oakes concluded that the church at Philippi comprised 36 per cent Romans and 64 per cent non-Romans. This is not true. The above is a model. It simplifies the world by use

22. Oakes, *Philippians*, 14–50.
23. Oakes, *Philippians*, 55–63.
24. Oakes, *Philippians*, 64–70.
25. Oakes, *Philippians*, 61, Table 2.

of arguments about probability, in order to give a realistic picture of what kinds of social structures were or were not likely. The more serious figures in the modelling exercise were ones given for the likely range of each of the figures, for example, slaves were estimated at 12–25 per cent:[26] beyond that range, it looks hard to fit the percentage of slaves in the church with what we might expect in a place such as Philippi. Even that allows that there could in fact have been a number outside those limits. The 12–25 per cent figures are trying to express what is reasonably probable, given the evidence. The figure of 16 per cent slaves is a notional one within the range, designed to give the overall model a reasonable pattern. Where this model gains a sharp edge is as a tool for comparison with the implicit models in use elsewhere, for example, in commentaries that assume a Philippian church entirely made up of Roman citizens or, more extremely, entirely made up of veteran Roman soldiers. The process for constructing our model shows that these all-Roman implicit models of the church at Philippi require a long string of improbable implicit assertions about the percentages of other groups in the population of Philippi and of the relationship of the social make-up of the church to that of the town.

A first step in using the above social model in interpretation of Phil. 1.27–2.5 is to combine the percentage figures with an estimate of the size of the Christian community. Based on the degree of organization evident in Phil. 1.1, I suggested 50–100.[27] If we take a notional figure of 75, this gives us a model church made up of:

Service groups 33; slaves 12; colonist farmers 11; poor 18; elite 1.

This would include 27 Romans and 48 non-Romans.

A second step is to take this group as the audience who Paul is expecting to hear his letter.[28] There are various possible directions to move in a third step. We could, for instance, begin looking at the structure of the letter as a whole, or at arguments about its specific situation and purposes. However, for this exercise, we will simply run through 1.27–2.5, pulling out a string of points made by Paul that look likely to interact in interesting ways with a social model of the audience. (If there are no significant such points to be found, that suggests that our model is not of substantial help for analysing this text.) Among the things that Paul calls for, or announces, are the following:

1. *Politeuesthe* worthily of the gospel of Christ (1.27)
2. Stand firm together, striving together for the *pistis* of the gospel
3. Do not be panicked (1.28)

26. Oakes, *Philippians*, 60.

27. Oakes, *Philippians*, 62.

28. For discussion of the idea of 'expected hearers', and the relationship between that and the idea of the 'implied reader' see Peter Oakes, *Galatians* (Paideia Commentaries on the New Testament; Grand Rapids: Baker Academic, 2015), 14.

4. You will receive salvation from God
5. You are suffering for the sake of Christ (1.29)
6. You are having the same experience as me (1.30)
7. You should consider your comfort from Christ and your compassion (2.1)
8. Be united in the same mind and purpose (2.2)
9. There should be no *eritheia* nor *kenodoxia* (2.3)
10. Show humility, considering others as more important than yourself
11. Look not to your interests but rather to those of others (2.4)
12. Have the same mind as Christ Jesus (2.5)

As a fourth step we can compare each of the twelve points with our model church. How, and to what extent, would each point relate to each group in the model? What would each point mean for relationships between groups in the model? Having attempted this, the key issues in the string of notes that I made could be summarized under five headings. Paul calls for or announces to his hearers the following, each of which has some element of *newness*, in the sense that they are not what would normally be expected for a set of first-century people with the social profile seen in the model (although some of the points are no doubt reinforcement of aspects of Christian life that were already in practice in the group at Philippi):

(A) The socially weaker people in the model are given *new roles*. All receive the instruction, *politeuesthe* (1.27). There is much debate about the meaning of this term. However, as a lexical choice (as opposed to, for instance, *peripateō*, a term which uses walking as a metaphor for behaviour, e.g. Phil. 3.17), *politeuesthe* carries connotations relating to the *polis*, the city.[29] Any elite men in the church would be used to public life, as would, to a lesser extent, other Roman men. Looking at a factor that we have not considered so far, if we took our model church to be 50–50 women and men (early Christian evidence suggests that, if anything, the proportion of women was probably higher), then the number of Roman men in our model church is 14 out of 75. Of these 14, about 6 are colonist farmers. The rest, apart from the possible member of the elite, are freed slaves or descendants of colonists who have lost use of land. The proportion of people in the model church likely to have engaged in political life in Philippi is very low. To the others, Paul gives a new kind of role. Either he is calling them to some kind of action that engages the public sphere in Philippi or he is presenting the Christian community, in which they are active, in the language of a political entity. The latter case links to points below about the rhetoric of identity. However, it also calls those who may have seen themselves as without responsibility for community decision and action, being solely at the beck and call of others, to a new existence as active participants in the 'civic' life of a community, even if it is a community just of Christians.[30] This

29. See G. F. Hawthorne, *Philippians*, revised Ralph P. Martin (Grand Rapids: Zondervan, 2004), 68–69, although they probably overread the civic aspect.

30. Cf. Annette Weissenrieder, 'Contested Spaces in 1 Corinthians 11:17–33 and 14:30: Sitting or Reclining in Ancient Houses, in Associations and in the Space of *ekklēsia*',

issue clearly also relates to discussion of Paul's use of the term, *politeuma*, in Phil. 3.20, in relation to the Christian community.[31]

There are further likely elements of call to new roles for those whose weakness in the Graeco-Roman social system would normally have precluded such action. For instance, when Paul evokes the ideas of mercy and compassion (2.1), if these relate to human (rather than purely to divine) mercy and compassion,[32] then, although clearly people of any socio-economic level can practice these, the terms would more frequently be used in appeals to those with greater economic resources, calling on them to share those. If, for instance, a Christian slave hears Paul's call as an encouragement to share some of the informal savings that they have from tips received, this small-scale benefactor role could well be a new (and difficult) one.

(B) The hearers are presented with *a new standard* by which they should orient their lives. 'Live (*politeuesthe*) worthily of the gospel of Christ' (1.27). Particularly when taken with *politeuesthe*, the phrase, 'worthily of the gospel of Christ', is evocative of the idea of a life lived according to a standard determined by the nature of an allegiance. The Philippian crowd in Acts 16.21 present Roman identity as being incompatible with certain actions. Cicero sees loyalty to Rome as all-encompassing:

> sed necesse est caritate eam praestare, qua rei publicae nomen universae civitatis est; pro qua mori et cui nos totos dedere et in qua nostra omnia ponere et quasi consecrare debemus.
>
> But that fatherland must stand first in our affection in which the name of republic signifies the common citizenship of all of us. For her it is our duty to die, to her to give ourselves entirely, to place on her altar, and, as it were, to dedicate to her service, all that we possess. (*De legibus* 2.2)[33]

For the Roman citizens in our model church, the primary determining standard can no longer be that of Romanness. For the non-citizens in the model, a standard

---

in *Contested Spaces: Houses and Temples in Roman Antiquity and the New Testament*, ed. D. L. Balch and A. Weissenrieder; WUNT 285(Tübingen: Mohr Siebeck, 2012), 59–107; here, 86–90. Weissenrieder sees the act of 'sitting' in the Christian community at Corinth (1 Cor. 14. 30) as indicative of a mode of meeting related to that of Greek citizen assemblies.

31. For discussion of this term see Peter Oakes, 'The Christians and their *Politeuma* in Heaven: Philippians 3:20 and the Herakleopolis Papyri', in *Citizenship(s) and Political/Religious Self-Definitions in the Roman Empire*, ed. Katell Berthelot, Interdisciplinary Studies in Ancient Culture and Religion (Leuven: Peeters, forthcoming).

32. See, for instance, Gordon D. Fee, *Paul's Letter to the Philippians*, NICNT (Grand Rapids: Eerdmans, 1995), 182.

33. Cicero, *On the Republic. On the Laws*, trans. Clinton W. Keyes, LCL 213 (Cambridge, MA: Harvard University Press, 1928), 374–77.

is being set up: an overall one, going beyond those determined by, for instance, household loyalty.

This takes us to a phrase at the end of 1.27: 'striving together for the *pistis* of the gospel'. The loyalty, trust, *pistis*, which is to be the object of the hearers' effort – a communal effort – is the loyalty constituted by the gospel. Again, we have here a loyalty that overrides the loyalties to household, to Rome, or to other entities, that various people in our model would have had. Teresa Morgan sees this in radical terms in Paul's letters, 'there is no longer any trustworthy relationship or community for them except that which exists with God and Christ in the kingdom of God'.[34] Whether or not we should go as far as this, Paul certainly presents this new *pistis* as becoming the most central point around which the lives of the hearers should now revolve.

(C) Still in 1.27, Paul calls his hearers to what are, in social terms, strange *new alliances*. For the set of types of people in our model, it would be very radical to call them to act 'in one spirit' and 'with one soul'. This point is then made repeatedly through 2.1-5: possibly in the references in 2.1 to love and *koinōnia* ('fellowship'); certainly in the insistent repetition of 2.2, 'thinking the same thing, having the same love, together in soul, thinking the one thing'; practically, in the call of 2.4 to consider the interests of each other. The alliances that this involves are not those of socially equal friends, nor are they family alliances, nor are they alliances of patron–client relationships. Paul puts the elite, the poor, slaves, shopkeepers, farmers, men, women, Romans and Greeks together, on a level with each other, in a relationship of mutual concern. The closest precedent for this is probably the existence of some ethnic groups resident far from their ethnic origin: for instance, diaspora Jewish synagogues and, related to those, ethnic *politeumata* such as the Jewish ones whose operation is seen in the papyri from Herakleopolis in the Ptolemaic period.[35] However, we do not have evidence, even in these kinds of settings, of the type of rhetoric that Paul deploys in drawing together the socially disparate group of hearers.

(D) Paul presents *new challenges*. We have already mentioned that poorer hearers may have perceived a challenging call to share even their meagre resources. There is also, more obviously, a challenge to the wealthier members of the congregation to do this. This goes with a rhetoric that is seen most starkly in 2.3-4, 'doing nothing according to *eritheia* or *kenodoxia* but in humility considering each other as more important than yourselves, each of you not looking to their own interests but rather[36] each looking to those of others'. As well as the clear challenge to sharing of resources, there are several likely

---

34. Teresa Morgan, *Roman Faith and Christian Faith: Pistis and Fides in the Early Roman Empire and Early Churches* (Oxford: Oxford University Press, 2015), 306.

35. For discussion, see Oakes, 'The Christians and their *Politeuma* in Heaven'.

36. For this translation of ἀλλὰ καί, see Markus Bockmuehl, *A Commentary on the Epistle to the Philippians* (London: A&C Black, 1997), 113–14.

challenges to the thinking of people in the higher status groups in our model. As Klaus Wengst argues, in a Graeco-Roman context, 'humility' (*tapeinophrosynē*) would typically be thought of as a characteristic of the poor, closely related to servility.[37] The rebuke to *kenodoxia*, 'empty glory', would also be likely to be heard as a challenge to the seeking for honour that was a key part of the life of the elite and of somewhat lower status groups who aped their practices. The term *eritheia* is hard to be clear about. It could be heard as relating to strife between political groups, or other factions (cf. Aristotle, *Politics*, 5.2): Paul sees it as driving those who are causing him trouble in his imprisonment (1.17). It could also be heard as relating to mercenary self-interest.[38] In that case, maybe it would be particularly disturbing to those engaged in trade. It would fit with the call not to look to one's own interests. This call would operate against a key responsibility of the Graeco-Roman wealthy, to maintain their wealth. Losing it was irresponsible to the family's status, resulting in loss of position in society. The challenge is further reinforced by the socially radical rhetoric of a call to consider others, no matter what their status was in comparison with yours, as more important than yourself.

(E) Paul offers a *new identity*. For all the people in the model, but especially for the great majority who were excluded from prestige in Philippi in one way or another, Paul offers an exalted new identity. They are receiving salvation from God (1.28); their sufferings are for the sake of Christ (1.29); their experience is like that of their leader, Paul (1.30), and their mind can be conformed to that of the cosmic Lord, Christ Jesus (2.5, cf. 2.9-11). Their community has something of the nature of citizen-soldiers fighting as a unit (1.27). It is also something like an elite male friendship group, sharing all things in common. Paul offers a way of life that lifts the church members from a range of low status identities into an existence as a significant group, trusted with the very work of God.

13.4 Conclusion

We all use models to manage complexity. For academic study, it is worth doing so consciously, thinking about what simplifications we do or do not make in constructing our models, trying to ensure that models are appropriate to the particular texts and tasks that we have in hand. The brief case study above uses a social model of the expected hearers of Philippians to alert us to a range of issues that are left invisible if we unreflectively treat the audience as an undifferentiated mass. Many other uses of models, social or otherwise, can shed still more light on a wide range of biblical texts.

---

37. Klaus Wengst, *Humility: Solidarity of the Humiliated – The Transformation of an Attitude and its Social Relevance in Graeco-Roman, Old Testament-Jewish and Early Christian Tradition*, trans. J. Bowden (London: SCM, 1988 [German 1987]), 4–18.

38. F. Büchsel, 'ἐριθεία', *TDNT*, vol. II, 660–61.

Bibliography

Bockmuehl, Markus. *A Commentary on the Epistle to the Philippians*. BNTC. London: A&C Black, 1997.

Büchsel, F. 'ἐριθεία'. *TDNT* II, edited by G. Kittel, trans. G. Bromiley, 660–61. Grand Rapids: Eerdmans, 1964.

Cicero. *On the Republic. On the Laws*, trans. Clinton W. Keyes. LCL 213. Cambridge: Harvard University Press, 1928.

Elliott, John. *Social Scientific Criticism of the New Testament*. London: SPCK; Minneapolis: Fortress, 1995; 1993.

Esler, Philip F. Review of *The Social Ethos of the Corinthian Correspondence*, by David G. Horrell. In *JTS* 49, no. 1 (1998): 253–60.

Esler, Philip F. 'Models in New Testament Interpretation: A Reply to David Horrell'. *JSNT* 78 (2000): 107–113.

Fee, Gordon D. *Paul's Letter to the Philippians*. NICNT. Grand Rapids: Eerdmans, 1995.

Giddens, Anthony. *New Rules of Sociological Method: A Positive Critique of Interpretative Sociologies*. London: Hutchinson, 1976.

Hawthorne, G. F. *Philippians*. Revised Ralph P. Martin. Grand Rapids: Zondervan, 2004.

Horrell, David G. *The Social Ethos of the Corinthian Correspondence: Interests and Ideology from 1 Corinthians to 1 Clement*. Edinburgh: T&T Clark, 1996.

Horrell, David G. 'Models and Methods in Social-Scientific Interpretation: A Response to Philip Esler'. *JSNT* 78 (2000): 83–105.

Keppie, Lawrence. *The Making of the Roman Army: From Republic to Empire*. London: Batsford, 1998.

Malina, Bruce J. *The New Testament World: Insights from Cultural Anthropology*. Atlanta: John Knox; London: SCM, 1981.

Meinhold, P. 'Polykarpos'. *PW* 21:2, 1686–7. Stuttgart: Alfred Drückenmüller, 1952.

Morgan, Teresa. *Roman Faith and Christian Faith: Pistis and Fides in the Early Roman Empire and Early Churches*. Oxford: Oxford University Press, 2015.

Neyrey, Jerome H., ed. *The Social World of Luke-Acts: Models for Interpretation*. Peabody: Hendrickson, 1991.

Oakes, Peter. *Philippians: From People to Letter*. SNTSMS 110. Cambridge: Cambridge University Press, 2001.

Oakes, Peter. 'Leadership and Suffering in the Letters of Polycarp and Paul to the Philippians'. In *The New Testament and the Apostolic Fathers 2: Trajectories through the New Testament and the Apostolic Fathers*, edited by Andrew Gregory and Christopher Tuckett, 353–73. Oxford: Oxford University Press, 2005.

Oakes, Peter. *Galatians*. Paideia Commentaries on the New Testament. Grand Rapids: Baker Academic, 2015.

Oakes, Peter. 'The Christians and their *Politeuma* in Heaven: Philippians 3:20 and the Herakleopolis Papyri'. In *Citizenship(s) and Political/Religious Self-Definitions in the Roman Empire*, edited by Katell Berthelot. Interdisciplinary Studies in Ancient Culture and Religion. Leuven: Peeters, forthcoming.

Weissenrieder, Annette. 'Contested Spaces in 1 Corinthians 11:17–33 and 14:30: Sitting or Reclining in Ancient Houses, in Associations and in the Space of *ekklēsia*'. In *Contested Spaces: Houses and Temples in Roman Antiquity and the New Testament*, edited by D. L. Balch and A. Weissenrieder. WUNT 285; 59–107. Tübingen: Mohr Siebeck, 2012.

Wengst, Klaus. *Humility: Solidarity of the Humiliated – The Transformation of an Attitude and its Social Relevance in Graeco-Roman, Old Testament-Jewish and Early Christian Tradition*, trans. J. Bowden. London: SCM, 1988.

Chapter 14

INSIDE THE BRIDAL CHAMBER: INDIVIDUAL, GROUP AND INTERTEXTUALITY IN *GOSPEL OF PHILIP* 65.1-26

Todd E. Klutz

Recent debates sparked by the critique of 'Gnosticism' as a category of analysis in the study of ancient Mediterranean religion have far-reaching but still largely unexplored implications for the interpretation of early Christian literature.[1] The implications of those debates for understanding a controversial unit of discourse in the fourth century CE Coptic writing known as the *Gospel of Philip* (Nag Hammadi Codex II, 3) – namely, the first passage in a sequence of several where the text includes explicit mention of 'the bridal chamber' (65.1-26)[2] – constitute an important part of the topic addressed by the present essay. Unlike several other units of bridal-chamber discourse in the *Gospel of Philip*, the teaching on that theme in *Gos. Phil.* 65.1-26 in particular has not been the focus of detailed criticism or exegesis in scholarship published to date.[3] The present essay is therefore

1. As noted by David Brakke, *The Gnostics: Myth, Ritual, and Diversity in Early Christianity* (Cambridge, MA: Harvard University Press, 2010), 23, the most influential contributions to the scholarly critique of 'Gnosticism' as a category are Michael A. Williams, *Rethinking 'Gnosticism': An Argument for Dismantling a Dubious Category* (Princeton: Princeton University Press, 1996); and Karen L. King, *What Is Gnosticism?* (Cambridge, MA: Harvard University Press, 2003).

2. The best-known English rendering of the Greek loanwords ⲚⲨⲘⲪⲰⲚ (the term used in 65.12), ⲠⲀⲤⲦⲞⲤ, ⲔⲞⲓⲦⲰⲚ, and ⲦⲀⲘⲉⲓⲟⲚ. Subtle differences of nuance between those terms may have interesting implications not yet explored by interpreters of the *Gospel of Philip*; but since only one of them (ⲚⲨⲘⲪⲰⲚ) is used in *Gos. Phil.* 65.1-26, detailed lexical study of the larger semantic field is not pursued in the present essay.

3. The most perceptive reading offered to date is probably Hugo Lundhaug, *Images of Rebirth: Cognitive Poetics and Transformational Soteriology in the Gospel of Philip and Exegesis on the Soul*, NHMS 37 (Leiden: E. J. Brill, 2010), 321–24, whose understanding of the bridal-chamber metaphors in the *Gospel of Philip* as referring to the body of either Christ (in some instances) or the individual believer (in others) has very much in its favour; but who also construes *Gos. Phil.* 65.1-26 more particularly as envisaging an apotropaic

primarily an attempt to heighten scholarly interest in *Gos. Phil.* 65.1-26 as a discrete unit of discourse, in the distinctive blend of interpretative possibilities and difficulties which that unit presents to its readers, and in the same passage's contribution to the larger bridal-chamber theme and related motifs in the *Gospel of Philip*; but in order to be properly critical and also informed by recent thought about the construction of abstract categories more generally, it is also intended to be an experiment in the integration of sociological, discourse-analytic and comparative method for the purpose of reconceptualizing 'Gnosticism' and closely related categories (e.g. 'Valentinianism').

The analysis below approaches the linguistic and conceptual aspects of *Gos. Phil.* 65.1-26 from a broadly discourse-analytic and intertextual perspective that compares the key unit and a few select intertexts, not with unrestricted interest in every possible effect of the intertextuality, but rather with particular regard to the position each text (especially *Gospel of Philip* 65) might be best assigned on a continuum between collectivist and individualist orientations.[4] For purposes of seeking, finding and organizing the information most relevant to that specific focus, my analysis also makes extensive use of the distinctions made by many sociologists between the family, the religious association and the state as discrete

---

union of the believer with Christ, where the grammar of the text – most especially, the use and entailments of the particle ⲙⲛ ('and', not 'or'!) in 65.9-11, 24 – implies on the contrary a prophylactic union of male and female spirit principles inside the bridal chamber (i.e. the body) of each individual Christian. In line with Lundhaug in that regard, and thus against the position developed below, are both Karen L. King, 'The Place of the *Gospel of Philip* in the Context of Early Christian Claims about Jesus' Marital Status', *NTS* 59 (2013): 575–76; and Einar Thomassen, *The Spiritual Seed: The Church of the 'Valentinians'*, NHMS 60 (Leiden: E. J. Brill, 2006), 456–57.

4. Here and below my assumption of the existence in late antiquity of a form of spirituality that can properly be described as 'individualistic' is not intended to equate the ancient moral universe of the *Gospel of Philip* and that of the modern North Atlantic world's individual self, especially where the latter is understood (as it now is by many historians and sociologists) as distinguished by experience of an introspective conscience, as plagued by inner guilt and as seeking salvation in the finding (or sometimes the creation) of its own self – perhaps with help from a psychoanalyst or professional counsellor. Instead, and because the individual Christian self in *Gos. Phil.* 65.1-26 is defined not merely as vulnerable to attack and in need of protection but also as possessing the inner resources required for victory, my use of the term is designed chiefly to identify the outlook of our passage with Hellenistic and Roman approaches to taking care of the (individual) self, a range of practices famously treated as a type of 'individualism' by Michel Foucault, *The Care of the Self*, trans. R. Hurley, vol. 3 of *The History of Sexuality* (New York: Random House, 1986), 41–68; and illuminated more recently by Troels Engberg-Pedersen, *Paul and the Stoics* (Louisville: Westminster John Knox, 2000), 13–14, 41–43, 65, 227–28, 294; and earlier by, among others, C. H. Moore, 'Individualism and Religion in the Early Roman Empire', *HTR* 2, no. 2 (1909): 221–29.

but interrelated levels of social structure.[5] The question of where the *Gospel of Philip* ought to be placed on the continuum of individual and group acquires much of its interest from the (largely unexamined) scholarly assumption that the text implies a context of group-oriented production and reception,[6] and that the particular group in question is best identified as Valentinian in character.[7] On those particular matters, the position developed below is that although it is of course impossible to preclude either a broadly group-oriented context or even a Valentinian setting in particular as the historical situation of the *Gospel of Philip*'s composition and early reception, the Coptic text of the *Gospel of Philip* extant in Nag Hammadi Codex II exemplifies a blend of features – both in terms of what the text includes and in regard to what it excludes – that pose serious difficulties for the default view.

The programme of inquiry just sketched is consciously motivated to a great degree by interest in whether 'Gnosticism' should perhaps be redefined partly in terms of a comparatively individualistic variety of early Christian self-understanding and religious practice. Such an idea is not entirely new. Interpreters as diverse as Risto Uro, Birger Pearson, Harold Bloom and Rudolf Bultmann have highlighted individualism as especially noteworthy either in gnostic discourse generally or in one particular gnostic text or another;[8] yet surprisingly, no major authority on 'Gnosticism' or on the writings from Nag Hammadi has hitherto explored the possible utility of including individualism as an essential element of a revised prototypical definition of the category.[9] The task of reconceptualizing

5. The conceptual triad of domestic society, religious society and political society is articulated explicitly in E. Durkheim, *Suicide: A Study in Sociology*, trans. J. A. Spaulding and G. Simpson (London: Routledge and Kegan Paul, 1952), 208–209, and is assumed throughout Durkheim's analysis of 'egoistic suicide' (chs 2 and 3) in the same work. Similar concepts and distinctions are assumed in a range of more recent sociological theorizing – see, e.g. Brigitte Berger and Peter L. Berger, *The War over the Family: Capturing the Middle Ground* (Harmondsworth: Penguin Books, 1984), 196–97.

6. See, e.g. Paul Foster, 'The Gospel of Philip', *ExpTim* 118 (2007): 417, 420–23, 425–26; Thomassen, *The Spiritual Seed*, 350–51; and Lundhaug, *Images of Rebirth*, 337–44.

7. Most recently, King, 'The Place of the *Gospel of Philip*', 566, 570; Nicola Denzey Lewis, *Introduction to 'Gnosticism': Ancient Voices, Christian Worlds* (Oxford: Oxford University Press, 2013), 89, 97–98; see also Foster, 'The Gospel of Philip', 424–26, where previous studies by Elaine Pagels, April DeConick and Einar Thomassen are cited in support of the same position.

8. See, e.g. R. Uro, *Thomas: Seeking the Historical Context of the Gospel of Thomas* (London and New York: T&T Clark, 2003), 76–79, 103–105, 124; B. Pearson, *Ancient Gnosticism: Traditions and Literature* (Minneapolis: Fortress Press, 2007), 336–37; H. Bloom, *The American Religion*, 2nd edn (New York: Chu Hartley Publishers, 2006), 9–10; and R. Bultmann, *Primitive Christianity in Its Contemporary Setting*, trans. R. H. Fuller (New York: Meridean Books, 1956), 170–71.

9. Williams, in *Rethinking 'Gnosticism'*, 134, 145–46, 151, 199, helpfully summarizes evidence from several Nag Hammadi tractates (*Gospel of Thomas, On the Origin of the*

'Gnosticism' along such lines and in a suitably rigorous manner, as opposed to embracing recent appeals that the category be consigned to the scrap-heap of failed scholarly ideas,[10] lies beyond the scope of the present contribution. However, by pursuing the course of analysis outlined above, the investigation below is able not only to produce fresh insight into the bridal chamber discourse in *Gos. Phil.* 65.12 and its literary co-text but also to show the promise of including individualism among whatever features might be considered in future scholarly attempts to redefine 'Gnosticism'.

14.1 *The Problem of Approach: Genealogy vs Analogy*

Published scholarship on the *Gospel of Philip* can be construed fairly as assuming that 65.1–26 in particular offers at best only meagre opportunity for comparative inquiry involving specifically biblical intertexts. For instance, although illuminating comparative material in Irenaeus and Hippolytus was cited in the treatment of my passage in the 1959 German translation of the *Gospel of Philip* by H. -M. Schenke and the commentary by R. McLachan Wilson in 1962,[11] neither of those studies even hinted at the possibility that the same passage in the *Gospel of Philip* might be significantly illuminated by one or more texts from Jewish or Christian Scripture. Similarly, Martha L. Turner's more recent source-critical and literary study of the *Gospel of Philip* as a whole, while noting the comparative potential of a couple of distinctively Thomasine sayings of Jesus in the *Gospel of Thomas* (22 and 114) for analysis of the bridal chamber as a general theme in the *Gospel of Philip*,[12] makes no reference to specifically biblical texts for purposes of intertextual study of

World, Zostrianos, Allogenes) pertaining either to solitude as a religious ideal or, relatedly, to spiritual exercises of withdrawal from urban society to the desert as a strategy of self-transformation – evidence that exemplifies the type of individualism defined above as germane to the interpretation of the *Gospel of Philip*; yet neither Williams himself nor any other recent scholarly authority (e.g. King, Brakke, Denzey Lewis, Dunderberg) gives serious attention – either constructively or even dismissively – to the value of individualism as part of a new typological construction of 'Gnosticism' as a category.

10. See, e.g. Williams, *Rethinking "Gnosticism"*; and King, *What Is Gnosticism?*

11. For references and discussion, see R. M. Wilson, *The Gospel of Philip* (London: A. R. Mowbray, 1962), 120–21.

12. Martha L. Turner, *The Gospel according to Philip: The Sources and Coherence of an Early Christian Collection* (Nag Hammadi and Manichaean Studies, 38; Leiden: E. J. Brill, 1996), 216–17. Extensive comment on Eph. 5.22-33 (part of which is treated at length below) as an intertext for the bridal-chamber theme in the *Gospel of Philip* as a whole – and especially in *Gos. Phil.* 58.10-14 (which does not include explicit reference to the bridal chamber); 67.9-18, 27-30; 69.36-70; and 71.3-15 – is offered in King, 'The Place of the *Gospel of Philip*', 571–76, but not for purposes of interpreting *Gos. Phil.* 65.1-26 in particular, which is unmentioned in King's analysis.

Gos. Phil. 65.1-26 or even of the bridal chamber theme more generally. The same tendency is apparent, moreover, even in the highly useful index edited by Craig Evans and others, *Nag Hammadi Texts and the Bible*,[13] and in numerous other scholarly works that include comment upon our passage.[14]

The reason for that state of affairs can be identified, at least in part, by means of an attentive reading of the 'Introduction' to *Nag Hammadi Texts and the Bible* in particular. In that context the editors' admirably clear emphasis on 'citations' and 'influence' signals to the reader that the type of comparative study they are intending to facilitate is what J. Z. Smith might characterize as 'genealogical' in orientation, in contradistinction to one that might be described as 'analogical' in nature.[15] The genealogical programme, as defined by Smith, is distinguished by an interest in establishing relations of causality, influence and borrowing.[16] It is also the approach taken, either consciously or by default, by all the studies just mentioned above. But more importantly in the present context, since *Gos. Phil.* 65.1-26 in itself is almost impossible to read as actually citing or even alluding to one passage or more from Jewish and Christian Scripture, the genealogical orientation of all these studies has the unfortunate effect of condemning interpreters of that passage and many others like it in the NH corpus to intertextually impoverished readings of the text(s). For purposes of facilitating a richer variety of reading, the analysis below is therefore interested less in questions about literary influence than in the heuristic value of comparing and contrasting a key primary text (i.e. *Gos. Phil.* 65.1-26) with a few other texts sufficiently similar to it to warrant the comparative analysis in the first place. It is also interested in ensuring that any significant differences between the texts are identified at least as carefully as the similarities are, and in giving the comparative work a disciplined focus upon well-defined questions whose significance is self-consciously derived from the scholarly context of the interpreter.[17]

The focus of comparison below, then, falls upon the ways in which *Gos. Phil.* 65.1-26 can be seen as differing, on a continuum between collectivism (i.e. strongly group-oriented values) on the one hand and an individualistic orientation on the other, from a few ancient intertexts that show promise for comparative analysis.

---

13. C. A. Evans, R. L Webb and R. A. Wiebe, ed., *Nag Hammadi Texts and the Bible: A Synopsis and Index* (NTTS 18; Leiden: E. J. Brill, 1993), 156.

14. See, e.g. I. Dunderberg, *Beyond Gnosticism: Myth, Lifestyle, and Society in the School of Valentinus* (New York: Columbia, 2008), 6, 137, 139, 194; and B. Layton, *The Gnostic Scriptures: A New Translation* (London: SCM Press, 1987), 339–40. An exception is H.-M. Schenke, *Das Philippus-Evangelium (Nag Hammadi-Codex II, 3): Neu Herausgegeben, übersetzt, und erklärt* (TU 143; Berlin: Akademie Verlag, 1997), 353–54, who strains hard to interpret the phrase ϫⲓ ⲉⲃⲟⲗ ⲍⲙ in *Gos. Phil.* 65.11-12 as an echo of the Sahidic version of 1 Cor. 10.16-17.

15. J. Z. Smith, *Drudgery Divine: On the Comparison of Early Christianities and the Religions of Late Antiquity* (Chicago: University of Chicago Press, 1990), 47–51.

16. Ibid.

17. I.e. an approach indebted to Smith, *Drudgery Divine*, 47–53, 115.

For purposes of the same comparison and as hinted above, 'collectivism' is to be understood in terms of interest shown in one or more of the constituents of the well-known sociological triad of family, religious community and prevailing structures of political power.[18] As a corollary, 'individualism' might be inferred wherever a discourse exemplifies either antipathy towards or conspicuous disinterest in the constituents of that same triad. And finally, although lexis referring to the bridal chamber (ⲡⲛⲩⲙⲫⲱⲛ) occurs in the key passage (65.12a), its modest degree of prominence in that context – it is neither repeated in 65.1-26 nor highlighted through other stylistic means – entails that the interpretative problems it poses need not be assigned central importance for the present inquiry.[19]

14.2 *Three Intertexts and a Chiasm*

Of the numerous potential intertexts that could be selected for the present sort of inquiry,[20] three in particular are given special attention in the analysis that follows. They are:

1. the analogy in Eph. 5.31-32 of the marital union between male and female, and the relationship between Christ and the church;
2. the description in Gen. 2.24 of the interpersonal processes whereby a man and a woman unite to become 'one flesh'; and
3. the discourse attributed in Plato, *Symp.* 189–193 to the comic playwright Aristophanes, on the origin and philanthropy of embodied love.

The selection here of only a few intertexts arises partly from constraints of space, and also from a conviction that careful comparative analysis of a few intertexts has obvious advantages over a superficial survey of the many that could be treated in a study lengthier than this one. But just as importantly, the special potential of all three of the intertexts just noted to be interpreted as sources of echoes in *Gos. Phil.*

18. See note 5 above.

19. An especially helpful statement of the problem, and summary of interpretative options, is King, 'The Place of the *Gospel of Philip*', 571–76. King's own suggestion, however, that the bridal chamber is presented throughout the *Gospel of Philip* as an aspect of a larger initiation ritual that includes baptism and effects both a union of the Christian believer with their heavenly twin (cf. Foster, 'The Gospel of Philip', 420–21; and Wilson, *The Gospel of Philip*, 121–22) and the establishment of the Church as the pre-existent body of Christ, is developed without reference to *Gos. Phil.* 65.1-26 in particular. In ways discussed below, *Gos. Phil.* 65.1-26 and its conceptualization of the bridal chamber in particular (65.12a) conflict with King's understanding of the bridal chamber in the *Gospel of Philip* as a whole and, at minimum, limit the scope of its applicability.

20. In addition to the intertexts analysed below, Tobit 6.14-18; 4Q560; Q11.24-26; 1 Cor. 7.1-7; 11.7-10; *Testament of Solomon* 1–15; *Gosp. Thom.* 75; and *Exeg. Soul* 131.13-133.9 would merit inclusion in any fuller study of potentially illuminating comparative texts.

65.1-26 protects the present essay against any charge of selecting its intertextual evidence either arbitrarily, or chiefly on the basis of its assumed potential to support its argument; thus, although my preferred approach to the texts is, as noted above, analogical, the coherence and force of my argument is enhanced by choosing my intertexts partly on the basis of genealogical considerations (i.e. the actual influence of the chosen intertexts on the target text).

No instance of intertextual analysis, however, can progress very far without a defensible understanding of the texts to be compared. While much of that understanding can of course emerge in the process of comparison, a few comments on the literary structure of my key primary source in particular will help to prepare the way for the intertextual analysis that follows. For that purpose, the English translation of *Gos. Phil.* 65.1-26 will prove useful.

Translation

A. As for the forms of unclean spirits, there are males among them and females. The male (spirits) are those that have sexual intercourse with (human) souls which inhabit a female form, whereas the female (spirits) are the ones that mingle sexually with those in a male form (that is, with the sort that can be seduced). And no one can [ⲘⲚ ⲀⲀⲀⲨ ⲚⲀⲰⲢ̄] **escape if attacked by them** [65.1–8]

B. unless he has a male power and a female power, the bridegroom and the bride. One gets those from the imaged [ⲈⲒⲔⲞⲚⲒⲔⲞⲤ] bridal chamber. [65. 9-12a]

C. Whenever uninstructed women see a man sitting alone, they leap down on him and play with him and defile him. So also uninstructed men, whenever they see a beautiful woman sitting alone, they persuade her and compel her, wishing to defile her. But whenever they see the man and his wife sitting beside one another, the female cannot go into the man, nor can the male go into the woman. [65.12b-23a]

B'. In this very same way, if the image [ⲈⲒⲔⲰⲚ] and the angel join with one another, [65.23b-25a]

A'. no one can [ⲘⲚ ⲀⲀⲀⲨ ⲚⲀⲰⲢ̄] **muster the courage to go into the man or the woman.**[21] [65.25b-26]

---

21. The translation is largely my own, though at numerous points it owes much to the renderings by W. Isenberg in *Nag Hammadi Codex II, 2-7, Together with XIII,2*, Brit. Lib. Or. 4926(1), and P. Oxy. 1, 654, 655*, vol. 1, ed. B. Layton (Leiden: E. J. Brill, 1989), 171; and by B. Layton, *The Gnostic Scriptures: A New Translation* (London: SCM Press, 1987), 340.

As indicated by the font-selections, alphabetic labelling, and use of indentation in the translation above, I understand *Gos. Phil.* 65.1-26 as having the schematic structure of an ABCBA chiasm. The correspondence of lines 25b-26 (i.e. segment A'), for instance, at the end of the passage as a whole, to lines 1–8 (i.e. segment A) can be seen not only in the foregrounding of concern about sexually motivated attacks by unclean spirits but also in the presence of a distinctive syntagm – ⲙⲛ̄ ⲗⲁⲁⲩ ⲛⲁϣⲡ̄ ('no one can ...', lines 7b-8, 25) – found only in those same two segments. The parallelism of lines 9–12a (i.e. segment B) and lines 23b-25a (i.e. segment B'), moreover, is instantiated not only by distinctive references to gender-complementary pairs of cosmic principles whose union in the 'bridal chamber' serves to provide the needed prophylaxis, but also by the occurrence of the cognate Greek-Coptic lexemes ⲉⲓⲕⲟⲛⲓⲕⲟⲥ ('imaged', line 12a) and ⲉⲓⲕⲱⲛ ('image', line 24), a word-group not used in the other segments of the chiasm. Finally, constituting the central segment of the scheme (i.e. C), lines 12b-23a stand out from the rest of the structure by (i) introducing and foregrounding the new theme of uninstructed men and women (i.e. non-initiates, perhaps including non-elite Christians);[22] (ii) referring exclusively to tangible realities in the familiar social world of human beings rather than to demonic and other abstract types of cosmic principles highlighted in lines 1–12a and 23b-26; and (iii) functioning in general as an analogy whose familiar, mundane referents serve to concretise and clarify the abstract teaching offered in the other parts of the chiasm.

A great deal more could be said about the chiastic structure just proposed and especially its possible implications for understanding *Gos. Phil.* 65.1-26 as a whole; but for my limited purpose of setting the stage for the analysis below, only one inference from the proposed scheme needs to be highlighted here. Namely, although ordinary heterosexual companionship is understood in the segment of analogy in lines 12b-23a as having the potential to prevent defiling entanglements with human seducers of the opposite sex, the related problem of sexual attack by demons is presented in the more newsworthy segments of the passage (especially lines 9-12a and 23b-26) as requiring a less dyadic, more individualistic, solution; for the protection commended in those lines consists neither of marriage between human beings – either carnal or spiritual – nor of social involvement in some religious or philosophical association, but rather of a gender-complementary pair of cosmic principles coming to be united inside the individual initiate, in an

---

22. In terms of information sequencing (i.e. 'given' and 'new'), the newness of the scenario described in line 12b is signalled not only by the occurrence of ⲁⲧⲥⲃⲱ ('uninstructed', lines 12b, 16), which is not used in the immediately preceding lines (1-12a) in connection with either the unclean demons or the humans (or any other referent) mentioned there, but also by the lexical shift from ϩⲟⲟⲩⲧ (lines 2, 3, 7, 9) to ⲣⲱⲙⲉ in line 16, the latter noun having far greater potential to denote human beings – in this particular line, uninstructed men (i.e. human males) – than male demons. Thus, *contra* Layton, *Gnostic Scriptures*, 340, the information structure of the Coptic text militates strongly against the use of 'male' as a rendering both for ϩⲟⲟⲩⲧ and for ⲣⲱⲙⲉ.

interior space conceptualized metaphorically as the 'bridal chamber'.[23] To be sure, the individualism of that programme is only implicit in the content of *Gos. Phil.* 65.1-26; but it acquires considerably greater salience and clarity when that unit is compared with contextually appropriate intertexts such as Eph. 5.31-32; Gen. 2.18-24; and Plato, *Symp.* 189c-193d.

14.3 *Marriage, Mystery and the Church in Eph. 5.31-32*

Near the end of a segment of teaching in which the relationship between believing husband and wife is compared to that between Christ and the church, the author of Ephesians uses the husband–wife union described in Gen. 2.24 – 'For this reason a man shall leave father and mother, and cleave to his wife, and the two shall become one flesh' (RSV) – as a store of meaning for his own discourse about the Christ–church union, a bond explicitly interpreted in Ephesians as 'a great mystery' (μυστήριον . . . μέγα, Eph. 5.32). Not surprisingly, therefore, the key clauses in the Ephesians text have sometimes been read as a probable influence on the development of the *Gospel of Philip*'s teaching about 'the bridal chamber' and related themes;[24] however, because the same passage in Ephesians has never been closely compared with *Gos. Phil.* 65.1-26 in particular, the basis for the ensuing comparison of the two passages ought to be stated clearly before proceeding further.

First, although *Gos. Phil.* 65.1-26 in itself neither cites nor even alludes to any of the clauses just quoted from Eph. 5.31-32, the immediately preceding co-text includes a clause – [ⲡⲙ]ⲩⲥⲧⲏⲣ ⲓ ⲟⲛ ⲙⲡⲅⲁⲙ[ⲟⲥ] ⲟⲩⲛⲟ6 [ⲡⲉ ('the mystery of marriage is great', 64.31-32) – which sounds very much like an echo of the Ephesians passage and thus has the potential to impact our reading of 65.1-26. Largely as a result of the presence of ⲙⲡⲅⲁⲙ[ⲟⲥ] in *Gos. Phil.* 64.31, our passage differs as much from the Sahidic versions of Eph. 5.32 as it does from the earliest Greek witnesses to the same text;[25] for even though the marital bond of husband and wife is highly

---

23. *Contra* Williams, *Rethinking 'Gnosticism'*, 149, whose inference that the passage envisages both 'spiritual marriage' (i.e. marriage lacking sexual intercourse) and the unification of individual believer and assumed angelic counterpart is undermined by the syntax of the key clauses in lines 9–11 and 24, and by the implications of the schematic structure of 65.1-26 as a whole.

24. Most recently, by King, 'The Place of the *Gospel of Philip*', 584–86; see also R. M. Wilson, 'The New Testament in the Nag Hammadi Gospel of Philip', *NTS* 9 (1963): 292, a brief but illuminating study surprisingly overlooked by E. Segelberg, 'The Gospel of Philip and the New Testament', in *The New Testament and Gnosis*, ed. A. H. B. Logan and A. J. M. Wedderburn (Edinburgh: T&T Clark, 1983), 204–12, in Segelberg's contribution to the festschrift dedicated to Wilson.

25. The edition of the Sahidic NT used for purposes of the present essay is H. Thompson, ed., *The Coptic Version of the Acts of the Apostles and the Pauline Epistles in the Sahidic Dialect* (Cambridge: Cambridge University Press, 1932).

salient in Eph. 5.21-33, the γαμος word group in particular is not attested in either the Greek or the Coptic witnesses to the Ephesians passage. But the collocation of that same distinctive feature (i.e. ⲘⲠⲄⲀⲘ[ⲞⲤ] in 64.31-32) and the motifs of sexual intercourse (ⲔⲞⲓⲚⲰⲚⲓⲀ, 64.35-36), defilement (ⲬⲰⲀⲘ, 64.36; 65.1) and image (ⲀⲓⲔⲰⲚ, 64.37) in *Gos. Phil.* 64.31-32 establishes a strong chain of lexical cohesion and discursive coherence across the transition from the antecedent co-text (most especially 64.31-37) to our passage (65.1-26) and thus impinges upon the present reading of the latter, in several ways that will emerge presently. And just as importantly, although the analogical character of the present exercise should be neither forgotten nor compromised, the justification for including Eph. 5.31-32 in it is scarcely weakened by considering the evidence of the *Gospel of Philip*'s actual knowledge and use of the Letter to the Ephesians more generally; for some part of Ephesians or another has probably conditioned the composition of at least nine different passages in the *Gospel of Philip*.[26]

A suitable foundation for comparison having thus been established, a few similarities between the two texts deserve special mention. Either as a web of conceptual metaphors, or as a description of a more physical sort of experience, or as both, a discourse of marital union is present in both passages (Eph. 5.31-32; *Gos. Phil.* 65.7b-11). Furthermore, either in each passage itself or in its co-text, a mood of concern over the possibility of attack by impure spirits is given expression;[27] indirectly, moreover, the effects of that sort of attack are understood in both situations as including sexual impurity in particular.[28] And finally, the spiritual power required for effective protection against the spirits of impurity is presented as being available in or through Christ (Eph. 6.10-17; *Gos. Phil.* 70.5-22).

Alongside the similarities between the two texts, however, are a number of noteworthy differences involving matters of marriage, family and religious community. As for marriage and closely related matters, the particular variety of marital union signified in *Gos. Phil.* 64.31-32 is, like that contrasted later in the *Gospel of Philip* (81.34–82.25) to undefiled marriage (i.e. the holy sort of marriage realized in the bridal chamber), closely associated with sexual intercourse and pollution; it possesses a physical or material quality and thus, for the ideal reader of the *Gospel of Philip*, is not being presented in that context as a paradigm of appropriate behaviour and relationships. In Ephesians, by contrast, while the potential of sexuality to become a site of evil or pollution can be identified as one of the letter's numerous interests,[29] at no point does the discourse of marriage – or more specifically, the conceptual domain of sexual intercourse within marriage – get recruited as a conceptual metaphor for sexual impurity or closely related phenomena.

For purposes of the present inquiry, the most noteworthy implication of that particular contrast is that it allows the author of Ephesians to extend the reference

---

26. See Evans, Webb and Wiebe, *Nag Hammadi Texts and the Bible*, 524–26.

27. Eph. 2.2; 4.27; 6.11-12; and *Gos. Phil.* 65.1–66.3.

28. Eph. 2.1-3; 5.3-5; and *Gos. Phil.* 65.1–66.6.

29. See, e.g., Eph. 2.3; 4.17-22; 5.3-5.

of his own source domain regarding marriage between believers and apply it in Eph. 5.33 to his new target domain of the relationship between Christ and the Church; whereas the implied author of *Gos. Phil.* 64.31–65.26 and its literary co-text is, at best, ambiguous both in regard to the ethics of sexual intercourse within Christian marriage[30] and regarding the value of marriage more generally. That same ambiguity, in fact, is almost certainly one of the most influential factors contributing to scholarly debates about the *Gospel of Philip*'s evaluation of conventional marriage.[31]

In harmony with the less ambiguous, more overtly positive estimation of conventional marriage between initiates in Ephesians, the key lines in Eph. 5.31-32 are embedded in a larger paraenetic discourse in which the instructions to husbands and wives in Christ are sandwiched by an exhortation to all members of the in-group audience to 'submit themselves to one another out of reverence to Christ' (Eph. 5.21), on one side, and by a sequence of commands pertaining to children and parents on the other (6.1-4). The collectivist overtones of this familial discourse in Ephesians are scarcely faint; from a comparative perspective, therefore, the absence of this kind of discourse about relationships in Christian households and communities is striking in *Gos. Phil.* 65.1-26 and its immediate co-text.[32] Instead of those kinds of interests, what one finds in the *Gospel of Philip* are a theological reflection regarding Christian baptism, conceptualized in conspicuously individualistic terms (64.22-31),[33] and a now lacunose discourse that seems to cohere around an interest in the mastery afforded by the holy spirit to the individual Christian over demons, fear and envy.

Those considerations by themselves suggest that at least in terms of marriage and family, *Gos. Phil.* 64.31-32 and its immediate co-text are considerably less group-oriented than Eph. 5.31-32 and its discursive environment. And since the whole semantic field of children and begetting is certainly very often metaphorical in character elsewhere in the *Gospel of Philip*,[34] a comprehensive study of its occurrence and effects throughout the tractate as a whole might be anticipated to produce results largely in line with the impression just sketched. A similar type of

---

30. From the standpoint of the author of the *Gospel of Philip*, the most positive aspect of sexual intercourse is probably its semiotic potential to serve as a source domain for metaphors that signify select aspects of higher and more abstract levels of religious experience for the benefit of the text's ideal Christian audience.

31. A valuable discussion of the interpretative options and relevant scholarship, along with a proposal different from that defended in the present study, is provided by Kimberley A. Fowler, 'From *The Apocryphon of John* to *Thomas the Contender*: Nag Hammadi Codex II in its Fourth-Century Context' (PhD thesis; University of Manchester, 2013), 108–27.

32. Cf. G. Beattie, *Women and Marriage in Paul and His Early Interpreters*, JSNTSup 296 (London: T&T Clark, 2005), 127.

33. In stark and very significant contrast, e.g. to 1 Cor. 12.12-13; Gal. 3.27-29; and Eph. 4.5.

34. See, e.g. *Gos. Phil.* 58.17–59.5; 59.31–60.1; 60.34–61.11; 69.4-13; 71.22–72.3; 80.23–82.25.

discourse about the family in a range of contemporaneous Sethian texts, three of which are attested together with the *Gospel of Philip* in Nag Hammadi Codex II, has been highlighted in a fine piece of analysis by I. S. Gilhus.[35]

Neither Eph. 5.31-32 nor the Ephesians letter as a whole offers ample opportunity for comparative analysis pertaining to the state. To be sure, interesting inferences can be drawn from discourse about aliens, citizens and the kingdom of Christ and of God;[36] but the metaphorical character of those and related concepts in Ephesians entails that their referents are abstract and spiritual in ways that do not differ greatly from the usage of political metaphors in the *Gospel of Philip*.[37] In that connection, a detailed comparative analysis could prove generally illuminating in future study; but its potential value for the present inquiry does not warrant further treatment here. More important insights are promised by a comparison of our two key passages with particular reference to the social phenomenon of religious community, the church(es) and related social structures.

As already noted, one of several interesting differences between the clause about 'mystery' in *Gos. Phil.* 64.31-32 and its intertext in Eph. 5.32 is the presence of ⲘⲠⲄⲀⲘ[ⲞⲤ] in the former. In *Gos. Phil.* 64.31-32 as also later in the *Gospel of Philip*, at 82.1-5, ⲄⲀⲘⲞⲤ does not refer to any sort of union the author would commend to his audience, even though the same term is sometimes used positively in the *Gospel of Philip* as a metaphor signifying certain higher and more abstract religious experiences.[38] A closely related and potentially even more significant difference is to be observed in connection with what directly follows the clause about 'mystery' in each of our texts respectively: in *Gos. Phil.* 64.31-32 what directly follows the mystery clause is a general observation about the causal role of marriage – and in particular marital intercourse as a private activity – in creating the whole 'world' (ⲔⲞⲤⲘⲞⲤ) of human beings, conceptualized as a single and undifferentiated mass; whereas in both the Greek text and the Sahidic versions of Eph. 5.32, the reference to the great 'mystery' of Gen. 2.24 – 'for this reason a man will leave his father and mother . . .' – is immediately explained by the author of Ephesians as a description of Christ and the Church (ἐκκλησια).

The Church, conceptualized metaphorically in Ephesians both as the wife or bride of Christ (5.23-32) and as Christ's body (e.g. 1.22-23; 5.25-30), the latter being constituted by believers as the ecclesial body's diverse 'members', can also

35. I. S. Gilhus, 'Family Structures in Gnostic Religion', in *Constructing Early Christian Families: Family as Social Reality and Metaphor*, ed. H. Moxnes (London: Routledge, 1997), 236, 243–47.

36. See, e.g. Eph. 2.12-19; and 5.5.

37. See especially *Gos. Phil.* 56.32–57.22, where kingdom discourse is part of a larger blend of metaphors whose cumulative force resides outside the domains of politics and the state. On the lack of reference in Ephesians to imperial aspects of civic life, see P. A. Harland, *Associations, Synagogues, and Congregations: Claiming a Place in Ancient Mediterranean Society* (Minneapolis: Fortress Press, 2003), 229.

38. See, e.g. *Gos. Phil.* 82.5; and 86.2.

be appropriately understood in the same letter as a network of associations of Christ-followers in western Asia Minor and a few other parts of the Mediterranean world,[39] and as unified (ideally) in one hope, 'one Lord, one faith, one baptism, one God and Father . . . who is above all and through all and in all' (Eph. 4.4-6). In Ephesians, therefore, the Church is an inherently collective phenomenon; and since explicit and consistently positive reference is made to the Church repeatedly in the letter, with the noun ἐκκλησια in particular occurring nine times, three in the first half of the letter (1.22; 2.10, 21) followed by the dense cluster of six in 5.23-32, the resultant group orientation of the implied author stands out against the background of the letter as a whole and is especially prominent in the unit under discussion here.

As already hinted, however, the situation in the *Gospel of Philip* is significantly different from that in Ephesians. In addition to the absence of the Greek-Coptic noun ⲉⲕⲕⲗⲏⲥⲓⲁ in *Gos. Phil.* 64.31–65.26, the same lexis is likewise absent in another unit of the *Gospel of Philip* where the motifs of marriage, mystery and the bridal chamber are blended, namely *Gos. Phil.* 81.34–82.35, which, like our passage, offers much potential for an intertextual dialogue with Eph. 5.31-32.[40] But perhaps even more importantly, the minor pattern of lexical absence just noted is part of a larger coherent tendency of the *Gospel of Philip* as a whole: consonant with its relative individualism vis-à-vis Ephesians in regard to matters of marriage and the family, the *Gospel of Philip* exemplifies comparatively little interest in the phenomenon of Christian assemblies and the social and communicative ties that hold them together. For instance, even though the *Gospel of Philip* as a whole is several times the length of Ephesians, it includes only a single occurrence of the noun ⲉⲕⲕⲗⲏⲥⲓⲁ; and significantly, in that context (53.32) the word is used to signify neither a particular Christian assembly nor, as in Ephesians, a larger social network of such assemblies. Instead, it is employed abstractly as one of several lexical tokens – pre-eminently ⲛⲟⲩⲧⲉ ('God'), but also ⲡⲉⲓⲱⲧ ('the Father'), ⲡϣⲏⲣⲉ ('the Son'), ⲡⲛ̅ⲁ̅ ⲉⲧⲟⲩⲁⲁⲃ ('the Holy Spirit'), ⲡⲱⲛ̅ⲁ̅ ('life'), ⲡⲟⲩⲟⲉⲓⲛ ('light'), ⲧⲁⲛⲁⲥⲧⲁⲥⲓⲥ ('resurrection') and so on – all of which serve in that context to illustrate the author's interest in the problem of names being frequently misunderstood or even used deceptively by the unenlightened (53.23–54.13).[41]

39. On early Christian assemblies as examples of association life in the Graeco-Roman world more generally, see Harland, *Associations, Synagogues, and Congregations*, 1–3 and passim.

40. Cf. Evans, Webb and Wiebe, *Nag Hammadi Texts and the Bible*, 168; and note esp. *G.Phil.* 82.2-6: 'Indeed, marriage in the world is a mystery for those who have taken a wife. If there is a hidden quality to the marriage of defilement, how much more is the undefiled marriage a true mystery!'

41. Notwithstanding the kinship overtones of ⲡⲉⲓⲱⲧ ('the Father') and ⲡϣⲏⲣⲉ ('the Son') in particular, neither kinship (even of the 'fictive' sort) nor any other social facet of this terminology is germane to the rhetorical function of *Gos. Phil.* 53.23–54.13.

To be sure, in several passages other than those just cited, the implied author of the *Gospel of Philip* exemplifies a positive attitude not only to friendship, both between different types of Christians and between religious insiders and outsiders, but also to the reality of religious authority;[42] so the tractate as a whole cannot be interpreted responsibly as either anti-social in orientation, anti-church, or even merely lacking interest in interpersonal matters. However, by comparison with a text such as Ephesians, the *Gospel of Philip* is best understood as significantly less collectivist, or more individualistic, in regard to matters of family and Church.

14.4 *From the Solitude of Adam to the Bride of Christ*

As hinted earlier, the mystery that the author of Ephesians interprets as referring to Christ and the Church also clearly relates to the text of Gen. 2.24: 'Therefore', asserts the narrator of Genesis, 'a man leaves his father and his mother and cleaves to his wife, and they become one flesh' (RSV). Leaving aside the various questions that a fuller study might ask here about extant Greek and Coptic translations of the Hebrew text of Genesis, I shall focus instead on a few key features of the Genesis passage's narrative co-text that invite comparison with *Gos. Phil.* 65.1-26 and its verbal surroundings. Perhaps most notably, since the creation of Eve in the immediately preceding co-text of Gen. 2.24 is implicitly conceptualized as a divine solution to the conspicuous difficulty of the man being 'alone' (Gen. 2.18) and not having 'a helper fit for him' (Gen. 2.20), the presence of a similar theme in *Gos. Phil.* 65.1-26 – namely, the familiar experience of heterosexual human males and females being most vulnerable to ordinary sexual seduction when they are alone, unaccompanied by a partner of the opposite sex (65.12b-19a) – invites closer attention, and all the more so since the description of that experience belongs to the central section (65.12b-24a) in the chiastic structure summarized above.

Not surprisingly, closer comparison of *Gos. Phil.* 65.12b-19a and Gen. 2.18-24 has the effect of complicating the impression of similarity just noted; and the way in which it does that is, chiefly, by helping us to see both a previously neglected example of subtlety and nuance in the *Gospel of Philip*'s self-presentation in regard to individual and group interest, and a tension which that same instance of subtlety opens up between the *Gospel of Philip* and Genesis. As for the subtle nuance within the *Gospel of Philip* itself, while the narrator of our passage shows full awareness and even approval of the conventional perception that human males and females are less vulnerable to sexual seduction and its polluting effects when they are accompanied by a partner of the opposite sex, that same perception is

---

42. On friendship between Christians: 72.17-28 (perhaps); and 78.32–79.4. On friendship between Christians and outsiders: 77.35–78.11. On interpersonal relationships more generally: 80.23–81.13. On lines of authority: 74.16-19. For further comparative analysis of the theme of friendship in the *Gospel of Philip*, see T. Klutz, 'Re-Reading 1 Corinthians after Rethinking Gnosticism', *JSNT* 26, no. 2 (2003): 210–11.

neither the main rhetorical emphasis in *Gos. Phil.* 65.1-26 nor even commended as advice to the implied Christian audience. Instead, it serves to present the familiar prophylaxis of ordinary heterosexual companionship as an analogy, an illustration, of something else, of something that may well be the most salient concern in this particular passage: namely, the protection which the bridal chamber, by virtue of its provision of both a male spirit principle and a female spirit principle (i.e. the bridegroom and the bride), affords the properly enlightened Christian initiate against sexually impure spirits.

Thus, whatever modest value the implied author of *Gos. Phil.* 65.12b-23a might ascribe to heterosexual companionship for its assumed contribution to sexual purity, he attributes far greater value to the apotropaic benefits provided by the bridal chamber. And since the bridal chamber in that same context is conceptualized as achieving its impressive prophylactic results not by joining together physical human beings but rather by providing a gender-complementary pair of male and female spirit-powers who are androgynously united inside each Christian initiate, it would seem to be a less group-orientated phenomenon than an individualistic one, to which there is no close analogue, moreover, in either Genesis 2 or Ephesians 5.

The tension just inferred between *Gos. Phil.* 65.1-26 and Gen. 2.18-24, particularly when the former is read with sensitivity to its own literary co-text, resists explanation as an instance of some imagined programme of 'protest exegesis' on the part of the implied author of the *Gospel of Philip*.[43] On the contrary, and as a patient reading of the other bridal chamber passages in the *Gospel of Philip* confirms,[44] the tension between the *Gospel of Philip* and Genesis has less to do with anti-traditionalism or, more specifically, with some imagined disdain for Jewish Scripture or Gen. 2.18-24 in particular, than with other ancient traditions familiar to the author of the *Gospel of Philip*, traditions that were highly influential in his cultural context and markedly different from Genesis on the perennial topics of human misery and its origins. While the particular extrabiblical tradition I have in mind, namely the myth of primal androgyny, best known from Aristophanes's encomium on Eros in Plato, *Symp.*189c-193d, is neither cited nor even alluded to in *Gos. Phil.* 65.1-26, the more overt adaptations of it elsewhere in the *Gospel of Philip* (68.22-26; and 70.9-22) invite us to wonder about its potential for intertextual conversation with the *Gospel of Philip* 65 as well.[45]

43. On the inability of formulae such as 'protest exegesis' and 'hermeneutic value reversal' to do justice to the variety of exegetical practices exemplified by ancient sources often categorized as 'gnostic', see Williams, *Rethinking 'Gnosticism'*, 54–79.

44. *Gos. Phil.* 67.2-29; 69.1–72.3; 72.17-28; 74.12-36; 75.25–76.16; 81.34–82.25; and 84.14–86.18.

45. On the relevance of the myth of the primal androgyny, and the version of it in Plato *Symp.* 189c-193d, to interpretation of the bridal chamber motif in the *Gospel of Philip* and other early Christian texts, see J. D. Turner, 'Ritual in Gnosticism', in *Gnosticism and Later Platonism: Themes, Figures, and Texts*, ed. J. D. Turner and R. Majercik, SBL Symposium Series, no. 12 (Atlanta: Society of Biblical Literature, 2000), 85–86, 111–19.

As in 65.1-26 so also in 68.22-26 and 70.9-22, a critical tension can be discerned between the implied author of the *Gospel of Philip* and the Genesis story concerning the creation of Eve. The relationship between that tension and our interest in the bridal chamber motif can be seen most clearly in *Gos. Phil.* 70.9-22:

> If the woman had not separated from the man, she should not die with the man. His separation became the beginning of death. Because of this, Christ came to repair the separation, which was from the beginning and again unite the two, and to give life to those who died as a result of the separation and unite them . . . Indeed, those who have united in the bridal chamber will no longer be separated. Thus Eve separated from Adam because it was not in the bridal chamber that she united with him. (Trans. W. Isenberg)

As noted by others, the author of the *Gospel of Philip* in this context is recalling some version or another of the Genesis story about the creation of Eve; but his evaluation of the biblical creator-god's separation of the previously united sexes differs from that implied in Genesis, where the creator's use of the man's flesh to fashion Eve as a physically separate person is conceptualized favourably as a solution to the problem of the man's lack of a helper-companion (Gen. 2.18-25). What the narrator of Genesis therefore understands as the solution of a problem – the problem, that is, of the solitariness of the man – the author of the *Gospel of Philip* construes as the origin of a catastrophe, an act of separation whose fateful consequences include the universal human experiences of feeling incomplete, of grievous longing for erotic union and of ill-conceived entanglements resulting in defilement and misery. In order to understand how the author of the *Gospel of Philip* could construe the events narrated in Gen. 2.21-24 as a disaster rather than a healing, at least brief attention must be given to the panegyric attributed to the Athenian comic playwright Aristophanes (c.446–386 BCE), regarding Eros, in Plato's dialogue *The Symposium*.

14.5 *Lovers, Cities and Self-Insufficiency in Plato, Symp. 189–193*

Originally, according to Plato's Aristophanes, human beings differed greatly in constitution from what they are now. More specifically, instead of the two sexes with which we are familiar today, there were three: a whole male consisting in effect of two male bodies joined so as to be spherical in form, a whole female consisting of two feminine bodies united in the same fashion, and a so-called hermaphroditic sex consisting of a combination of the other two but physically joined together in the same way (*Symp.* 189d–190b). As a consequence of the constitution just described, these primal humans possessed strength and abilities so formidable that they became proud and attacked the gods (190b–c); whereupon Zeus and the other deities agreed to put an end to the rebellion by bisecting all these human beings regardless of their sex (190c–e). In addition to explaining why today's human beings possess a navel in the middle of their belly (191a), the tale told by Aristophanes serves as an explanation of why human reproduction now takes place as it does (191b–c), why some human couplings are now heterosexual while others are homoerotic (191d–b), what sorts of wounds are healed by human experiences of love (192d–e) and why people feel complete only once they have been united with their 'other half' (192e–193d).[46]

As in Aristophanes's tale so also in *Gos. Phil.* 65.1-26 and other units of discourse about marriage and the bridal chamber in the same tractate, the separation of formerly united and erotically charged human beings is understood as the defining problem of the human condition. In contrast to Plato's Aristophanes, however, who gives high praise to the experience of love and affection that result from finding one's other half, and even defines the quest for wholeness in the arms of a congenial lover as essential to human well-being (*Symp.* 193a–d), the author of the *Gospel of Philip* has no interest in presenting the embodied union of human males and females (*Gos. Phil.* 65.12b–23a) as paradigmatic or commendable for his intended audience; instead, and as strongly suggested by the chiastic structure inferred above from *Gos. Phil.* 65.1-26 as a whole, the implied author of our passage sees the value of heterosexual intercourse – interestingly, the possibility of homoerotic coupling is not entertained, a silence that reinforces the sense of the *Gospel of Philip*'s comparative individualism[47] – as residing either largely or entirely in its potential to illustrate a less earthy, more abstract facet of the relationship between the sexes: namely, each individual Christian can experience a powerful reunion of male and female by receiving both a bride-spirit and a bridegroom-spirit in the bridal chamber (*Gos. Phil.* 65.9-12a, 23b–26), an event best understood as taking place inwardly at baptism and providing protection against the demons of sexual impurity.[48]

On the basis of the foregoing comparison, the Aristophanes figure in *The Symposium* emerges as considerably more sympathetic than the author of the *Gospel*

---

46. On the significance of the theme of human incompletion, needfulness and self-insufficiency in the speech of Aristophanes, see especially Arlene W. Saxonhouse, *Fear of Diversity: The Birth of Political Science in Ancient Greek Thought* (Chicago: University of Chicago, 1992), 161–73. The blending of that same theme and an interest in its sexual implications in both the *Symposium* and the *Gospel of Philip* constitutes an area of substantive similarity between the two texts.

47. With only a moderate risk of anachronism, and even though the world view of the *Gospel of Philip* 65 as a whole is certainly strange from the standpoint of a typical Western reader today, its sexual ethics and related assumptions are consonant with what is now familiarly labelled as heteronormativity. By contrast, the sexual values implied by Aristophanes, like those assumed in many of the *Symposium*'s arguments, remind us of the high potential for ancient patterns of experience and meaning to be unfamiliar, strange, or even nearly unintelligible to the modern reader; on which see especially R. B. Rutherford, *The Art of Plato: Ten Essays in Platonic Interpretation* (London: Duckworth, 1995), 179.

48. In addition to the analysis above of the literary structure of *Gos. Phil.* 65.1-26, see *Gos. Phil.* 68.8-16; 69.27-28; and 84.20-24.

of Philip to lifelong embodied partnerships between human beings, regardless of sexual orientation; to the desire for experience of wholeness that includes not only the mind or spirit but also the body; and to the search for completion in the form of another human being or, should that quest fail, then at least 'a sympathetic and congenial object for our affections'.[49]

The speech of Aristophanes includes at least one other detail pertinent to the present investigation. The detail in question has less relevance to matters of the family or religious association, moreover, than to the only level of social organization not yet explored in the present comparative exercise, namely the experience of the state. In Aristophanes's colourful account of the various types of couplings that resulted from the gods' punitive bisection of humans from all three of the primal sexes, he evaluates males who seek wholeness in the form of an exclusively male dyad as the best variety of human among the familiar sexual types. In defence of that judgement, Aristophanes maintains that men who love other men do so not because they are shameless, as some people suggest, but rather because those men are supremely high-spirited and superior in virility; but most importantly for the present study, the proof which Aristophanes offers for the greater masculinity of men who love other males is that when those males reach maturity, they devote themselves to life and action in the public sphere.

In contrast to Plato's Aristophanes, the author of the *Gospel of Philip* shows no overt interest in the world of politics and government; and since Aristophanes's affirmation of life in the public sphere is blended with his predilection for the exclusively male type of dyadic bonding, his discourse helps us to see the silence in the *Gospel of Philip* about male homoerotic coupling as more conspicuous and ideologically significant than it might otherwise seem. In regard to both the dyadic union of lovers and the macro-social world of politics and the state, the difference in perspective between the *Gospel of Philip* and the speech of Aristophanes is very stark and strongly reinforces the air of comparative individualism already identified with the *Gospel of Philip* on the basis of other considerations.

On the other hand, the wider literary co-text of *Gos. Phil.* 65.1-26 contains at least a few passages that might be read best as having subtle political undertones,[50] and which therefore invite us to ask whether the text's lack of direct reference

49. Plato *Symp.* 193c, in the delightful rendering by W. Hamilton, *The Symposium by Plato* (Harmondsworth: Penguin Books, 1951), 65.

50. E.g. of the seven passages in which the bridal chamber is described as protecting the initiate against being 'detained' (ⲀⲘⲀ2ⲦⲈ/ⲈⲘⲀ2ⲦⲈ in 65.8, 28, 32; 70.7; 76.23, 25; 86.8) by antagonists, the last three offer no support for identifying the opponents as the same sorts of figures implied in the first four, where demonic powers seem to be envisaged. In the last three occurrences, by contrast, and especially in 86.8, the identity of the detainers is surrounded by much greater ambiguity, a feature more consonant with politically sensitive discourse than with a demonological reference.

to the state might be an example of a loud and meaningful silence. In order to address that question properly, the comparative analysis undertaken in the present study would need to be expanded so as to include several other texts, including for instance *Tri. Trac.* 121.31–122.27; and Irenaeus, *Adv. Haer.* 1.24.5–6, both of which offer evidence of Christian concern over the possibility of the church's persecution by Roman officials. In the former the 'church' is put in the foreground of an interdiscursive blend that also includes both the bridal chamber metaphor and an interpretation of the church's possible persecution by Roman officials as redemptive; while in the latter a combination of motifs attributed to the Basilideans but likewise collocated in the *Gospel of Philip*[51] is criticized by Irenaeus as a despicable ruse enabling heretical initiates to recant their religious opinions in the presence of civic authorities and thus escape persecution.

For purposes of the present study the most significant implication of those observations is that, on a continuum between individualism and collectivism, the *Gospel of Philip* stands much closer than either Irenaeus or the implied author of the *Tripartite Tractate* to the individualism end of the scale. With its correspondingly lower interest in the definition or maintenance of familial and socio-religious boundaries, the *Gospel of Philip* would also thus appear to be less deviant, sociopolitically, than either of the other texts, less sectarian, more typical of a movement seeking low sociocultural tension with its environment, and to that extent also more 'gnostic'. Of course, in regard to the relationship between the *Gospel of Philip* and Irenaeus, none of that will surprise students familiar with the pertinent sources and debates; but what may prove newsworthy to many is the considerable distance which that sort of analysis could open up between the *Gospel of Philip* and the *Tripartite Tractate*, texts whose religious and theological affinities, as Ismo Dunderberg has recently argued, are not as strong as has normally been assumed.[52] Indeed, the time may now be at hand for the still popular notion of 'Valentinianism' (or a Valentinian school), constructed in good measure out of materials as dissimilar as the *Gospel of Philip* and the *Tripartite Tractate*, to be scrutinized with the same kind of critical intensity that has distinguished the recent rethinking of 'Gnosticism'.

---

51. Most notably: (1) the invisibility of the initiate to all the powers (*Gos. Phil.* 70.5-9; 86.4-8; *Adv. Haer.* 1.24.6); (2) the salvific power of knowledge (*Gos. Phil.* 83.9–84.11; *Adv. Haer.* 1.24.6); (3) an ambivalent attitude towards the noun 'Christian' (*Gos. Phil.* 64.24; 67.26-27; *Adv. Haer.* 1.24.6); and (4) an anthropological dualism in which the soul is esteemed but the body is viewed with contempt (*Gos. Phil.* 56.20-26; *Adv. Haer.* 1.24.5).

52. Dunderberg, *Beyond Gnosticism*, 172. For a recent reaffirmation of Valentinian literature as including both the *Gospel of Philip* and the *Tripartite Tractate*, see A. H. B. Logan, 'Gnosticism', in *The Early Christian World*, ed. P. F. Esler, 2nd edn. (London and New York: Routledge, 2017), 865, n. 19; the same grouping is embraced earlier, despite awareness of the problem of classification, by M. R. Desjardins, *Sin in Valentinianism*, SBLDS 108 (Atlanta: Scholars, 1990), 6.

14.6 *Summary and Conclusion*

The recent scholarly dismantling of 'Gnosticism' has been accompanied by constructive appeals that the various writings in the Nag Hammadi corpus and related collections no longer be read through the lenses of inherited categories tainted by the history of religious conflict and polemic, but instead be contextualized as distinctive instances of social discourse and theological rhetoric. In sympathy with such appeals, the analysis above offers a close reading and contextualization of *Gos. Phil.* 65.1-26 and, for that purpose, employs the notion of a continuum of collectivism and individualism whereby that passage's theological point of view might be compared with those of a few contextually appropriate intertexts.

One noteworthy outcome of the foregoing analysis is that, against the prevailing scholarly assumption that the *Gospel of Philip* as a whole and its bridal-chamber discourse more particularly imply a group-oriented context of production in an assumed 'Valentinian church', *Gos. Phil.* 65.1-26 is best understood in relation to its various layers of context as implying a rhetorical situation that is, comparatively, individualistic. The individualistic orientation deduced above from *Gos. Phil.* 65.1-26 and its literary co-text is, largely or at least partly, a consequence of comparing the target text with three very different but contextually relevant intertexts – namely, Eph. 5.31-32; Gen. 2.18-24; and the encomium to love attributed to the comic playwright Aristophanes in Plato's *Symposium* (189c-193d) – specifically in terms of their respective interests in matters of the family or household, the religious association or 'church' and the dominant structures of political power at the time. The same strategy of analysis, moreover, by highlighting significant differences between the *Gospel of Philip* as a whole and the *Tripartite Tractate* in regard to the individual–group continuum and sociocultural accommodation, nurtures emerging scholarly doubts about the coherence of any notion of 'Valentinianism' (or at least 'Valentinian' literature) that gives roughly equivalent weightings to those two writings in the assumed definitions of the category.

At the same time, though, while fostering suspicions about the coherence of received scholarly constructions of 'Valentinianism', the perspective inferred above from *Gos. Phil.* 65.1-26 has the effect of strengthening a minority scholarly intuition that any future efforts to construct a new typological definition of 'Gnosticism' might be well advised to include comparative individualism among the constituent features of the revised category.

Finally, two questions that are very closely related to the present essay but could not be addressed satisfactorily in the available space, ought to be mentioned as potential items for future study. One of them is: what relationship (if any) is to be seen in the *Gospel of Philip* and other early Christian writings – especially other tractates in the Nag Hammadi corpus – between individualistic tendencies wherever they might be deduced on the one hand, and the phenomenon denoted by Michael Williams and others as 'sociocultural accommodation' on the other hand? The other is: what insights might be gained by applying the same blend of methodological concepts used above – the comparative analysis of select target writings (or key passages thereof) and their intertexts in particular regard to the individual–group continuum – for purposes of testing and refining scholarly contextualizations of a wider range of early Christian, Jewish and other writings from antiquity? In an intellectual context where knowledge of the social sciences has taught so many of us to look for and expect an encounter with the social, the collective, the group-oriented dimensions of the ancient texts and other artefacts that have captured our attention, any methodological instrument that can help us to avoid losing sight of the individual, with all of his or her potential for the making of new meanings, should be a welcome addition to our interpretative toolkit.

Bibliography

Beattie, G. *Women and Marriage in Paul and His Early Interpreters*. JSNTSup 296. London: T&T Clark, 2005.

Berger, Brigitte, and Peter Berger. *The War over the Family: Capturing the Middle Ground*. Harmondsworth: Penguin Books, 1984.

Bloom, H. *The American Religion*. 2nd edn. New York: Chu Hartley Publishers, 2006.

Brakke, David. *The Gnostics: Myth, Ritual, and Diversity in Early Christianity*. Cambridge, MA: Harvard University Press, 2010.

Bultmann, R. *Primitive Christianity in Its Contemporary Setting*, trans. R. H. Fuller. New York: Meridean Books, 1956.

Denzey Lewis, Nicola. *Introduction to 'Gnosticism': Ancient Voices, Christian Worlds*. Oxford: Oxford University Press, 2013.

Desjardins, M. R. *Sin in Valentinianism*. SBLDS 108. Atlanta: Scholars, 1990.

Dunderberg, I. *Beyond Gnosticism: Myth, Lifestyle, and Society in the School of Valentinus*. New York: Columbia, 2008.

Durkheim, E. *Suicide: A Study in Sociology*, trans. J. A. Spaulding and G. Simpson. London: Routledge and Kegan Paul, 1952.

Engberg-Pedersen, Troels. *Paul and the Stoics*. Louisville: Westminster John Knox, 2000.

Evans, C. A., R. L. Webb and R. A. Wiebe, eds. *Nag Hammadi Texts and the Bible: A Synopsis and Index*. New Testament Tools and Studies, 18. Leiden: E. J. Brill, 1993.

Foster, Paul. 'The Gospel of Philip'. *ExpTim* 118 (2007): 417–27.

Fowler, Kimberley A. 'From *The Apocryphon of John* to *Thomas the Contender*: Nag Hammadi Codex II in its Fourth-Century Context'. PhD thesis, University of Manchester, 2013.

Foucault, Michel. *The History of Sexuality*, vol. 3: *The Care of the Self*, trans. R. Hurley. New York: Random House, 1986.

Gilhus, I. S. 'Family Structures in Gnostic Religion'. In *Constructing Early Christian Families: Family as Social Reality and Metaphor*, edited by H. Moxnes. London: Routledge, 1997.

Harland, P. A. *Associations, Synagogues, and Congregations: Claiming a Place in Ancient Mediterranean Society*. Minneapolis: Fortress Press, 2003.

King, Karen L. *What Is Gnosticism?* Cambridge, MA: Belknap Press of Harvard University Press, 2003.

King, Karen L. 'The Place of the *Gospel of Philip* in the Context of Early Christian Claims about Jesus' Marital Status'. *NTS* 59 (2013): 565–87.

Klutz, T. 'Re-Reading 1 Corinthians after Rethinking Gnosticism'. *JSNT* 26, no. 2 (2003): 210–11.

Layton, B. *The Gnostic Scriptures: A New Translation*. London: SCM Press, 1987.

Layton, B., ed. *Nag Hammadi Codex II,2–7, Together with XIII,2*, Brit. Lib. Or. 4926(1), and P. Oxy. 1, 654, 655*. vol. 1. Leiden: E. J. Brill, 1989.

Logan, A. H. B. 'Gnosticism'. In *The Early Christian World*, edited by P. F. Esler, 2nd edn. London and New York: Routledge, 2017.

Lundhaug, Hugo. *Images of Rebirth: Cognitive Poetics and Transformational Soteriology in the Gospel of Philip and Exegesis on the Soul*. NHMS 37. Leiden: E. J. Brill, 2010.

Moore, C. H. 'Individualism and Religion in the Early Roman Empire'. *HTR* 2, no. 2 (1909): 221–29.

Pearson, Birger. *Ancient Gnosticism: Traditions and Literature*. Minneapolis: Fortress Press, 2007.

Plato. *The Symposium*. Trans. W. Hamilton. Harmondsworth: Penguin Books, 1951.

Rutherford, R. B. *The Art of Plato: Ten Essays in Platonic Interpretation*. London: Duckworth, 1995.

Saxonhouse, Arlene W. *Fear of Diversity: The Birth of Political Science in Ancient Greek Thought*. Chicago: University of Chicago, 1992.

Schenke, W. *Das Philippus-Evangelium (Nag Hammadi-Codex II,3): neu Herausgegeben, übersetzt, und erklärt*. TU 143. Berlin: Akademie Verlag, 1997.

Segelberg, E. 'The Gospel of Philip and the New Testament'. In *The New Testament and Gnosis*, edited by A. H. B. Logan and A. J. M. Wedderburn, 204–12. Edinburgh: T&T Clark, 1983.

Smith, J. Z. *Drudgery Divine: On the Comparison of Early Christianities and the Religions of Late Antiquity*. Chicago: University of Chicago Press, 1990.

Thomassen, Einar. *The Spiritual Seed: The Church of the 'Valentinians'*. NHMS 60. Leiden: E. J. Brill, 2006.

Thompson, H., ed. *The Coptic Version of the Acts of the Apostles and the Pauline Epistles in the Sahidic Dialect*. Cambridge: Cambridge University Press, 1932.

Turner, J. D. 'Ritual in Gnosticism'. In *Gnosticism and Later Platonism: Themes, Figures, and Texts*, edited by J. D. Turner and R. Majercik; SBL Symposium Series 12; 83–139. Atlanta: Society of Biblical Literature, 2000.

Turner, M. L. *The Gospel according to Philip: The Sources and Coherence of an Early Christian Collection*. NHMS 38. Leiden: E. J. Brill, 1996.

Uro, R. *Thomas: Seeking the Historical Context of the Gospel of Thomas*. London and New York: T&T Clark, 2003.

Williams, M. A. *Rethinking 'Gnosticism': An Argument for Dismantling a Dubious Category*. Princeton: Princeton University Press, 1996.

Wilson, R. M. *The Gospel of Philip*. London: A. R. Mowbray, 1962.

Wilson, R. M. 'The New Testament in the Nag Hammadi Gospel of Philip'. *NTS* 9 (1963): 291–94.

Chapter 15

SHIFTING SOCIAL CONTEXTS AT NAG HAMMADI: IMAGINING A FOURTH-CENTURY MONASTIC RESPONSE TO THE ROLES OF KNOWLEDGE AND LOVE IN THE *GOSPEL OF PHILIP*

Kimberley A. Fowler

Social scientific studies of the New Testament seeking to illuminate the social contexts of the 'communities' implied by certain texts, and the particular situations being addressed by their authors, have been plentiful.[1] Similar approaches have naturally been taken by scholars of the Coptic Nag Hammadi Codices. Those attempting to reconstruct the identities of the authors and earliest readers of these texts, however, have faced a difficult task, as our knowledge of these details is in many instances sketchy, and interpretations of the documents have often been influenced by the pejorative descriptions of 'Gnostic' teachers and groups offered by Christian heresiographers. Building on recent studies which seek to understand the Nag Hammadi Codices within the fourth or early-fifth century Egyptian context in which they were produced, this essay proposes that illuminating comparisons can be drawn between the *Gospel of Philip* (Nag Hammadi Codex II, 3) and contemporary monastic material from the fourth century. Specifically, I will argue that the *Gospel of Philip*'s engagement with Paul's affirmation of the priority of love over knowledge in 1 Corinthians, culminating in the famous statement from 1 Pet. 4.8 – 'love covers a multitude of sins' – would have resonated with the ethos of the Pachomian monastic movement. Without suggesting that the Pachomians were the producers or *sole* readers/owners of the codices, I offer this particular case study in order to demonstrate that the *Gospel of Philip* would have been quite at home in the spiritual environment of fourth-century Upper Egypt, and could have been used in monastic circles to reinforce coenobitic Christianity

---

1. Just as many New Testament scholars are now reluctant to suggest that specific 'communities' originally lay behind certain texts, so too are many working with the Nag Hammadi literature. For a recent critique of the community paradigm in New Testament studies see David Lamb, *Text, Context and the Johannine Community: A Socio-Linguistic Analysis of the Johannine Writings*, LNTS 477 (London: Bloomsbury, 2014).

centred on renouncing material wealth, promoting bodily (particularly sexual) asceticism and encouraging the pursuit of spiritual knowledge.

15.1 *The Gospel of Philip*

Uncertainty has long surrounded the compositional origins of the *Gospel of Philip*, partly due to its apparently piecemeal format that scholars have understood as the compilation of multiple sources. Based on the presence of Syrian language and etymology in sections 56, 62, 63 and 71 it has been suggested that the text originated in Antioch, and existed originally in Greek.[2] Early estimates for dates ranged from the second right through to the late-third century.[3] Central to the debate surrounding the *Gospel of Philip* has been its supposed place within Valentinian Christianity, and scholars have gone to great lengths to establish which particular schools and teachers influenced its theology.[4] Several scholars have subsequently viewed the text as a Valentinian compendium intended for didactic purposes.[5] The *Gospel of Philip* is concerned largely with the nature of the resurrection and the roles that the sacraments play in the spiritual transformation of the Christian initiate. We read that 'some' (ϨΟΕΙΝΕ) are afraid that they will be resurrected naked (56.26-29), and that there are 'others' (ΚΟΟΥΕ) who deny the resurrection of the flesh altogether (57.9-10). It has been tempting for interpreters to understand these two sets of people as disillusioned members and/or external antagonists of an implied second or third-century community that the *Gospel of Philip* is

2. See Martin Krause, 'Coptic Sources', in *Gnosis: A Selection of Gnostic Texts*, vol. II, ed. W. Foerster, trans. R. McL. Wilson (Oxford: Clarendon Press, 1974), 76–101; and Hans-Martin Schenke, 'Das Evangelium nach Philippus', *TLZ* 84 (1959): 321–32.

3. Krause, 'Coptic Sources', 77, suggests the latter half of the second century, while Wesley Isenberg, 'Introduction' to the *Gospel of Philip*, in *Nag Hammadi Codex II, 2–7 together with XIII, 2*, Brit. Lib. Or. 4926 (1), and P. Oxy. 1, 654, 655*, vol. I, ed. B. Layton, NHMS 20 (Leiden, E. J. Brill, 1989), 131–39 (131), posits the late third century.

4. Prominent in this debate has been Einar Thomassen, whose voluminous 2006 study of the 'Valentinian Church' as a whole argued that the *Gospel of Philip* conforms to the Eastern School of Valentinian thought, which understood the Saviour to be a spiritual being in a material body. See *The Spiritual Seed: The Church of the 'Valentinians'*, NHMS 60 (Leiden: E. J. Brill, 2006), 93. For an earlier treatment of the *Gospel of Philip* as an Eastern, or 'Oriental' representation of Valentinianism, see Jean-Daniel Kaestli, 'Valentinisme italien et valentinism oriental: leurs divergences à propos de la nature du corps de Jésus', in *The Rediscovery of Gnosticism*, vol. I, ed. B. Layton (Leiden: E. J. Brill, 1980), 398–99.

5. Schenke, 'Das Evangelium nach Philippus'; Gerald L. Borchert, 'An Analysis of the Literary Arrangement and Theological Views in the Gnostic Gospel of Philip', Th.D. dissertation, Princeton Theological Seminary, 1966; and Bentley Layton, *The Gnostic Scriptures: A New Translation* (London: SCM Press, 1987), 14.

addressing directly.[6] The fact remains, however, that Nag Hammadi Codex II, which contains the *Gospel of Philip*, simply does not come from the second or third century. Rather, it is a product of the fourth century.[7] The codex has been dated on the grounds of its physical similarity to the other codices with which it was found, most notably Nag Hammadi Codex VII, which contained cartonnage (scrap paper used for strengthening) in its covers dated to between 341 and 348 CE, giving the collection a *terminus post quem* of 348 CE. Any reconstruction of second and third-century Valentinian communities, therefore, is at best hypothetical and at worst entirely misleading.[8]

15.2 A Fresh Approach

Largely due to the complexity and opacity of its theological/ideological statements, the coherence of the *Gospel of Philip* has been repeatedly called into question, with early commentators such as Grant and Wilson condemning it as 'chaotic',

6. See T. E. Klutz. 'Re-reading 1 Corinthians after '*Rethinking Gnosticism*', *JSNT* 26 (2003): 193–216, who suggests that it might be possible to identify the 'Strong' antagonists of the Corinthian congregation with the type of Christianity that the author of the *Gospel of Philip* promotes – both share, for instance, the idealization of knowledge (compare *Gos. Phil.* 77.27-29, which emphasizes the importance of spiritual knowledge, and 1 Cor. 8.1-11, in which the 'Strong' of Corinth are attempting to share their greater understanding about idol meat with the less enlightened members of the congregation). More recently, Eduard Iricinschi has argued that the *Gospel of Philip* was addressing its own 'Pauline textual community' who were having problems deciding between the message of the *Gospel of Philip* and that of other similar 'Pauline groups'; see 'If You Got It Flaunt It: Religious Advertising in the Gospel of Philip', in *Heresy and Identity in Late Antiquity*, ed. E. Iricinschi and H. M. Zellentin, TSAJ 119 (Tübingen: Mohr Siebeck, 2008), 253–72 (253–54).

7. Hugo Lundhaug posits that due to the *Gospel of Philip*'s engagement with issues such as the virgin birth, the resurrection, ritual practice and Christology, all of which were crucial to the post-Nicene writings of the likes of Theophilus, Cyril and Athanasius, the text might even be dated to as late as the early fifth century, up until which time controversy over Origenist notions of the resurrection and Arian teachings about the nature of Christ were prominent. See below for further discussion, and Hugo Lundhaug, 'Begotten, Not Made, to Arise in this Flesh: The Post-Nicene Soteriology of the *Gospel of Philip*', in *Beyond the Gnostic Gospels: Studies Building on the Work of Elaine Pagels*, ed. E. Iricinschi et al., STAC 82 (Tübingen: Mohr Siebeck, 2013), 235–71.

8. For further details pertaining to the cartonnage in the covers of the Nag Hammadi Codices, see John B. W. Barns, 'Greek and Coptic Papyri from the Covers of the Nag Hammadi Codices: A Preliminary Report', in *Essays on the Nag Hammadi Texts in Honour of Pahor Labib*, ed. M. Krause, NHS 6 (Leiden: E. J. Brill, 1975), 9–17, and John B. W. Barns et al., eds, *The Nag Hammadi Codices: Greek and Coptic Papyri from the Cartonnage of the Covers*, NHS 16 (Leiden: E. J. Brill, 1981).

'rambling and inconsequential'.[9] David Tripp's attempt to defend the text against these charges argued that concern for the role of the sacraments in Christian initiation connects every section of the text, and a progressive journey through these rites can be traced throughout.[10] The problem with this is that many of the passages dealing with the sacraments are not concerned so much with their place in the initiate's spiritual transformation as clarifying their particular function. More recently, Hugo Lundhaug has convincingly elucidated a consistent and systematic soteriology in the *Gospel of Philip* by drawing on theories of conceptual metaphor and intertextual blending from the field of cognitive linguistics.[11] Lundhaug examines how the *Gospel of Philip* is able to cultivate contemplation of salvation, the self and the world into the minds of its readers, partly through the use of scriptural intertextual links which 're-pattern and recombine'[12] certain texts in order to bring new meanings that contribute to an overall soteriological outlook. Conceptual blending is essentially a mental function which enables the comprehension of new insights from a range of 'inputs' (e.g. words, images or ideas) that otherwise might be difficult to grasp.[13] When applied to the *Gospel of Philip's* often confusingly ordered material, where topics are addressed and then abandoned in ways that do not always seem immediately logical, this theory brings some much needed clarity to its overall message. For Lundhaug, the *Gospel of Philip* is in essence a lengthy contemplation on the conceptual blend found within the statement 'that one [the initiated] is no longer a Christian but a Christ' (67.26-27). The tractate draws a series of parallels between the believer and the Saviour, whereby his birth, baptism, anointing, death and resurrection are all re-enacted by the Christian initiate through the ritual sacraments and the following of Christ's example as laid out in the Scriptures.[14]

Significantly, Lundhaug also identifies intertextual links in the *Gospel of Philip* with both the Nicene and Constantinopolitan creeds, particularly relating to the notions of creating and begetting. The significance of creating and begetting in the Arian controversy, Lundhaug argues, supports a compositional date for the text during the fourth, or even early fifth century, much later than scholarship has previously considered. This line of enquiry is developed in his article of 2013, which adds that the *Gospel of Philip's* stance on the resurrection brings

9. Robert M. Grant, 'Two Gnostic Gospels', *JBL* 79 (1960): 1–11; and Robert McL. Wilson, *The Gospel of Philip* (London: A. R. Mowbray, 1962).

10. David H. Tripp, '"The Sacramental System" of the Gospel of Philip', in *Studia Patristica*, ed. E. A. Livingstone (Oxford: Pergamon, 1982), 251–60.

11. Hugo Lundhaug, *Images of Rebirth: Cognitive Poetics and Transformational Soteriology in the Gospel of Philip and the Exegesis on the Soul*, NHMS 73 (Leiden: E. J. Brill, 2010).

12. See Lundhaug, *Images of Rebirth*, 3–4.

13. For the pioneering study in this area see Gilles Fauconnier and Mark Turner, *The Way We Think: Conceptual Blending and the Mind's Hidden Complexities* (New York: Basic Books, 2002).

14. See Lundhaug, *Images of Rebirth*, 344.

to mind the Origenist controversy of the late fourth century.[15] For Lundhaug, a preoccupation with situating the *Gospel of Philip* in an imaginary Valentinian setting has prevented scholars from viewing the text for what it really is – a fourth-century or early fifth century tractate that would have been perfectly at home within the milieu of Egyptian Christianity of the time. As Lundhaug explains, during the fourth and early fifth centuries, Alexandrian archbishops such as Theophilus, Cyril and Athanasius were well known for their writings against 'heretics' such as Nestorius and Arius, particularly on issues such as the physical resurrection of the body, the virgin birth and Christology. It is no coincidence, Lundhaug argues, that the *Gospel of Philip* deals with each of these issues.[16] The *Gospel of Philip* takes care not to step outside the boundaries of the Nicene Creed, bringing its understanding of the resurrection in line with 'orthodox' views, yet subtly subverting it at the same time. The complex language of the text disguises any views that might have been particularly controversial. *Gos. Phil.* 56.26–57.19 argues that there is a resurrection in the flesh, but not in the sense of the believer's body rising. Rather, by partaking in the sacrament of the Eucharist, the Christian initiate becomes 'clothed' with Christ's flesh, thereby taking part in his physical resurrection when their own mortal bodies die. Epiphanius, for example, complains of certain Origenist ascetics who perverted the meaning of the resurrection by saying that the resurrection in the flesh occurred in a flesh distinct to that of the human body (*Panarion* 82.3).[17] This is not far removed from the view outlined above in the *Gospel of Philip*. The author has situated himself carefully between those who argue against the resurrection in the flesh and those who argue in favour of it. Scholarship must move forward, then, and cease looking to the second and third centuries in order to understand the Christians who read the *Gospel of Philip*. Focus needs to shift to the fourth, and possibly even early fifth centuries.

Scholarship from the 1970s and 1980s gave some consideration to the fourth-century context of the Nag Hammadi Codices,[18] seeing scholars divided over whether a monastic community of Upper Egypt, possibly the Pachomians,[19]

---

15. Hugo Lundhaug, 'Begotten, Not Made', 235–71.

16. Lundhaug, 'Begotten, Not Made', 241.

17. Lundhaug, 'Begotten, Not Made', 257.

18. See particularly Armand Veilleux, 'Monasticism and Gnosis in Egypt', in *The Roots of Egyptian Christianity*, ed. B. Pearson and J. E. Goehring (Philadelphia: Fortress Press, 1986), 271–306; Charles W. Hedrick, 'Gnostic Proclivities in the Greek Life of Pachomius and the *Sitz im Leben* of the Nag Hammadi Library', *NovT* 22 (1980): 78–96; Dwight W. Young, 'The Milieu of Nag Hammadi: Some Historical Considerations', *VC* 24 (1970): 127–37, and Frederick Wisse, 'Gnosticism and Early Monasticism in Egypt', in *Gnosis: Festschrift für Hans Jonas*, ed. B. Aland (Göttingen: Vandenhoeck & Ruprecht, 1978), 431–40.

19. One objector to the Pachomian theory is the papyrologist Ewa Wipszycka, 'The Nag Hammadi Library and the Monks: A Papyrologist's Point of View', *JJP* 30 (2000): 179–91 (182–83), who argues that the cartonnage in the covers of the Nag Hammadi Codices contains documents evidencing financial transactions that the monks would not have had any part in. Contra Wipszycka are James Goehring's assertions that such activity by Egyptian

whose significant monasteries at Pbow and Chenoboskia were located just a few miles from the site of the Nag Hammadi Codices' discovery, might have owned and buried them – perhaps due to pressure from the Alexandrian Church.[20] Unfortunately, these speculations were based largely on the presence of monastic material in the cartonnage found in the covers of the codices, which could easily have been sold by a monastery to a waste paper dealer and bought by the producer of the codices. What has been lacking until quite recently is comparative work between the Nag Hammadi texts and contemporary Egyptian Christian literature. The topic has recently attracted new interest, however. Particularly notable is Jenott and Pagels's 2010 article, which compares the tractates of Nag Hammadi Codex I with the fourth-century Letters of St Antony, illuminating more than superficial similarities in the way that both sets of texts centralize and understand the themes of self-knowledge, the notion of a spiritual resurrection and the seeking of revelations.[21] In a similar vein, Iricinschi suggests that the whole of Nag Hammadi Codex II is a monastic teaching aid advocating renunciation as a remedy for the detrimental influences of the material world.[22] The points of contact that these scholars have found between the Nag Hammadi texts and contemporary monastic material warrants further investigation. I suggest that one such point of harmony

ascetics is in fact evidenced in the sources, but has been glossed over by scholarship; see James Goehring, *Ascetics, Society and the Desert: Studies in Early Egyptian Monasticism* (Harrisburg: Trinity Press International, 1999), 41.

20. A common suggestion has been that Athanasius of Alexandria's Festal Epistle of 367 CE might have prompted the monastery to purge their library of what would have been considered 'heretical' material, but as Nicola Denzey Lewis and Justine Blount have recently argued, there is no firm evidence linking the two events. See Nicola Denzey Lewis and Justine Blount, 'Rethinking the Origins of the Nag Hammadi Codices', *JBL* 133 (2014): 397–417 (410–11).

21. Elaine Pagels and Lance Jenott, 'Antony's Letters and Nag Hammadi Codex I: Sources of Religious Conflict in Fourth-Century Egypt', *JECS* 18 (2010): 557–89. See also Philip Rousseau, 'The Successors of Pachomius and the Nag Hammadi Codices: Exegetical Themes and Literary Structure', in *The World of Early Egyptian Christianity: Language, Literature and Social Context. Essays in Honour of David W. Johnson*, ed. J. E. Goehring and J. A. Timbie (Washington DC: The Catholic University of America Press, 2007), 140–57.

22. Eduard Iricinschi, 'The Teaching Hidden in Silence (NHC II 1,4): Questions, Answers and Secrets in a Fourth-Century Egyptian Book', in *Beyond the Gnostic Gospels*, 297–319. My own doctoral thesis similarly argued that Codex II can be read meaningfully as a collection that would have been instructive to the Pachomian monastic community of Upper Egypt, whose spiritual outlook, as evidenced by the rich collection of writings which survive from the movement, bears many similarities to the views of asceticism, spiritual knowledge and communal ethic advanced by the tractates of the codex; see Kimberley A. Fowler, 'From the Apocryphon of John to Thomas the Contender: Nag Hammadi Codex II in its Fourth-Century Context', PhD dissertation, University of Manchester, 2013.

can be found in the concern expressed in both the *Gospel of Philip* and the Pachomian literature for the relationship between knowledge and spiritual love.

The sympathies that Lundhaug highlights in the *Gospel of Philip* with Origenist claims about the resurrection could have been a deal breaker for Pachomian monastic readers, and it is therefore significant that stories in the Pachomian sources where Pachomius is portrayed as distinctly anti-Origen are likely to be later additions by writers conscious of their relationship with Alexandria. In the First Greek *Vita* (31)[23] Pachomius throws a work of Origen into the water (31), and he is also said to have advised visiting anchorites whom he suspects of reading Origen's work that they should do the same (*Paralipomena* 7). That these pericopes were a later addition might be indicated in that Palladius (a follower of Origen) describes the monks of Pachomius's first monastery at Tabennese in very positive terms in his *Lausiac History*. Surely Pachomius would not have been so hospitable to Palladius had they differed on this crucial matter.

15.3 *Pachomian Ideology and the Gospel of Philip*

Following its lively engagement with Paul's teaching on the resurrection in 1 Corinthians, the *Gospel of Philip* goes on to discuss the relative importance of knowledge and love, again drawing on the apostle's arguments for the superiority of the latter. The discussion climaxes with a quotation of 1 Pet. 4.8: 'love covers a multitude of sins'. Before considering this discussion against the comparable attitudes of the Pachomian literature, I will begin by briefly introducing the Pachomian sources in question. In addition to the *Vitae*, which survive to us in various Coptic, Greek, Arabic and Latin versions, we have the *Rule of Pachomius*, surviving in Coptic and Greek fragments, and translated into Latin by Jerome, as well as the *Rule of Horsiesios*, and letters and instructions from Pachomius and his successors. There are also the *Paralipomena* (Greek anecdotes integrated into nearly all the Greek *Vitae*), and Palladius's *Lausiac History*, which refers several times to the monasteries which used the Pachomian *Rule*. The earliest sources, Pachomius's letters and the *Instruction of Pachomius*, are from within the founder's lifetime (*c.* 323–346 CE). Most of the other evidence, however, dates to between 346 and 400 CE, when the monastery was under the control of Pachomius's successors, Theodore and Horsiesios.[24]

The Pachomians characterized themselves as ἀποτακτικοί (renouncers).[25] However, their renunciation took on a form different from that of the anchoritic hermits in that their ascesis was regulated within a community of comrades. The

---

23. References to the Pachomian sources are taken from the translations of Armand Veilleux, *Pachomian Koinonia: The Lives, Rules, and Other Writings of Saint Pachomius and his Disciples*, 3 vols (Kalamazoo, MI: Cistercian Publications, 1980).

24. For more details see the helpful illustrations of Goehring in *Ascetics*, 164.

25. Goehring, *Ascetics*, 58.

Koinonia (the collective name given to the Pachomian monasteries) emphasized the responsibility of each brother to edify those around him and take care not to lead them astray. Despite the numerous accounts of Pachomius's own ascetic feats in the *Vitae*, he is described as stating explicitly that the lowliest in the Koinonia, who do not practice such excessive ascesis will be greater in God's eyes than the anchorite (Bohairic *Vita* 105). Unlike the anchorite, the coenobite is able not only to develop his own spirituality but also to impact upon those around him as well. Competitive ascesis with oneself or others is condemned, as illustrated vividly in the Bohairic *Vita* (64), where one monk who ignores a warning from Pachomius for excessive fasting is subjected to his vainglory manifesting itself as a murderous devil.

Palladius states that the Pachomian *Rule* ensured that even 'the little ones' were given the chance to attain spiritual fulfilment through the nurturing community ethic of the Koinonia (*Lausiac History* 32.7). Endangering the spiritual health of another brother was met with harsh punishment. The *Rule* warns that anyone found guilty of perverting the soul of a simpler brother, or imploring him with words will be subject to a beating before the monastery gates, and is to be fed only bread and water if he remains unrepentant (*Precepts and Judgements* 4).The brothers were encouraged to develop at their own pace. Indeed, Pachomius is described as reacting badly when a certain Theodore (not to be confused with Pachomius's successor of the same name) refuses to take his own brother under his wing when he pleads to enter the monastery. Pachomius insists that new members require special care and instruction to enable their full immersion into the community (Bohairic *Vita* 37–38, First Greek *Vita* 37, 65). The sources portray Pachomius as particularly concerned with equality among the brethren, seeking to avoid schism in the community. The *Vitae* claim that Pachomius required any clergy wishing to be a part of the monastery to embrace the rules in the same way as the rest of the community (Bohairic *Vita* 25, First Greek *Vita* 27).

The emphasis that the Pachomians placed upon responsibility for the spiritual health of others allows us to reconsider the shared concern for this topic in the *Gospel of Philip*, which has been overlooked in previous scholarship, despite constituting a significant portion of the text's use of and engagement with the New Testament. Prior relegation of the *Gospel of Philip* to second or third-century 'Valentinian Gnosticism' makes this oversight unsurprising. Until Michael Williams's influential rejection of 'Gnosticism' as a heuristic category, the view that 'Gnostic' texts advocated only certain individuals or groups as spiritually privileged or predisposed to salvation was widely held.[26] The *Gospel of Philip*, however, makes explicit the need for those possessing of greater spiritual knowledge to be vigilant lest they allow it to consume them to the detriment of others. Paul's similar chastisement of the enlightened members of the Corinthian congregation

---

26. Michael A. Williams, *Rethinking 'Gnosticism': An Argument for Dismantling a Dubious Category* (Princeton: University Press, 1996), 189–212.

here becomes a supportive tool for the *Gospel of Philip*. The central passage that concerns us here (*Gos. Phil.* 77.15–78.11) is worth citing in full:

> He who has knowledge (ΓΝΦΟΙϹ) of the truth is a free man, and the free man does not sin. For 'he who sins is a slave to sin' (cf. Jn 8.34). Truth is the mother, but knowledge (ΓΝΦΟΙϹ) is the mingling. Those to whom it is not given to sin are called 'free' by the world. The knowledge (ΓΝΦΟΙϹ) of the truth makes these to whom it is not given to sin arrogant, that is, they are made free, and it elevates them over everything, but love (ἀΓΑΠΗ) edifies (cf. 1 Cor. 8.1). And he who has been made free through knowledge (ΓΝΦΟΙϹ) is a slave because of love (ἀΓΑΠΗ) for those who have not yet been able to take up [the] freedom of knowledge (ΓΝΦΟΙϹ), [but] knowledge makes them capable [to] become free. Love (ἀΓΑΠΗ) [. . .] anything that it [is] its [. . .] is its, it does not [say that, . . .] or this is mine [. . .] are yours. Spiritual love (ἀΓΑΠΗ ΠΝΕΥΜΑΤΙΚΗ) is wine and fragrance. All those who will anoint themselves with it [benefit from] it. Those who stand near them also benefit, like those who are anointed who stand there. If those who are anointed with ointment leave their side and go, those who are not anointed, who are only standing near them, once again remain in their (own) stench. The Samaritan did not give anything to the wounded man but wine and oil. It was nothing else except the ointment, and healed the wounds. For 'love covers a multitude of sins' (cf. 1 Pet. 4.8).[27]

It becomes clear that love (ἀΓΑΠΗ) is valued above knowledge (ΓΝΦΟΙϹ) and freedom, with the *Gospel of Philip* agreeing with Paul that the freedom one believes that they receive as a consequence of knowledge risks inciting a superiority complex over other believers. The *Gospel of Philip* refers to Paul's preference for love and its ability to 'edify', or 'build up' (ΚΦΤ), through loving service to other Christians (1 Cor. 8.1; *Gos. Phil.* 77.25-27). Knowledge must be imparted with extreme care, just as Paul advises those who possess knowledge not to flaunt their liberty so that it becomes 'a stumbling block to the weak' (1 Cor. 8.8). Indeed, the *Gospel of Philip* argues elsewhere that while ΓΝΦΟΙϹ makes a 'free man' (77.16-17), it also brought death (74.5-12). What is perfectly clear is that the *Gospel of Philip* sees the benefit of interaction between more and less enlightened believers. By identifying knowledge as something that enslaves (77.27), the *Gospel of Philip* emphasizes the duty of those with knowledge to instruct those still in pursuit. Just the mere presence of those 'anointed' in spiritual love can positively impact others. Moreover, an awareness of the appropriate level of instruction is also necessary:

27. I borrow the translation of Hugo Lundhaug throughout; see his *Images of Rebirth*, 468–537. Unlike many scholars, Lundhaug compares biblical citations and quotations to the Sahidic Coptic New Testament in addition to the Greek, thereby avoiding the potential oversight of hermeneutically significant features in the Coptic translation of the Greek text.

A master of a house acquired everything, whether child or slave or cattle or dog or pig or wheat [or] barley or chaff or hay or [. . .] or meat and acorn. [But he is] wise and knows the food of each [one]. He placed bread before the children, [. . .], but he placed [. . . and (a simple) meal before] the slaves, and [he threw barley] and chaff and hay before the cattle. He threw bones before the dogs, [and] he threw acorns and slops before [the pigs]. Thus the disciple of God, if he is wise he understands what it is to be a disciple. The bodily forms will not deceive him, but he will look at the condition of the soul of each one and speak with him. (*Gos. Phil.* 80.23–81.6)

The comparison is crude, but the message is extremely clear – giving someone reasonably advanced in knowledge only the basic level of instruction is useless. Equally, giving those who are just beginning advanced tuition is inappropriate. Just as Paul advises the Corinthians, all the knowledge in the world is useless if one cannot be a positive influence upon those around him. In fact, this passage seems to say something very similar to Paul in 1 Cor. 9.19-23, where he explains his tactic for making his message accessible to everyone that he encounters, 'to the Jews I became as a Jew . . . to those under the law I became as one under the law . . . to the weak I have become weak'. This would resonate clearly with an ascetic community where individual spiritual pursuits could lead to a blinkered view of their role to 'build up' those around them.

The First Greek *Vita* (49) emphasizes that great care must be taken of children (best understood as new monastic recruits) from the very beginning, in order to enable them to be receptive to good. The *Vita* argues that just as ground that is attentively cultivated from the start is easier to keep clean, those instructed appropriately in spiritual knowledge are more likely to succeed. Even ground that is planted with good seed can turn wild if not tended properly. Similarly, fragment II of the Tenth Sahidic *Vita* contains instructions on how to receive young monks and teach them to keep their bodies pure. The shared sentiment of the *Gospel of Philip* and the Pachomian movement is nicely summarized in the *Testament of Horsiesios*:

After we have rendered an account of our own life, we shall likewise render an account for those who were entrusted to us. And not only is this to be understood of the housemasters but also of the superiors of the monasteries and of each of the brothers belonging to the rank and file, because all must 'carry each other's burdens and so fulfil the law of Christ'. (cf. Gal. 6.2) (*Testament of Horsiesios* 11)

15.4 *Concluding Remarks*

The Pachomian literature, like the *Gospel of Philip*, makes quite explicit that quashing individualistic spirituality and promoting communal responsibility to maintain a unified, mutually supportive environment was of central importance. I am not suggesting that the Pachomians were the ones responsible for the production of the Nag Hammadi Codices, or even that they were responsible for burying them in the desert.[28] Moreover, I do not claim that the Pachomians were the only group in Upper Egypt to engage with the Nag Hammadi Codices during the course of the fourth and possibly early fifth centuries. Which precise groups encountered and engaged with the texts (either as a collection or as individual tractates or codices) prior to their concealment at some point after 348 CE remains unclear. I have presented here just one case study which highlights the similar concerns of the Pachomian writers and one author from Nag Hammadi Codex II; other scholars have found significant parallels between the Nag Hammadi texts and other inhabitants of fourth-century Upper Egypt, such as the Shenoutians.[29] The tractates within the Nag Hammadi collection offer us a dynamic glimpse into a period of early Christianity that saw some of its most central issues repeatedly debated and reinterpreted. As more studies begin to recognize that the codices can be read harmoniously alongside contemporary material from Christian Egypt, scholarship draws ever closer to understanding much of the Nag Hammadi Library simply as evidence *for* fourth and fifth-century Christianity, rather than a 'heretical' perversion of it.

Bibliography

Barns, John B. W. 'Greek and Coptic Papyri from the Covers of the Nag Hammadi Codices: A Preliminary Report'. In *Essays on the Nag Hammadi Texts in Honour of Pahor Labib*, edited by M. Krause. NHS 6; 9–17. Leiden: E. J. Brill, 1975.

Barns, John B. W. et al., ed. *The Nag Hammadi Codices: Greek and Coptic Papyri from the Cartonnage of the Covers.* NHS 16. Leiden: E. J. Brill, 1981.

Borchert, Gerald L. 'An Analysis of the Literary Arrangement and Theological Views in the Gnostic Gospel of Philip'. Th.D. dissertation, Princeton Theological Seminary, 1966.

Denzey Lewis, Nicola, and Justine Blount. 'Rethinking the Origins of the Nag Hammadi Codices'. *JBL* 133 (2014): 397–417.

Fauconnier, Gilles, and Mark Turner. *The Way We Think: Conceptual Blending and the Mind's Hidden Complexities.* New York: Basic Books, 2002.

28. See Denzey Lewis and Blount, 'Rethinking the Origins of the Nag Hammadi Codices', 412–19, who argue that the library was buried according to common late-antique Egyptian practice as grave goods with its owner, who was likely a collector of esoteric literature. In addition to rejecting the idea of monastic burial of the codices, these authors argue that the uncertainties surrounding the find story of the codices (see 401–405) cast doubt upon the assumed proximity of this site to the Pachomian monasteries (see 405–407). I see no reason, however, why their conclusions rule out the possibility of one or more groups, including the Pachomians, having read the codices at some point – a private owner may simply have been their final owner.

29. See Lundhaug, *Images of Rebirth*, 145–49, who argues for similarities between the Shenoutian corpus and the *Exegesis on the Soul* (Nag Hammadi Codex II, 6), notably on the theme of repentance.

Fowler, Kimberley A. 'From the *Apocryphon of John* to *Thomas the Contender*: Nag Hammadi Codex II in its Fourth-Century Context'. PhD dissertation, University of Manchester, 2013.

Goehring, James. *Ascetics, Society and the Desert: Studies in Early Egyptian Monasticism*. Harrisburg: Trinity Press International, 1999.

Grant, Robert M. 'Two Gnostic Gospels'. *JBL* 79 (1960): 1–11.

Hedrick, Charles W. 'Gnostic Proclivities in the Greek Life of Pachomius and the *Sitz im Leben* of the Nag Hammadi Library'. *NovT* 22 (1980): 78–96.

Iricinschi, Eduard. 'If You Got It Flaunt It: Religious Advertising in the Gospel of Philip'. In *Heresy and Identity in Late Antiquity*, edited by E. Iricinschi and H. M. Zellentin. TSAJ 119; 253–72. Tübingen: Mohr Siebeck, 2008.

Iricinschi, Eduard. 'The Teaching Hidden in Silence (NHC II 1,4): Questions, Answers and Secrets in a Fourth-Century Egyptian Book'. In *Beyond the Gnostic Gospels*, 297–319. Tübingen: Mohr Siebeck, 2013.

Isenberg, Wesley. 'Introduction' (to the *Gospel of Philip*). In *Nag Hammadi Codex II, 2–7 together with XIII, 2*, Brit. Lib. Or. 4926 (1), and P. Oxy. 1, 654, 655*, vol. I, edited by B. Layton. NHMS 20; 131–39. Leiden: E. J. Brill, 1989.

Kaestli, Jean-Daniel. 'Valentinisme italien et valentinism oriental: leurs divergences à propos de la nature du corps de Jésus'. In *The Rediscovery of Gnosticism*, vol. I, edited by B. Layton; 398–99. Leiden: E. J. Brill, 1980.

Klutz, T. E. 'Re-reading 1 Corinthians after *Rethinking "Gnosticism"*'. *JSNT* 26 (2003): 193–216.

Krause, Martin. 'Coptic Sources'. In *Gnosis: A Selection of Gnostic Texts*, vol. II, edited by W. Foerster, trans. R. McL. Wilson, 76–101. Oxford: Clarendon Press, 1974.

Lamb, David. *Text, Context and the Johannine Community: A Socio-Linguistic Analysis of the Johannine Writings*. London: Bloomsbury, 2014.

Layton, Bentley. *The Gnostic Scriptures: A New Translation*. London: SCM Press, 1987.

Lundhaug, Hugo. *Images of Rebirth: Cognitive Poetics and Transformational Soteriology in the Gospel of Philip and the Exegesis on the Soul*. NHMS 73. Leiden: E. J. Brill, 2010.

Lundhaug, Hugo. 'Begotten, Not Made, to Arise in this Flesh: The Post-Nicene Soteriology of the *Gospel of Philip*'. In *Beyond the Gnostic Gospels: Studies Building on the Work of Elaine Pagels*, edited by E. Iricinschi, L. Jenott, N. Denzey Lewis, and P. Townsend. STAC 82; 235–71. Tübingen: Mohr Siebeck, 2013.

Pagels, Elaine, and Lance Jenott. 'Antony's Letters and Nag Hammadi Codex I: Sources of Religious Conflict in Fourth-Century Egypt'. *JECS* 18 (2010): 557–89.

Rousseau, Philip. 'The Successors of Pachomius and the Nag Hammadi Codices; Exegetical Themes and Literary Structure'. In *The World of Early Egyptian Christianity: Language, Literature and Social Context. Essays in Honour of David W. Johnson*, edited by J. E. Goehring and J. A. Timbie; 140–57. Washington DC: The Catholic University of America Press, 2007.

Schenke, Hans-Martin. 'Das Evangelium nach Philippus'. *TLZ* 84 (1959): 321–32.

Thomassen, Einar. *The Spiritual Seed: The Church of the 'Valentinians'*. NHMS 60. Leiden: E. J. Brill, 2006.

Tripp, David H. '"The Sacramental System" of the Gospel of Philip'. In *Studia Patristica*, edited by E. A. Livingstone; 251–60. Oxford: Pergamon, 1982.

Veilleux, Armand. *Pachomian Koinonia: The Lives, Rules, and Other Writings of Saint Pachomius and his Disciples*. 3 vols. Kalamazoo, MI: Cistercian Publications, 1980.

Veilleux, Armand. 'Monasticism and Gnosis in Egypt'. In *The Roots of Egyptian Christianity*, edited by B. Pearson and J. E. Goehring; 271–306. Philadelphia: Fortress Press, 1986.

Williams, Michael Allen. *Rethinking 'Gnosticism': An Argument for Dismantling a Dubious Category*. Princeton: University Press, 1996.

Wilson, Robert McL. *The Gospel of Philip*. London: A. R. Mowbray, 1962.

Wipszycka, Ewa. 'The Nag Hammadi Library and the Monks: A Papyrologist's Point of View'. *JJP* 30 (2000): 179–91.

Wisse, Frederick. 'Gnosticism and Early Monasticism in Egypt'. In *Gnosis: Festschrift für Hans Jonas*, edited by B. Aland; 431–40. Göttingen: Vandenhoeck & Ruprecht, 1978.

Young, Dwight W. 'The Milieu of Nag Hammadi: Some Historical Considerations'. *VC* 24 (1970): 127–37.

AUTHOR INDEX

SUBJECT INDEX

Qumran community 14, 18–19, 160
  Teacher of Righteousness 162–75
Qumran literature 34, 37, 125, 163
  anthropology 130–4
  economics 139–40
  gender 130–1, 149–50
  identity of groups 129
  liminality 132–3
  multiple identities 128
  political history 137–9
  poor, identity of 140
  poverty and common ownership 139–40
  psychology 134–7
  purity and impurity 133–4
  rite and rituals 131–2
  scarce resources theory 140
  sectarianism 126–7, 128, 132–3
  sociology 126–30
  terminology use 128

Rebekah 15, 51–2 n.2, 54–5, 66
reciprocity 15, 72, 73, 74, 76, 79
redistribution 15, 72, 74, 75
refugee 15, 51–2, 53, 54
  Hutu refugee 66
  Jacob as *see* Jacob narrative, of
    migration
religious movements 167–9, 171
resurrection 234, 235 n.7, 236–8, 239
rhetoric 5, 10–11, 14, 58, 129, 152, 166,
    174, 176, 190, 205, 207–8, 225, 230
rites 131, 133 n.35, 236
rituals 15–16, 18, 35, 40–1, 90–4, 131–2,
    136, 236
  temple rituals 100
  textualization in Leviticus 83–4
ritual space 15–16, 86, 88–9
Rule of Horsiesios 239
Rule of Pachomius 239, 240
Rule of the Congregation (1QSa) 134, 137

Samaritans 38 n.4, 241
Samuel–Kings 30
science 5–7
Second Temple period 91, 100, 129, 134,
    137, 140 n.65, 149, 151, 152
sectarianism 18, 126, 127, 129, 159, 161
shame 9, 19–20, 76, 154, 168, 171, 174,
    175, 177, 188, 288

Sinai 86, 87, 88 *see also* Mount Sinai
social identity 160 *see also* identity
social memory 13, 14, 16, 20, 32, 35, 175
    see also memory
social models
  advantages of 202–3
  construction 21
  definition of 197, 201–2
  inherent interdisciplinarity 199
  and language 198
  Philippians 1.27–2.5 (case study) 203–8
  and research framework 200–1
  social categories 203
  structuration theory 200
  use of 197–8, 202
social-scientific perspectives, concept of
    6–7, 9–10, 12–23
society 33, 51, 72, 74, 76, 78, 97, 108, 114,
    133–4, 150, 151–2, 154, 185, 189,
    197, 208, 213 n.5
socio-literary approach 9–10
sociology, of organizations 162–4
socio-rhetorical criticism 10–12
socio-scientific approaches 162
space 83–4
  critical studies 85–6
  imaginative spaces 90–2
  and memory 86–8
  mental space 85
  symbolic space 85–6
spirituality 212 n.4, 220, 222, 233–4, 235
    n.6, 236, 238–9, 240–2
spiritual marriage 219 n.23
structuration theory 200
Sukkôt 90
Symposium, The 226–9
  Aristophanes 226–8, 230
  love in 227
  sexual orientation in 226–7
systemic linguistics 11, 16

Teacher of Righteousness 19, 162–75
  functions of 172–3
  maximalist hypothesis 170–1
  memorial figure 174–5, 176–7
  memory in Essene community 173–4
  minimalist hypothesis 170
  power of 175–8, 176–7
  voice of 173, 174

INDEX OF REFERENCES